The Paladin

Brian Garfield, born in 1939 in New York City, graduated with an MA from the University of Arizona.

He has written nearly sixty books, both fiction and non-fiction, including *Deep Cover*, *Line of Succession* and *Death Wish*, which was made into a highly successful film, directed by Michael Winner and starring Charles Bronson.

His novels *Wild Times*, *Recoil*, *The Romanov Succession*, *Hopscotch*, *Kolchak's Gold* and *Death Sentence* (the sequel to *Death Wish*) are also published in Pan.

Also by Brian Garfield
in Pan Books

Kolchak's Gold
Hopscotch
Death Sentence
The Romanov Succession
Recoil
Wild Times

The Paladin

Brian Garfield

in collaboration with
'Christopher Creighton'

Pan Books in association with
Macmillan London

First published 1980 by Macmillan London Ltd
This edition published 1981 by Pan Books Ltd,
Cavaye Place, London SW10 9PG
in association with Macmillan London Ltd
3rd printing 1982
© Brian Garfield and Crick Limited 1980
ISBN 0 330 26455 9
Printed and bound in Great Britain by
Cox & Wyman Ltd, Reading

For John, Greta and Crick

Foreword

The hero of this narrative is a real person. He is now in his fifties. His name is not Christopher Creighton.

This book is based on his extraordinary story, but the book is a novel and it employs the sort of license that is customary in a work of fiction. Perhaps only 'Christopher' can say how closely and at what points the narrative coincides with the truth. I have done my best to insure that there are no errors of chronological or historical fact; if there are any such errors, they are mine alone, possibly the result of those reorderings of reality that sometimes are done for dramatic purposes.

For generous assistance in the preparation of the book I should like to thank Jack and Rita Botley, Bill Cosgrove, Ted and Marjorie Hayes, Michael Korda, Marc Jaffe, Dan Johnson, Gaynor Johnson, Alan Maclean, Henry Morrison, Police Sergeant Donald Rumbelow, Ed Victor, and — especially — James Wright. And of course my very special thanks to 'Christopher Creighton'. He is a remarkable man.

Brian Garfield
London and New York, 1979

Prologue

London – 1965

In the crowd stood a tall fair-haired man, fortyish, lean, muscular. His eyes were alert and his head, unlike most others, was not bowed. His swift glance swept along the route of the procession – Whitehall, the Cenotaph, a glimpse from here of Downing Street – and it was as if he were memorizing everything in sight so as never to forget this hour.

There was a dry bitter-cold east wind. The throng was immense and Londoners were still arriving to swell it. No-one spoke. The only sounds came from drubbing feet and the mournful pound of the slow drums. The raised flags of many nations fluttered above the heads of standard-bearers in the crowd; the man recognized two of the people who held French flags aloft – he recalled their faces from the Resistance a quarter century ago and he was pleased to see they were still alive. The Frenchman was very old now and the woman, middle-aged, had an oriental sort of face. She had saved his life once. But he made no effort to make himself known to her.

In the biting cold the coffin, adorned by the chivalric insignia of a knight of the Order of the Garter, progressed slowly towards Trafalgar Square and the man watched its progress as he watched everything · with alert eyes that missed nothing. Beside him a woman wept openly and the man moved on past her, past men who were removing their hats and bowing their heads; he moved along behind the front rank of the crowd, keeping parallel to the procession. Newsreel and television cameras played across the scene, their lenses glinting dully in the grey cold air, and upon a rooftop he saw a man in an old RAF uniform draw himself to attention and raise his arm in a quivering salute.

Drawn by a compulsion he only half understood, he made his way steadily forward – he had a catlike ability to manoeuvre among them without drawing anyone's attention more than momentarily – and once in Trafalgar Square he moved away from the procession's route and increased his pace, walking swiftly on his long legs through Chandos Place and Henrietta

Street and on behind the Aldwych, everything deserted back here, shops closed up; he crossed Kingsway and skirted Lincoln's Inn Fields – across Chancery Lane and finally through the back streets to post himself on a raised step from which, over the heads of the teeming silent crowds, he could see the face of St Paul's Cathedral. For an instant he remembered quite clearly the occasion on which that venerated structure had stood out alone amid the devastating fires of the Blitz.

His breath came in long easy streams of white vapour. He waited with the patience of a hunter.

He did not need to be nearer than this. He watched the royal car draw away and knew well enough what he'd see if he were inside: kings, queens, presidents, dictators, public servants, figures of substance, men and women of the armed services. By now Queen Elizabeth II and the royal party would be settled into their seats to await the cortège – the first occasion in recorded history when a reigning British monarch had attended the funeral services of a commoner.

The stray thought struck him that by exercising a bit of influence and persuasion he himself might have been marching in place of one of the one hundred and eight Royal Navy officers and ratings who drew the lead coffin on its gun-carriage up to St Paul's Cathedral. But it was better to remain anonymous as he always had done.

Mine eyes have seen the glory. . . The crowd was so still he could hear the ring of the hymn from within the cathedral but he was thinking not of this solemn ceremony and not of the great deeds of the statesman who after ninety years of strife and triumph was on his way to his final place of peace accompanied by such stately pageantry. No; he was thinking of the person, not the Prime Minister; the friend, not the hero. *Tigger. . .*

The man turned – put his back to the crowd and walked away into the silent cold streets of winter. Now for the first time he ceased to withhold his tears; his eyes went opaque and moist – not so much in grief as in memory.

Chapter One

Seeking adventure the boy prowled through a jungle of rhodo-
dendron and found before him a wall of fresh red bricks. It was
a bit higher than his head, even when he stood on tiptoe, and
its top was unfinished, bricks lying askew. The boy looked all
round, in case a gardener might be lurking, and then launched
himself boldly on to the wall, clutching at bricks, shinning himself up to see what might lie on the other side.

To his dismay the bricks gave way. As his weight fell across
them the wall collapsed: the boy felt himself tumbling, bricks
all round.

At the same time he heard a man's bellowing roar. It seemed
to come from just beneath him.

Several tiers of bricks plummeted away and the boy found
himself sprawling across the waist-high base of the wall; there
was a tremendous clattering, a continuing bellow, a vague sense
of someone very bulky trying to scramble out of the way of the
tumbling bricks.

When the rubble stopped collapsing the boy managed to
swing a leg over and sit up on top of the base and then he had
his first clear look at the man he had so rudely disturbed. The
man seemed very large and fat as he struggled to his feet and
loomed ferociously over the boy. A barrow full of wet mortar
stood half-capsized by the wall; several bricks had fallen into it,
splashing the grey paste about — some of it on the old man's
overalls. The man had a flat bricklayer's trowel in his hand
which he now raised overhead as he roared like a bull: the boy
cringed.

The man seemed about to strike him but then relented; the
trowel slowly descended and the old man peered at him.
'What the devil do you think you're doing?'

'I'm so sorry sir. . ." Then he swung the other leg over and
glanced about him at the destruction. He felt his cheeks flush-
ing; he said in a loud piping voice, 'How was I to know there
wasn't any mortar in those bricks?'

'And just who gave you permission to climb this wall, young man?' The old man was very angry indeed.

The boy tossed his head back to clear the hair from his eyes and defiantly met the fat man's stare. 'I only wanted to see what was on the other side.'

'Did you now?' There was a note of warning in the old man's growl. He turned and looked down at himself. 'Lord – look at me. Here I stand – drenched, begrimed and bedraggled.'

The boy said stoutly, 'You really should put up a warning sign or something.'

'Don't be impertinent.'

His pulse raced and he thought perhaps he had gone too far; he made a show of contrition, hanging his head. 'I am sorry, sir. Honestly I am.'

The fat man made ineffectual efforts to brush the brick-dust off his overalls; it only smeared the wet mortar about, caking his hands. 'Who are you?'

'I live here.'

'Here? Where is "here"?'

The boy flung his arm and pointed back towards the rhododendrons. 'In the cottage just there, sir.'

'Chartwell Cottage? You're one of Mrs Creighton's children then?'

'Yes sir.'

Ominously the fat man glowered at him. 'Well then, young man, you've just met your landlord. It might have been a more auspicious introduction, I should have thought.'

Muttering, the fat man stooped with a grunt and began to pick up bricks. The boy slid down off the wall and sought to placate him by assisting; following the old man's lead he gathered up the tumbled bricks and began to stack them by the base of the wall. After a moment the boy said anxiously, 'You're not hurt, are you, sir?'

'No thanks to you.'

'I should like to make amends, sir.'

The old man scowled. 'How?'

'I shall accept whatever punishment you think appropriate.' He squared his shoulders.

The fat man's lips began to twitch and quiver; for a moment

he averted his face. When he presented it again it was stern. 'How old are you?'

'Eleven, sir.'

'And what is your name?'

'Christopher, sir.'

'And you've just come home for the school holidays, I suppose. Do you know who I am, then?'

'No.'

'My name is Winston Churchill. And although I am merely an elderly parliamentarian,' the fat man said, 'I am still the owner of this place, you see, and I can't very well have eleven-year-old boys rampaging about my estate without so much as by-your-leave. As you suggest, we shall have to find a suitable punishment, shan't we?'

'Yes sir,' he said with a sinking heart. He had hoped his boldness might encourage the fat man to set him free, but it was not to be.

'Come along, then.' And the old man set off briskly towards the row of low outbuildings that squatted some distance down the slope.

Brick pathways carried them between the lawns. Beyond the sheds and cottages were a pair of ponds in a hollow. White foxgloves and a few small trees grew round the ponds; on the water the boy saw black swans and several geese.

'Wait here.' The man disappeared inside a cottage and after a moment the boy heard running water. Presently the fat man reappeared; now he carried a long-handled garden hoe. He thrust it into the boy's hands. 'Pray observe that the grass tends to overstep its mark, here at the edges of the paths, much as you overstepped the mark by climbing upon a wall that wasn't yours to climb. Now I should like you to go along the paths and make a neat edge to the lawn, on both sides. Here, let me demonstrate.'

Retrieving the hoe from him, the fat man stooped awkwardly, hefted the hoe in both hands and brought it down smartly so that the blade chopped off the grass that had begun to creep over the brick.

'Do you think you can do that?'

The boy contemplated the paths that curled about the lawns — they seemed endless. Without enthusiasm he said, 'Yes sir.'

5

'Then bestir yourself.' The old man handed him the tool and walked away, throwing a parting shot over his shoulder: 'I shall return in time to inspect your progress.'

At about noontime the fat man appeared from the trees and gave the boy a glance and walked up to the big brick house and disappeared into it. The sun became hot on the boy's head but he worked on with dedication; he meant to show he could take the punishment – he wasn't going to have the fat man think him a shirker. *I'll show him.*

He went on without reckoning time, ignoring hunger. Then he scented the strong sour aroma of cigar. Looking up he saw a puff of smoke slowly dissipating from beyond the branches of a tree. The boy stooped to his work and made a show of his weariness, sighing, making heavy weather of lifting the hoe each time; he paused, dramatically dragged the sleeve across his forehead, sighed again, and began to chop.

The fat man appeared from behind the tree. The boy made a show of being surprised.

'I was lurking,' the old man explained. 'Spying on you. You've worked very hard, haven't you?'

'Yes sir.'

'I suppose you're tired and hungry and thirsty now.'

'Yes sir.'

'Come along then.'

In that manner the boy made the acquaintance of his mother's landlord. It was June 1935; the boy's parents had divorced that previous winter and Uncle John, who lived nearby at Crockham Hill, had found lodgings for the boy, his two sisters and his mother in the cottage on the Churchills' estate near the village of Westerham in Kent.

In the ensuing school holidays he came to know the fat man a bit and to think of him as an old grump. He seemed to spend much of his time complaining that he was finished in politics, his career in ruins, nothing left but walls to build and pictures to paint and books to write that nobody would read.

The boy would see him painting under his great broad hat, sitting before an easel on the tiny wooded island he had built in the lower Chartwell pond. On one occasion he crept up towards the old man from behind but the wooden footbridge betrayed him, creaking underfoot, and the fat man's hat-brim turned quickly:

'Playing at Red Indians, are you?'

'Sorry, sir. I wanted to see the painting.'

'Whenever I catch sight of you you're up to mischief!'

In the main the boy did not think unkindly of the fat man; he did not think of him at all. The boy spent very little time in the company of adults. Mostly he was away at boarding school.

Hitler's first aggression – the Nazi occupation of the Rhineland in March 1936, unopposed by the French – was remarked upon by Mr Churchill in an I-told-them-so manner but the boy had no interest in such things and hardly had an idea who Mr Hitler might be; the only German politician with whom he was familiar was the Ambassador to the Court of St James's, Herr Joachim von Ribbentrop, who had dined several times at the boy's father's house in Harley Street before the divorce. Ribbentrop had been a fellow student with the boy's father, who had spent two years in a German school before the Great War.

In spring 1938, when Christopher was at public school, German troops marched into Austria. There was no resistance. Austria ceased to exist; not a shot was fired. By now the boy and his schoolmates were aware of the meaning of the sabres being rattled on the Continent. There was civil war in Spain; and at Munich in September the Prime Minister, Mr Chamberlain, allowed himself to be intimidated into letting Czechoslovakia fall into German hands. When Christopher visited Chartwell at the bank holiday Mr Churchill was in a fury: 'Czechs freeze and starve so that Hitler and his gang may be clothed and fed in luxury – and we won't lift a finger! Pray explain to me how we may avoid having them on the beaches of Britain.'

The fat man sat bundled in a heavy coat on the terrace. He was sipping hot soup from a spoon. Christopher couldn't help laughing; Mr Churchill's perverseness and bounce put him in mind of a favourite character from earlier childhood.

The fat man glared pugnaciously. 'What do you find so amusing?'

'Sorry, sir. That's not, by any chance, extract of malt?'

Quick as a flash the fat man responded as if reading his mind: 'Roo's medicine, eh? "What Tiggers like" — you look astonished. D'you think you're the only person on the planet who's read *The House at Pooh Corner*? So I'm Tigger, am I?'

'I'm sorry. Seeing you eat with a spoon like that. . .'

'*Bloody* cheek!' Then the fat man smiled. His smile was infrequent and rare — but it could be dazzling. 'Well if I'm Tigger then you, I suppose, are Christopher Robin?'

In the late summer of 1939 when the boy was fourteen Germany invaded Poland. England declared war on Germany and Mr Churchill snapped, 'So much for peace in our time.'

At school the boys went round singing *We're going to hang out our washing on the Siegfried Line*. A British expeditionary force had crossed the Channel to take up positions and the new First Lord of the Admiralty — Mr Churchill — had gone to France to review the Maginot Line defences. Christopher followed it all keenly in the newspapers and kept his wireless switched on in case there were bulletins. It excited him to realize he knew someone in the corridors of power. But the Phoney War dragged on into one of the bitterest winters on record; and after a time the interests of the boys returned to other things.

Then in April the Germans invaded Denmark and Norway; British forces went north to meet them and the war was on.

Christopher was summoned to the telephone in his housemaster's study. The voice on the line was Uncle John's. 'I've got the headmaster's permission for you to come down to London.'

'Whatever for?'

'There's something rather important I should like to talk to you about.'

'Me, sir?'

'You, Christopher. Will you come?'

'Of course,' he replied, mystified.

'A Colonel Metcalf will collect you at the station. He's seen your photographs — he'll recognize you. And Christopher — absolute hush. Understand?'

On the train he sat with his head against the window watching the spring landscapes roll by. Two men in bowler hats sat opposite him arguing about Norway. 'It's all the First Lord's doing. Hitler would have honoured Norway's neutrality if Churchill hadn't ordered the Navy to lay minefields in Norwegian waters to prevent them getting iron ore shipments out to Germany.'

'Well – rather clever of the old boy, you must admit. Provoke them into attacking the poor old Norwegians instead of ourselves.'

'Our turn will come soon enough. I'm sure Hitler's laid on the plans.'

Christopher, baffled by Uncle John's mysterious summons, reviewed the trunk-call conversation but could find no clues in it. Uncle John had one of those icy even-toned voices that never gave anything away.

Uncle John was unmarried; often he had taken supper at Harley Street and stayed in one of the guest bedrooms there when he was up in London on his business trips. He and the boy's father had become friends during the Great War; he wasn't a real uncle.

He was involved in some vague way with foreign trade. He had a sinister aspect that enhanced the chills of the ghost stories he sometimes told to Christopher and his sisters, sitting on the edge of the children's beds. The tales were deliciously alarming but in other respects it was difficult to warm to Uncle John. His brown hair was sleek and polished like cordovan; he wore expensive Savile Row suits and a trimmed military moustache and he was known to most people simply as 'the Major' because he had been an officer in the 1914–18 war. It was said of him that he had been shot while in the trenches and that the 7.62mm bullet had lodged near his heart and was still there, too close to the vital organ for safe removal, and that he never knew from one day to the next when the fragile membrane might burst and the bullet penetrate and his life gutter out. It was said that he never made personal plans, never booked reservations ahead, and lived a gloomy life in sepulchral surroundings.

It was Uncle John who provided the connection between the boy's family and the Churchills. At different times during the Great War he had served in the same mess with the boy's father, who had been an RFC pilot, and with Mr Churchill, who after leaving the war cabinet had served at the front with a combat regiment; Uncle John had become Mr Churchill's aide and they had remained friends ever since. Later, after the boy's father had become an important surgeon and had begun to practise in Harley Street, Uncle John had introduced the two men.

But Christopher had never altogether liked him. Uncle John talked through his teeth in an unattractive way and his polite interest in the children seemed forced. His eyes were a brilliant cold blue, luminous with shrewd confidence but frightening.

When the train arrived Christopher looked round the platform for the Colonel Metcalf who was supposed to collect him. He saw several stiff tall gentlemen in the crowds who might be colonels, but none of them paid him any attention. Then a podgy man with a moustache, in an ill-fitting officer's uniform, carrying a grubby raincoat, came prowling forward squinting at faces. He hurried over when he saw Christopher, his swagger stick tapping against his thigh. 'Christopher Creighton?'

'Yes sir.'

'The Major asked me to collect you. Colonel Metcalf.' The Colonel beamed and thrust out an unexpectedly firm hand. 'Come along, please.'

The car was a Daimler, black and long. The Colonel gripped the strap when it moved off. He said to the chauffeur, 'Back to the Admiralty now,' and settled back. 'Madness this afternoon,' he confided wearily to the boy. 'Everyone rushing about like lunatics. You'd think they hadn't had all these months to pre-pare for it.'

'Sir, do you have any idea why Uncle John wants me?'

'I'm sure you'll learn soon enough. Oh, by the way, you're to call me Winnie the Pooh.' The Colonel winked at him. 'Code name, don't you know.'

Christopher tried to conceal his astonishment.

Winnie the Pooh chatted away amiably until the car drew up before the Admiralty. 'Here we are then.'

Men and women bustled along the corridors. The red-cheeked colonel guided Christopher with a hand on his shoulder. Quite a few of the uniformed ratings carried arms and this prompted Christopher to ask, 'Are they fighting in Norway, sir? Actually shooting, I mean?'

'Oh yes, I'm afraid so. Rather heavy fighting, especially round Narvik.'

'I wish I could be there.'

'That's the spirit.'

Colonel Metcalf delivered him to a small room, asked him to wait, and left him alone there. There was an unoccupied desk, a high window, several maps pinned to the walls. Busy footsteps hurried by outside the door. The boy felt as if he'd been sent up for punishment. Unnerved, he went to the window and looked out across Horse Guards' Parade. A convoy crept along Horse Guards' Road – troop-carrier lorries: soldiers going off to the ships. He heard the chime of Big Ben striking the hour.

The latch clicked and he turned in time to see Uncle John enter; and behind him came Winston Churchill, dressed in a black coat, pin-striped trousers and a spotted bow tie. Uncle John quickly closed the door behind Mr Churchill, who gave Christopher a brief glance and shifted it almost immediately towards one of the wall maps, at which he glared belligerently. Uncle John said, 'Thank you for coming at such short notice. I suppose you find this very mysterious – I'm sorry I wasn't free to speak more plainly on the telephone. You didn't tell any of the other boys where you were going, did you?'

'No sir. You asked me not to.'

'You're quite sure you've told no-one?'

'Yes sir. No-one.'

Mr Churchill turned away from the map. 'You don't need to cross-examine him all afternoon, Major. Christopher, pray come and sit down. We've a favour to ask of you.'

The fat man pointed to a chair and Christopher settled on the edge of it, sitting up very straight.

'We first met, what – nearly five years ago, isn't it? From the first I was impressed with you.' The fat man waggled his finger roguishly at the boy. 'When I was a young man – a few years older than you are now, to be sure – I was taken prisoner by the Boers in South Africa. You put it back in my mind that morning when you crashed into my garden. I climbed a wall then, you see, to make my escape. Of course I was, shall we say, somewhat less clumsy in my attempt than you in yours. I managed to get safely over the wall without attracting attention. Then I had to cover some three hundred miles of hostile country to our own lines.'

The boy saw Uncle John's eyes roll impatiently towards the ceiling. Mr Churchill, who did not see Uncle John's rude expression of exasperation, went on with hearty enthusiasm for his narrative:

'How hopeless it appeared. But I went on alone, walking boldly through the streets of Pretoria, humming a tune, and boarded a train just coming out of the station. I clambered into a filthy carriage filled with empty coal bags. Some hours later, at midmorning, I was quenching my thirst in a stream with a lean and hungry vulture as my only companion. Those were indeed adventurous days. We faced danger at every turning – but with great good cheer.'

Then the fat man subjected the boy to an alarming silent scrutiny. He had strange pale eyes; his skin was pale and pink; he had a way of overwhelming one with his gaze.

He said abruptly, 'So many adventures – my youth was filled with them. Omdurman – the reconquest of the Sudan, 1898. I shot five men for certain, perhaps more. I was the very first of Kitchener's army to see the enemy, you know. I was on patrol that day and we of that privileged band were the first to hear the war songs of the forty thousand Dervishes – enough to put awe into the heart of any civilized man. They opened fire upon us and we galloped across their front firing into them – I have never experienced anything like the exhilaration of that charge. Nothing touched me, somehow, but the smell, which was quite beyond description – ten thousand bodies lying about, at the end.'

The old man was garrulous: it wasn't the first time Christopher had heard those tales. His war stories were quite thrilling the first time but they quickly became boring with repetition. Christopher was not disappointed when Uncle John cleared his throat noisily and said, 'The appointment with Lord Beaverbrook. . .'

'Yes, yes, all right John.' Then the fat man squinted at Christopher. When he pursed his lips that way he seemed to pout. 'You're still in the Scouts, aren't you?'

'Yes. I'm a Sea Scout.'

'I believe St George is the patron saint of the Scouts?'

'Yes sir.'

'Unfortunately St George is not readily available to use. In the circumstances, I wonder whether you, Christopher, are prepared to help us slay this dragon?'

Christopher knew that when the fat man's eyes twinkled it meant he had mischief in mind.

Uncle John said, 'I'm still not convinced it's a wise. . .'

'I know, I know. I admit it's a dreadful burden for one so young. But at least let's put it to the boy and see how he feels. John, you weren't there the day he faced that juggernaut. It was most impressive – an example of dogged courage one rarely finds in young men nowadays. Do you remember the old gypsy woman, Christopher?'

The old woman had lived in a caravan near Chartwell Manor; she had been a source of cruel amusement to the Westerham boys as she hobbled about, bent over her gnarled stick, smacking her gums. On a grey afternoon Christopher had been riding his bike down the hill, pedalling swiftly as he was late for tea; his mother would scold him roundly, as it was to be the first occasion on which the Churchills had consented to come round to tea in the cottage. Out of breath, he'd sped madly down the road past the manor gate. Then he'd seen the old woman, hobbling slowly up the road, smack in the middle of the narrow lane and clearly oblivious to the fact that a large open touring car was bearing swiftly down on her from behind.

The car hooted imperiously and the driver shouted at the old woman. She must be deaf as a post, the boy realized. It seemed possible the driver might run her down.

The boy whipped his bike past the old woman and slithered it round in the lane, sliding to an abrupt stop; he put one foot out to stand upright and faced the car. The pale young driver laughed superciliously, skidded the car across to the left-hand verge and at the last moment sliced it past the boy and the old woman. A young couple in the rear seat shook their heads at Christopher; the girl in the driver's arms laughed cruelly; and the driver tossed his head and sneered: 'Take good care of your lady friend, Sir Galahad.' Then the car accelerated towards the top of the hill, laughter ringing back.

The old woman had scowled at the boy, then turned and

resumed her slow crawl up the lane as if nothing had happened. The boy had watched her go. 'Stay off the road then, you old fool.' But she hadn't heard him. Then he'd recalled the urgency of his errand and pointed the bike towards the cottage.

That was when Mr and Mrs Churchill had emerged from the trees by the side of the road. The fat man had bellowed, 'There's that cheeky boy on his blasted bike again!' Then the man had turned to his wife and said, 'That was really quite extraordinary. Seldom have I seen anyone face danger with such ruthless disregard for his own safety.'

Mrs Churchill had smiled. 'But, my dear, I thought he was a precocious brat?'

For once, at that moment, the fat man had had nothing to say. But henceforth the boy's bicycle had been forever dubbed the 'blasted bike'.

. . . 'Yes sir,' he replied, 'I remember the old woman.'

Mr Churchill nodded and smiled, a bit oddly, and then returned to the map. He jabbed a finger at the north of France. 'The Maginot Line. Facing it, the German Siegfried Line. Do schoolboys take an interest in these things?'

'Some, sir.'

'And what do they think will happen here?' Mr Churchill tapped the map.

'Well I suppose it will be like the last war, sir. Trenches, fortifications, tanks, masses of artillery. . .'

'Not this time, lad. No, the Hun is a bit cleverer than that. Look here – what would you do if you were Jerry and had it in your mind to take France?' And without waiting for an answer Mr Churchill slid his finger boldly to the left along the map. 'I shall tell you. Herr Hitler intends to repeat the Schlieffen Plan of 1914 by running his offensive round the end, through the Ardennes and the Low Countries. Originally he planned to put his Blitzkrieg into effect last November but it has been postponed for a number of reasons. If you'd like to know how I know this, ask Uncle John – intelligence is his job, and I can assure you he's quite good at it.'

So that is what his business interests are, thought Christopher.

Uncle John said, 'One can't really expect full information of the enemy's intentions, can one. But we've been fortunate. Not long ago a German aeroplane crashed in Belgium and the plans for the Schlieffen route were found on the German officer in the aircraft. We think this accident caused another postponement in the German schedules. . .'

'But we believe in the end they will carry out the plan,' Mr Churchill concluded. 'We believe we know where they intend to strike. What we don't know is when.'

Christopher found himself staring at the fat man's small finger, which was still pressed against the map of Belgium. Mr Churchill's cherubic face seemed inconsistent with the hard growl of his words. 'Next week your school chum Prince Paul will return home for the holidays to his parents' château near Antwerp.'

'Yes sir.'

'Lord Gort's Expeditionary Force has been placed here – on the left flank of the Maginot Line, along the Franco-Belgian border, together with four French armies,' Mr Churchill said, thumping the map.

'Yes,' said Christopher doubtfully, mystified by the abrupt change of subject.

Mr Churchill scowled abstractedly out of the window. 'Christopher, you must understand the delicacy of our predicament. The Belgians are our friends and we are pledged to defend them; but Belgium is a small nation under the shadow of Germany and it is a frightened nation, living in the memory of the Great War. King Leopold, perhaps understandably, does not wish to offend his powerful German neighbour and is attempting to maintain a precarious neutrality. To placate the Germans not only has he denied his friends the right to keep an army on his eastern border to defend him from the Hun, but he has gone so far as to ask all staff officers to leave Belgium. No British military officer now remains on Belgian soil. Of course this stricture applies to German officers as well, and French and so on; but what it means to us is that we have been blindfolded and our ears covered. We don't know as much as we need to know about Belgium's plans for defence or the disposition of her armies. Therefore how can we shape our own tactics? Do you understand?'

'Yes sir.'

Mr Churchill turned at last away from the map and confronted the boy squarely. 'Now young Christopher, keeping all this in mind, I want to ask whether you might be willing to do a job for us – a dangerous job for King and country? Before you answer', Mr Churchill added, 'I should like to assure you that this matter has been brought to the King's attention and has his approval, and that the major and I have discussed it in general terms with your mother. Of course you may wish to discuss it with her yourself, but we've had her consent – naturally she's in favour of your assisting us.'

'Naturally?' Uncle John said drily. 'I shouldn't go that far but in any case she's agreed to it. Christopher, the one thing we must ask you to refrain from doing is discussing it with your father. It's not a question of his disapproving – I'm sure if he knew the facts he'd give us his support – but your father would ask far too many questions and there's a great deal we should be unable to tell him. I'm afraid he'd resent that.'

Christopher said, 'What is it you'd like me to do?'

'Oh that's quite simple,' Mr Churchill said. 'We'd like you to persuade your friend Prince Paul to invite you to accompany him to Belgium for the school holiday. And when you arrive there we'd like you to engage in espionage in that château – to discover, if you can, the dispositions of the Belgian army, and to report anything else you consider of import.'

Uncle John stood near the window toying with a waistcoat button, looking at neither of them.

Mr Churchill said, 'The choice is entirely yours. No-one can force you to do such a job. And I should be a fool if I led you to believe that you were to be the only British spy in all Belgium. We've many sources of information. Unfortunately at the moment most of them are producing unreliable information or, in some cases, none at all. We should like to have someone inside the Belgian centre of power – someone who's not suspect. A young boy on his blasted bike – well I'm sure you can see how you might make yourself useful. Adults will ignore young boys at play when they speak confidences to one another. Who'd suspect a boy your age of spying on state secrets?'

Christopher felt Uncle John's eyes on him: Uncle John was studying him with a suspicious scrutiny. It wasn't to do with placing burdens on him. Uncle John was worried about whether he could be trusted to keep things to himself.

Christopher sat up very straight. 'You can count on me, sir.'

Uncle John said, 'You'll want to think it over more carefully than that, I think.'

'No sir. I'm quite ready to do as you ask.' *To be a spy for England* . . . his heart raced.

'It may not be as adventurous as you think. You may learn nothing at all. And if you do learn something and you're discovered – well, it's a dangerous business. It's not a game.' Uncle John shook his head. 'I should think twice if I were you.'

'Don't you want me to do it, sir? Then why did you ask me down here?'

'I'm afraid the major sometimes doesn't know his own mind,' Mr Churchill said. 'The idea seems to strike him alternately hot and cold, you see.' To Uncle John he added, 'I wish I'd never mentioned that ridiculous Christopher Robin business to you.'

'It should serve the purpose,' Uncle John said, distractedly.

Mr Churchill said, 'Uncle John's always been one for Byzantine deceptions – silly secret code names and the like. It appears he was very much smitten with the idea that I should be referred to in all secret communications in this affair as "Tigger". You're to blame for that.'

'You needn't have told him about that.'

Mr Churchill laughed. 'Stout lad. Quite right. I mustn't pass the blame to you.'

Uncle John said, 'It's an amusing idea, really.'

'If that sort of thing entertains you.'

'Christopher, the point is that an agent in the field must disguise his communications from eavesdroppers,' Uncle John explained rather stuffily. 'A spy can't very well switch on his wireless transmitter and broadcast to the world the fact that he's addressing a message to the First Lord of the Admiralty. Code identifications are vital to the transmission of intelligence. I've proposed – based on your own initiative – that the First Lord be referred to as "Tigger", that my own code name be "Owl", that my associate Colonel Metcalf be called "Winnie the Pooh", and that you yourself be dubbed "Christopher Robin". We've also discussed the possibility of seconding Winnie the Pooh to Lord Gort's staff in France, where he may act as your contact with home. You've met Winnie the Pooh of course – he collected you from the train.'

'Yes sir.'

'Do you like him?'

'He seems quite nice.'

Uncle John nodded. 'He is. He's also quite brilliant – don't let his dull appearance mislead you.'

'No sir,' Christopher said, and turned his eyes towards the fat man. 'Sir – if it's not rude, may I ask a question?'

'Ask away.'

'Why did you choose me for this?'

'For a number of very good reasons. You happen to be a friend of the Belgian boy. Your French is good. You happen to be possessed of an uncannily innocent appearance. You happen to be so young as to allay suspicion, you're tough as nails, and you happen to be well known to us. We believe you can be trusted.' Then he turned fully from the window and for the first time faced Christopher squarely. 'I very much hope we shan't learn our trust has been misplaced. You have, not to put too fine a point on it, a well-deserved reputation for misbehaviour.'

'I won't let you down, sir.'

'We shall rely on that', said Tigger.

It was all, Christopher thought, quite unbelievable.

Chapter Two

When he reached the door a servant appeared farther along the corridor; it made him jump a bit and he kept on walking, glad the servant hadn't come a few seconds later and seen him actually enter the room. Christopher gave the man a vague smile as he passed. At the turning he loitered until he heard the servant's footsteps dwindle; then he put his head back round the corner, saw the corridor was empty, and hurried back to the door. He stopped just outside it, bent as if to tie his shoelace and looked both ways along the hall. No-one lurked among the statues and busts and chandeliers and paintings. He tried the door and crept into the room and stood looking about him with wide-eyed innocence for the benefit of anyone who might be in the room, but it was empty and he pushed the door silently shut behind him and went down the length of the long elegant table past the high wing-chairs to the far end.

The windows at the far end of the room were small and set high in the walls, for ventilation rather than view. During the meetings that had taken place on the past two evenings the windows had remained shut, as he'd discovered to his annoyance when he'd gone over the château roof in the dark.

A gilt-edged side-table against the wall supported two telephones. He stepped up on to it, stood on tiptoe, and found he could just reach the centre window. He took the small coil of copper wire from his pocket and twisted the end of the wire to the simple latch-handle on the inside of the window, tossed the coil outside, and pulled the window gently shut. When he examined it from the floor the wire was barely visible against the dark brass fitting and it looked as if the scheme would work: pull the wire to one side from the outside and it ought to disengage the latch; then pull outward and it ought to open the window.

He rubbed the tabletop with the heel of his hand in case his shoes had left marks. Then he hurried back to the door and held his breath while he put his ear to the crack.

Footsteps rang in the corridor, growing louder – approaching.

He shrank back against the wall, but the footsteps clicked on by; then there was silence and he let himself out of the room and hurried towards the garden.

The children were still at lunch, picnicking on the lawn. Prince Paul rolled his eyes at Christopher. 'Where were you?'

'In the lav. Sorry I'm late.'

'Ah, what foods these morsels be.' Paul stuffed his mouth with a sausage and passed the plate to Christopher. By the flower-beds Paul's sisters were giggling at something. The governess sat in the shade wrapped in a heavy shawl sipping tea.

The château was one of the centres of Belgian and Luxembourgeois politics: during the past week ministers and ambassadors had been frequent visitors; once King Leopold and his entourage had come to dinner – the children were kept at a distance – and the Grand Duchess of Luxembourg had arrived on Tuesday afternoon; everyone seemed to call her 'Tante Charlotte'. Paul's father had some sort of position in the Belgian government but Christopher had been unable to define it exactly and his efforts to question Paul had been unsuccessful: 'Well, my father's a sort of military adviser and aide-de-camp to the King. Not officially, of course. The families have been close for hundreds of years; you know how it is with these things.'

In the past few days the Germans had defeated the British troops in Norway; the British forces had had to be evacuated and there was talk that the Prime Minister, Mr Chamberlain, might resign; there was also great concern over what the next Nazi target for conquest might be. Fear of air raids had driven some of the politicians out of Brussels and Antwerp – and some of them had arrived at the château, either to stay or to stop briefly en route to their own country houses. Conferences took place nightly; the King himself had attended one of them. Everything was uncertain and everyone seemed afraid: they all seemed to be trying to read Hitler's mind; yet sometimes in the balmy afternoons they sat about the courtyard with their glasses of wine and whisky talking of trivial things.

He kept remembering Mr Churchill's parting words to him in the Admiralty: *We're at war, Christopher – make no mistake about that.* But it seemed an odd sort of war to him.

*

He climbed silently over the tile roof, wearing plimsoles, and lay flat at the edge. He reached down to feel for the coil of copper wire. At first he couldn't find it — the light that came out of the windows blinded him to what lay in the shadows. He shifted along the roof a bit and stretched his arm down, aware of the two-storey drop to the flagstones beneath.

When he found the wire he gave it a little tug and heard the latch squeak. He froze, peering down at an acute angle through the window — all he could see was a small piece of the table and part of the edge of the room; one man sat there, the top of his head bald, talking to someone out of sight. The bald head didn't rise or turn; after a moment Christopher tugged again and felt the latch slide open. He pulled the window out just a few inches.

'. . . no tanks, very few aircraft, an obsolete cavalry corps, a brigade of cyclists — cyclists, *mon dieu*! — with what are we supposed to fight?' The bald man spoke in French.

Christopher tugged out his notebook and scribbled with the stub of his pencil, unable to see what he was writing, hoping he could recall it later: *o tks, few arcrft, obslt cav corp, brg cyclists. . .*

'We've an army of nine hundred thousand men —' Another voice, hidden somewhere in the room; the bald man replied, interrupting:

'Nearly half of them conscripts brought in after the order for general mobilization. With what we have we can hardly hope to withstand the machine that overran Poland.'

'We must try.'

Christopher inched forward, snaking his head out over the tiles. The room crept into his view, upside-down. He began to lose equilibrium and pulled himself back and looked behind him — there was a vent-pipe a foot or so to the right and he positioned himself below it, hooking the instep of his foot round it, and let himself slide down again until his elbows barely made purchase on the rim and his head drooped over so that he could see through the pane beside the open window.

'We must continue to rely on the established plan,' one of the men was saying. 'To hold our delaying position along the Meuse and the Albert Canal — to defend the fortresses of Liège and to rely upon our British and French friends, to counter-attack if we are invaded.'

'If the Germans give them time to counter-attack,' the bald man replied drily. 'Judging by the Polish and Norwegian experiences I rather wonder whether Monsieur Hitler will be so kind as to conform to the needs of the Allied timetable. It takes time to move armies.'

'We shall just have to hope the next German target is not Belgium.'

The discussions went on and on. Christopher made the occasional note. He became cramped and chilled. Finally, after midnight, the room emptied and he slithered back across the roof and went down through the branches of the elm tree by the rear coachway. He did not enter the château; he set off across the lane into the wood and made his way slowly through the trees, feeling his way in the dark from trunk to trunk. In the distance an aircraft droned across the horizon.

The army camp was about a mile from the château and his destination was just short of it. He could see the soldiers' lights beyond the wire fence. Using them as a guide he found his way to the tent that sat in a cul-de-sac off the lane that led into the Belgian army camp. It was only an outpost — a single company street of tents; it couldn't have been here long. Some farmer had given up his north-west field for it.

The young man and woman were waiting in the tent. Christopher let the flap fall behind him. 'Is something wrong?'

'They've sent patrols out twice today.' The young man spoke with a Scottish accent. He had pale hair and a pleasant youthful face. The woman was red-haired and comely. They were posing as a honeymoon couple on a camping trip.

The woman said, 'They asked us questions this afternoon.'

'A few too many questions,' the young man said. 'They'll be asking us to move on soon. I don't know how long we'll be able to remain here.'

The W/T was a bulky B-Mark-II short-wave set. Christopher helped the young man run out the full seventy-foot aerial, winding it round tree trunks and carrying it high into the branches. Then the woman switched it on. The valves began to glow and the young man sat down with Christopher's notepad to encode the message.

None of it seemed all that important to Christopher. It was probably information London already had. But Uncle John — Owl — wanted everything. It was what he was here for and he didn't intend to botch it.

The woman was at the mouth of the tent listening to the night. Christopher could hear nothing except the wind. The woman said, 'All right,' and the young man began to tap the Morse key.

Christopher pushed the rook forward and lifted a black pawn off the board. Paul looked at him with a bemused shake of his head. 'You ruddy fool.' And brought his knight out of hiding.

The dark cloud-bellies were pregnant with the menace of rain, and they sat at the marble garden-table ready to dash for cover. Paul said, 'I'll push you right back in that corner and jump on your king with both feet.'

It gave Christopher a picture of his opponent's plan and forearmed with that knowledge he opened a new drive with his white bishop in the opposite corner of the board; ten minutes and a dozen moves later Paul tipped his king over, resigning with a rueful shake of his head. 'How did you do that? I didn't even see it coming.'

'You gave your game away. A closed mouth gathers no foot, old chum.' Christopher felt the first warning droplets on his hands. They collected the chess pieces and made for the pagoda shelter in the centre of the formal garden. The masses of tulips were ready to be cut; the azaleas were beginning to come out.

Paul put down the board and they began to set the pieces in place. 'Oh, I forgot to tell you — there seems to be a spy among us.' His eyes flashed with excitement. 'They've intercepted radio signals coming from nearby.'

'Near here?' Christopher's heart raced. He put his hands in his lap to keep Paul from seeing them tremble; he pretended to concentrate on the chessboard. 'In German or what?'

'Nobody sends short-wave signals in plain language, dolt. They say it's in numbers — a cipher. Who knows what language it might be? But you're probably right — it's got to be a German spy.'

'I wonder who it is.'

'It could be nearly anyone, I suppose. But I shouldn't want

to be in his shoes if he's caught.' His head turned towards the front of the house then; so did Christopher's, drawn by the sound of tyres crunching on the gravel drive. A car came slowly in view along the curve of the driveway and Paul said, 'Speaking of German spies!'

On the wings of the large car insignia flags flapped red, white and black – the German swastika. The car came to a sedate stop; the chauffeur, in grey German uniform, leapt out and unfurled a black umbrella as he opened the passenger's door. Christopher stiffened when he saw the big square-faced German emerge under the umbrella.

'You know him, Christopher?'

'Ribbentrop.'

'The foreign minister?'

'He was ambassador to Britain when I met him.' Ribbentrop had drawn up before the house in Harley Street in a car very similar to this one – the same long black bonnet with the same Nazi flags. His accent had seemed peculiar to Christopher, who was a boy of eleven at the time; he had sniggered at him and Ribbentrop had caught him at it – the boy's father had begun to reprimand him but Ribbentrop had swept it aside and laughed. He'd patted Christopher awkwardly on the head and said that the boy was absolutely correct, his accent was amusing but he was doing all he could to improve it and he hoped the boy would bear with him. Then the German had clapped the boy's father on the arm and they had gone on into the sitting room reminiscing about their schooldays together in Germany before the Great War. Herr von Ribbentrop had come to the house several times in 1936 and 1937; the boy had seen him there twice on his visits to his father after the move to Chartwell. The German had never quite forgiven him for laughing at him, but he pretended to take it in good part. 'Ah, the young man who was so bold to tease an ambassador!' It was mainly Ribbentrop's way of showing that he remembered who Christopher was. He took great pride in his memory for names and faces.

In 1938 Hitler had appointed Ribbentrop his foreign secretary. Ribbentrop had concluded the infamous Non-Aggression Pact between Germany and Russia. Now, when the tall German disappeared into the château, Christopher said, 'What do you suppose brings such an important Nazi to Belgium?'

'I suppose,' Paul said drily, 'he's come to dictate the terms of surrender to us. He may find a few surprises — we shan't go under as easily as the Poles did.'

Christopher said nothing; but he remembered the dour arguments he'd overheard the night before and wondered whether indeed the Belgians would have any chance at all against the Nazi armies.

Late in the afternoon the rain moved on. In the steamy dusk more cars arrived, some of them apparently from the nearby-grass-strip air station, for several of them were preceded by the low landing-approaches of light aircraft. Christopher and Paul raced each other across the lawns chasing a football and no-one paid them much attention, but Christopher took note of the fact that three of the visitors — men in trilby hats and dark raincoats, collars turned up, arriving separately from the aerodrome at ten- or fifteen-minute intervals — entered the château by side doors and were neither seen by nor introduced to the other guests.

Christopher went up to his room to prepare for dinner. Washed, changed and presentable in his Sea Scout uniform, he went along the wide central hall towards the small dining room in the rear of the château where the children ate. He was passing a doorway when a man emerged from it and he recognized Herr Joachim von Ribbentrop. The German glanced at him without recognition and began to turn away. On impulse Christopher turned. 'Herr von Ribbentrop? What a surprise — don't you remember me?'

Ribbentrop's eyes widened. He scowled. Then a quick smile of belated recognition. 'Why, of course — Christopher Creighton. Whatever are you doing *here*?' he asked in his thick accent.

'Visiting my schoolfriend, Prince Paul.' Without allowing his reluctance to show, he accepted the German's handshake and then, remembering Ribbentrop's polite questions about his nautical progress on the occasion of their last meeting, he contrived to grin proudly. 'I've been made troop leader in the Sea Scouts, your excellency.'

'That is good, Christopher — that is good. And how is your dear father?'

'Very well, thank you sir.'

Ribbentrop said, 'A brilliant surgeon, your father. And a loyal friend. It's ludicrous the way war interrupts such valued friendships. When you return to England perhaps you might suggest to your father that he use his influence in London to persuade his friends to abandon their aggressive warlike course towards Germany. My country only wants peace and it's a terrible shame that England should oppose us. The English have always been our friends. I've made every effort to convince Whitehall that war between our countries is not inevitable. Far from it. If only a bit of reason can be employed. . .'

'Yes sir. I'm sure no-one wants war.' You bloody hypocrite.

'Speak to your father of these things, then. He's a most influential man.' With a distracted smile, Ribbentrop snapped his head down in a quick bow, turned and clicked heavily away through the forest of sculpture.

Christopher watched him go, wondering what audacity had prompted him to confront the Nazi minister. He certainly hadn't learnt anything useful from it. It had been a stupid mistake to reveal his presence to the German. Someone was already aware that coded messages were being broadcast from near the estate.

Worried, he went on to dinner.

Canted vertiginously over the lip of the tile roof he lay with his feet hooked round the ventilation pipe and the notebook clutched awkwardly in his hand, the pencil scratching hurriedly across it making tracks that were invisible in the night.

His legs and shoulders burnt with cramp; he'd been there three hours and if they went on much longer he'd run out of pages in the notebook. Twice it had begun to rain halfheartedly, and he hoped the pencil marks hadn't run; he'd tried to shelter the notebook under his chin. Twice he'd had to take out his Scout knife and sharpen the pencil – it was down to an inch-long stub.

Herr von Ribbentrop had taken command of the meeting from the beginning – as if it were a German headquarters rather than a neutral one. Paul's father had tried to assume the chair at the outset but the German foreign minister had cut him dead.

Ribbentrop was flanked by four German officers. Amazingly they were in uniform – a measure of their arrogance. Three of them were grey – one bearing the red tabs of the General Staff – the fourth grey–green with black trim, the uniform of the SS. The wearing of foreign uniforms had been forbidden by King Leopold. The colonel in the General Staff uniform seemed to be in charge of maps and charts; other men would cluster round the map and Ribbentrop would move his pointer from place to place as he spoke.

In response to Ribbentrop's questions, Paul's father's aide and the other Belgian – an elderly army general – delivered in flat tones precise information about strong-points, troop concentrations, defences, lines of communications and supply.

They were selling their country out to the Germans.

The first hour of the meeting had been devoted to excuses and reluctance on the part of the Belgians. Ribbentrop had ridden harshly over their arguments with vulgar threats.

Paul's father from the outset expressed nothing but agony. He wished only to spare his countrymen the horrors of destruction that had befallen Poland – the horrors that Belgians remembered too well from a war hardly more than twenty years ago. 'We cannot win against the Wehrmacht,' he kept saying, as if to persuade himself of the truth of it; and Christopher felt tears squeeze from his eyes as he listened. 'We cannot win – we cannot win.' *You can't always go by that* – he wanted to shout it at the stupid timid man.

Ribbentrop was relentless. 'No. You cannot win. You can, however, be spared the worst. Germany's quarrel is not with Belgium.'

'It is,' said the Belgian aide, 'with France, this German quarrel, yes?'

Ribbentrop gave the man a blank look. 'With France, yes. When Belgium executes her surrender, the British and French armies will be exposed on their flank – we shall divide and destroy them and' – Ribbentrop smiled with cool menace across the map at the Belgian – 'the war will be over in a matter of weeks.'

'And you will claim all Europe from the Russian border to the Atlantic Ocean, yes?'

'The Third Reich honours its commitments, monsieur. This you may confirm simply by inquiring of the government of Spain. So long as you gentlemen honour your part of our agree-

27

ment, Belgium and her King will remain independent.' Ribbentrop's smile never changed: it was as rigid as a painted mask.

Paul's father, like his son, had the habitual mannerism of shaking his head back and forth to express any number of things. Ribbentrop saw the gesture and drew his own conclusions from it. He snapped, 'The choice before you is between a Belgian government willing to ally itself with Germany in friendship, and a military government imposed by Berlin. Which do you prefer?'

'We haven't lost the war yet,' Paul's father said. It was the only spark to flash from him.

'You will, soon enough. Please don't count on the support of your British and French friends. They were of no use to Poland, were they?'

In the end, Paul's father got to his feet and said broodingly to the others round the table, 'Gentlemen, I wish with all my heart to spare my country. But I shall not betray her.' And he walked swiftly from the room, his back very straight.

Well done, old man! Christopher found himself grinning in the dark. Then he scribbled another note.

That was when the remaining two Belgians – the aide and the old general – began to deliver specific defence information into the hands of the Germans; it had gone on now for more than two hours and Ribbentrop was standing back with a satisfied smirk while the German officers made lengthy notes and drew symbols on the maps.

For a moment the old Belgian general took the floor. 'Germany has many friends in Belgium – we see the folly of a strong resistance to the German advance. If war is inevitable then we must take the reasonable position that a short war is less destructive than a long one. I am sure our host would agree with me on this matter if he were here.'

'I'm sure he would,' Ribbentrop purred, so softly that Christopher barely heard him.

The general moved forward. 'With your permission?' He borrowed Ribbentrop's pointer. With its tip he touched a position on the map. Christopher strained to see but the distance was too great.

'Here, a petrol dump – half a million gallons.' The tip of the pointer moved; one of the German colonels made a note. 'Here, explosives and ammunition dumps – our cartridges are for the most part compatible, as you know.' The pointer moved again. 'Petrol again, and diesel fuel as well. This dump is concealed in the ruins of a village destroyed in the Great War.' The old general looked up. 'It is to prevent a repetition of such destruction that I reveal these matters.'

'Yes, yes, we understand that, Herr General.'

'Here' – the pointer moved again – 'a large supply dump of rations; some bedding and clothing as well. Your men will have little use for the clothing, of course, since the uniforms are not German, but the food will be helpful.' He began to recite figures – tonnages of food, quantities of oil and petrol, so many artillery shells, so many thousands of rounds of small-arms ammunition. Mortars, grenades, rubber tyres for lorries, stocks of powder and phosphorus, stores of medicines and spare parts.

'For the most part the dumps are concealed, as an alternative to being heavily guarded. They should be easy enough to capture if you know where to find them. By my order two days ago, demolition charges have been removed from the petrol and ammunition dumps.'

'What reason did you give for that order?'

'The risk of accident. We've a great many hastily trained conscripts in the Belgian forces.'

'Excellent. The information is invaluable – the Reich will not forget your generosity.'

The general replied, 'I do this for Belgium, not to curry favour with Germany.'

'Of course.'

Ribbentrop turned to one of the German generals. 'These dumps will speed our advance. I'm certain now that the Blitzkrieg will take the Allies completely by surprise. They won't have time to react. The French and British expect to be able to march into central Belgium to meet our attack – they'll find themselves left flat-footed. We shall drive across Belgium and Luxembourg, through the Ardennes where the English and French believe tanks cannot travel. Thanks to your supply dumps, we shall move so quickly they'll have no time to prepare defensive positions. We shall catch them as they move up from the French border, and then, at the crucial moment, you will surrender. They'll be surrounded and forced to capitulate. It will take no more than three weeks. And Belgium will be spared the destruction that so concerns you, General.'

The old general bowed his head; perhaps he could not meet anyone's eyes.

It was nothing less than treason, so far as Christopher could see. These Belgian officers were planning a traitorous Belgian surrender: one of them even went so far as to say, 'We have the ear of the King and we can persuade him, at the proper time, that Belgium must surrender, for the good of the people.'

Finally Ribbentrop, looking at his wristwatch, motioned to one of the German officers, who began to roll up the maps. Ribbentrop said, 'We must be leaving. Our aircraft is waiting.'

The old Belgian lifted his head. 'When may we expect the attack, then?'

Ribbentrop delayed his reply until the maps were put away in their tubes, the charts gathered up, and the German officers assembled at the door ready to leave. Then he said, 'In about five hours' time.' He smiled politely to the others and walked swiftly out of the room.

Five hours. . .

Christopher felt the notebook fall from his fingers. Just then he heard a car on the gravel: the headlamps swept across the château and he heard the thump when his notebook fell on the stones and he held himself flat, motionless on the roof because the first thing they'd spot would be movement. The lights ran across him and went on turning and then someone in the distance shouted. He couldn't make out the words but the shout so startled him that he jerked back in a sort of involuntary spasm, and his foot slipped off the pipe and he felt himself sliding away. He clutched desperately at the edge of the roof but a tile came away in his hand and he was falling then, tumbling past the open window, catching his ankle painfully against it as he hurtled past.

Some instinct made him fling himself over: he'd been falling head-first and he managed a somersault to bring his legs under him and he couldn't see the ground — later he realized that was what must have saved him; he hadn't gone tense at the wrong moment. He shut his eyes in terror and then he hit ground, both feet, very hard — a flash of sudden pain — and went asprawl, breaking the fall with his hands, scraping the heels of both palms painfully on the stones as he slid and tumbled.

Then he was lying flat with the memory echoing through him of the clattering racket he'd made. Someone cried out; someone else answered; then a door whacked open and a man appeared in the rectangle of light silhouetted with a rifle across his chest. They'd heard him; they were coming for him.

He scrambled towards the hedge as fast as he could. All his limbs seemed to be functioning; there were bruises everywhere and he couldn't sort out individual pains from the general agony. He had a feeling his left palm was bleeding; it felt damp. *The notebook*.

But there wasn't time: two more men had reached the open door and they were coming out into the garden, spreading out, searching the night. The light from the doorway and windows didn't reach under the hedge but a fourth man was emerging from the house and the beam of his electric torch played across the bushes and Christopher shoved himself back under the hedge, clambered through and backed away on his knees, scrabbling feverishly on the grass until he was amid the tulips.

He began to get to his feet for the first time and when he put his weight on his right ankle a blade of incredible pain jabbed up his leg and he fell down, crushing the tulip stems, biting his lip to keep from crying out.

There were several men searching by now—at the moment they were spreading out away from the house and he was to one side of the direction of their search but it would only be moments before they widened it. He had to get away from there.

He crawled swiftly past the pagoda and reached the lawn beyond it, got his left foot under him, windmilled himself upright and hobbled one-footed towards the woods. Behind him the searching men were talking to each other; the torch beams stabbed the night but he was beyond their reach now. They weren't sure of what they'd heard. It could have been anything—but if they found the notebook he'd dropped. . .

He clutched a birch trunk for support and tested the earth gingerly with the injured foot. It didn't hurt unless he put his weight on it; it moved—painfully, but he could move it. Not broken them. Twisted—strained. He had to go on hobbling on his left foot, swinging from tree trunk to tree trunk, moving as fast as he could, but if they came after him now there was no way he'd be able to run away from them. He felt the brass of terror on his tongue.

A car growled, roared away: Ribbentrop and his entourage, probably. The same four or five men were still talking across the lawns behind him but the excitement was dwindling in their voices. He could no longer see the beams of their torches; he'd put quite a bit of forest behind him. He kept listening for the shout of discovery that would mean they'd found the notebook.

The attack—*five hours*—less, now; time was rushing by and he stood embracing a birch tree, gathering breath, willing the adrenalin to stop thudding through his system.

He was lightheaded with the shock, the pain of the fall, the fear—he knew he had to collect himself: one stupid mistake and he'd be lost.

The wireless. He had to warn Pooh.

He pushed through the wood. At times his weight came down inadvertently on the bad foot and agony shot through the ankle. He was beyond earshot of the gardens now; even if they found the notebook he wouldn't hear it. It didn't matter. He crawled across a ditch and hobbled on. There were hardly any stars; he went along as much by feel as by sight. Then finally he was coming up to the cul-de-sac, guided by the lights of the army camp beyond.

He swung past a tree ready to whisper his signal to the honeymooners' tent, but when he came into the open it wasn't there.

No tent, no young couple, no wireless.

Then he remembered the young man's nervousness during the last rendezvous: *They'll be asking us to move on soon.*

His heart pounded painfully. Suddenly for the first time he was in the grip of the fear of being utterly alone.

Had they found the transmitter and arrested the young couple? Or had they simply forced them to move on? If it was the latter, he ought to wait here. The young man and woman were trained professional agents with a job to do; they'd make contact with him. But how long could he afford to wait?

He remembered Paul's talk earlier in the day: *They've inter-*

cepted radio signals coming from nearby. . . I shouldn't want to be in his shoes if he's caught.

He didn't know what to do. Wait for the young couple or return to the château and brazen it out by pretending he'd been in bed all night asleep?

If it weren't for the ankle that would be the sensible course. But word of that crashing fall would be all over the château by morning.

Morning. How far away? Three and a half hours? Four?

He'd give it half an hour, he decided. If the young man or woman didn't appear by then he'd have to go back.

In the end he wasn't certain whether it had been five minutes or an hour; fear pounded in him, distorting judgment.

Sitting with his back to a tree, he took the ankle in both hands and manipulated it. He knew enough to tell whether it was fractured or not. It wasn't. He wiggled it, flinching with pain, and determined that it probably was a bad muscle strain — he'd clipped the side of his ankle bone against the window when he'd fallen past it and that was the source of part of his pain now, but mainly it hurt because he'd landed badly on it and the foot had twisted up too far, pulling the muscles. When he felt around the ligament at the back of the heel, it didn't seem torn. He remembered the time when a schoolfriend had suffered a similar injury on the rugger field. It had taken him about three weeks to regain full use of his foot.

The young man and woman did not appear and he was aware that a blind sort of panic was creeping up within him. He had to move; he couldn't wait any longer; by morning the German attack would begin: Luftwaffe planes grinding overhead — Panzer tanks gnashing up the roads. He'd seen the cinema newsreels from Poland. Would anyone bother about an English spy amid all that confusion?

And there was the notebook — perhaps, it hadn't been found. . .

He got to his feet and began to hop towards the woods, going back the way he'd come.

He lay under the hedge scanning the outlines of the château. Crouched in hiding he felt humiliated.

Not too far away a railway engine hooted; he heard the clacking of wheels on the rail. He was afraid. Childhood dreams of railway trains had always frightened him.

An hour or two left before dawn, perhaps; he had no watch, no way of reckoning time except guesswork. No-one seemed to be about. A few lights burnt, throwing pale yellow glows against windows towards the farther end of the château. The windows of the conference room were dark. He crawled forward without sound; beneath the centre window he began to search the ground, sliding his palms across it, sweeping back and forth by touch. Nothing. They must have found it.

But he continued to search methodically square by square. If there was any chance at all – it was the only evidence; without it they'd have no proof against him. He'd make up some story about the injuries, insist he had to be returned at once to England; if they got him as far as a railway station or an aerodrome he could reach his contacts by telephone somehow. But if they had the notebook they'd know he was the spy; they'd arrest him and he'd have no chance at all of getting word through.

The British would know soon enough of the German attack through the Ardennes. But they wouldn't know about the supply dumps that had been betrayed to speed the German advance; and they wouldn't know about the treacherously planned Belgian surrender. If they were caught by surprise and encircled. . .

It had been impressed upon him in the briefings with Owl and Winnie the Pooh that a quarter of a million regular troops – the cream of Britain's forces – had been committed to the defensive line. And it was the job of British intelligence to make certain those soldiers were not taken by surprise.

Christopher's job now. Somehow he had to get through to Winnie the Pooh. . .

A faint grey line of pre-dawn light seeped across the horizon. Within a few moments he could see the earth about him and there was no notebook anywhere. There was a coarse metal grating below the rainspout at the base of the corner of the château, and the slots between its bars were wide enough to have allowed the notebook to slip through, but it would have taken a freak bounce for it to have gone down there. He put his face over the grating but the drain was dark and he couldn't see a thing. He heard a faint gurgling; by the sound it seemed quite deep. If the notebook had gone down there it was irretrievable.

'Is this what you're looking for?'

The voice made him jump; he nearly went over; he wheeled clumsily in a crouch – it was Paul. He had the notebook in his hand and something else in the other: a revolver.

He slowly got upright, one foot and the wall for support. Paul was opening his mouth to speak but a sound reached both of them just then – an advancing high-pitched drone of aircraft engines. A faint thumping in the distance. Was that artillery?

He glanced at Paul's revolver. Paul watched his face; Paul's expression was unreadable.

In the sky the planes appeared, dropping out of the clouds, black crosses on pale green gull wings. The Stukas put their noses down and screamed towards the earth and then, screaming wickedly, they shot past the turrets of the château and ran on, diving towards the army encampment beyond the estate. He saw the planes pull up and let their bombs go: the engine notes dropped to a straining growl; the bombs detached themselves and described their short arcs, disappeared beyond the trees and burst with great smashing thuds of sound.

Behind him something rattled faintly; he thought it might be the cartridges in the chambers of Paul's revolver. Paul said, 'Get inside,' in a bleak tone of voice that made the short hairs prickle at the back of Christopher's neck.

He hopped in through the side entrance and Paul touched his arm; he stopped there, propped against the wall, and Paul went ahead of him down the narrow servants' hall, pushed a door open, put his head inside for a quick look, switched on a light and beckoned with the revolver. 'Down here – quickly.'

Alarmed, uncertain, Christopher made his way painfully forward. Planes roared overhead again and just as he reached the doorway he heard the heavy dull thumps of the bombs; the explosions were near enough to make the floor shiver underfoot.

He found himself at the head of some narrow wooden stairs leading down into the earth. Damp stone walls, a heavy wooden door with an iron ring for a handle.

'Go on – get cracking.'

'What do you think you're? . . .'

'*Move!*' An urgent forceful whisper.

He heard the planes thunder away. He put both hands on the railing and went down two steps at a time, one-footed. A distant rumbling just reached his ears; perhaps it was something he felt rather than heard. At the bottom he twisted the iron ring. The heavy door scraped open. Christopher saw high rows of racked wine bottles.

Paul closed the door and put the revolver away in his belt.

'Are you going to turn me in, then?'

'To whom? The bloody Germans?' Paul's laugh was off-key. He tossed him the notebook and Christopher nearly dropped it in surprise. 'I managed to decipher a good deal of that. I used to think you had quite good handwriting but. . .'

I had to write in the dark, he thought.

'Spying. Like a fly on the wall spying on *my* father!' Paul shook his head. 'You've betrayed me – your *friend!*'

The cold stone floor trembled steadily now: it had to be big guns, field artillery.

'I ought to beat you to a bloody pulp,' Paul said.

'You could try. Even with this ankle I think I might beat you.'

'Never without pluck, are you, Christopher?' The twist of Paul's mouth expressed his mockery.

'It's your friends who're the traitors,' Christopher said. '*I* haven't betrayed anyone to the bloody Germans.'

'Did you get the signal off?'

'No.'

Paul's eyes dropped towards the notebook in Christopher's hand. 'Who was that for?'

'Who do you think?'

'Not the bloody Sea Scout leader, I imagine.'

'Belgium never told London anything about its defence plans. They needed to know what was going on. I came here to find out. I didn't expect to find Belgians selling Belgium out to the Nazis.'

'They sent a fifteen-year-old schoolboy to spy on us?' Paul shook his head. 'I thought I knew you.'

'I haven't betrayed *you*.'

'You would have, if my father'd been one of the traitors.'

'Yes.' No point in denying it. 'Did you read it all? If you did,

36

you know what those guns are — what it means. Your country's the front line for my country now.'

Paul didn't speak. Christopher said, 'What do you intend doing?'

'If I turned you in — with that notebook—'

'Do it, then. I'll tell my story and we'll see who's in trouble.'

Paul brooded at him. Christopher said, 'You haven't turned me in and you're not going to, are you? Because if King Leopold saw this notebook he'd have to have your father arrested along with the others. He was in that meeting — that's all they'd need to hear. Perhaps your father didn't know what they were about. Perhaps he didn't want to know. Probably that's why he left when he did. All the same, he didn't lift a finger to stop them. He could have called in the soldiers. He didn't. Paul, I'm sorry I've put you in this mess but you won't help anything by turning me over to them. You've got to let me go.'

Paul faced him bitterly; his shoulders lifted; then abruptly he turned towards the door. 'I'm locking you in. I'll be back.'

'Paul, you've got to listen to me. They're going to invade. . .'

But Paul was gone and Christopher felt the walls begin to contract.

The pounding vibration went on endlessly and its changes were imperceptible, but a time came when he realized the tremors were heavier; the guns were coming nearer.

He had no way to judge the passage of time. When the door rattled he hid himself behind a stack of wine bottles until he was sure it was Paul. Then he said, 'What time is it?'

'Nearly nightfall. The château's been a madhouse but most of them have gone now. The telephone lines went down and they've had to make for the military stations to keep in touch with their departments. Some of the guests made for Antwerp but I doubt they'll get there. The roads are jammed with refugees. The Germans have come through the Ardennes — they're coming on like a train. The Panzer tanks may be here by this evening.'

Paul delivered the information in a flat voice devoid of feeling. He opened the bag he'd brought and set things out — plaster and tape; cheese, bread, lemon squash; a copy in English of *Vanity Fair*.

'What's the book for?'

'To help pass the time.'

'You're going to lock me in and leave me here. I thought as much.'

'No. I shan't lock it. You may leave at any time. But I shouldn't hurry if I were you. Where do you expect to get on that foot?'

'And if the Germans come—'

'Then we'll all have to run for it, won't we?'

'You just said they'd be here in a few hours.'

'No. I said they might be. Giraud and Lord Gort and King Leopold are driving up to the front. They still hope to stop the German advance along the Albert Canal and the Meuse.'

The Albert Canal was only about ten miles from the château. Christopher thought about that. If the Allies came forward past the château he could join them. Perhaps Paul was right: it was best to wait.

Paul said, 'My father's arranged for an aeroplane to come and collect us – my mother and my sisters and I, some of our friends who're still hanging about. It's coming from France and it's to take us to England. My father refuses to accompany us. He's packing now to go down to Ghent and join his old regiment. My father doesn't know you spied on that meeting and I daren't tell him that I know – he's in enough anguish already.'

'You've thought about shooting me with that revolver, haven't you?'

'To protect my father – yes.'

'It wouldn't make anything any better.'

'No, I suppose not. Otherwise I'd have done it, wouldn't I?' Paul managed a bit of a smile. 'I had time to think – it's not your doing. But I wish you'd let me in on the game earlier. I don't like not being trusted by my friends.'

'Friendship doesn't come into that sort of thing.'

'I suppose it doesn't. But just the same. . .' Then Paul unstrapped his wristwatch and gave it to Christopher. 'Within a few hours everyone should be gone from the château – unless the Germans arrive first, in which case we'll all be blown up. I think the lines should hold till tomorrow, though. They can't keep rushing forward forever, can they – they've got to sleep. You should be free to leave here soon. You know where the bicycle stands are – in the courtyard. Can you cycle on that?' He gestured towards Christopher's foot.

'I think so.' He wasn't sure but he didn't want to burden his friend with it.

'Bloody Boche,' Paul murmured, putting great feeling into it. 'I expect I shall join the army. I doubt if I'm cut out for it, but one must do one's bit.' With a shy sort of hesitation he thrust out his hand.

Christopher took his grasp and smiled to reassure him.

'When you reach London, go to the Admiralty. Tell the First Lord what was in the notebook. It's important, Paul. He must know about those dumps and the plans to surrender. The moment you reach London you must tell the First Lord, Mr Churchill.'

'Churchill's no longer First Lord. As of today he's Prime Minister. It's just been on the wireless.'

Christopher gave a bark of pleased laughter. The washed-up elderly parliamentarian had done it, then. Tigger at 10 Downing Street!

'I'll tell them – if they'll listen to me.'

'Good luck, then.'

'It's for me to wish you luck. I've got a ticket out of here, haven't I? It's more than I can say for you.'

'I'll get to England all right.'

'I believe you will. I'll tell you a secret – the reason I wanted to be your friend from the beginning. I envied you your courage. I still do.'

'Look where it's got me.'

'You'll come through with flying colours. You always land on your feet.' Paul smiled. 'The game's begun. I shall expect to hear all your adventures when I see you in England.'

They shook hands.

Then he was alone in the wine cellar. The floor shook under him with the thunder of the advancing German guns.

Chapter Three

He wound Paul's Rolex and hopped on one foot up the stairs; he found the château deserted, made a quick visit to a bathroom, cleaned up as best he could, and then went out into the courtyard.

The Sitzkrieg was over. The noise of the war was loud and near and incessant. For a while he stood stunned by it.

Half a dozen bicycles remained in the rack. Anyone who'd had faster means of transport would have left his cycle behind but these remaining were in poor shape. He selected the best of the poor lot and walked it away, his haunch resting on the seat and the bad foot dangling, pushing at the earth with his good foot, moving very slowly until he was away from the château and into the wood. The thump of gunfire seemed to quake the branches overhead and he heard the scream of Stukas somewhere nearby. It was too close to be the Albert Canal line; the Germans must have breached it and crossed the canal but he saw nothing except the occasional aeroplane sliding among the clouds. One of them, he was nearly certain, was an RAF Hurricane but he had only a glimpse of it.

He settled himself astride the bicycle and rested the good foot on the pedal and propelled himself forward, but the pedal wouldn't come up to complete the circle and he stopped, nearly falling off when he forgot the bad foot and came down on it. He positioned the machine again, kicking the pedal to the top, this time resting the bad foot on the lower pedal for ballast and hoping it wouldn't drive pain straight up through the top of his head when he moved it.

He leant forward to push his weight down against his leg and the cycle began to roll forward; the bad foot rode without force up and round. The ankle throbbed and complained but it seemed bearable and he went along at a snail's pace in that manner, pushing down each time the good foot came to the top of the arc. He wobbled a good deal and when the earth began to tilt found it was impossible to ride uphill without the use of both feet: he had to hop beside the machine, employing it as if it were a wheeled crutch, and that meant using the handbrake whenever his weight was on it because otherwise it rolled back.

He made his way out of the wood into the country lane that ran down to the south behind the château. It would take him past the aerodrome to the army camp. He would report to the Belgian army and find some way to convince them to allow him wireless communication with Winnie the Pooh at Lord Gort's headquarters.

The aerodrome was a grass strip with a single small hangar; it belonged to the château. Christopher pedalled slowly along the verge and glanced through the trees at the field. He was surprised to see an aeroplane there – half a dozen people sitting round in the hangar's shade on their suitcases, and a man in a pilot's cap working at one of the engines: the nacelle covering had been opened back on its hinge and the man had both hands up in the machinery.

He stopped in the trees and watched. It was too far for recognition but he thought one of the figures in the shade might be Paul. There were several women; he recognized one of Paul's sisters by her pink dress. They hadn't got off yet because mechanical trouble had delayed them. Heavy guns thundered all round – a few miles away to the left, nearer to the right; and when Christopher turned his head he picked up more gunfire. It sounded as if the war were to the west as well, behind him, and that was alarming because if it was true it meant the Germans must have leapfrogged ahead of the canal. Had they dropped parachutists behind the lines?

He could show himself; he could ask to be taken aboard the aircraft. Paul's father wasn't there. Perhaps none of them would want to arrest him. But he couldn't count on it – and every seat was certainly filled. The risk wasn't worth taking since the army camp was only a short distance down the lane. And in any case Paul had the secret, too; between them they could surely warn the BEF of the German plan.

The pilot latched the cowling-cover shut and turned, rubbing his hands; he spoke and the wind carried his voice to Christopher. The passengers got to their feet and the pilot and his partner helped them carry their luggage to the plane. Paul, walking across the strip, was easily recognizable by his size and shambling gait. Christopher grinned.

The two engines sputtered to life and when the plane began its turning roll he thrust his hand out, thumb up, wishing them luck. He stayed to watch the take-off and that was when he saw another plane overhead, a dot in the sky at first but it grew quickly as it dived and Christopher leapt off the bike, falling to one knee, hobbling as fast as he could go, out into the field waving both arms to get the attention of Paul's pilot. But no-one saw him and the plane lifted off the grass strip and banked to clear the trees.

'No—look out!' He kept waving at them but the plane was climbing away from him and then the diving Messerschmidt began to shoot as it spiralled in. He heard the distant pop-pop-pop of its guns and saw the tracer streaks as they sought the unarmed French plane.

He watched Paul's plane explode in the air, a great burst of yellow fire and tumbling black debris.

Stubbornly he pushed himself along the lane on the bicycle, weeping; he could hardly see where he was going.

The Messerschmidt buzzed overhead, coming out of its dive. He shook his fist at it and yelled oaths at the top of his voice. The plane dwindled away into the clouds.

Amid the rumbling of the distant guns he inched his way on. It took him the next half hour to get over the hump of a long hill; then he began to coast slowly down a narrow hedge-bordered lane. He stopped several times to blow his nose; finally his stomach began to churn and he tumbled off his cycle and lay in the weeds on the verge. He was violently sick.

Paul. . .

I'll see you in England, old friend.

Bastard Boche. *Bastards!*

He rolled away from the stench, tore off a leafy branch, and scraped it roughly across his mouth to wipe it clean; he lay under the hedge and had a hard time getting his breath.

He had to get to the army camp. There was no-one to ring Mr Churchill in London and tell him the German plot. Paul wouldn't be there. . .

Stop thinking about it. The only thing that mattered now was to get to the army camp, get his message through.

He climbed back on to the bicycle and rolled forward, coasting. The army camp was just round the next bend, then over a slight hill. The hill gave him trouble and he thrust feverishly with his one foot; finally he abandoned the bicycle and hopped up the road, arms pumping, leaping on one foot. From the top he could see the camp. He couldn't see a living soul. There wasn't a single lorry in sight. The tents had been taken down. There was a bit of damage from the Stuka bombs. That was all. The place was abandoned.

'Bloody hell.' He felt dizzy. His groin went tight and he stood with one arm round a tree, breath heaving in and out of his chest, the one good leg trembling under him.

'*Bloody* hell.'

He cycled slowly from one farm gate to the next, seeking evidence of overhead wires that would indicate a telephone from which he might be able to get through to BEF Headquarters.

But he hadn't yet found one when he heard the squeaking clattering gnash of tanks in the lane behind him. It was a fast-moving column of German armour and he lay under the hedge while they screeched past. The steel treads clanked within six feet of his face and the noise was astonishing. He covered his ears.

They were running at a good clip – perhaps twenty-five or thirty miles an hour, he thought; they drove forward contemptuously, their tops wide open, commanders sitting in the sun in caps and goggles and wide-shouldered grey Panzer uniforms. The leader sped ahead of the others by several hundred yards as a scout. Then came the clanking pack, strung out at forty-yard intervals, probably as a dispersal against air or artillery attack. He counted twenty-four of the behemoths; behind them came a dozen open half-tracks with tripod-mounted machine-guns and then nine or ten troop lorries with their canvas pinned up, each carrying a squad of Wehrmacht soldiers. From his place of concealment Christopher watched them bitterly as they roared on down the road away from him.

When their sound faded he heard once more the rumble of war in the near distance. He couldn't place its direction and he wondered if in fact it was all round him. The tank column was ahead of him now and the realization came to him that he was behind enemy lines.

He dragged the bicycle out from under the bushes and propped himself against it, got his leg over, and resumed the slow ride. The stink of the tanks' exhausts hung in the air for a long while.

He considered briefly the bold idea of simply placing himself in the hands of the Germans. He could do a haughty upper-class act on them and insist that he be taken to see Herr von Ribbentrop, who would vouch for him; probably Ribbentrop would see to it that Christopher got safe passage back to England by way of some neutral third country like Switzerland. Ribbentrop would have no reason to connect Christopher's presence with the suspicion that there'd been a spy at the château.

No reason except the strained ankle. That might give him away; Ribbentrop had been among the men who'd heard the crash of his fall.

And in any case it would take too long and he couldn't very well send signals back from Germany. He had to get through to the British lines – it was the only chance to get his information to Lord Gort in time.

Still, as exhaustion overtook him he had to fight off the temptation to deliver himself into German hands. He could satisfy them easily enough by telling part of the truth. He'd been visiting a school chum and been caught up in the Blitz-krieg: nothing sinister in that. They'd give him fair treatment.

Stop thinking like a treacherous bloody idiot.

He had a vital job yet to do and it was no good trying to think up excuses for not doing it. This wasn't some unpleasant school chore to be got out of. He wasn't here on some headmaster's account; he was here for Tigger – and he wasn't going to let Tigger down.

Twice more during the morning he had to hide from columns of German armour. He pedalled south, wanting to avoid the outskirts of Antwerp because the city would be jammed and confused and probably an early German target. He had a rough map of the country in his head and he had it vaguely in mind to cross the Dyle about midway between Antwerp and Brussels and try to make his way southwest to find British GHQ.

He was coasting down a shady lane when he heard men's voices nearby; he slowed silently and stopped the bicycle to listen. He couldn't make out much of it but they were talking in a language he didn't recognize – then he realized it was probably Flemish.

There was a field beyond the hedgerow; the voices seemed to issue from there. He stopped at the edge of the trees, the sun warm on his face. The breeze tousled the mown grass and its smell seemed peculiarly English. He was about to announce himself when a blast of hot air flung him across the road – the bicycle shot away and broke itself across a tree; noise flattened him and then he was pelted by clots of debris.

Now bloody what?

There was a rushing express-train roar. The air, and his head, felt split open by the deafening impact of the shell.

Out in the field men rose from the ground and began to run in every direction. Another shell tumbled in; the noise of the hit rattled his teeth – earth shot into the air and he was pelted with clods. Christopher hugged the ground.

The artillery came one shot at a time, marching erratically away from him across the field, flinging Belgians into the air. There'd been at least a squad of them concealed in the field – eighteen or twenty men – and the incoming shells seemed to find them wherever they ran. He saw a severed arm fly through the air like a Catherine wheel, spraying blood. Bile crept into his throat. The shellfire ceased and there was abrupt silence; his ears still rang but nothing stirred except slow-drifting dust and smoke. The neatly mown field had been changed into a cratered moonscape.

A light plane buzzed low overhead and wheeled away; he saw the Luftwaffe markings on its wings and knew its meaning. The plane was a spotter and had called down the artillery fire on to this field where it had discovered the Belgian soldiers resting. Now it banked away out of sight, looking for another target.

Christopher pulled himself upright against a tree. He glanced at the mangled ruin of his bicycle and began to hobble out into the field to see if anyone had survived the terrible smashing. He didn't see anything move. He found only four bodies and stayed well clear of them, frightened of approaching; he was surprised there didn't seem to be more dead. The others must have fled through the smoke and got away into the woods beyond; possibly even now they were regrouping but he hadn't the agility to catch them up. He hopped wearily into the shadows of the trees and sat down hugging his knees, feeling hungry, thirsty and very tired.

No more bicycle; he had only the vaguest idea where he was; there were Germans behind him and Germans ahead of him. He had bruises and scrapes all over his body; there was one particularly nasty lump on his forehead where something — probably a clod of earth — had struck him a hard blow. From where he sat he could see two of the dead Belgian soldiers out in the cratered field; they both lay as they had fallen — mangled, twisted; sickening distortions of human figures.

He began to cry.

The farm was a poor place. The stone walls of the house were centuries old and in need of repair. Stalls in the barn showed where horses had been kept; tracks in the farmyard indicated there'd been a wagon. Horses and wagon were gone now — the occupants had fled. He found scraps of food in the house and made a meal of them, washing it down with water he pulled up in a bucket from the well; the place had no plumbing. He found plasters in a cabinet and used them to put patches on the three cuts that were still bleeding.

The bed was merely a straw ticking on a crude wooden frame. Christopher regarded it morosely; it might be filled with bugs. In the end he simply lay down on the floor and groaned and fell into a state that was more unconsciousness than sleep.

He woke once. It was quite dark. 'Paul?' For a moment he forgot where he was, thought he'd fallen asleep in Paul's wine cellar and had a bad dream. Then it all flooded back. He shivered with cold, listening to the infernal racket that had woken him — a roaring and whining that seemed to be just outside the window.

He dragged himself to the sill and peered out and had a glimpse of faint wheeling shapes against the stars. They were planes, he realized. It was a battle between opposing air squadrons. He heard the sharp stutter of machine-guns and the heavier thudding of cannon. Exhaust sparks flickered from the screaming engines and while he watched he saw one plane burst brilliantly into flame and spiral away towards the earth a mile or two away. He had no way of telling whether it was friend or foe.

The battle soared away; soon he could hardly hear it for the rumble of distant artillery, which went on apparently without respite. He was so accustomed to it now that he would have noticed its absence. He slid back to the floor and passed out again. He did not wake again until the screech and clatter of rolling armour warned him. He was at the window in time to see the tanks roll past in the road. It was nearly noon; the sun high and watery through a grey layer of cloud. Christopher stood away from the window in the shadows and wondered whether the Germans would ever run out of tanks; even on the side roads he'd counted nearly a hundred of them, and he recalled that the Belgian army had no tanks. Unless the Allies had swung into line against the swift Panzers they must have reached the sea by now.

He retreated deeper into the room and began to turn towards the door. A shadow fell across the doorway then. Fear enveloped him. He looked about him for a place to hide but there was no time. A huge man filled the doorway and Christopher looked into the muzzle of a shotgun.

By his garb the man was a farmer. He squinted ferociously. Christopher heard soft footsteps in the next room; then a girl appeared beside the big man. She couldn't have been more than seven or eight years old – all eyes and legs; thin as a twig. She wore a torn grey woollen dress and her pigtailed hair was matted.

When she saw Christopher she rushed against the big man and clutched him in fear.

Christopher slowly held up his hands, open palms out. His heart pounded.

None of them spoke. The tank convoy's noise was intense.

The big farmer blinked slowly. His face was drawn and pale. Then he moved slightly – towards the window; a grimace of pain – and then Christopher saw the dark stain of blood on the cloth under his arm.

The shotgun slid away towards the window – it was as if, expecting a German tank to push itself through the wall, the farmer intended to ward it off with his puny bird-hunter's weapon.

Christopher put his hands down slowly and backed towards the wall, hopping, to avoid using the useless ankle; the farmer's eyes shifted towards him but the shotgun did not stir. The tanks moved on and the farmer lurched across to the window and looked out into the sunshine, sagging slowly against the sill while the shotgun drooped in his grasp.

Christopher spoke in French: 'You're wounded. We'd better see to that.'

The farmer didn't seem to hear him but the girl's face changed on hearing his words; she had trailed after the farmer to the window, afraid to be parted from him, but now she swayed a bit farther away from him and the ghost of a smile twitched across her mouth. Christopher said, 'Don't be afraid.'

He went one-legged to the wall cupboard where he'd found the plasters last night. There was still a roll of surgical tape there and a half bottle of clear alcohol and a few small plasters. He got them down and made his shambling awkward way round the room to the window. The farmer's fevered eyes were suspicious but his strength was draining away and he sagged back against the frame of the window, his hip on the sill. The shotgun clattered on the floor and the little girl pounced on it, dragging it away, not quite knowing how to hold it but determined to menace Christopher with it.

He said, 'Don't be afraid. I'm not going to hurt him. He needs help.'

The girl bit her lip and Christopher said, 'I've got to cut his shirt away – I'm taking out my knife now. Don't be afraid of it.'

She watched narrowly. He opened the knife and gently worked it through the loose grimy cloth.

'Well that doesn't look too bad,' Christopher said, keeping the truth from the little girl. 'More of a bruise than anything else. What was it – a rifle bullet?'

The farmer didn't reply. There was an open groove across his ribs, oozing dark blood; the flesh all about the area was discoloured. Christopher said, 'This will sting,' and soaked a wadded bit of cotton plaster with alcohol and bathed the open cut tenderly. If it hurt the farmer he made no indication of it. His eyes were nearly shut; his head lolled against the frame of the window. Christopher put the small plasters in a row along the bullet-groove and wrapped tape round the man's torso to hold them in place. He was an enormous man; Christopher couldn't span his waist with both arms.

'You ought to rest now.'

The farmer made no sign he'd heard. His eyes tried to find the girl but turned up into his head and he slid down until he sat on the floor, back to the wall, legs splayed and chin on his chest. The little girl whispered, 'Is he dead?'

'No. Asleep.' More accurately, Christopher thought, he'd passed out. 'Is he your father?'

'No.'

'What's your name?'

She wasn't sure she'd give it to him. She pouted, her eyes ran vaguely round the room. Finally she muttered, 'Geneviève.'

'That's a pretty name.'

'Is my uncle going to die?'

'No, I don't think so. Do you live round here?'

'No.'

It appeared she was from somewhere near Verviers — a long way off in the east. She talked reluctantly at first but then the dam burst and she wept. He couldn't understand all she said because it came too fast and her accent was difficult. He had to ask her to repeat things. They'd had a small dairy farm and Belgian troops had bivouacked at the edge of their land. The Boche blackbirds — Stukas — had dive-bombed the soldiers and one of the bombs had bounced into the house before exploding. The soldiers had fired their rifles fruitlessly at the diving planes. She didn't know what had become of them.

Her Uncle Charles had smashed his way into the debris of the kitchen and rescued her from where she'd taken shelter under the table. He'd lifted her up piggy-back upon his shoulders and begun to walk.

A few hours ago they'd been coming across a freshly ploughed field when something had clicked under Uncle Charles's foot and he'd flung the girl away from him so hard she'd fallen and bruised herself badly. He'd dived away himself but not in time to avoid all the shrapnel from the land-mine and he'd started bleeding; but he'd told her it was nothing to be alarmed about. He'd lifted her up on his shoulders again and picked a path out of the minefield, and then they had come upon this farm.

They'd heard the approaching tanks and sought shelter in the farmhouse and found Christopher there.

'What will become of me?'

'Let's wait for your uncle to wake up.'

In the dusk a motorcycle came up the lane and Christopher stood in the doorway's shadows with the shotgun watching the cyclist stop and get off and stretch. It had a sidecar but no passenger. Christopher thought of shooting the cyclist and taking the motorcycle but he didn't know how to ride it and Uncle Charles didn't seem strong enough to be moved. Remembering his Sea Scout first aid, and conversations with his father, Christopher knew there was a chance the farmer was bleeding internally and therefore should not be moved.

The German dispatch rider was fixing a narrow slitted air raid protection mask over the headlamp of his machine. Then he turned to the side of the lane and watered the hedge, buttoned his trousers and looked all round him. Christopher stiffened, for it seemed the soldier was staring right at him, but then the head kept turning and finally the man swung his leg over the saddle and kicked the engine into life, switched on the headlamp and went sputtering away.

Christopher stepped outside. The little girl Geneviève had got on his nerves with her incessant questions, to which he had few answers. He limped out to the lane and threw his head back and studied the stars, getting his bearings. He found he was chewing his lip. *I ought to leave them here. They've fended for themselves this long – they can go on doing it.* It was vital that he get his message through to Winnie the Pooh.

'Are you taking my uncle's gun with you?'

Her voice made him jump. He found her in the gateway, arms akimbo, eyes very large and accusing.

He sighed. 'No. Get back in the house.' And went back inside with her.

Uncle Charles woke some time in the morning. He seemed very feeble; his eyes had no spark. 'What are you? You're not Belgian.'

'I'm English.'

'What the devil are you doing here?' The man tried to sit up;

he fell back. Christopher supported his head while he drank water from the mug. Its handle was broken and it had been left behind. 'Hungry,' the man muttered.

'There's nothing here to eat. I'm going to have a look round. There must be other farms nearby.'

The little girl sat down crosslegged and clutched Uncle Charles's hand.

'The little one is an orphan now,' the farmer said to Christopher. He took it to mean her parents must have been killed by the Stukas. He'd guessed as much.

'She has a brother somewhere in the army. His name is Robert Desrosiers. Can you remember that, boy?'

'Robert Desrosiers.'

Uncle Charles had to lie silent a while, gathering breath. 'God will bless you if you take Geneviève with you.'

'You'll take her yourself, I imagine. As soon as you've got your strength back.'

'We haven't time for that. The Boche—'

'They won't have any interest in this poor farm.'

'You don't know them. I know them from the last war. Listen to me, the first armies rush through but the second echelon comes behind and they search everything. House to house, tree to tree. They'll find us if we stay here. Today, tomorrow, a week from now, I don't know, but they'll come here.'

Let's hope they don't come today, he thought. Neither Christopher nor the wounded farmer was in any condition to move at speed.

There must be farms nearby—perhaps a vehicle; even a horse would do. Food; and he needed a telephone. He stood up and tested his weight on the bad ankle. It didn't seem any better than it had been before. 'I'm going to look for food,' he said. 'Stay here with your uncle.' Then he left.

Uncle Charles rallied slowly and Christopher watched him take food and blink drowsily and try his muscles and fall back exhausted. The farmer's eyes were terribly bloodshot and did not seem to clear. It might be concussion.

Christopher counted the days anxiously. He had thought it out. It couldn't be helped: they needed a few days for his ankle to heal and for the big farmer to recover, if he was going to. It was no good trying to get through German lines with a useless foot and a half-conscious man. Dead, he could give no messages to Winnie the Pooh.

He used the time in exploring every farm within two miles of the place. The largest of them had a telephone but the lines were dead and his disappointment was keen. He wiped his tears and filled a sack with food which had been left behind and dragged it wearily back with him, hobbling along with the aid of a knobbly walking-stick he'd found.

Not a single horse or wheeled vehicle remained in the valley. The place was pocked everywhere with craters. Dead soldiers of both armies lay in the woods where burial parties must have failed to find them. Maggots crawled on the carcases of caisson horses. The stench of battle still hung around.

On the tenth day he discovered a tiny village along the stream about three kilometres south of the farm. There were tinned foods in the litter of what had once been a village shop; nearly every building had been destroyed. He saw dead dogs and swarms of insects but there was nothing else alive in the place and he left it swiftly, frightened. Uncle Charles was right: they were in a sort of no-man's-land between the front lines and the rear echelon. The second wave would come through any time now, making a slow thorough sweep, consolidating the German advance. It was a backwater, nowhere near strategic centres; but soon the Nazis would come.

In a tumbledown barn on the outskirts of the village he found a two-wheeled cart with long tongues and a single narrow seat. It was meant to be drawn by an animal smaller than a horse — perhaps a goat.

It was very slow going but he dragged it along with him. It took him the rest of the afternoon to get it home. On the way he sought any sign that might lead him to an animal, but nothing stirred in the dead landscape.

The foot still gave him pain but he was able to put weight on it by then and with Geneviève's help on the tongues they made a few miles' progress on the first day. Uncle Charles sat dazed in the little seat, his head lolling as he swayed; once he fell out and they had to hoist him back into the cart. Christopher knew they had to get Uncle Charles to a doctor.

Many of the lanes were like English ones: bordered on either side by high hedges. Christopher avoided these because they couldn't risk being trapped there if an enemy tank or motor-cycle should come along. The limitation narrowed their choices; several times they had to double back on their tracks.

The most intense noise of battle was due west of them and Christopher chose a southwesterly course in the hope of sliding between the battlegrounds. But at midday on the third or fourth day he and the girl struggled with the cart to the top of a low knoll only to see, from that slight elevation, a line of tents and lorries and field guns stretched below the crest of a distant ridge. It was, he saw immediately, the German line: the fortified rear of the battle zone. No chance of getting through that.

They turned back into the trees.

He woke in dismal mood. The light was too bright; it took a long time for his tired eyes to adjust to it. A convoy of lorries crawled over the hill to the north—German soldiers. Nearly a mile away but he could hear their singing; the song was cheerful and had a lusty beat to it. He dug out the last of their tins of peaches and soup. They'd eat the food cold, as they always did; it was no good building fires when the smoke might draw attention.

But when he turned to offer Uncle Charles his breakfast the farmer was dead.

He hadn't the tools to dig a grave for the big man. The best he could do was to leave the body and the goat-cart beside the road where someone would soon find them.

'Come on, then.' He put out his hand.

'Leave me alone!' She pulled away.

'You must come with me now.' He spoke gently; he put out his hand again—'*Tu me tiens très fort, vite.*'

She hesitated; finally she took his hand and he pulled her away quickly into the wood before her attention could return to her uncle.

The din of battle was close. The earth now was littered with the debris of great armies in retreat. Some of the flat tin helmets were British and Christopher felt weak with the shock of it. The British army always won in the Royal Tournament and the

53

Aldershot Tattoo and the manoeuvres on Salisbury Plain. It was invincible, every schoolboy knew that. Yet the debris spoke a different tale: here a smashed Bren gun, there a twisted mortar; an Enfield with a splintered butt; a single boot; a scorched light tank half overturned in a muddy shell hole.

He tugged Geneviève with him – they lurched among the craters and the mud sucked at their feet; once it had been a hay field. At the top was a low stone wall. He made for that.

The ankle was growing stronger; he was able to walk on it. There was still pain but it was part of the life now, as if he'd always lived with it. They reached the wall and he straightened up to peer over it and that was when a voice shot at him from behind his right shoulder: 'What they bloody hell do you think you're up to?'

He wheeled. First he saw the Lee-Enfield rifle. It hung by its webbing sling from the shoulder of a gaunt man with a narrow smoke-grimed face and raw bright eyes. He wore a British uniform: sergeant of Guards.

'Thank God,' Christopher said.

Geneviève clung to his leg. The thin sergeant poked his chin suspiciously towards the boy. 'Who're you, then?'

'I'm English. . .'

There were seven of them – tattered shapes who emerged from their hiding places along the crest of the ridge. They gathered round Christopher and the little girl and stared at them as if they'd never seen children before.

'Look here – you got any papers to show who you are?'

'No. Can't you tell I'm British? Look at my bloody arm!' He pointed to his Scout badge.

'Less of your lip, son. Who's this, then?'

'She's Belgian. Her parents were killed.'

'A right bloody balls-up,' the sergeant muttered. 'Nobby, let them have a tin of something – they look starved. You lot get back to your positions – or do you want Jerry pushing bayonets up your arses?'

When Christopher got the sergeant's attention he said, 'I've a vital message that must get through to Lord Gort's headquarters.'

The sergeant laughed at that. It took quite a long time to get through to him; by that time Christopher knew it wasn't going to be much good anyway. The seven men were the remnant of a detachment of Guards that had been cut off in the maelstrom. They were isolated now, far behind the German lines without wireless communication. They had a bit of food left and a bit of ammunition for their small arms. Two of the seven were wounded and couldn't move very fast; they'd been debating what to do.

'They're using Belgian supply dumps,' Christopher insisted. 'Panzers. They'll cut us off from the sea if the army's not warned.'

It dawned on Christopher that the sergeant actually believed him now. When the sergeant laughed again it was with brutal irony.

The little girl clung to him like a leech. She ate corned beef from a tin with a soldier's mess spoon and rolled her eyes fearfully from Christopher to the Guards sergeant.

He sucked tepid brassy water from a flask and gave it back to the sergeant. 'Isn't there any way we can get the word through?'

'Sprout bloody wings,' the sergeant replied. 'You can't get through to the west there – it's bloody madness. We'll have to go south, try to get through to the French lines.'

'There's a dozen rivers to cross. It would take weeks getting through that way.'

'Aye. But with luck we'll get there alive, won't we? If we can keep out of Jerry's sight.' The sergeant turned him roughly by the shoulder. 'There's my blanket. Get your head down.'

Curled up in the chill damp night he felt his stomach turn when the wind carried the stench of death across the ridge. Until a fortnight ago he'd never seen death, let alone smelt it; now it seemed the most natural thing in the world.

In the small hours of the darkness he crawled out of the blanket. The little girl lay curled up under a soldier's battle-dress tunic. Several times she had hurtled into Christopher's arms for protection: each time a soldier spoke to her in English she bawled. He'd tried to soothe her but they were alarming apparitions, the tattered soldiers – none of them had shaved in

55

days; they stank of sweat and war; smoke and muck had grimed them, fatigue had dulled their eyes.

He'd tried to get up before but his stirring had woken her and she'd clutched his arm with both hands: 'Don't leave me.'

'I've got to go off to the bushes,' he'd growled. He hadn't really needed to but he went off to see how she'd take it. When he returned she was curled up in a ball, snivelling. He'd made her sit up. 'Now you listen to me, little girl. These are your friends. They may not look like much but they're English soldiers—the finest men in the world. You're a lot safer with them than you were with me.'

'They're strangers!' she wailed.

'Ten days ago I was a stranger.'

She gazed at him, puzzled; it was as if she didn't remember that far back.

'Trust them, Geneviève. I may have to go away.'

'I'll go with you.'

'No, you can't do that.'

'Why not?' She pouted at him.

'You just can't,' he murmured. 'Now go back to sleep.'

'Stay with me,' she insisted, lying down obediently.

Christopher had tucked the battledress tunic about her and watched her fall asleep; then his own weariness had overtaken him and he'd slept till now.

He crept away, inching slowly so as not to disturb her; he eeled past the thicket on his elbows. The sergeant sat awake on watch, Lee-Enfield in his lap; without turning his head towards Christopher he said very softly, 'And the best of luck to you, lad.'

'Will you do something for me? Will you look after the little girl?'

'As best we can.'

'Her name's Geneviève.'

'Right.'

'She's got a brother in the Belgian army. His name's Robert Desrosiers.'

'What unit?'

'I don't know. It's all they told me.'

'Desrosiers. Spell it.'

Christopher spelt it; the sergeant wrote it down. Then the pencil and paper went back into his pocket. 'Now listen, lad.

Alone you may get across but you've got to keep your head down and look before you march, right? If a field hasn't got shell holes, avoid it – it may be mined. Don't walk in the roads, walk on the verges. Don't trust anybody at all if he doesn't wear the right uniform. These Frogs don't quite know which side they're on, some of them – there's farmers and refugees who'd turn you in to the Germans for a scrap of bread. Here, take this ration tin. You'll find ample water all right. When you come to the canals and streams don't use the bridges, they'll be watched. Can you swim? Right. Underwater's best, and don't go splashing about.' He flung up an arm. 'That way – west. You'll come to the front. What's your name, then?'

'Christopher,' he replied. 'Christopher Robin.' Then he slipped away into the darkness.

The German guns were formed up behind a hedge pumping shells towards a position on the spine of a long mound of earth half a mile away; the racket was infernal. He went along behind the Germans, keeping low, darting from shrub to shrub, dashing at full speed to test the ankle. It gave no pain. If he could get round the end of the line he might make it across to the back of the mound. That had to be the Allied line; otherwise the Germans wouldn't be pounding it so relentlessly.

Behind a low ridge a mass of German armour waited in the afternoon drizzle, ready for a surprise attack. When the artillery stopped, he thought – that was when the Panzers would move. Just now the tank crew sat about in the light rain, oilskins over their shoulders, drinking coffee and smoking.

He made his way past the rear of the armoured column, darting across the road and tumbling into the trees on the far side, waiting a moment to learn whether he'd been seen, then getting up and walking steadily uphill. The ankle twinged now and then but he had no difficulty walking on it. He hadn't yet tried much of a run but the short dashes had been all right.

Beyond the wood he saw a great sprawl of men and machines – a brigade, perhaps. He clamped his teeth together and retreated into the trees and turned, wondering whether he could get through simply by staying within the wood and pressing forward towards the crest. Was it possible that he could get through under cover of the thick forest? It was that or turn back. Worth a try, in any case. He pushed ahead.

An hour's careful walking brought him to the narrowing end of the wood, still a hundred yards or so short of the crest. Shells whistled and rumbled as they went directly above his head towards targets in either direction. He could hear the thump of the Allied guns now and realized he was out in the unoccupied zone between the guns: no-man's-land.

He nearly stumbled into clear sight of the bunker before he spotted it – a machine-gun's barrel poking through the slitted concrete. It must have been a Belgian position once, taken over by the Germans now; he could see two or three pot-helmeted heads in the shadows behind the gun barrel. A forward outpost. He saw the wireless antennae stretching up into a tree. If the Allies tried a counter-attack into the wood the outpost would warn the German army of it.

He slipped back into the trees and tried to find another way but after half an hour's exploration he realized the only way over the top was to cross the open slope, a hundred yards or more of featureless ground, then the no-man's-land on the other side. No way to predict what he might find there; but to get that far he'd have to get across the open stretch first – and that was right across the field of fire of the machine-gun in the bunker.

The steady drizzle made everything grey and misty but he could see as far as the crest easily enough and that meant the Germans could see it too.

The best thing to do, he decided reasonably, was to wait until dark – another three or four hours – and then make his run. He'd crawl the first bit, as far as the crest. Then he'd try to get his bearings and run down towards the Allied positions, taking cover when he got nearer the lines so they wouldn't shoot him by mistake. When he got near enough he'd call out to them in English and French and he'd wait for a reply before he showed himself.

But he'd hardly settled when the sudden silence astonished him. The abruptness of it left a ringing in his ears. He could hear the patter of rain in the leaves.

Then he knew what it meant. The bombardment had ended:

the attack was ready to begin. If he stayed here he'd be caught in it. He had to make his run *now*.

Long ago, not far from here, his father had won a gold medal in the Olympic Games running in a track event; but his father hadn't had to make his run under the muzzle of a waiting enemy machine-gun.

We're all runners in this family, Christopher. It comes from our ancestors—carrying dispatches across the Highlands for the MacAlpine Kings of Scotland.

The ankle seemed fully healed. But would it hold?

He burst low out of the wood and began his run. He was thinking it would be best to run straight for the crest at first; it would take them a few moments to see him and to swing the machine-gun towards him.

After fourteen paces he threw himself to one side and ran six more paces and broke stride again, moving to the right, and that was when the bullets started to crack around him. The popping sounds of the bullets were explosive, like handclaps against the ear, and he dodged and ran, diving and zigzagging, flinging himself flat and rolling, digging his toes in and leaping forward again. The gun snapped at him in short bursts and he was out on the exposed face of the slope with nowhere to seek cover and there was nothing else to do but keep running because if he stopped they'd find the range.

Bullets pinged off stones all round him. He jinked left, then left again, then right; he stopped—just one beat—then he was running again, arms windmilling for balance. It fooled the gun again and the bullets chopped ahead of him briefly and he leapt to one side and heard the bullets crack past his left ear. He dived, rolled, scrambled, felt a stinging pain in the bad ankle, tried to see through eyes gone suddenly awry; then a shell crater opened before him and he dived into it, somersaulting flat on his back.

He lay stunned. The machine-gun bullets passed over his head. The aim dropped and the tracer began to chew up the earth parapet above him. He pressed lower in the hole, grinning, blood pounding in his head.

The gun stopped. He thought he heard the distant clattering

squeak of tanks. The machine-gun stuttered a few times. *Just to let me know they're still there.*

He gathered breath in his lungs and shouted, 'Why don't you come and get me?'

Then he laughed and burst out of the crater running. Someone behind him shouted with discovery and the gun opened up almost immediately but its aim was too low.

There was another crater to his right and he dived into it before the gun found the range.

'Missed me again!' His laughter filled the crater.

It was pounding through him – like the thrill of running for the line at rugger – and he knew he had to keep the tension at high pitch because if he remained in the hole long enough to get his breath the urgency would subside and he might not be able to go out under the gun again.

It was a wide crater and he crawled swiftly to the far side, to the right. He got purchase with both feet, curled his knees up and grasped the rim with both hands. 'Right, chaps, here I go!'

Then he was running up the slope again. The gun's aim was off to his left and he watched the tracers fly towards him until they were too close and then he leapt up in the air, came down to the right, zigzagged, dived, rolled into another crater, and hooted his mocking laughter at them.

The tanks were definitely nearer – approaching, he guessed, right along the edge of the wood. If he could hear them that clearly they'd be on him in a matter of minutes.

'You Jerries *need* a whole Panzer division to catch an English schoolboy!'

He bolted again, straight for the top. He hurled himself over the top and dropped flat behind a boulder while bullets bounced off the rock.

A green valley pocked with brown holes – a shattered farm below – and half a mile away a great army waited on the high facing slope. Eerie now because it was so silent. He heard the advancing squeak of the Panzers behind him, nothing else. The rain had stopped; he hadn't noticed when.

He turned back to taunt the German gunners once more and that was when he saw a tiny figure break out of the trees below him.

How in God's name had she followed him so far?

He shouted, 'Go back! Go back! Go back, Geneviève!'

She moved fast for her size, little arms pumping, feet skittering on the damp ground with plucky determination. She kept running up towards him and the machine-gun began to fire – the *bastards*, using a seven-year-old girl for target practice. . .

He began to run towards her but he'd hardly come off the rock when the gunner found her. The tracers cut her apart and began to sew a swift stitch up the slope towards Christopher. He slipped on the wet weeds, went down, found a purchase and flung himself back to shelter as the bullets found the rock.

When the burst ended he lifted himself and looked down the slope. She lay broken in her blood and he stared for a long time. The thrill of his triumph vanished. A bleak emptiness possessed him.

A rough fist gripped his arm and he nearly screamed. A hoarse voice grated at him, 'Bloody fool boy!'

An outpost, it must be. A helmeted face swam into his vision. Counterpart to the German bunker: a forward spotter. An English soldier.

Christopher felt his face screw up. 'Let me have your rifle, will you?'

'Don't be an ass.' The soldier reached for his arm.

Christopher yelled at him: 'Look – look down there – use your eyes then!' He snatched the soldier's collar, turning his face towards the slope.

The soldier's face changed. 'Oh the bloody swine,' he breathed. He braced his elbow on the boulder and brought the Lee-Enfield up. Right close to Christopher's ear the rifle shots were deafeningly loud. The soldier fired until his magazine was empty. By then the machine-gun had started up and Christopher dropped behind the boulder with the soldier, who reloaded his rifle and looked at the boy. 'They've got concrete, haven't they. It's a bunker? Speak to me, lad.'

'Yes, it's a bunker.' Then his stomach lurched and he rolled away to be sick.

When the dry heaves finally ended he wiped his mouth and shut his eyes and squatted, hunched over, waiting to be sure it was over. Nearby he heard the soldier talking in a dulled voice. 'Map coordinates Baker Seven Point Five. Fire.'

He heard the hurtling projectile quite close overhead; he turned his head in time to see it burst in the trees.

'Spotter here. Correction. Deflect forty yards left. Lower elevation twenty yards. Fire.'

The soldier was talking into a field telephone. Its wire ran down the back of the slope into the weeds.

The skyrocket *whoosh* of the shell filled the air and the explosion threw trees about like matchsticks. The soldier waited for the smoke to lift. 'Correction. Traverse ten yards right. Lower elevation five yards. Fire.'

The German tanks crawled into sight along the edge of the trees. The first tank stopped and the man on the turret swung his field glasses slowly across the crest. Christopher ducked. He heard the shell go over and strike.

'Spot on,' the soldier exulted. 'That'll have the roof off them. Put one more in there. . . Hold on. We've got Panzers.'

The German tank commander stooped to talk down into the hatch to his driver. The other tanks closed up behind him.

'Bring it two hundred yards to the right of your last shot. Try raising the elevation one hundred and fifty. Fire.'

Christopher ran across to him. 'The Germans are still alive in that bunker.'

'Got to stop the tanks, lad.'

'Then give me your rifle!'

'Bonkers,' the hoarse weary voice muttered. 'The boy's bonkers.'

Tears filled his eyes and he struggled to free the rifle from the soldier's grasp. Then the soldier clouted him across the cheek and wheeled to watch the shell strike. Christopher picked himself up and crawled to the lip of the boulder. In the broken trees the Germans were running back into the wood from the crumpled bunker. A shell threw earth across the column of tanks. He saw the last of the Germans, carrying their machine-guns, disappear into the wood.

'Get your head down, lad.'

'We could have shot them. We could have killed at least *some* of them.'

'Can't do two things at a time.' Then the soldier was barking aim-corrections into his telephone and the big howitzers began to seek the German armour.

'Stay close — you'll go back with me, lad.'

'You could have killed some of them,' he said again, hurt and accusing.

'Well there's no shortage of Germans to kill. Correction. Raise your elevation another bloody twenty yards and then start walking them back at ten-yard intervals. Got it? Right. I've got to come home now — it's a bit noisy up here. Signing off.'

The soldier dropped the telephone, smashed it with the butt of his rifle, took Christopher's arm and hauled him roughly down the slope, running flat out. Christopher ran and the chant drummed through his mind in time to his running footfalls: *Kill the bastards. . . Kill the bastards. . . Kill the bastards. . .*

Chapter Four

The refugees trudged empty-eyed: no end to them. When the Stukas wailed overhead the old ones seemed indifferent, as if they knew it was useless seeking shelter; they remembered Flanders twenty-five years before.

In a dead man's outsize uniform and on a commandeered bicycle Christopher screwed up his courage and pedalled straight up to a French checkpoint and gave a cheery wave and rolled right through. No-one stopped him.

No-one was quite sure where Lord Gort's headquarters had gone. Communications were a shambles. South and west – the officers and men pointed that way and turned their backs; they had no time for a boy on a bicycle. But the Grenadier Guards lieutenant who'd provided the clothes and the bicycle had believed him. Stukas had knocked out half the Guardsmen and the wireless with them. He knew only that headquarters was somewhere between here and the sea.

The roads were jammed with wagons, donkeys, oxen, children, old people, men and women. The verges were littered with lorries and vans and cars that had run out of petrol or broken down; most of them had been looted – the seats, even the wheels; he saw wagons running on pneumatic tyres. He had never seen such a crush of human beings; and it went on endlessly, the dead lying beside the roads, their bodies stripped; beside them those who were too weak to go on.

He inched his way through the crowd. Soon he'd given away his food and his water bottle. He'd left his soldier's tunic across an old woman's shoulders and was cycling on in shirtsleeves. The plimsoles on his feet were ragged.

Time and again came the terrifying screams of the diving Stukas. The crowd tried to get off the roads but the sheer mass prevented it and the Stukas tore up the mob. Here and there a detachment of soldiers – Belgian, French, British – would return the divebombers' fire with small arms but it was ineffectual.

Finally he chanced upon a Belgian armoured car broken down by the road. Its driver was attempting repairs and four young officers stood about waiting. Their faces were expressionless. Christopher asked if they had a wireless. No. He asked if they knew where Lord Gort's headquarters was. They'd just come from there. They pointed south.

'Go on with you. I've no time for schoolboys.'

'I've a vital message for Colonel Metcalf.'

'Can't say I've ever heard of him.'

'He's on Lord Gort's staff.'

'Sure and he is. And I'm the Queen Mother. Be off with you.'

Finally a corporal took pity on him, gripped his shoulder with one hand, turned him and pointed with the other hand to one of many staff tents. 'You might find the Colonel's batman in that one.'

'Thank you Corporal.'

After an argument – Colonel Metcalf had been up without sleep for seventy-two hours – the batman took him inside and shook Winnie the Pooh awake.

The old man sat up with a start. 'What – what?'

'The lad insisted, sir.'

'Who? What?' Pooh's puffy eyes came round. 'Good Lord. Is that Christopher Robin?'

Christopher neither saluted nor nodded. Suddenly all the strength had run out of him.

'We'd given you up for dead, lad.'

General the Viscount Gort, VC, was an elderly man with lively blue eyes. 'We're being driven back pellmell as it is,' he protested to Pooh. 'Every ten minutes I'm in receipt of another set of strident orders from Weygand and the French High Command to turn my army south and join forces with them. And how the bloody hell am I to do that? The Panzers have reached the coast at Abbeville – they've cut us off from the main French armies. Boulogne has fallen and the 10th Panzer is hammering away at Calais—'

'And the Belgians are collapsing at Zonnebeke,' said Pooh.

Gort swung round on his chief of staff, Lieutenant-General Pownall, and gave one of the decisive orders that was to save the British Expeditionary Force. 'I think the 5th and 50th will have to plug that gap, Henry. Get Franklyn and Martel rolling at once. Maximum effort.'

'Very good, sir.'

The general's blue eyes turned on Christopher. They set off, strikingly, the maroon of his Victoria Cross. 'And how much can I rely on you, Creighton?'

'Absolutely, sir. I've told you the truth.'

Pooh said, 'The Prime Minister chose him for the job, sir.'

'I know that, Metcalf.' Lord Gort scowled at the officers who crowded round their maps behind him. 'But it is I, not the Prime Minister, who must decide whether to rely on the Belgians holding our left flank to the sea, or to abandon them and retire to Dunkirk in the hope of evacuating our army.'

'And the supply dumps, sir?' asked Pooh.

'Obsolete,' said Gort, 'as we know to our cost. The Panzers have only some twenty miles to go to occupy all of Belgium — hardly a strain on their fuel supplies.'

Lord Gort's bright eyes turned on Christopher once more. 'How sure can we be that the Belgians are going to surrender?'

'It was agreed with the Germans, sir, before all this started.'

Lord Gort's mouth worked. After studying Christopher for what seemed to the boy an eternity he said in a decisive voice, 'Very well. The army will make a fighting withdrawal to the perimeter at Dunkirk in accordance with the orders circulated by General Pownall yesterday. Inform the War Office and signal Admiral Ramsay at Dover that we shall require a little assistance from the Royal Navy in the shape of operation "Dynamo" as soon as practicable. Since he's a matelot, you'd better send him my compliments.'

He turned; and heads lifted to attend him. 'I'll want the navy to take off the useless mouths cluttering up the ground between my fighting men and the beaches. I mean to have an orderly retirement. We'll get as many off as we can — before the evacuation is terminated by enemy action.' He smiled bleakly at the stuffiness of his own phrase. 'Convey my regrets to General Weygand, and inform London of our decision. Let's get cracking, gentlemen.'

Gort's humour at such a tense moment was not lost on his staff as they saluted and went to carry out their orders.

*

The British Expeditionary Force fell back towards the sea and Christopher went with it, swept up in the madness of withdrawal. German guns and planes pressed them all the while.

Towards Dunkirk the crush was unbelievable. The terrifying speed of the defeat had destroyed the army's morale. Overhead the RAF somehow fought back the Junkers and Messerschmidts, Dorniers and Stukas; tiny brittle RAF open biplanes ran along the German front and dropped bombs – mostly by hand. The oiled German war machine hesitated for the first time but it was poised for the kill.

Christopher pedalled carefully through the crowds, passing under shattered bits of trees with the spring blossoms still on them. Finally he had to abandon the bike. He walked on, keeping close to Pooh, pushing through the muck and mud – fields, once, but trampled nearly to bedrock now.

Dunkirk. He never saw the city itself but for miles he saw treacly columns of black smoke where huge oil storage tanks burnt. The whole coastline seemed ablaze and he wondered how they could get off.

They found Lord Gort in Bastion 32, smoke-filled, with a battery of field telephones and a retinue of staff officers and messengers. When Lord Gort saw Christopher there was a flash of blue eyes. 'The Belgians', he said, 'have surrendered.' With a bleak sad smile he squeezed Christopher's arm and went on past, raising his voice to an aide: 'Have you made contact with Franklyn yet?'

That first night Christopher saw German planes flying across the horizon, working back and forth offshore, and he said, 'What are they up to?'

'What did you say?' Pooh said politely.

'What are the buggers doing?'

'Laying mines in the water, I expect.' And Pooh went back to his charts.

The boats began to come in at dawn, thrusting their prows through heavy rolling billows of black smoke, sliding up on to the beaches and pulling back off. The sea became carpeted with vessels – hundreds and hundreds of them: fishing boats, ferries, broad-arsed Thames barges towed by little London police boats, even a paddle steamer.

'You might lend a hand, Christopher,' Pooh said mildly, but it was not a rebuke; it was irony, for Christopher lay exhausted after a full day's carrying wounded men to the boats. Then Pooh smiled. 'We'll get ourselves off in due course, lad. But there are men in greater need than us.' Some of the men hadn't eaten for days; some were so badly injured it was pointless to move them. A charnel stink clung to everything.

Picking paths through enemy minefields, the little boats came in under the German guns; men up to their chests in water stood in the queues to get aboard and Lewis guns banged away from the decks of the small craft to ward off the Stukas that got through the RAF screen.

Christopher learnt in the ensuing days to recognize the symptoms of tetanus: the arched back, the gaping mouth and staring eyes. He learnt how to peel back a man's eyelid and judge him alive or dead. He learnt to live with the stink and the noise.

The noise drove stray dogs insane; they rushed about frothing at the mouth. 'Shoot the poor buggers,' Pooh said in his sad quiet voice, and a soldier began to go among them, picking them off.

The nine days of Dunkirk had begun on Sunday 26 May. On Friday 31 May, Lord Gort was evacuated, by the Prime Minister's order and despite his objections, aboard *Hebe*. Pooh was ordered to go with him but said to Christopher, 'I imagine it's an order I won't be court-martialled for disobeying.' He smiled and took Christopher by the shoulder and trudged back towards the acres of wounded who waited on their stretchers.

The perimeter had shrunk and the German guns had the range. By Sunday the coastline was broken up into pockets ringed by their artillery. The guns were picking off the boats as they appeared in the channels; not many were getting through any more. Pooh said, 'I suppose it's time we left. This will be the last day, I think.' Towards evening they made their way down to the shore. The few boats lying offshore taking on passengers were nearly swamped by the masses of men clinging to them. Christopher saw a British officer forcing his way on to a boat while his men were still on the beaches; finally someone shot the officer and he pitched overboard. A power launch ran into a small sailing boat, nearly capsizing it; the power launch backed away and the captain shouted through his megaphone, 'Can you stay afloat?'

'Why?' replied the helmsman of the sailing boat. 'Are you thinking of trying it again?'

There was a tremendous roar. Tons of metal careened past Christopher and plunged into the green–black water and he was drenched to the skin. Through the cascade he saw the sailing boat curtsey past the stern of the power launch – men on both decks were laughing like idiots. Aboard the sailing boat men clung to the gunwales and as it tacked out towards the Channel he saw men gently push floating mines off with their bare feet, taking care to avoid the spiked horns.

With Pooh and a crowd of soldiers he found himself in a rubber dinghy pushing off. The soldiers used their rifle butts for oars. A shell hit near enough to toss them about – one man fell into the water but Christopher stretched over the side and got his hand. The man in the water grinned at him. 'A bit dodgy there, mate.'

Pooh and Christopher helped the man aboard. The rubber boat pitched in the choppy water and a soldier bawled at them to keep an eye out for floating mines. One man sat open-mouthed and stunned, not moving, and Christopher took the man's rifle and began to paddle with it. There were fourteen in the dinghy; he doubted it had been designed for more than eight. The swollen gunwales rode down close to the water and each time she pitched into a trough she took water over the blunt bow. Several of the men began to bail with their helmets. Pooh had taken a position in the stern; he was trying to steer with an oar – one of the two oars aboard – but he had to keep shouting corrections to the soldiers because one side or the other would pull ahead and the boat would turn. 'Make for that destroyer.'

Smoke rolled heavy across the sea – the entire shore was ablaze. Smoke stung Christopher's eyes and made him cough. He could hardly see the ship ahead of them.

Then a man said in disbelief, 'She's turning away. . .'

'Cor, she's leavin' us here!'

'Bleedin' sods.'

They filled their chests and coughed and bellowed at the

destroyer but the ship neither saw nor heard them and within moments it disappeared into the fog of smoke.

'Right chaps,' Pooh said. 'Keep bailing. There'll be another ship. And if there's not then I think it might be a nice night for rowing to England.'

'We only need to keep her prow into the waves.'

'Why's that, lad?'

'It's a north wind tonight, sir.'

'Well we're all ignorant landlubbers here, Christopher, and you must be patient with us. How do you know the wind won't shift?'

'Not likely in this sort of weather, sir. It might veer a couple of points but no more than that.'

'You know these waters, then?'

'I know the weather patterns, sir.'

'But he's never bloody *been* here, has he?' shouted one of the soldiers.

Pooh roared, 'Shut your mouth! Or would you rather float adrift till we all die of thirst? Right, then. Christopher, if you'd be so kind as to navigate us home?'

Pooh let him out of the car in Harley Street. 'Get a good rest.'

'Would you like to come in for a moment, sir?'

'Thank you, but you ought to get to bed. My best wishes to your father.'

They'd cleaned him up and fed him full of eggs and hot chocolate at Dover; he'd slept standing up in the corridor of the packed train to London, protected by Pooh's thick arm across his shoulders. The borrowed clothes were too large and he kept tripping over the trouser turn-ups; he worried about looking a fool. His key was lost somewhere in Belgium and he had to stand on the step waiting for someone to answer his ring.

When the door opened it was a stranger's face – a young woman in a Wren uniform. She was small – quite a lot smaller than Christopher – and she had glossy dark hair; her eyes danced with merriment. 'Well what've we here? Can I help you?'

Christopher looked about. Had he come to the wrong house? No. 'I live here,' he said, and began to push past her.

The girl put out an arm. 'Wait a moment.'

'What's all this? Who're you?' Had his father taken up with a girl this young? It was ludicrous.

She still barred his way. Christopher dislodged her arm firmly. 'Let me pass.'

'You can't come in here.'

'I can't? We'll see about that. It's my bloody house!'

'No, wait. Please. You must be Mr Creighton's son, then?'

'And who else might I be?'

'Well your father doesn't live here now.'

'What?'

'He's given the house over to the services for the duration, you see. He's gone off to serve in the RAF.'

Christopher stared at her.

'Weren't you told?'

'I've – I've been away. I only got back to England today.' Then because he could not resist it he said, 'I was at Dunkirk, you see.'

Her dark eyes went round with astonishment. 'You're pulling my leg!'

'Where did you say my father is?'

'I've no idea, actually. Some RAF station or other, I suppose.' The girl scowled; pretty wrinkles corrugated her delicate brow. 'Haven't you got anywhere to stay then?'

He saw WAAF, Wren, ATS hats and greatcoats on the coat rack in the hall.

'Do you mean to tell me my house is full of women?'

It inspired the girl's bawdy laughter. 'You'd better come in. My name's Anne, with an "e" – what's yours?'

'Christopher, with a "ph".'

'Well then, Christopher, welcome to the Vicious Circle. That's what we call this place. There are sixteen of us packed in here. Luxurious digs for the junior women officers, wouldn't you say? We were awfully lucky to be billeted here.'

His mind was racing. 'Look, I shan't keep you but I've got some of my things here. I need my clothes as you can see – these rags came off a relief cart at Dover. My things must be somewhere about.'

'There are trunks in the cellars. Perhaps down there.'

'I know the way.' He set off for the cellar stairs but Anne came along behind him. Her call rang up the stairs:

'Man in the house!' Then, with a giggle, the revision: '*Boy* in the house! Boy in the house!'

He heard a slamming of doors from above.

The girls sat round the table chorusing the robbers' song from the West End musical *Chu Chin Chow*. The woman who led them in song had a rich contralto; she was big, with an opulent figure and a face that was just beginning to get heavy, and she was obviously the senior WAAF officer in the house. Her name, he'd learnt, was Flight Officer Jennifer Lister. She seemed more amused than annoyed by his presence at the dinner table. She was good-natured and matter-of-fact. She arranged for three girls to move out of his old room on the top floor. He'd been ushered in with great courtesy. 'You may make it your home whenever you're in London, Christopher, so long as you don't betray us to our superiors for having you here. Now have a nice long hot bath and get into your own clothes and come downstairs when you're ready. We'll have supper laid on for you.'

Christopher went back to school and found it boring.

'It's bloody arrogant,' he told Patrick McBride, a schoolfriend. 'It's false pride and pointless cruelty.'

'That's so,' Patrick agreed, 'but do remember, old boy, that without the old school tie you can't make your mark.'

I've made my mark, Christopher thought, but he said nothing.

His voice began to change, alarmingly. He had to give up his prized position as first treble in the school choir. Some of the senior boys ridiculed his unintentional and unexpected yodellings; he boxed two of them into submission. The third boy was too small to attack but he was the class bugler and Christopher stuffed his instrument with chewing gum and had the satisfaction of watching him turn purple while all the other boys sniggered.

France capitulated. In the countryside round the school the Local Defence Volunteers drilled with pitchforks, dreaming of knocking the Jerries for six; and Christopher noted that along the verges of the nearby RAF training station pillboxes and trenches and barbed-wire entanglements were appearing while

72

men in steel helmets watched the skies. Officers with identification silhouette books went round warning them not to confuse Blenheims with Junkers 88s.

He explained his absence much as he had explained it to the girls in Harley Street – visiting his friend in Belgium he'd been caught up in the German advance and after Prince Paul had been killed he'd made his way to Dunkirk – and his schoolmates were suitably impressed and went round hailing him as the school hero for a bit. Then he suffered the humiliation of going down with chickenpox and was in quarantine for three weeks, during which time German planes dropped 'Call to Surrender' leaflets on the school. Then early in July air battles began over the Channel and by the middle of the month the German planes were coming over in waves and the Battle of Britain was on.

Chapter Five

Owl was prompt, as always, and sat in the dining room until the Prime Minister arrived – late, as usual. Handing his hat to the butler the Prime Minister said, 'Where is Mrs Churchill?'

'I believe she is lunching out, sir.'

'Good. We'll be able to discuss cloaks and daggers.' Metcalf came in behind him and the three of them sat down to the meal and were served by the butler and a parlourmaid, both wearing white gloves with unbuttoned wrists. The Prime Minister said to Metcalf, 'I've a preference for round tables. It's not an Arthurian delusion. Actually it's sensible. No matter how many are at table, anyone can see anyone else. Well then, John – what is it?'

'We've just lost four more of our agents in Ireland.'

'That was very careless of you.'

'We have to assume at least one of them was squeezed before he was thrown away. The question is how much the enemy's learnt.'

Nearly every evening the Prime Minister met Brendan Bracken and Lord Beaverbrook to decide matters of strategy and logistics. For weeks Owl had been trying to persuade each of the three men, separately as well as jointly, that the Irish difficulty needed more of their attention than it was getting. Now he felt he had the ammunition. 'Four men, the best. All lost. It means they're concerned – it means we've rattled them. And it means whatever they're up to, they're determined that we don't get wind of it.'

The Prime Minister glared at him, evidently afraid Owl was about to produce figures and tables. People with statistics and charts and graphs always annoyed Winston; he tended to despise staff-officers' minds, except for a few bold ones (like Harris and Gort). It was astonishing how often he bullied or ignored his chiefs of staff. Owl had the feeling it stemmed from the way the army had cast Winston out, in early life; the PM had never quite forgiven them. Of course it had been his own bloody fault: his know-it-all arrogance had made him unpopular among his fellow officers and they'd ostracized him.

Just now the PM's attitude seemed especially truculent. Part of it, Owl thought, was the presence in the room of Winnie the Pooh Metcalf in his bloody army uniform. Metcalf wore the gold badge of the Intelligence Corps – the roses of York and Lancaster on a laurel wreath; what Winston in his unkinder moments liked to describe as two pansies resting on their laurels. Metcalf was a big man whose false appearance of complacency was bound to irritate the PM in any case; he had no visible dash. His stubborn bravery at Dunkirk had only confirmed Owl's confidence in him – Metcalf was the most thorough man he had, and one of the brightest – but the PM's prejudices wouldn't let him see that.

Winston was in mid-tirade at the moment and Owl waited it out. Winston was on again about air power: 'The navy can lose us the war, I suppose, but only the air force can win it. Harris has assured me that the RAF can win it by bombing alone, and not with any silliness of airborne troops – what's the use of dropping men? They don't explode when they hit the ground.'

'If I might interject the matter of U-boats,' Owl said drily.

Winston scowled combatively at him. 'Very well. Get on to the ruddy Irish if you must.'

'Colonel?'

Metcalf poked a toe in tentatively. 'Sir, we've got two issues intertwined. The German submarines and the Irish coast.'

The PM pointedly looked at the clock and sighed.

'Doenitz is the man we have to watch,' Owl insisted. 'In the long run he's a much greater threat to our survival than Goering. It's not the Luftwaffe that has this island in a state of armed siege – it's Doenitz's U-boat pack. Look – you've ordered my section to set Europe ablaze. A fine phrase, Prime Minister, but I've got to be able to feed my people and get them across the water before they can set any fires.'

'Will you get to the *point*?'

It was one of Owl's constant and greatest difficulties. You couldn't sneak up on Winston. The PM had no small talk. None.

'In a way,' Winston muttered, 'I nearly wish the Huns would try to invade. I am sure we should smash them up – certainly we should deal them a big blow.' He glowered at Metcalf.

'Instead it's pick-pick-pick-pick. They'll pick-pick me to death, and you'll pick-pick away at the remains like scavenging vultures and jackals. How many agents have you lost in Ireland to date?'

'It's reached double figures, sir.'

Winston snorted. 'Double figures. We can't deal the enemy a decisive blow without wiping out *millions* – and you're talking about a dozen men or so?'

'Nine men, sir. Four women.'

Winston's face changed. 'The sods.' Owl had difficulty in not laughing at the peculiar display of archaic gallantry. He could talk blithely of the murder of millions of Germans but the deaths of four Englishwomen shocked him.

'Sir,' said Metcalf, 'we're ringed by enemy bases from Norway to Brittany. Our only openings are to the west and north-west – a good part of which is blocked by the position of Ireland on the map. Our ships passing to the south of Ireland are exposed to murderous U-boat attacks and the Irish have denied us access to their ports. We know that de Valera's government is terrified that Germany may invade Ireland. At least he's had the courage to refuse Hitler's request that Ireland provide him with aerodromes and aircraft repair stations, and that may be because it would be too obvious a violation of their precious neutrality, but what happens under the sea is a different matter.'

Winston opened his mouth as if to interrupt, but then scowled and closed it.

Metcalf went on doggedly as if determined to bore the PM into an outburst. 'It was bad enough before – we know the U-boats were coming out of submarine pens in the Bay of Biscay. They were able to sortie quite far into the Atlantic from there, beyond the western reaches of Ireland. That's where they sank the carrier *Courageous*. Our losses to Doenitz's U-boats have been very great; over a million tons, including the battleship *Royal Oak* dead at anchor in Scapa Flow.'

'We all know that,' said the PM testily. 'I've sent messages to de Valera already. I've reminded him that Eire depends for her livelihood on the supplies our convoys bring in to HMS *Ferret*.'

'Yes,' Owl said. 'But Ireland continues to refuse to help us and her refusal's been a huge contribution to our losses in the Atlantic.'

'Only our hold on Northern Ireland and Iceland keeps open the sea lanes from America,' Metcalf said. 'Doenitz is building new U-boats faster than we can sink them. The armoured welded pressure-hulls of the new models are vastly stronger than our own riveted hulls – it takes virtually a direct hit by a depth charge to kill them. The situation, Prime Minister, is – not to put too fine a point on it – precarious.'

Owl said in his dryest voice, 'What profit is it to win the Battle of Britain if we lose the Battle of the Atlantic?'

'Well put,' Winston applauded, approving the phrasing, not the sentiment. 'Granted, the U-boats are masters of the Atlantic. Granted, we're throwing everything we have into the struggle against them and it's touch and go. Nevertheless, I have assurances our new Asdic sound gear will effect a major change in the predicament within a very short time.'

'I shouldn't count on it. You know how long it's taken to work the bugs out of our radar.' Owl refrained from pointing out that Winston's tendency to rely on untried gadgets was notorious. He had that – among other things – in common with Adolf Hitler.

'Well go on,' he said gruffly.

'It comes down to the basic fact that all our plans depend on the defeat of the U-boat menace. Hitler is depending on Doenitz to win the war for him by starving us to death. At this moment, sir, Germany feels so secure she is actually demobilizing forty of the two hundred divisions she called up last month.'

'I suspect Corporal Hitler will find that's a mistake,' Winston murmured happily.

'We've got to stop Jerry from sinking our transports. It's bad enough having them lie in wait for us off the Irish coast – but if the hints we've had are true, then in a matter of weeks the last convoy corridors will be closed against us.'

Churchill glared at Owl. 'What do you propose? What do you want me to do?'

'It might be wise to increase the pressure on de Valera,' Owl said. 'Let him know we suspect it. Diplomatically, of course.'

'Naturally. And?'

'We might try sending an agent to Donegal.'

'Yes?'

'Christopher Robin, for instance. A boy on a bicycle might get through where grown men with pistols under their armpits haven't been able to.' Owl added, 'He's a blooded veteran. We can depend on him. If I may be so bold, we're pursuing total aims with limited means. Christopher is one means available to us. We've got to stop Jerry from sinking every last British ship on the Atlantic – can we afford, out of sentiment, not to make use of a valuable weapon of intelligence?'

'You overestimate him.'

'If I may throw your own words back at you – if we lose this war the world will enter a new Dark Age. Not merely for one boy but for all boys.'

'For a realist and a cynic you've got the most incredibly melodramatic flair sometimes, John. Now you imply this one schoolboy could win the war for us. Has he got his finger in the dike, then?'

'He's already helped us avoid losing the war,' Owl pointed out with a sly smile. 'The least we can do is give him a chance to help us win it.'

A plain-clothes policeman and several of the Prime Minister's staff followed Mr Churchill on the short walk from 10 Downing Street through the Foreign Office Yard to the Office of Works Annexe. Christopher and Owl followed the party at a discreet distance. Tigger walked beaming through the passers-by; when one woman smiled at him he lifted his pink hand in the V-for-victory sign.

From outside, the building looked innocent enough – too innocent to house the nerve centre of the entire British war effort. It stood between King Charles Street and Great George Street overlooking the corner of St James's Park. Those who knew its interior never called the building anything but the 'Hole in the Ground'. Along the pavements were barbed-wire barricades, mountains of sandbags and armed sentries – Royal Marines and Grenadier Guardsmen for the most part. There were entrances on three sides of the building but the party led by Mr Churchill walked down Clive Steps to the park entrance; when the Prime Minister had gone inside, Owl took Christopher up the steps past more Grenadiers and a quartet of Royal Marine pensioners and a corporal to whom Owl and Christopher showed their passes. Through a slit in the wall beside a green metal door, Royal Marines with Thompson submachine-guns guarded the entire approach.

Owl led Christopher inside, down a narrow spiral staircase at the bottom of which stood more Guardsmen, still at attention from the Prime Minister's recent passage. Owl said to Christopher, 'Whenever you come here make sure you have your identity card and your pass. Be careful here – I've tripped half a dozen times myself over the bloody bulkhead frames at the bottoms of these doorways. They're watertight, you see – notice the heavy steel plate. We're below the level of the Thames here and if a few of Hitler's bombs should breach the banks of the river we might have a bit of a flood. . .' He poked his finger towards the low ceiling. 'We've fourteen feet of concrete above our heads here so there's no need to worry about direct hits. Come along – this is the PM's set of cubicles.'

Christopher was fascinated by the warren of tunnels and the thick clammy walls. Air banged in the sheet-metal ventilation conduits; fans rattled and footsteps echoed and telephones rang. Then Owl ushered him into a cell and withdrew, and Christopher was alone with Tigger.

Mr Churchill shut the door and pointed him to a chair. 'Welcome to the "Hole". We're on the top of three levels, actually. We haven't expanded into the third level yet – it's got quite a population of rats, I'm told. Now then. Let me describe the blasted U-boat situation to you.'

It was quite a long monologue but the boy listened to it with far more interest than he had to the fat man's discourses of earlier years. But there were, of course, digressions.

Mr Churchill said, 'We were able to take a third of a million men off the beach at Dunkirk – the finest men in British uniform. It might have been only half that number had we not received your information in time. We are in your debt. But now – now Armageddon is upon our doorstep. We must defend our island. We must employ every stratagem.' The fat man rolled the phrases off his tongue as if testing them for further use. 'The BEF has had to leave nearly all its heavy equipment behind at

Dunkirk, as you may know, and we are strapped for material. Corporal Hitler knows this, of course, and is attempting to ensure that our supply by the Atlantic convoys is destroyed by his submarines and his Luftwaffe.' Tigger's tongue made a shambles of the German word and he made a face. 'I can never pronounce that beastly language.'

He rambled on about Britain's plight and the need for boldness and daring; it was rather the sort of thing you got from the captain before a rugger match, Christopher thought, but all the same he was powerless to prevent his own feelings from rising to the surface: Mr Churchill's voice and words created in him an odd and heady feeling that electrified the skin over Christopher's spine.

Finally Mr Churchill said, 'I have told the English people that the Battle of Britain will be recalled as our finest hour. But it is also our most precarious hour. We are on the brink of losing the war. I've no doubt the RAF can hold back the Luftwaffe, but these submarines are another matter. If indeed they are receiving succour from clandestine pens on the northern coast of Ireland – an allegation which remains to be substantiated – then the last of our sea lanes may soon be closed.'

Christopher swallowed and blinked.

'The outlaw Irish Republican Army wields unduly strong influence in Dublin. The IRA is known to support the German side in the war, perhaps on the cynical theory that my enemy's enemy is perforce my friend. Your Uncle John rather dislikes the Irish, as you may know, and takes the position that it would serve them right if they were occupied by the Huns, but I rather think we shouldn't like to have the Germans based on that side of us – we'd be well and truly surrounded then, wouldn't we? Therefore, if we cannot persuade the Irish government to come in on our side, we must at least help them maintain their neutrality, lest they fall into the enemy's camp. For that reason, Christopher, we must conduct our intelligence quietly with the Irish government. Yet at the same time we cannot afford to allow Admiral Doenitz blithely to employ the coast of Ireland as a diesel station for his bloody wolf packs, if in fact that's what he's up to. If the submarines are there, they must be evicted – but first they must be found, and proof of their presence obtained, and it all must be accomplished without fuss or publicity. Given proof of their presence in Ireland we then will be armed with sufficient ammunition against Ireland to confront Dublin with an ultimatum.'

Mr Churchill had a habit of leaping up from his chair to illustrate a point with a finger-stab at a wall map. He did so now, thrusting his finger against the very northern tip of Ireland. 'Donegal, as you know, is a part of the Republic which actually lies to the north of Northern Ireland. It is here, along this northern coast, that your Uncle John believes the U-boat pens to be located. His agents have tried to find them. Four have been found dead.'

Mr Churchill turned. 'The job, as you can see, is a most perilous one.'

'Yes sir.'

'I shouldn't ask it of you at all. But Europe has fallen, Christopher, and we must face the storm alone. We must use every advantage to counteract this pitiless venal Nazi oppression and aggression. In this hour we need every one of our fire-eaters, whether they be old men like myself or adolescent schoolboys with an ardour for action. You've proved yourself a young man of lionhearted pluck and resourceful tenacity. It's our opinion that you may just pull the job off – Sea Scout on a camping holiday on that blasted bike. Beneath suspicion, as it were.'

'I shall do my very best, sir.'

'You're quite free to decline, you know. I'm not giving you an order. I'm asking a favour – not for myself, but for England.'

Christopher grinned at him. 'Do or die, sir.'

'Pray do it carefully, then.' Mr Churchill went towards the desk. 'Off you go. Uncle John will fill in the lurid details.'

'One must appreciate the irony,' Owl told Christopher. 'The facts are enough to make a cynic weep. Our government provides insurance policies for the convoy transports that carry goods to our shores. These are the only insurance policies on earth that cover acts of war. And we are inundated with honourable businessmen' – he spat the phrase out as if it were an insect that had flown into his mouth – 'who make it a practice to buy old tubs, register them in Liberia, coax them to work long enough to attract the U-boats with their smoke and their six- or seven-knot top speeds, and then collect the insurance if the boat is sunk, the profits if it somehow survives. Is it for these profiteers we're fighting this unholy war?'

Then he looked up. 'Well never mind. Colonel Metcalf? Brief the boy.'

Winnie the Pooh beckoned him to the map. 'HMS *Ferret* is the RN base on the River Foyle in Londonderry. I shall be there while you're in Ireland. You'll have a wireless and I shall be standing by for your signals. You'll take the Irish Channel ferry from Stranraer to Larne, then cycle to Londonderry. Crossing the border into the Republic is easy enough. There's a wood on the hill above Londonderry, a few British patrols now and then, but no fence. If they stop you you're in Sea Scout uniform and you'll have your identity card.' His fingers moved north. 'The fragmentary reports we've managed to acquire indicate that this northernmost coast is the most likely area for them. There are several long narrow sea loughs with high cliffs down to the water and fairly large caves at the waterline. They'd be more likely to use existing caves than to draw attention by blasting new ones.'

Pooh went back to his desk and sat down. Owl sat to one side scowling, smoothing the hair at his temples. 'I wish I had more information to give you,' said Pooh, 'but then if I did, we probably wouldn't need to ask you to go.'

'Yes sir.'

Pooh twisted his head to look back at the map. 'You see, our difficulty is that by refuelling in north Eire, the U-boats save a steaming distance, return-trip, of about a thousand miles. They extend their range into the north and west by that much. It effectively shuts down the Iceland passage to us. Another few weeks of the sort of losses we're sustaining. . .' He didn't need to finish it. But he added, 'One more thing. We've lost a number of agents over there. I don't believe they'd have been so careless as to have turned their back on a German. If they were betrayed or trapped, it was done by Irishmen, not Germans. Do you take my meaning, lad?'

'I think so.'

'Right. Trust no-one.' Then Pooh said, 'Your schoolfriend Patrick O'Shea McBride — his father's got a country place in Donegal. That's your pretext for visiting Ireland. But don't turn up at the McBride house unless circumstances force you to do it. Go there if you know you're being watched, but say nothing to anyone in that house.'

'You can't suspect Patrick, sir – he hates the Nazis!'

'It's not your friend we suspect.'

Owl said, 'We'd rather not have it like Belgium again. You might not get out of the wine cellar a second time. Avoid your friend if you can.'

Chagrin must have showed in Christopher's face. Winnie the Pooh said in a gentle voice, 'One of the prices we pay in the sort of games we play here is that we all must avoid our friends. We can never reveal anything to anyone who's an outsider. You must never tell your friend Patrick or anyone else about this mission, or the one in Belgium. Not your sisters or your mother or your father – not anyone at all.'

'Yes sir.'

'You see,' said Pooh, 'our little detachment is rather secret, old lad. In fact it's so secret it doesn't even have a formal name.'

'What do we call ourselves, then?'

Pooh and Owl exchanged glances; both men smiled – it was probably a response to his use of the first-person pronoun.

'We're known here and there,' Owl said, 'as "The Section". We're amateurs – gifted amateurs, but amateurs nonetheless. Our paymaster was His Majesty the King – the budget used to come out of his pocket, you see, rather than from government allocations. We are now on the official budget but I think we may regret that in the long term. We've avoided bureaucracy up to now. We've functioned as a private little team and we've had to report to no-one except the King and Mr Churchill. They tell us now that we're going to have to coordinate our activities with the formal intelligence services and I suppose they're right, if only to prevent us from blundering into one another's operations, but I suspect as long as the war lasts there'll still be a need for a section that can function privately without the knowledge of the staff or the Cabinet. The Prime Minister,' he added in a voice as dry as wind through autumn-yellow leaves, 'has need of a hatchet-man or two.'

Pooh stood up. 'Come along then, Christopher. We'll have a run out to Northways and see to your equipment.'

On the heights the wind roughed up his hair and he stopped to pump up the rear tyre again. It really wanted a patch but the leak was quite slow and he'd been able to nurse it along, stopping every five or six miles to pump air into it.

There were rain squalls over the sea but between them he saw a convoy coming in towards the coastline – destroyers and minesweepers moving along on station. He counted fourteen ships and wondered how many more had been with the convoy when it had left North America.

It was time to move the wireless again. He propped the bike against a tree and ducked into the wood to retrieve the set. They called it, officially, a portable transceiver but it was a heavy bulky thing.

He'd explored the route by daylight; now in the falling dusk he rolled along it again, covering eleven miles by midnight, packing the W/T into a loose natural cairn of rocks and covering it over with stones after preparing his brief negative report to Pooh, coding it with care and tapping out his Sea Scout Morse. Then he cycled half a mile, found a pleasant hillside, set up his Scout tent and made his fire. He'd ridgewalked and cycled a hundred miles of coastline in the past four days and had found nothing at all to stir his suspicions. He'd gone into village pubs, all wide-eyed and innocent and claiming to be lost, and encouraged the garrulous locals to talk, but there'd been no hints, no clues.

It was high summer and the days were long but the climate along that jagged northern coast was raw – chilly and grey with squalls over the sea and a green mist over the scrub-dotted rock cliffs. The loughs were long and narrow; the sides were cut by steep ravines. The best way to study them, he'd found, was to go along one side studying the base of the opposite cliff through his binoculars, then go round the landward end and back along the far side repeating the process in reverse. It was thorough but slow; at this rate it would be Christmas before he'd finished surveying the coast. Then after the second day it had occurred to him that they probably wouldn't try to maintain submarine pens in the exposed ocean coast, but rather in the sheltered cliffs within the loughs; so rather than exploring the seacoast he'd begun to cut across from one lough to the next, sometimes saving fifteen of twenty miles that way and at the same time avoiding the seaside villages.

On the fifth day he pedalled round a bend and found himself in the midst of a double column of Irish soldiers taking their rest on either side of the lane. Wary sentries presented the muzzles of their Enfields. Christopher leant weakly on one leg, holding his bike, and tried to work saliva into his mouth.

'What's this – what's this?'

'Sorry, Corporal. I didn't mean to startle you.'

'Who're you?'

'Christopher Creighton.' He piped it up stoutly and dazzled the corporal with his most boyish smile.

'English?'

'Yes.'

'And a Sea Scout, I see. Shouldn't you be in a boat?'

'I'm on a cycling holiday.'

'By yourself?' The dark brows beetled suspiciously.

'I'm on my way to visit my friend Patrick.'

'Patrick who, then?'

'Patrick McBride. At Donneally House.'

One of the soldiers, propped on an elbow spooning fruit from a tin, looked up and said mildly, 'You'll be after findin' it, then. Donneally House is another eighteen, twenty miles up the road here.'

'Yes, I know. Thank you.'

The corporal's hair had distributed a powdering of dandruff on the shoulders of his tunic. His suspicion waned and he sat down upon a rock at the side of the road.

'May I go?'

'You may – and you'll be finding your friend's house by tea time.'

The boy pedalled nonchalantly away, waving and smiling at the soldiers.

Once round the bend he stopped. What was a detachment of well-armed soldiers doing along this deserted stretch? They weren't carrying food; there were no tents. It meant they came from somewhere in the immediate vicinity – and the intelligence map showed no army stations in the area.

The rifles and submachine-guns indicated they were guarding something. Guarding what? He hid the bike in bullrushes and crept back to the bend to spy on them.

85

He followed them along the road, two or three miles to a crossroads where a farm lane wove drunkenly away over the hills. The soldiers stopped and relaxed for ten minutes and then turned back, retracing their line of march. There was the occasional laughter, the occasional bark of pain as someone twisted his foot on a stone. He sensed no urgency or secretiveness in them but they were here for some reason and he intended to find out what it was.

They led him past the point where his bicycle was concealed and he let them get beyond the hilltop and then retrieved the bike and pedalled slowly up to the crest, where he dismounted and walked through a little stand of stunted trees to scout the road ahead.

The soldiers were strolling past a small cottage. Beyond the cottage was the edge of a cliff top — the ragged promontory above Lough Swilly, which was the next lough on his map. The cliff meandered away to his left and beyond it through the green mist he could see the top of the opposite lough wall, a twisting steep slope of crags and crevasses.

The corporal spoke. From that distance Christopher couldn't make out the words but four of the soldiers detached themselves from the column and went to the cottage door, whereupon another soldier appeared from within; there was a brief colloquy and then the soldier in the doorway was joined by three companions from inside. The four of them came out and joined the corporal's column, while the corporal's four men went inside with their rifles. Obviously it was some sort of changing-of-the-guard; the cottage was a sentry station of a lookout of some sort.

What did the Irish army have to hide here? Then he saw the corporal lead his men off the road into a nearly hidden path to the right. The line of men dwindled towards the rim of the cliff and then, one by one, disappeared between two large boulders.

He glanced towards the sun and judged the number of hours to darkness and went back into the trees to have a kip beside his bicycle.

He crept round wide behind the cottage, keeping to the shadows of the rocks and moving silently on his dark plimsoles. No lamps burnt in the cottage but he could hear the laughter of the men inside; the wind carried the clink of glass to him. For sentries they were casual enough; he counted it his good fortune and made his way circuitously to the great pair of looming boulders between which he'd seen the army column disappear.

There was a slight mist and the night was chilly. He slipped into the narrow stone passage between the boulders and moved an inch at a time because he didn't want to be surprised by any-one in the passage but he saw no-one when he emerged; there was nothing very exciting in sight – moonlight came down through the mist and put a silver glow on the dewy grass and the damp black rocks. The ground sloped away from him but what took his interest was the heavily rutted tyre tracks that ran along to the edge. They were so deep as to be nearly trenches; there were smears of oil on the hump of grass between them.

A good many lorries had come this way, he thought. He padded along the track. It seemed to go straight out to the edge and plunge down, but that couldn't be. The mist worked on his nerves and he proceeded to the edge with slow care, alert to the danger: suppose someone came up from below? There was no place to hide.

As he approached the edge he heard the splash of surf below. The opposite face of the cliff was not visible through the mist but he'd seen it earlier by daylight – it wasn't far away. The water was deep and the currents treacherous; it would take expert pilotage to navigate these waters in anything so large as a submarine without smashing on the rocks, and he began to wonder if this possibly could be the right place.

He reached the edge. It wasn't a sharp-cut rim; the road simply went down more steeply and turned along the face of the slope, switchbacking to the bottom. The cliffs at either side had been eroded here and this part wasn't nearly vertical, though it was steep enough. If you fell you'd probably roll clear to the bottom, bouncing off boulders; the bottom wasn't more than two hundred feet away. He saw the glow of white froth where the sea broke on the rocks.

He went out to the edge of the road for a better look, moving with care. At the bottom was a flat of rock the size of a village green and he saw structures there, half obscured by the shoulders of the slope; there were no lights but he made out people moving about in the darkness, stealthy and silent, going from one building to another. Lorries were parked in rows and he caught the metal glint of a high chain-steel fence that surrounded three sides of the camp.

He couldn't make out detail – he needed to get closer. He went slowly along the road and there was a scrape of sound and he wheeled in alarm to meet it. Something hurtled at him and he dropped instinctively to one knee. It slid across above his shoulder – a bayonet fixed to the muzzle of a rifle. Christopher tumbled to one side. The earth seemed to tilt, he had no bearings for a moment, and he heard the sound of his attacker's sharp intake of breath. Then he saw the blade wheeling in silhouette against the sky – coming right at him.

He felt the wall of stone at his shoulder and thrust himself away from it. The bayonet scraped rock where he'd just been. His flailing arm blindly found his assailant's leg and he heaved on it. The man let out a cry of pain and Christopher pounded his shin again. The man fell across him; the rifle clattered on the ground. Christopher scrambled about, making wild grabs in the dark – it was deep shadow here under the great boulder and he could hardly see a thing against the rock.

Then something whacked painfully into his ribs and he was flung violently back. He was rolled over by the blow, and he found he was near the edge, lying flat, afraid to move lest he go over the cliff.

He heard the man scratching about in the darkness, probably searching for the rifle he'd dropped; in a corner of his mind Christopher coolly realized that was a mistake because it gave him a moment in which to gather breath and claw his way back on to the centre of the shelf. Then he saw the man loom against the mist, bayoneted rifle extended warily, and with a fevered heave Christopher flung himself into a rolling attack, swinging his leg up, aiming his foot at the man's groin.

The kick knocked the man down. There was a cry of alarm and pain, then a savage grunted oath. Christopher's groping hands found cloth, snatched at it, and it came away – the soldier's soft cap. He flung it away and groped again, found hair, gripped it in his fist and pulled.

The man yelled again. There was a thrashing of boots on the

rock. Christopher swayed on his knees, reached out blindly and found the rifle, pulling with all his strength.

It must have taken the man by surprise. The rifle came away in Christopher's grip and he swung it by the barrel. He felt the heavy buttstock collide with flesh; there was a solid thump and the metal was nearly jarred from his grasp. Then he heard a strange sigh and a sort of scraping, crumpling sound. He found the rifle's grip and trigger, reversed it in his hands and played the bayonet back and forth, whipping it from side to side to keep his opponent back, but the tip found nothing except the stone of the cliff – a slight spark, a small ring of sound.

He stood frozen for what seemed an age. His assailant didn't stir; there was no sound.

He cringed back against the wall and thrust the rifle out before him.

He crept forward. When his fingers brushed warm flesh he recoiled. He touched it again and it didn't move under his fingers.

The man was unconscious or dead. Christopher dragged him out towards the edge of the shelf, into the moonlight, and when he saw what the blow of the rifle butt had done to the soldier's head he knew the man was dead.

The soldier looked terribly young. Hardly more than Christopher's age; pale blond hair; acne spots on his cheeks.

You're in it now, he thought. You're right in it.

He squatted in the path, trembling. The young sentry, he supposed, had been surprised – they'd shared those things and Christopher had had some sort of grisly luck or he'd be the one lying dead on the stone.

He got his breath and became aware that he was doing the necessary things: dragging the sentry back into the cleft of rock from which he'd sprung, thrusting the heavy rifle back into the stone, turning to examine the sky to judge how many hours of darkness remained.

Then he remembered something that stunned him motionless. In his shock of panic during the fight the young sentry had cried out in alarm – *in German.*

Wedged into a craggy cleft of rock Christopher felt suddenly hot, then cold. Water burbled off stones at the foot of the cliff and he contemplated the height of the vine-covered steel fence with the bleak realization that he could get over it easily enough but not without drawing the attention of the sentries in the guard tower.

The uniform -- that of an Irish soldier -- was not a bad fit but the boots were too large and he'd had to stuff cloth round his feet. It wasn't comfortable but it would do. He'd stripped it off the body and carried the dead man some distance and pushed his body off the cliff into the sea. It had been in his mind to take the sentry's place but when he'd got closer to the encampment he'd realized the uniform would not be enough to get him into the place. The gate was well guarded. For the past hour he'd watched it. Once a patrol of eight soldiers had entered the gate and they'd had to stop there while the sentries studied their identity cards and shone torches in their faces to compare their likenesses with the identity-card photographs.

Finally he gave up the idea. He went along outside the fence, some distance from it, clambering through a jumble of fallen boulders until he reached the water. He was thinking of going in the water, swimming round the end of the fence, and climbing ashore inside the camp. But the water smashed the great rocks furiously and from the look of the currents he wouldn't stand a chance.

There had to be *some* way. He crawled back across the field of boulders and lay down in the shadows to stare at the gate. Above it loomed a sentry tower disguised as a windmill. It appeared to house a swivel-mounted searchlight. He saw a lorry come crawling down the hillside road -- a tanker. A strange hour of the night for deliveries, he thought, but if this place was what he thought it was then they'd be obliged to bring it in by night, safe from aerial observation.

The lorry stopped at the gate and the sentries gave the driver's papers an inspection. They shone their torches in his face; then they passed the lorry through and it went along into the camp behind a low building and out of Christopher's sight. Five minutes later a second lorry came down the hill and the ritual was repeated.

It gave him his method. He made his way back up the slope climbing from rock to rock until he reached one of the hairpin bends of the road. Then he lurked. He found himself grinning and he felt a bit ashamed. He remembered the young German. He wasn't sure how he felt about killing him.

Don't think about it.

A third fuel-tank lorry came growling down the road, running in low gear, whining, coming into the hairpin turn at a crawl, and Christopher made his run when its rear wheels were passing him. He gripped the back of it and hooked himself up underneath the inward-sloping bottom of the cylindrical tank; he was in plain sight but only to someone on the left-hand side of the lorry and the sentries had approached the first two lorries from the right-hand – the driver's – side. Unless they came round the lorry they wouldn't see him.

He rode it down to the gate and held his breath when it stopped. He heard the sentry and the driver talk to each other in German. He waited, clad in Irish uniform; if they caught him he'd try to bluff his way out, claim he'd merely hitched a ride on the truck because his feet were sore. . . But it wasn't necessary. The truck gnashed into gear and he gripped a pipe coupling to hold himself in place while it bumped forward into the camp.

When it went round the end of the long hangar structure he dropped off the lorry; rolled and came up with his back to the corner of the building, clutching the rifle. The lorry, feeling its way with slitted blackout headlamps, went on along the wall and stopped at the end of a queue of tankers; he crept a bit closer and saw that they were hooking the lorry tanks up to filler-hoses that ran inside the hangar. The building's roofline was cleverly broken up – from the air it would look like fishermen's huts.

A number of men stood about – the lorry drivers and five workmen. They were talking casually in German.

Christopher went back round the inland end of the hangar; the main gate was in plain sight but he walked boldly across the face of the building, past its door, relying on his uniform, and no-one challenged him.

He trotted down the long far side of the structure towards the sea, excitement pounding in him, and when he came to a window he peered in but it was opaque – blackout curtains, he supposed – and he went on. If anyone challenged him he would be in trouble because he didn't speak German, but he could try an Irish accent.

The hangar ended at the sea. From the corner, peering round, all he could see was a high flat corrugated wall, painted some dark dull colour. There were several bushes and trees growing against it. He squinted, trying to understand – then he realized this foliage would be immersed at high tide; therefore it had to be fake. He made his way back along the side wall to the first of the rows of windows he'd passed; but it was as opaque as before and he turned, wondering what to do next.

There was a little structure nearby – a portable lavatory; beyond it was an open shed and when he explored inside it he found welding gear: tanks, torches, helmets. Nothing very useful there. He couldn't very well go cutting his way inside through the wall of the hangar and wake up everybody in the camp; in any case he had no idea how to use welding equipment.

He heard the soft crunch of footsteps and crouched down in the welding shack. Two soldiers appeared, rifles slung over their shoulders. They walked down towards the sea. 'No, it wasn't him at all, John, it was Seamus.'

'They told me it was Curley.'

'They told you wrong.'

The men reached the shore, turned and walked towards the end of the fence. Guard patrol, Christopher guessed, but they seemed casual enough about it.

Opposite him a door in the wall of the hangar came open. There was a brief splash of lamplight from within. Someone emerged; the door thudded shut and a man walked away into the camp.

Skulking about by night would do nothing but draw attention to himself, he decided. The thing to do was to wait for daylight. He crossed swiftly to the lavatory and eased inside. It had three cubicles. He went into one of them and shut the door, sat down on the toilet, and leant his head back.

He kept rehearsing the fight with the German sentry and he was still awake when light crept into the lavatory. He was hungry, thirsty, cramped and sweaty in the coarse uniform. He willed the camp to wake up, but for ages nothing seemed to stir. He heard footsteps now and then but judged them to be guards, walking in twos. Once someone came into the lavatory. The man went into the next cubicle, did what he'd come to do and left, slamming the door behind him. Christopher felt imprisoned. Fear began to grow in him until he wondered if he'd be capable of moving at all.

Gradually the morning came alive. He went to the door, opened it a crack and peered out. Workmen and soldiers in various uniforms and outfits were milling about; the hangar door stood open now and men passed through it. Some of those who stood about outside were smoking cigarettes and chatting with one another, looking at their watches; evidently a new shift was about to go in.

He screwed up the courage to come out of the lavatory and walk unhurriedly towards the welding shed. He felt that dozens of eyes were staring at him but he avoided looking at anyone and went into the shed with his shoulders braced.

Two men were leaving the shed, carrying canisters and torches and helmets in their arms. Christopher went back among the equipment and had to lean against a bench, getting his breath and waiting for the dizziness to clear. This was the most foolish thing he'd ever done. *How was he ever going to get out of here?*

Think about it later, he told himself. He'd got in; he'd get out. He gathered up a torch and an acetylene canister and pulled the welder's helmet down over his face. The view through the thick glass plate was distorted and restricted; he felt confined but he went out wearing the blasted thing and followed a group of men into the hangar.

There were two of them, side-by-side, resting silently in the water inside the big hangar: camouflaged blue-grey German submarines with numbers painted on their high conning towers. Men crawled about, fixing hoses to couplings, scraping, daubing paint, repairing cable. A steady stream of men carried heavy crates and sacks on board. Wooden gangways ran round three sides of the hangar. At the far end there were massive steel gates at the waterline like canal locks. That would be on account of the tides, he realized; the U-boats could only go in and out at high tide, when the end wall of the hangar would be rolled up into the ceiling and the U-boats floated out. It looked crude but it served the purpose well enough. He had time to wonder briefly at the skills of the men who had to pilot them in here.

His eyes flicked from point to point, taking in detail; he tried to make a rough count of the number of men working, the number of soldiers. No way of telling how many were German, how many Irish. A few submariners lounged about – pale bearded men with anxious eyes in trim navy-blue uniforms.

He'd seen more than enough; it was time to get out. He turned back towards the door, pushing into the stream of incoming men – then a hand fell on his shoulder.

He nearly jumped a foot. Somebody was talking to him in rapid German. Christopher swallowed. Attempting a brogue he said, 'Oi wouldn't be understandin' German, sir,' but his voice cracked infuriatingly and the hand maintained its grip upon his shoulder and in a panic he thrust desperately through the crowd, squeezing through the door, yanking the welder's helmet off his head. The German was right behind him, yelling. Christopher wheeled, gripping a welder with both hands, bodily lifting the man round with him, and the blow meant for Christopher hit the welder across the neck. Several people stumbled together and he heard an angry bellowing and then he was running full pelt, flinging the tunic off as he ran; he leapt past the end of the hangar with the half-formed thought in his head that there wouldn't be rocks in that water because that was where the submarines entered the locks and then he was soaring in a flat racer's dive and the bullets began to chatter all round him and he hit the water too flat and dragged himself desperately down into it, shocked by the terrible cold. He opened his eyes underwater but the stuff was nearly black and he pulled himself forward with powerful strokes feeling the drag of the soldier's boots. He followed his Sea Scout training and curled up in the water and wrenched at them. As always the worst job was undoing the laces but finally he got them off and swam on, hearing bullets slap the surface overhead and feeling his chest grow tight for want of air. Then the current began to pull him and he was sucked down into the undertow.

From the window Pooh contemplated the chilly misty landscape above the rooftops of HMS *Ferret* and waited for the wireless to stutter, but he'd been waiting a long time now and his hands were trembling from all the coffee he'd drunk. The signal was more than forty hours overdue and his hope had dwindled.

It was too much to ask of a schoolboy, he thought. Somehow he'd convinced himself, as Mr Churchill had, of an invincibility in the boy – the plucky lad playing the game of 'Christopher Robin goes to war' on his blasted bike. Well it wasn't on after all. The bloody IRA had nailed the others and now it must have nailed young Christopher as well, and if Doenitz had wolf-pack pens in Donegal they were still there, undiscovered.

'What time is it, yeoman?'

'0415 hours sir.'

Bloody hell.

He went across to the coffee pot and poured another cup and lifted it unsteadily. The foul stuff had gone stone cold now. He sat down and then got up again, spilling a splash of coffee, bestirred by rising anger. Damn Owl, he thought, the boy's death was on Owl's doorstep – in his callousness Owl had sent a boy on a man's job, not caring a fig for the boy's life.

Before he'd come to *Ferret* to monitor Christopher's signals Pooh had received an invitation, or perhaps it was a summons, to go round to Owl's house in Chelsea for a chat. Owl was pathologically solitary by choice and it was no good feeling sympathetic about his lack of friends; he preferred it that way – a secretive bleak existence, no private social life at all. But now and then he seemed to feel a need to unburden himself and in recent months he'd chosen Pooh as his *confidant*, perhaps because Owl's only real friend was now Prime Minister and the formalities of office precluded the old cameraderies.

Pooh had had misgivings ever since Owl had recruited him into Churchill's quasi-official intelligence section in 1939. Pooh had had a satisfactory career in army intelligence and had retired from it that year to settle in Bearsted with Maida, potter in the garden and write his history of the Napoleonic spies. Then Owl had rung and asked him over to Crockham Hill for a chat and delivered himself of a rather hollow-sounding 'England needs you, old chap' speech, and ever since he'd taken the job Pooh had felt he'd been tricked. He complained of it to Maida but of course she saw through him: 'You hate gardening, you're not a writer; and you were becoming a pill. You're happy now with a job to do – shut up and get on with it.' She said it with a comfortable smile and of course she was right; he'd nothing but boredom since his retirement – the boys were away in Sandhurst,

Emily was living with her new husband on the Isle of Man and there was nothing to keep him at home except stubbornness so he'd taken a flat in Knightsbridge and plunged into Owl's intrigues.

That night in Chelsea, Owl had been in a particularly bleak mood. Owl's house reflected his person: airless, cheerless, claustrophobic, the confinement emphasized by its heavy blackout curtains. Owl had poured port into a pair of stemmed crystals and sat down facing Pooh across the inlaid card table. He'd held the crystal in both hands and looked down into it as though it contained oracular entrails. 'Unless Christopher can provide some kind of hard evidence, Winston will do nothing. He'll wait for his bloody Asdic to defeat the submarines for him and that will be too late. God knows I love the man but he's never outgrown the imperious stage of infancy in which every wail is sure to summon a nurse to see to his needs – he's never had to learn that he's not the centre of the universe. Do you know he doesn't even dress himself? He puts out his foot and Sawyers puts the sock on it. When he wants something he assumes he can have it – he never thinks of realities. He thinks that by telling the navy to sink more U-boats and lose fewer transports he can make it happen, just like that. My God, sometimes I despair. I feel I've been infected by his own black dog.'

The Prime Minister had fits of depression; the black dog had been a familiar visitor and sometimes, in the wilderness years, a constant companion. It was a melancholia he was usually at pains to conceal from the outside world by putting on bursts of energy, but at times the depression showed through, even to strangers: Pooh thought himself a stranger, though he'd spent enough time in the PM's company to qualify as a minor member of the circle.

Owl said, 'He was on again today about winning the war with bombs and Asdic. I tried to point out that our production isn't keeping up with the rate at which the Germans are destroying our ships and planes. But when you disagree with him he only pouts and says, "You are not on my side", as if he believes you guilty of treachery.'

'He's not that much of a fool,' Pooh replied firmly.

'He can be. He tosses out these fatuous ideas – bombing Germany into defeat, outwitting Doenitz with Asdic that doesn't exist beyond the drawing-boards; he's got a child's enthusiasm for clever conjuror's tricks and crackpot stunts. He's sentimental. Emotion should never be allowed to cloud a war leader's judgment but it clouds Winston's at every turn – it's up to us to try and set him straight, to do the basic toil that he despises. Real work has always been alien to him. He was a poor student, you know. At Harrow he got other boys to write his papers for him. I doubt he has any idea of the work we all do for him.'

'That's what a leader has aides for.'

'To be sure,' Owl said, his voice dropping dismally. 'But unless the aides impress realities upon him he'll tip right over into adolescent fantasies.'

Pooh said, 'His leadership has united the country and inspired it. That heroic voice of his is the one thing that's kept us going. That's the important thing, isn't it?'

'Ah, Metcalf, don't be so naïve. It takes more than heroic words. You've got to guard against that tendency to subscribe to the gospel according to Winston – thou shalt have no other gods but me.'

'Oh it's not quite like that, really. But I do find him unaccountably endearing.'

Oddly, Owl smiled in response. 'He is, you know. He inspires such ridiculous affection in all of us.' But then the smile fell away. 'The irony is that this devotion is largely a mystery to Winston. He's a total opportunist. Do you see much difference between his opinion of his generals and Hitler's? You know the common wisdom has it that Germany's main military weakness is the fact that Hitler constantly interferes with his generals. Winston does exactly the same thing, doesn't he? Sometimes I think his solipsism's going to drive us all round the bend. He assumes we're all wrong except when we happen to agree with him. He could lose the war for us, you know, unless we can persuade him to bring more weight to bear upon this U-boat issue. It's the one crucial matter before him but he refuses to see it. We've *got* to protect those convoys.'

Owl drained his glass and, with surprising ferocity, banged it down on the table. 'And the thing that terrifies me, you know, is that at this precise moment we've managed to drop all our fragile eggs into the basket of a schoolboy's ruddy bicycle.'

Pooh tried to reassure him. 'Heaven lies about us in our infancy,' he said.

Owl favoured him with his most scathing frown. 'Aphorisms. Wordsworth. For God's sake.'

'I think the lad will come through.'

'Crystal ball is it – or ouija board?'

'Call it what you like. If there's anything to be found on the Irish coast I believe Christopher will find it.'

That had been in Chelsea; now his faith had dwindled and he stood near the wireless with an empty coffee cup trying to will the bloody thing to start clicking but it remained as silent as death and finally, quivering with exhaustion, Pooh gathered up his raincoat and umbrella. 'I shall be in my quarters if there's any news,' he muttered to the yeoman, and turned unsteadily towards the door.

It opened under his hand; he stepped back, surprised, and then the familiar face was in the doorway grinning at him and a great wave of feeling rushed to Pooh's throat. 'Christopher – thank God!'

'I couldn't go back to the W/T or the bicycle, you see, sir. They were combing the hills. I saw the patrols searching every foot of the ridge. I kept to the sea and swam out nearly to the ocean. When I got tired I'd lie up on a rock.'

'And you *walked* all the way to Londonderry?'

'Yes sir. There wasn't much choice.'

'You must have sore feet,' Pooh remarked.

Owl had the signal in his hand; he was reading it into the telephone: '. . . two U-boats, full crews. At least a company of support personnel, some of them Germans and others Irish. I gather he didn't have time to sort out quite what the command relationship may be between the two. They're using fifteen hundredweight lorries to carry fuel oil and they run them in by night. They. . .'

On the other end of the line Winston suddenly roared in outrage.

Owl held the scrambler receiver away from his ear and glowered at it. 'What?'

'No, not you, John. The cat's just bitten my toe. It's what I get for waggling it.' Then the Prime Minister chortled. 'So Christopher Robin's brought home the prize, has he? I thought he might — he's a buccaneer after my own heart. Now let me have the exact location on the map, will you? I'll get right on to Dublin with it. Who is our man in Dublin? You were right all along, John. I didn't believe de Valera would have the effrontery but that's that. I shall pressure the man mercilessly now. If the Irish don't expel the Germans instantly then we will — and we'll inform the world what we're doing. Given the divided loyalties of the Irish populace, de Valera may have a civil war on his hands if he leaves it to us to evict the Boche for him. No, he's got no choice now — he'll have to throw them out. We'll do it quietly at the outset — give them a chance to get rid of the submarines and keep it hush-hush.'

'Right.'

'Good work,' Winston said, 'absolutely first class. Convey my congratulations to the lad.'

'Straight away,' Owl said.

'Is he all right, then?'

'He will be. Metcalf's looking after him at HMS *Ferret*. We'll bring him back across the Irish Sea tomorrow.'

'We'll want air photographs of that place, of course.'

'Of course.'

'What an adventure that boy is living!'

Chapter Six

Christopher swayed towards the girl and leered. 'Give us a kiss then.'

'I'll do no such thing.' She got up from the couch and stood over him, feigning indignation. 'You're drunk.'

'What of it?'

'You'll feel terrible in the morning.'

He'd come back to the Harley Street house because he'd nowhere else to go. It hadn't changed since his last visit; it was still being used as a hostel for service women. One look at his bedraggled appearance and he'd been taken in, as before; Anne and the formidable Flight Officer Lister had tucked him up in his secluded corner of the top floor. They'd told him he was the only man ever to sleep in the house since the girls had taken possession of it.

Then they'd wormed from him the information that he had just turned sixteen. There was nothing for it, then, but to celebrate the occasion. Christopher hadn't developed a taste for alcohol; he'd chosen the sweet wine, as the least objectionable alternative, and had tasted it tentatively, making idiotic remarks about its bouquet until the girls had laughed at him.

Anne was right about one thing. When he woke in the morning he felt dreadful. He rang Pooh and put his appointment off till the next day, pleading exhaustion. He had a tentative breakfast of toast and tea, served up by the Wren steward, a laconic old woman who disapproved of his presence in the house. Finally in the afternoon he screwed up the courage to ring his mother.

She came down to London on the six o'clock train and took him to dinner at the Savoy. When they sat down Christopher remarked how nice she looked in her ATS senior officer's uniform. She gave a gracious, if distracted, smile and then she said with sharp concern, 'You look as if the better part of you is in some other country.'

'Perhaps it is. I've killed a man.'

His mother wasn't the sort of woman to utter protestations of ladylike shock. She looked sideways at him – handsome eyes over a patrician nose – and her words were measured. 'On duty?'

'Yes.'

'That's all right then.' She unfolded her napkin. 'Was he a German?'

'Yes.'

'I shan't pry any more. Uncle John's made it clear I'm not to.'

'I know.'

'What do you want to do, then?'

'I honestly don't know, mother.'

'You've only a few days' school holiday left. Do you want to go back there?'

'I'd taken that for granted. It's not a matter of wanting, is it?'

She sat tall and straight, as always. 'I think the Prime Minister would like you to go on working for him. How does the idea strike you?'

'I know about it. I suppose it might depend on what sort of work it was.'

'They seem awfully pleased with what you've done so far.'

'Yes. Well I've been rather lucky.'

'Are you afraid? Is it dangerous? Well of course it must be. If you've had to kill a German – I suppose the German was a soldier?'

'Yes.'

'Are you afraid, then?'

'Not in that way, no.' He grinned in spite of himself. 'I've been sort of – playing at war. I suppose they've told you a bit?'

'They've told me enough.' She paused. 'In normal circumstances I suppose I should be horrified by the whole idea,' she said, 'but circumstances aren't exactly normal. Still, I don't want to let them force you to do anything you don't wish to do.'

He said, 'I got drunk last night. On some dreadful sweet wine.'

She made a face. 'Are you trying to impress me with your maturity? Any fool can get drunk.'

'I shan't do it again,' he promised.

'Of course you won't. Have you spoken to your father?'

'No. I thought of ringing him but—'

'Don't.'

'No?' He was surprised.

She said, 'You can't trust him to be discreet. He's never been the sort of man to be entrusted with secrets. Don't misunderstand me – there are qualities to be admired in your father; but if you should tell him anything of what you've been up to, he'd react with horror and he'd immediately begin posting broadsides to his friends in the government, complaining of the uses to which his young son has been put. The result would be great embarrassment for the Prime Minister. Your father, I'm afraid, still thinks of war as a sort of gentleman's sport. You know he deplores the idea of my being in uniform. It's not the sort of thing an Englishwoman should do.'

Her smile was infectious; he laughed in response.

Then she said, 'If it pleases you, I should be happy if you chose to serve the Prime Minister. I regard him as the personification of valour. Mr Churchill is a prophet, a visionary, a dynamic romanticist, a true hero. He's the one great man of our time, Christopher, and he'll be the victor in this shabby war. There are those who detract him and those who hate him and those who are contemptuous of him – don't let them influence you; every great man has enemies. Stick by him and you won't go wrong. When you've grown up you'll be thankful to have played a part in making history.'

Mr Churchill paced rapidly up and down, head thrust forward, a sombre scowl on his face. He turned his pale blue eyes on Christopher. 'You had great good luck out there, didn't you? That German might have done for you.'

'He didn't.'

'But you're a boy playing a man's game. An amateur on the playing field against professionals. It won't do.'

'Am I to go back to school, then? I'd much rather go on working for you.'

The Prime Minister was visibly pleased. 'If you ever fail me it won't be for lack of cheek. Your mother's been speaking to me, you know.'

'Yes sir.'

' A remarkable woman.'

'Yes sir.'

'Would you care to be my paladin?'

Mr Churchill had to explain to him what a paladin had been:

one of Charlemagne's twelve heroic knightly peers. The words 'Charlemagne' and 'peers' rolled off his tongue.

Mr Churchill resumed his pacing as if the matter were settled. 'They accuse me of draconian designs. Well that may be true enough. God knows there are dark hours when I envy the dictators their ability to shoot people who refuse to agree with them.'

Christopher thought it best not to reply to this.

'You could be of great use to me, Christopher. You're willing enough. You've the stout spirit for the challenge. But if that German sentry had been a little more experienced. . . Look here, you need training in the arts of war. We'd like to send you to school. A rather special school.'

England endured the winter of the Blitz and Christopher endured the course of training under cover of Number Two RAF Initial Training Wing in a small room in the Fens.

Herndon, the warrant officer, had a way of shouting obscene orders into your eardrums from two inches away and when you couldn't obey his impossible orders he would make you run six miles in full pack or dig bloody great excavations with a tiny trenching spade. You stood to attention for hours in foul blizzards; you scoured walls with soap and cotton waste; you went to Scotland and ran up towering wooden walls and over the top and down the other side; you climbed ropes and crawled under concertinas of barbed wire; you hurled grenades and fired all manner of weapons.

You didn't need to do anything to provoke Herndon. Your existence was enough. Herndon called your father a ponce and your mother a tart, and defied you to do anything about it. He kept on at you until you did; then he pinned you flat and laughed in your face and sent you on another six-mile run.

You worked out in the gymnasium until your muscles were cramped with fiery pain. You studied the properties and applications of a dozen varieties of explosives. You went through a course in parachute-jump training, beginning in the gymnasium where you were taught how to fall, then jumping off the back of a slow-moving lorry, then by degrees jumping off the back of the same lorry at speeds up to 25 mph so that you would be prepared for parachuting in strong winds, then off high towers with slide-cables and finally from the jump door of a throbbing transport plane at two and a half thousand feet, falling terrifyingly through space and waiting for the chute to spring open.

You studied languages – different ones from Herndon's basic English – wireless codes and ciphers, hand-to-hand combat, demolition, disguise, deception. You learnt how to dismantle and assemble a submachine-gun in pitch darkness, and how to kill with it. Occasionally you saw some of the young women who were also trainees but were housed elsewhere; they wore WAAF uniform and occasionally your lot shared a lecture hall with them and you marvelled at their courage.

You were the youngest trainee and the others treated you somewhat as a mascot until you taught them better.

It was the first time he'd been alone with Herndon in Herndon's private quarters.

'Sit down, Hamilton.'

Christopher was Peter Hamilton there. Owl had laid on his identity with care. Files and records had been slipped into numerous archives to support the existence of Peter Hamilton, nineteen years old.

He sat on the edge of the bunk. Herndon leant forward, sticking out his chin. 'Like to tear me limb from limb, wouldn't you.'

Christopher smiled.

'You want to prove I can't break you, isn't that it? The others learn obedience – you've only tested your defiance. What am I to do with you? We've taught the rest of them well because we know what to train them for. They'll have one another for support – they'll be working in teams and squads and companies. You're another sort of bloke, aren't you. You'll be on your own, I think. No, I'm not prying; I'm merely trying to explain to you why I've been rather harder on you than on the others. If you've got a team behind you, you can afford the occasional mistake because someone else is there to set it right. But if you're working alone you haven't got that cushion. How old are you? Never mind. I know you're not ruddy nineteen.'

Herndon lowered himself on to a chair. His body was as trim and as deftly tuned as a Stradivarius. 'I haven't been able to shout you into it. Perhaps I can reason you into it. Look, lad,

I'd be failing my duty if I let you pass out of here without learning how to live off the land and how not to die on it. This course isn't so much to teach you how to do things — it's to prepare you for when things go wrong. You've got to learn to react without thinking about it. That's why you trouble me, Hamilton. You keep thinking when you ought to be reacting out of instinct. I find myself wondering what you'll do when you find a gun in your face and a German's finger going white on the trigger.'

'I'll kill him, I suppose.'

'You *suppose*?'

'I'll kill him.' *I already have.*

'You never show fear — that troubles me too.'

'Well, I suppose there's fear — and then there's the even greater fear of showing fear.' Christopher smiled.

'You're an awkward sod,' Herndon said.

'Don't I obey orders?'

'You do. As though you were humouring me. It's not good form to patronize your superiors, lad.' The big jaw came forward again. 'Would you kill a man simply because you were ordered to do it?'

Christopher made no reply. Then Herndon said, 'We're going to have to learn the answer to that one, aren't we. But understand one thing — I am not your enemy.'

'I know that.'

'Do you?'

'I've played your game. I don't hate you any more than you hate me.'

'Haven't you got any bloody feelings at all then?' Herndon got up, driven by frustration. 'You're good, you know. You're always right at the top of the form. It's as if you were born two days ahead of the rest of them. But you stand back from yourself and you keep smiling as if it's all a bloody joke; as if you know things the rest of us don't know — as if you've already been there.'

'In a way I suppose I have.'

'You were at Dunkirk, weren't you?'

'Who told you that?'

'No-one needed to,' Herndon said. 'But it's more than that. I suppose some of it's the ruddy upper-class thing.'

Christopher said, 'You don't really need to worry about me, you know. You've taught me well. I shan't let you down.'

Herndon gave him an unhappy look. 'Lad, we've hardly started.'

The girl tapped the table smartly with her ruler. After a time the whistling died away and the girl said, 'And keep it quiet. My name is Falkiner.' She was a Wren third officer; from his seat in the third row Christopher watched her with awed fascination. She swung the tip of the pointer against the chart on the easel beside her. 'We are here to discuss ciphers, and only ciphers.'

It provoked laughter and Falkiner smiled a bit to show she was not made entirely if ice. 'We'll start with basic principles – the five-digit cluster. . .'

It was the last lecture period of the evening and afterwards a crowd assembled round the striking lecturer. Christopher's chum Roberts came along to the door beside him, grinning lewdly. 'I've always wondered what sort of underclothes they wear under those uniforms. She'd be a lovely one to help me find out.'

'Most likely she's got a stiletto under there, just for blokes like you.'

Roberts said airily, 'Christ, Hamilton, where's your barefoot dash? Come on, it's Friday. Shall we mount a frontal assault on the King's Arms?'

The public house was awash in airmen and smoke. The din was earsplitting. Someone was banging a piano but it could hardly be heard. Then he heard a bawdy hoot and turned to see Wren third officer Falkiner flinging herself leggily through a group of admirers, lithe and unselfconscious. Christopher's heartbeat picked up and he realized he'd been staring at her only after she disappeared from sight in the crowd.

'Right,' Roberts breathed close to his ear, 'there'll be a few self-induced wet dreams in the billet tonight, old chap. Well never mind. Drink up.'

'I haven't seen her round here before,' Christopher said.

'She's new, right enough. We'd have noticed. I say, did you get the hang of that bridge nonsense this morning?'

'I think so.'

'Go over it with me tomorrow then, will you? Didn't make any sense to me at all. You need to be a ruddy engineer to understand all that rot about stresses and thrust.' Roberts shook his head. 'I know there's a war on but they take it too fast by half for me; if I didn't have you for an interpreter I'd have been sent down weeks ago. Here, put that away, it's my round. I owe you a lot more than a beer.'

'You'll be all right,' Christopher told him. 'Just don't push it too hard. Don't get rattled. If you get rattled you start making mistakes.'

'Well they never give you enough bloody *time*, do they?'

Falkiner came in sight again through a gap in the crowd. Someone was pointing a uniformed arm this way. The Wren said something and made her way forward. Roberts touched Christopher's arm. 'My word. The vision's headed this way.'

She came right up, laughing as she fended off hands and puckered lips; she wasn't nearly as tall as she'd seemed on the platform. She looked up into Roberts's face. 'You're Hamilton, aren't you?'

Crushed, Roberts shook his head and poked a thumb towards Christopher.

Christopher executed a courteous and elaborate bow. 'Very much at your service, ma'am.'

'May I have a word with you?' Then she shot over her shoulder: 'Keep your hands to yourselves if you don't want to be up before the CO tomorrow morning.'

'Sorry, ma'am – I slipped.'

She laughed to take the edge off it; then, amazingly, his arm was in the warm grasp of her fingers and she was guiding him away from the bar.

She led him outside. Hoots and whistles followed them. 'Ignore them,' she said.

'I'm very flattered by this attention, ma'am, but what could you possibly want with me?'

They were walking along to the corner; she still had his arm. 'I wanted to talk to you.'

'Me? Why?'

'I've heard a bit about you. Perhaps I need to explain a bit. I'm in GCCS at Bletchley. Quite a few signals come across my table there. From Belgium, for example, and from Ireland.' She gave him a meaningful look. 'I wanted to see what you looked like. Is that too brazen for you?'

He stopped, nearly unbalancing her. 'Who sent you?'

The tea-shop was virtually deserted. He laid out one and six for tea and biscuits and they took seats at a table barely large enough for two cups and four elbows. She said, 'I'm from Devon.'

'Oh yes. It's beautiful there.'

'You've been there, then.'

'Well – no.' He smiled. 'But I can see it in your eyes.'

'You're a bit too gallant for your age.'

'Well then, how old are *you*?'

'And a bit too bold. I'm older than you are, child.' She stirred a lump of sugar into her tea. 'Your friends in the pub seem to be from some other planet, don't they. They're as enthusiastic as small boys looking for mischief. Dear God, they're talking about war, they're talking about killing and being killed. What did it feel like to kill that man in Ireland?'

'He didn't say.'

'That's not funny. It's cruel.'

'Sorry, ma'am. What did you want me to say?'

'That's a fair-sized chip on your shoulder, isn't it?'

'I'm wondering who sent you to pump me.'

She put the spoon down. It rattled a bit. 'I suppose I've been awfully clumsy, haven't I? Well I've never done this sort of thing before. I don't think I'm cut out for it. I don't think I'll do it again.'

'It's all right. There couldn't have been anything in those signals about Peter Hamilton. Someone had to give you that name or you wouldn't have connected it up. You should have pretended you didn't know my name.'

'I suppose I'm not much of a Mata Hari. Well thank you for the tea.' She began to rise.

'Don't go.'

'Well I've embarrassed you – and myself.'

'Stay,' he said. 'Please.'

He had to take a fair amount of ragging at the camp. He laughed but he said nothing. In the morning he found Herndon's reptilian attention on him and he gave in to the opiate of repetitive training and at four, when he was tugging off his boots to massage his feet, Herndon came through the barrack and said, 'That's better, lad,' and went on past him to berate someone else.

She was in the tea-shop when he arrived and he couldn't help beaming. 'I wasn't sure you'd come.'

'I said I would.'

Sitting down he studied her face. 'Falkiner,' he said, 'isn't quite enough of a name for me to know you by.'

'It's Patricia.'

'I suppose you ought to call me Peter.'

'I'd prefer Christopher. I won't call you that where anyone else can hear.'

'They've appointed you down here from P–5 Section. You've told me that much – but for how long?'

'A fortnight.'

'That seems awfully short.' Then he provoked her smile, which was as good as a kiss: 'I doubt we're quick enough to learn it all in a fortnight. We're a slow lot. Particularly your obedient servant. I may need a great deal of supplementary tutoring.'

She said, 'This is silly, isn't it? They asked me to do a little job on the side and I mucked it up in the first five minutes. I don't know what I'm doing sitting here with you. I've made such a fool of myself.'

'Never mind,' he said. 'Come on, let's walk down by the river.'

Patricia Falkiner looked into his eyes, not sure whether to smile. Christopher said, 'Look here, do you want me to clear off?'

'I don't think so.'

'You're not very sure.'

'I've been going through rather a sticky patch,' she said. 'I'm not very sure of anything.'

Goaded by an intuition he said, 'You had a chap, didn't you?'

'Yes.'

'Was he shot down?'

'Nothing so heroic. We decided to go our separate ways.' She took his elbow and they began to walk back. 'We'd been happy with each other. In a way it might be easier if he'd died. He'd never have disillusioned me then, would he?'

'He's a fool,' he blurted, 'letting you go.'

She laughed. 'He knew me better than you do, Christopher. But that's very gallant.'

The park was empty, the light fading; he nearly didn't see them in time. There were four of them, rushing him in menacing silence, and he turned to meet it with everything Herndon had taught him. He interposed himself between them and Patricia and he met the first one with an out-thrust boot, the second with an arm across the windpipe. But then they had him down and one of them was dragging Patricia back into the trees, a hand over her mouth. He was pinned by the weight of three of them and they knew what they were about. He got a few digs in — one of them got careless and Christopher flapped an elbow into his nose; another one, shifting his weight, put his ear too close and Christopher gnawed it like a bulldog until someone popped him across the cheek and sparks blazed behind his eyeballs. He kicked and felt his toe connect with flesh.

'Right. Pull him over there.'

'Fierce bugger, this one.'

'Get cracking.'

They were dragging him on the grass on his backside; they had his wrists and ankles. He tried to heave himself about but it was no go. He had time to realize that if they'd meant to kill him they'd have done it by now; and he had time to wonder who the hell they were and what they could possibly want from him. They weren't going to all this trouble just to rob him and he doubted they had designs on Patricia; they were too efficient for that.

He hadn't got much of a look at them — big young men in macs and turned-down hats — but he caught sight of a pair of boots and they looked military.

Anger swelled in him but he didn't cry out; it would only have invited a clout across the mouth. He let himself go slack and his dead weight made their work a little harder; he took what satisfaction he could from that. He rolled his head from side to side but he couldn't see Patricia; the fourth man had her somewhere back in the trees above the embankment. Now they tossed him into the bushes but before he could get his feet under him they were on him again. Two of them pinned him down and the third dropped on his belly with both knees. It hurt like fire and it drove all the wind out of him. Then the man was slapping him, right and left, swinging like some relentless pendular machine, not terribly hard but after the first few goes it began to sting and he felt the blood rush into his cheeks. The battering went on until he thought he'd lost his mind.

When it stopped he had no feeling left above his neck and his vision was awash in red.

'All right.' The voice was calm, businesslike. 'What's your name?'

'Peter Hamilton.'

Something cracked his shin; pain went through him like a white-hot blade.

'Your *name*.'

That time he said nothing at all and they did something to his shin again and he cried out; he couldn't help it.

'Talk to me, boy.'

'You know my name.'

'Who do you work for, then? Who gives you orders?'

'The Royal bloody Air Force.'

'Try again.'

It was accompanied by a crack on the shin that made him arch his back; he screamed into the palm that clapped across his mouth; he tried to bite it but the man was ready for that one and cupped his hand away from the teeth. The smell of acrid sweat came into his nostrils. His mouth was regaining its feeling; he could taste the metallic bitterness of his own fear.

'Who sent you to Ireland? What were your instructions?'

'I've never been to Ireland in my—'

They cut him off with a crack across the shinbone that nearly catapulted him right up to the treetops and he lay panting with his teeth locked together, hissing through them until he got control of the pain.

'We can keep hitting that spot all night, boy. It's time you talked to us.'

'I can't tell you anything I don't know. What do you want me to say? Tell me and I'll say it.'

'What's your name?'

'Hamilton.'

Crack.

He passed out for a while. When he came to he didn't stir; they still had him pinned and he didn't want them to know he'd come round. But they must have detected a subtle modulation in his breathing. The hated voice grated at him:

'Tell us about Ireland. Tell us.'

'I've never been—'

'Heads up. Someone coming.'

'Christ, it's the bloody coppers.'

'Hold him still. They can't see in here.'

It had got dark. He'd thought it was his eyes but it was night and he saw the glimmer of the torches' beams through the branches. He began to heave and struggle. The hard palm came down across his mouth again and a warning hand closed round his windpipe but his rage was too great and he didn't let it stop him; he kicked out and heaved his back off the earth and tried to flail and it knocked one of them loose and he had a leg free and he kicked savagely, connected with something, felt steel fingers close round his throat and kicked again. It made a racket in the brittle branches. His breath was cut off and he felt his larynx go soft and he knew he was done for. Nothing to lose, so he kept thrashing and they grunted at him in rage and then the cut-off of oxygen burnt a hot flame right up through his chest into his head and everything went black.

It was only for a bit and he heard them walking away. He heard someone's sharp question: 'Who's over there? What's happened to him?'

'A bit much to drink, I fancy. He seems to have fainted. We only just came across him ourselves.'

'Leave it to us, then.'

'Right. Cheerio.'

He wanted to shout but his throat was on fire and it was all he could do to squeeze ragged bits of breath in and out of the raw pinched passage. The torch beams hurt his eyes and he closed them.

*

He hadn't any voice and he had to whisper; even that hurt. 'Are you all right?'

She said, 'Yes. Dear God, what have they done to you?'

It was a narrow bed with starched hospital sheets; they felt like gravel against his punished flesh. He said, 'You didn't happen to recognize any of them, did you?'

'No.' That was a bit curt because she'd recognized the accusation concealed in his question. 'Do you think I had something to do with it, Christopher?'

'I hate the world just now. Never mind – I'm sorry. He didn't hurt you?'

'No.'

A fat nurse came along. 'That's enough for now. He'll want his rest, miss.'

'Sergeant Byrne, lad. My colleague's Constable Atterton. Feel up to talking?'

'Yes.'

'You've taken a bit of a beating, they tell us. We didn't find much in your pockets. Did you have much worth taking?'

'I had about ten quid,' he lied. 'I suppose that's what they wanted. They must have seen me take out my wallet in the tea-shop.'

'Did you recognize them from the tea-shop, then?'

'No. But I was with a young lady. I wasn't paying attention.'

'Gave a good account of yourself, didn't you, lad. You didn't know any of these men, then?'

'No.'

'Would you mind describing them as best you can?'

He had a glimpse of himself in a mirror on the way out. They'd broken a great many blood vessels in his cheeks; his face looked like an old drunk's. But it was his shins that still hurt the most. He hobbled arthritically down the steps, using Patricia Falkiner's arm for support.

She said, 'They won't expect you to report in until you're well enough to run. Come on, I've got the use of a car and a few gallons of petrol.'

'Where are we going?'

'My digs. A bit outside the town. Listen, I've told the landlady you're my brother.'

She had a shabbily furnished bed-and-breakfast room on the first floor at the back above a newsagent's shop. She pushed his trouser legs gently up to his knees and folded damp warm towels across his shins. 'There. They said that would be the best. Those bruises – I've never seen anything so ugly. What did they want?'

'Information.'

'About what?'

He smiled. 'I didn't tell them.'

'And you're not likely to tell me. Well that's all right. I shan't pry. I do feel somehow responsible for this, though.'

'Why?'

'I don't know. I hadn't anything to do with it – you must believe that.'

'Is it so important to you what I believe?'

'Yes.'

It took forever to get a trunk call through the phone kiosk in the shop. Finally he had Pooh on the line and he breathed deeply to contain his anger. 'I was beset by four highwaymen.'

'I know,' Pooh said. 'We've had the police reports. You put up quite a fight, didn't you? Are you all right?'

'I've a few more bruises than I need. There were four of them. Do you want descriptions?'

'No. It's a police matter, isn't it?'

'They wanted to know about Ireland.'

There was a silence of static on the line. After a moment Pooh said, 'What did you tell them?'

'Ask them.' He banged the receiver down on to its cradle.

Five minutes later the shopkeeper called him to the telephone. It was Pooh again and Christopher shouted into the phone, 'How did you know where to find me? I didn't leave a number.'

'We're keeping track of you, old lad. It seems only sensible after what's happened. Why did you ring off?'

'To let you know what I think of your little practical joke.'

'It wasn't mine, Christopher. I'm saddened you'd think it of me.'

'Look, they were *Englishmen*. Do you understand me? In

English bloody army boots. They had orders and it wasn't orders from Berlin, was it?'

'I'm going to have to look into this. I'll ring you back.'

'What's the bloody use? I'm on to your games.'

'They weren't mine, Christopher. I promise you that.'

'Then whose were they?'

'I shall endeavour to find out, you can be sure of that.'

'You might start by looking under the carpet in your own office.'

'I understand your anger but please don't jump to conclusions.' Then there was a pause after which Pooh said, 'I must ask you this again and I'd like a proper answer. What did you tell them?'

'Nothing.'

'Good on you, lad.'

'I warn you, Colonel, if this was someone's idea of a passing-out examination —'

'I'll let you know what we find out. Apart from that are you quite all right? Is there anything you'd like?'

'A new pair of shins and a skin-graft on my face. And an hour alone with each one of those four blokes.'

'That's the spirit. Onwards and upwards, old chap.'

He made his way up to the room like an old man and warmed the towels and spread them across his legs. Waiting for Patricia to return from her lectures he tried to read a dusty copy of *Ivanhoe* someone had left in the drawer but he couldn't keep his mind from wandering. He lurched with his chair to the window and sat with his feet propped up on the edge of the bed, neck twisted so he could look out on to the countryside. The trees in the hedgerows were bare and there was a rime of ice round the window but the gas fire kept the room comfortable enough. He saw a formation of Blenheims climbing towards the east, heading for the Channel and targets in occupied Europe beyond. The morning's *Telegraph* from the shop below lay on the bed and he put his feet down to retrieve it and, for want of anything better to do, reread the day's news. Lord Beaverbrook was encouraged by the increase in aircraft production. The Prime Minister had made a speech in the Commons saying that the victory in the Battle of Britain had proved that England could hold on. The Luftwaffe's switch to London, as the target of its Blitz, merely demonstrated that the German air force was too weak to continue its fight against the RAF. There was a brief article in which General Sir Hastings 'Pug' Ismay issued a warning that Japan's recent signing of the Tripartite Pact with Germany and Italy must not be ignored, for it constituted a threat against Britain's possessions in the Far East.

What no-one dared say was that England clung to its survival by her fingernails and that Mr Churchill's hated Nahzees were poised just over the Channel awaiting the order from the Führer to invade.

The room had Patricia's subtle scent in it. His awareness of her was gradually becoming the size of a house. Abruptly he got out of the chair, steadied his legs under him, ignored the lances of pain and made his way downstairs. Mrs Davies gave him a kindly smile and he said, 'Is there anywhere nearby where I might buy some flowers?'

'The greengrocer keeps a greenhouse just up the lane. You might try there.' Then her eyes changed. 'Flowers?'

'For my sister,' he explained. 'She's been awfully kind.'

Suspicion deserted the woman's eyes. She smiled and nodded.

When he returned with a bunch of chrysanthemums she gave him a tall glass for a vase and, desperate for company, he sat about the shop making small talk with her.

When Patricia returned she looked tired; she'd had to fend off a pack of over-eager blokes who'd tried to take her along to the pub for an evening meal. She was a bit cross until they went upstairs and she saw the flowers in the glass of water. Then she turned her face towards him and wept helplessly.

Puzzled and a bit frightened he stepped forward, wincing because he'd forgotten the shins, and clumsily put his arms round her; she sagged against him and cried against his chest. It was the first time he'd embraced her and the softness of her body sent a thrill through him. He sank his face in her hair and breathed deeply in her clean scent.

Finally she drew away gently and he proffered his handkerchief; she dabbed her eyes. He said, 'What's that all about?'

'I'm sorry to be such a fool.' She snuffled. 'Nobody ever gave me flowers before.' Then she bawled again.

'I grew up rather sheltered,' she said. 'Our lives centred round the parish church – Girl Guides, choir practice, Saturday night dances, amateur dramatics. It was rather High Church. I went through a desperately fervent religious phase. I was going to be a missionary in darkest places.'

'Then you joined the Wrens.'

'Oh that was years and years ago – the missionary fervour, I mean. Then I took my school certificates and decided to take up nursing. Then the war came along. Actually I've been in nearly two years now, since before the war. It was Derek, that chap I told you about, who recruited me into the crypto-analysis section.'

'The one you broke up with.'

'Yes.'

He pictured a lanky blond chap with receding chin, long scarf and sports car. He hated Derek.

He said, perfectly sober this time, 'Give us a kiss.'

She smiled and obliged.

'You'll want to be jolly careful with this.' Herndon placed the bundle of blasting sticks – in his hands. 'When you've set the fuse remember you've got fifteen seconds. And I'll remind you fifteen seconds is not sixteen seconds.'

He crept towards the stack of weathered planks which for training purposes represented an enemy bridge. He set the charge, wrapping it in place with tape, uncoiling the fusewire. He looked over his shoulder; the others were watching from behind their sandbags. Herndon gave him thumbs-up and Christopher struck a match and made sure the fusewire was well and truly sputtering. Then he ran for it. The shins gave a twinge or two. He dived into the slit trench and tugged his helmet down firmly. It was just as well he did because a bit of wood clanged off the helmet and made his ears ring. The explosion echoed round the field and he looked up through the rolling smoke and saw he'd set the charge in the right place; there wasn't a stick left anywhere near the detonation point.

'Right. Gather round now, let's have your attention. There'll be a lorry arriving soon and people coming off it in German uniforms. You six are out here today for special training and I know you've been wondering why you've been kept on after the others have passed out of the course. You're here to deal with the six Jerries we're bringing in from the Isle of Man. I assume you're all familiar with Defence Regulation 18B under which enemy aliens and other suspicious types were gathered up at the start of the war and sent off to the internment camp on the Isle of Man. Two of the men on the lorry are from that camp. The other four are from the Prisoner of War camp. All six of them come from condemned cells.'

Roberts gave Christopher a worried scowl; the other two commando trainees squatted with their elbows round their knees watching Herndon without expression; the two girls, in baggy combat togs, stood close together as if for mutual support; one of the girls was testing her commando knife in the scabbard. She had quite a pretty face and curls of blonde hair that peeped out beneath her balaclava.

'Let me tell you about these six German gentlemen.' Herndon pronounced the word with contempt. 'Kreisler, first. Kreisler was passing himself off as a Swedish businessman in Oxford Street. He'd been in this country four years and he'd married an Englishwoman and they had two daughters, aged two years one month and one year one month. Kreisler was a sleeper agent. He got orders from Berlin to activate himself and get hold of information about our RAF coastal radar installations and pass the information back to the Abwehr. Kreisler wasn't taking any chances on being betrayed. We don't know whether his English wife stumbled on to a clue to his true mission but we know he went out of the flat one night at three o'clock in the morning while his wife and the two infants were asleep. He filled the gas meter and turned on the cooker, but he didn't light it. He waited outside the flat half an hour and then he wrapped four inches of petrol-soaked rag round a brick, set it alight and threw it in through the window from the street. There was enough left of the wife and the two little girls to identify them, but only just.'

Herndon paused for breath and his eyes flicked from face to face. 'Right. Next we have Beck. Charming fellow, Beck. He'd been over here since '34, flogging second-class diamonds from Amsterdam. All quite legal but the stones were flawed. Shabby little man but his job gave him an excuse to travel round the country and he kept his eyes open and reported back what he saw — military installations, training manoeuvres, and so on. Again, standard espionage. But Beck turned out to be a bit over-eager and a bit over-ardent about his Nazi principles. When the war came we were on to him, enough to have surveillance on him, and our intelligence blokes were near enough to witness it but not near enough to stop it when Beck took a pistol to a family of harmless Jews in a shop in Bristol. We're not quite sure what came over him, for it clearly wasn't any part of his orders from Germany. He simply wiped them out, two bullets each. The grandfather was eighty-six, the shopkeeper's widow was fifty-three, the son who ran the shop was twenty-six and confined to a wheelchair with polio, and the daughter who was visiting was twenty-four. I needn't add that none of them was armed, nor were they seen to provoke Herr Beck in any way. Their crime, apparently, was that they were Jews.'

Herndon addressed the last bit to the two girls and Christopher wondered whether one of them might be Jewish. Herndon said, 'Right, that's the two Section 18Bs. Now the other four are POWs and two of them were SS, both corporals, taken prisoner by a squad of Belgian soldiers during the retreat to Dunkirk. Our two SS chaps came into a village near Liège along with two other Germans – we understand they were SS officers – and the two officers were shot from ambush by a sniper. In reprisal for those two killings these SS corporals went round the village shooting everything that moved. By all accounts they massacred some forty-two civilians, including old people and children and two pregnant women, before they ran out of ammunition and were taken prisoner. Why the Belgians didn't shoot them dead on the spot I've no idea.

'Finally there are two junior naval ratings. They were gun crew aboard an E-boat in the Channel. About four months ago a flight of Blenheims was returning from a raid over occupied France and the E-Boat shot one of them down. The observer was killed but the rest of the crew got out and parachuted. The pilot happened to land in the water not too far from the E-boat. At this moment one of our own MTBs came into range and there was something of a duel between our boat and the German E-boat; the Blenheim pilot was near enough to get scorched by some of the burning debris. The E-boat had bigger armament and it sank our MTB – the crew of fourteen managed to get off before she went down, and they'd fired a last salvo that broke up the E-boat and sent most of the German crew to their life-rafts. But these two diligent bastards remained on board until the last possible moment because they were having a bit of sport shooting up the survivors of the MTB who were swimming round in the water trying to stay alive. They killed eleven of the fourteen. Then their E-boat sank and they swam to their life-raft but the Blenheim pilot, wearing his life jacket, held them both at the point of his revolver until the RAF air–sea rescue picked them all up.'

Herndon closed his eyes a moment and Christopher saw one of his fists tighten, the knuckles going white. Then Herndon said in quite a gentle voice, 'I'm sure my point is taken. These men aren't merely spies and soldiers. They're criminals – war criminals. Their murders aren't justified by any code of war or justice that we recognize. Each of the six has been tried by a jury and found guilty of murder. They have been sentenced to death.'

Then Herndon looked up and met each pair of eyes in turn.

'You will be their executioners.'

The lorry appeared at the top of the lane and came grinding slowly down across the field. Nothing else stirred on the wintry field. The cold seeped into Christopher's bones and he heard the chatter of Roberts's teeth. The lorry came forward – too slowly, it seemed.

Herndon was still talking. 'Part of your training has been in assassination. You've been chosen as the execution squad to carry out death sentences on these six prisoners. There are no rules here – you're simply to regard these six as live practice targets. I'd recommend you don't spend much time reflecting on the histories I've just told you. If you go into this arena in hot blood it may cost you your life. Rage breeds haste, and haste breeds mistakes. Keep cold.'

The lorry was fifty yards away. Herndon said, 'They've each been told what this is about. They're unarmed – you've got your knives – but they've been told this. If any of them can beat the lot of you and stay alive, his sentence will be commuted to life imprisonment. So these Jerries have got a bloody good incentive to kill you lot. Keep that in mind.'

Herndon swung his Sten to bear on the back of the lorry as

it slewed to a stop. The driver got down and two armed men came out of the canvas-covered back; they stood facing the tailboard, submachine-guns lifted, and six men climbed awkwardly down with their hands manacled behind them.

The blonde girl cleared her throat nervously. Herndon said, 'You may decline if you wish. It will put a black mark on your records.'

Christopher's throat grew tight. He swallowed. He heard the sawing of Roberts's breath, harsh and abrasive.

The two lean young blond ones would be the SS lads and they'd be the most dangerous; he studied the six of them with care. They stood thirty feet away and the lorry driver was tossing a ring of keys—it struck the ground at the feet of one of the Germans, a burly man with enormous shoulders. The German never took his eyes off the waiting executioners: he got down on both knees and felt behind him for the ring of keys and worked with it for a while until his hands came free and then he shook off the handcuffs and turned to one of his companions and set him free.

When the first SS youth was freed he reached down and picked up two sets of handcuffs and locked them together and swung the chain into his palm. One of the armed guards gestured with his submachine-gun. *'Nein.'*

The SS smiled bleakly and tossed the chain of cuffs; the guard caught and pocketed them.

Then Herndon joined the lorry driver and the guards. Weapons levelled, the four of them backed slowly away and Christopher kept his eyes on the six Germans in the field while Herndon and the guards got in the lorry and drove it back up the lane. It stopped a hundred yards away with a good field of fire and Christopher saw one of the SS men look over his shoulder to judge his chances of making a run for the hedgerow. It was a quarter of a mile away and under the guns all the way. The SS swung his face back and Christopher saw it close up, the eyes going down to slits, the jaw creeping forward to lie in a hard line.

Roberts bounced the knife in his fist. Christopher saw him lick his lips. 'Right then. Let's get it done, shall we.' Roberts began to walk down the slight slope.

Christopher stood perfectly still until he realized the other five were walking forward; then he followed them.

They circled the six Germans who stood together in a knot. The two SS stood at either side of the group, facing out, palms rising and falling in the *en-garde* position of men who'd been trained to fight with their hands. Their knees were flexed and their eyes darted everywhere. If there was any fear in those two they didn't show it. The other Germans were plainly afraid but trying to cover it and one of them began to splay his fingers and wave his palms about in imitation of the two SS. It was clear enough he was unsure of himself. His eyes were dismal.

The unreality of it was chilling; Christopher found himself trembling. The hilt of the fighting-knife slipped in his moist hand.

Roberts gave a shout and darted in, light dancing along the blade. It was a feint. The SS dodged away from it and that was what Roberts had wanted. Knife into flesh and a twist to expose the wound—the blade pulled out and Roberts made another lunge. Christopher went for the other SS but even as he closed he thought, *Not like this.* When he hit the SS it was with the blunt hilt of the knife, a blow across the chest; then, deliberately, he opened his hand and let the knife fall away and went into the fight on equal terms.

One of the girls shouted; there was a din of scuffling. He grappled with the SS and they were tumbling in a crowd which separated quickly. One of the Germans was diving for the discarded knife. There was a confusion of slithering and grasping. Someone cried out in pain. Christopher still had the SS in a hold but it wasn't a disabling hold and the SS rolled him off. After that it was feint, parry, lunge, kick, guard, attack. The SS went for his eyes with spread rigid fingers. Christopher batted it aside, took a jump-kick on the turned side of his thigh, parried that one by kicking the other foot out from under the SS and then leapt on him but the SS was too quick for that one and rolled aside. Christopher dropped on to one shoulder and swivelled to get to his feet but the SS came at him with both hands. Christopher's windpipe was still tender after last week's mauling. He made the mistake of trying to wrestle the hold off by gripping the two wrists and of course he hadn't the leverage for that and in a fraction of a second his larynx would be crushed but he used the fraction as he'd been taught; the base of his palm straight up against the tip of the man's nose.

That finished it instantly. It was the most wicked of simple blows. Struck hard enough and with precise aim it was calculated to snap the brittle cartilege of the nose and drive it straight up into the brain. It destroyed motor power immediately and death was virtually instantaneous. The German was dead before he fell; everything went loose, there was a sudden stink of excrement. Christopher crawled out from under and wheeled but he was the last. The others stood clutching their blood-soaked knives. Roberts was staring reproachfully at him and one of the girls, the blonde, was turning round and bending over to retch; but she'd made her kill and Herndon was riding down the slope on the running board of the lorry, not smiling but satisfied with his students. Christopher watched the hard soldier's face while something died in his heart.

He sat not moving in the darkness until the door opened and a fan of light fell across his shoes from the hall. He was aware of it when she came in, shut the door, switched on the light, came round to look down at him. She didn't remove her cap or the service respirator; she only watched him. 'What's the matter? Sitting here in the dark like a ghost.'

It was as if he stood outside watching himself. He heard her clearly enough. But he hadn't the will to respond. He went on staring into darkness.

'Come on then.' She pressed the side of his face against her hip, ran her fingers along his scalp. 'What is it?'

'Bloody little pimp.'

'What?'

'Herndon.'

'What on earth did he do to you?'

'Cold-blooded bastards.'

She didn't stir. His arms went up around her. She said, very softly, 'If you don't snap out of it you'll get yourself into a rare old state.'

He patted her rump and stretched to ease the tension. 'I'm all right. Sorry. We had a rough exercise today.'

'Well it's nearly over, isn't it? Two more days and we're both out of here.'

'You're off back to Bletchley then?'

'Yes.'

'I'd like to come round and see you. When I can.'

'I'd like you to do that,' she replied. Her hand kept touching his shoulder. She sat down beside him; her voice modulated subtly, sharpening his awareness of her sexuality. 'In fact I shall insist upon it.'

He felt better. He strode to the door and back; couldn't decide what to do with his hands and finally put them in his pockets. Then he said, 'I can't fathom what you see in me. I'm too young for you. I've been nothing but trouble ever since we met.'

She said, 'Let's be honest then. I think it's because you need me. It's a thing to treasure, being needed. It doesn't happen all that often, you know.'

'The same instincts that make you want to take up missionary work and nursing. Is that what you mean?'

'No. I don't think so. That's not personal, is it? You're very personal. And don't go on so about the age difference. It's only two years and in any case you're a hundred years older than I am. I've never had any patience with adolescent boys but there's nothing adolescent about you. It's one of the things that troubles me, you know. You're getting old before your time. You might be thirty-five just now.'

'It was rather an adventure at first.'

'It still can be, can't it? If you don't let it get you down so.'

He said, 'I suppose it depends what sort of jobs they find for me to do.'

'If you don't like them you can leave. You're under age — they can't force you to do things.'

'They haven't spent all this time on my learning to let me go now.'

'They can't stop you.'

He thought, *They could kill me off*, but that immediately struck him as a melodramatic fantasy. They wouldn't kill a sixteen-year-old boy just for turning his back, would they?

'Why don't you wait and see what they've got laid on for you?'

She was right; he must wait and see.

She said, 'I wish you'd be a bit less withdrawn. You don't need to tell me secrets but you can talk to me. I'm the one who knows about Christopher Robin, remember?'

'That bloody childish name.'

'You could do with a bit more childishness.'

He said, 'Come here then and give the child a kiss.'

Chapter Seven

It was getting on for six o'clock and people were making their way to the tube. Some of them deliberately went round by Whitehall and Downing Street in the hope of catching a glimpse of the Prime Minister. The sky was clear and the autumn air warm; the crowd at the barricade at the top of the street was larger than usual and the Prime Minister, on his way to the Hole in the Ground, waved happily at the sea of smiling faces and went on into the Foreign Office Yard.

Following along in the knot of staff officers and aides, Owl marvelled how Winston – no matter what his mood might have been a moment earlier – always managed to obey the strident calls of patriotism, grinning ferociously at any crowd with his heroic V-for-victory salute.

A workman at the end of King Charles Street stepped up from his manhole cover, a wide shining smile of adoration on his leathery gaunt face, and held up a flame at arm's length and Winston bowed into it, pausing in his stride, twisting his cigar in the flame until it was well and truly burning, meeting the workman's beaming glance and clearly overcome by the moment so that he stood his ground and the eyes of both men began to shine with tears; and then Winston moved on.

In truth, Owl thought, the war had not saddened Winston at all. He had risen zestfully to the great adventure, paying no more than lip-service to its dark tragedies. He would go about London viewing bomb destruction after a raid and tears would roll down his face; they were quite genuine, Owl thought, but strictly for the moment. Ten minutes later he'd have forgotten about it. The German bombers came over again and they'd have to haul him down off the roof where he'd gone to watch the display of searchlights and flak, grinning from ear to ear like a small boy at a fireworks display.

Winston as always chose the narrow spiral stairs to go down into the Hole in the Ground because it gave him the feeling of going down into a submarine for action stations. Owl wondered if he was aware that submarines did not normally have spiral staircases.

Owl trailed after him; it would be a while before he got the PM's attention and he was resigned to waiting. The staff dispersed into various tunnels, Ismay and Hollis proceeding along to the War Cabinet Room while Winston went into his cell accompanied by Sawyers, his valet, and one of his private secretaries. Owl sat down in the outer room to wait.

They hadn't shut the door and he heard Winston dictating a memorandum in somewhat acidulous tones:

'No view can be taken of the future until we know how "Crusader" goes. A battle is a veil through which it is unwise to peer. No, let me rephrase that. . .'

Auchinleck was ranged against Rommel in the Western Desert but nothing was going right and it was remarkable how well Winston had stood up under the setbacks of the past months – most recently the sinking off Gibraltar of the leviathan *Ark Royal* by Doenitz's pestilential U-boats. His moods seemed unaffected by the ups and downs of the war; they came from within. On a day of victory he might well be supine under the jaws of terrible depression, his black dog; glum awareness that all life, including his own, ended in death. Then unaccountably the weight would lift and in the midst of disappointment he might be filled with ebullient cheer.

The year had started on a good note. The Battle of Britain had been won, the denial of Irish bases had reduced the appetite of the wolf packs in the Atlantic, and the American Harry Hopkins, that gentle dying man, had brought over a note from President Roosevelt – handwritten on White House notepaper – hailing Winston in the words of Longfellow:

> Sail on, O ship of State!
> Sail on, O Union strong and great!
> Humanity with all its fears,
> With all the hopes of future years,
> Is hanging breathless on thy fate!

That had brought tears and not to Winston's eyes alone. But Owl had felt obliged to qualify optimism: 'Our intelligence persuades me that the chance of the United States coming into the war this year is nil.' And so it still appeared ten months later. 'Even if they did come in,' he'd had to point out, 'the entire American army has fewer than a quarter of a million men.' The isolationists had a firm grip on both houses of Congress, without which Roosevelt could not declare war.

Three months earlier Winston had sailed secretly aboard *Prince of Wales* to meet the President off the coast of New-foundland; in the four-day conference at anchor they had drawn up the Atlantic Charter but that was a long way yet from real alliance.

For the most part it had gone badly on all fronts. The bomb-ing of London had gone on incessantly into the spring of the year; Rommel's Afrika Korps appeared in the desert and Winston had gone along to the closed-up estate at Chartwell to await word of Wavell's progress against the German tanks. The failure of Wavell's attack had depressed him. Then the ULTRA cryptographers at Bletchley had revealed Hitler's plan to attack Russia – and Winston, in an inspired but unsuccessful effort to divide the German army and thereby prevent Hitler from defeating the Soviets, had ordered Wavell into Greece with an inadequate force to keep the Wehrmacht occupied there. Not only had he failed in that aim but a month later the Germans had parachuted into Crete in force and seven days later, having lost another sixteen thousand men, Winston had been obliged to agree to the evacuation of British forces from the island.

When Germany invaded the Soviet Union, Owl had found the hour exciting because he felt it marked the war's turning-point; it was Hitler's great blunder. By way of immediate effect it relieved London of a considerable burden, for the Blitz came to an abrupt end so that the Luftwaffe could be diverted east. Winston, however, was phlegmatic in the extreme about the Russians. On the heels of the German attack – about which Winston had repeatedly warned Stalin but to no avail since Stalin believed him to be lying – the Soviets had appeared at Downing Street, slouch-hats in hand, begging for handouts of equipment and ammunition. Winston had gone about the War Rooms in a rage: 'Where were those bloody Bolshevik baboons when we were being bombed by German planes fuelled with Russian oil?'

That hadn't been the turning-point after all; or at least it didn't appear to have helped in the next few months. Hitler had a big enough army to fight both wars. And now it looked likely that the desert army would be defeated again by Rommel. One more major defeat and Winston might be out of office and that would be catastrophic, Owl thought, because despite his impatience, his tendency to rashness and his tyrannical bad temper, Winston was a remarkable man, and irreplaceable. He might lose the war – anyone might – but he was the only man who could win it.

His troubles just now were political more than military. Winston was the most peculiar sort of politician: he did not mirror. He seldom moved with the tide of opinion; he had in the past changed his party allegiance blithely and chosen to disregard old obligations whenever it suited him. His habit of miscalculation had made enemies – perhaps too many enemies for him to withstand; and he was not likely to keep fending them off forever with mere words, no matter how eloquent. Indeed Winston was far too impressed by the importance of words: 'I live from mouth to hand.' His words had been inspirational, courageous, brilliant (but rarely wise), audacious, dynamic; he had rallied the people but not always the politicians. In the end all he had left was his mystical communion with the people and his hot-headed sense of destiny; but he didn't know how to be conciliatory and that could be his downfall.

It had become Owl's mission to protect Winston from himself. Clearly it hadn't entered Winston's head that he could possibly be removed from office, and there was no way of calling his attention to it. But the rumblings were becoming alarming. He had won the last vote of confidence easily but the next one might be a close thing, and if there were another major set-back it was on the cards that he'd have nowhere to go but out.

What was needed just now, Owl thought, was not so much victory as the appearance of victory: the promise of it. It didn't need arguments or reason; it needed something symbolic. A flash of hope, a cause for celebration.

A victory on the battlefield could achieve this but only momentarily – until the next defeat obscured it. There was one thing that certainly could do it. *We have to get the Americans into the war.*

*

When the sweeping searchlight reached Christopher he was standing quite still; they would spot movement before anything else. He didn't stir, and the light moved on. He jinked from cover to cover along the fence and stood with the sweat drying on him; it was not long to sunrise.

He was acting in support on this one; it was Roberts's show and Christopher merely had to cover the break. He'd clipped the holster-stock on to the Mauser before breaking out of the trees and now he waited, his shadow merging with the telegraph pole, a round ready in the breech. Roberts was late.

The searchlight swept across the pole. It didn't pick him up. This operation was dicey because at first they'd had nearly a week to set it up and they'd gone about it methodically but then suddenly they'd been told to go in. Roberts was inside the camp now but they hadn't been able to lay on the ruse they'd planned (a drug-induced illness inside the camp and Roberts to effect entry as the ambulance driver), and Roberts had simply gone in over the fence with a switched-off torch in one hand and a Walther automatic in the other. He'd been inside nearly an hour now and Christopher was no longer sure that he'd be coming out again.

The searchlight went by again and right behind it Roberts flew against the fence. He had a small figure beside him. Christopher hurled the end of the rope over the top and Roberts threw the girl across his shoulders and went up hand-over-hand. Christopher waited for the shout of discovery from the tower; he had the stock of the Mauser against his shoulder.

They nearly made it clean. The searchlight was three-quarters of the way round its circuit and Roberts was balanced on top of the fence handing the girl down. Christopher slung the Mauser and leapt forward to catch her, then Roberts jumped down and between them they lifted the girl off the ground. They were actually into the get-away run when a German bellowed into the night and the game was on.

He let Roberts run on towards the trees carrying the girl. Christopher wheeled, got down on one knee, aimed the Mauser, and smashed the searchlight before it found him. Then he sprayed the tower left-to-right and heard someone's cry of pain. He ran then, zigzagging, and made it into the trees just behind

Roberts. Then the three of them slammed through the wood, Roberts shaking the torch until its beam strengthened.

It was a half-mile run through the wood to where they'd left the Peugeot parked in the trees near the lane. They heard the rush of German lorries along the main road to the left, coming out of the prison camp gate. The lorries would get there ahead of them but with luck the Germans wouldn't spot the Peugeot because they'd covered it with brush and left it back off the lane. He heard dogs baying – still in the lorries but excited by the anticipation of the hunt.

But when they came in sight of the lane a fifteen-hundred-weight lorry was blocking it. The windscreen was stained with mud thrown up by the wheels and the two soldiers on the open bed were stripping the canvas off its mounted Spandau machine-gun.

Two soldiers, one driver. Roberts pushed the girl down flat between two trees and touched Christopher's arm. 'Three of them. Let's take them out and run for it.'

'No. Give them a minute or two. They'll get restless and move on.'

'Your trouble in life, Peter,' Roberts whispered cheerfully, 'is that you weren't born with an English gentleman's love of slaughter.' Then Roberts lifted his Walther but Christopher closed his hand over it.

'No. The noise. Don't be a bloody fool.'

The lorry began to grind slowly along the lane. When it went out of sight they pushed the girl into the back of the Peugeot and Roberts took the wheel and they ran straight across the lane, driving without lights, smashing through a screen of uprooted shrubbery and bumping down a narrow track. They'd spent three nights clearing saplings to prepare the track through the wood; on the far side it brought them out on to the main Saintes road and two kilometres later they were turning into another back lane, losing themselves amid the dark farms. By dawn they were round the back of the town and the chance of discovery was down to nothing. Roberts turned to glance over the back of his seat: 'How is she?'

'More dead than alive.'

'Well, they wanted to get as much out of her as they could before they executed her. I wonder how much she's told them.'

'Lorraine? She won't have given them a thing.'

Roberts said, 'But we've got to know, haven't we? I mean that was the whole purpose of this job. We've got to keep her alive. If she's exposed the circuit we've all got to go to ground.'

'We'll patch her up and bring her round and she'll tell us she didn't tell them a thing.' You had to go through the motions but there hadn't been any new faces and the circuit had kept security very tight. They kept it tight by keeping a distance between each member and all the others. No two of them communicated with one another directly; most of them didn't even know one another's identities. All communications came through Rollo and nobody had approached him. If anyone did, the network would go to ground within an hour. It was a sensible arrangement, achieved by experience; discipline of a high order was maintained and finding out whether the girl had talked or not was merely an excuse for getting her out. The real reason was humanitarian: they'd saved her life and that was what made Christopher enjoy these jobs.

He supposed it was a good thing he'd been put under Roberts, however. Roberts had a far more brutal outlook – he'd changed dramatically since Christopher had first met him at the training centre. Roberts had started out as a diffident youth, unsure of himself and anxious to please; but cameraderie and self-confident leadership had fallen comfortably round his shoulders like a well-tailored cloak and he enjoyed most of all the sabotage and assassination jobs. He had discovered a savage appetite for blowing things up. Christopher wondered what would become of him if he survived the war; either he would turn to crime or he'd have to go into some line of work where he could go on playing with detonators and incendiaries.

The safe-house was a farm on the Loire. They relinquished Lorraine to the doctor and retired into the kitchen for breakfast. Rollo turned to Christopher: 'We've had a signal. You're to return to London – they're recalling you.'

'What for?'

'I've no idea, *mon ami*.'

'It's not disciplinary,' Owl told him. 'You've done nothing wrong. In fact you've been commended by the Resistance.'

'Then why was I recalled?'

'I want you on hand,' Owl said. 'You're wasted over there – anybody in the SOE can do the job you've been doing. We sent you out there for an apprenticeship. You've got the experience now; you're a blooded veteran, you've earned a bit of leave. There's still enjoyment to be had in London even if it's behind blackout curtains.'

Christopher grinned then. 'I shan't complain. When shall I report in?'

'Just keep us appraised of your whereabouts. We'll be in touch when we want you.'

'What's my cover?'

'None. You're Christopher Creighton. You've been away at school for the past year. If anyone asks, tell them you've been at school in Australia or whatever you like. You know how to fend off questions.'

He rang Patricia straight away but got no reply at her flat and when he rang Bletchley on the Northways scrambler line, using his priority identification, a woman with starch in her voice informed him that Wren third officer Falkiner had been appointed temporarily to Bermuda signals station and would not be back in England before mid-December. Would the gentleman care to leave a message?

He left the Sub-Section MO/D office in Dorset Square – the old offices of Bertram Mills Circus and now the headquarters of the Section – and walked a good part of the afternoon, taking special enjoyment from the opportunity to stroll through a friendly city without having to keep an eye open for the Gestapo and SS thugs.

On impulse he bought a bottle of whisky and carried it with him to Harley Street. The Lister was still in residence and informed him Anne would be returning within the hour; he was welcomed by the girls with some restraint, for they seemed a bit alarmed by how much of a man he'd become.

'Would you prefer me to find digs somewhere else, then?'

'Don't be silly,' the Lister said. 'This is still your home.'

Reassured, he collected his luggage. He was unpacking and tossing things into drawers in his room when Anne entered.

'My goodness. You've grown so tall!'

'School cooking,' he explained.

'Some school. How scrummy!' Her tongue spoke one language, her eyes another; she appraised him coolly, admiring what she saw. 'How old are you now?'

'Seventeen this past birthday.'

She was pert; her saucy little breasts stirred the fabric of her shirt; her eyes had the same wide shining innocence but she'd done her own growing up; this was evident in the languor with which she crossed the room, hips swaying just enough to communicate invitation.

'Well then,' he murmured, 'how about a kiss now?'

This time she made no pretence of reluctance. 'You shut the door,' she whispered, 'and I'll turn down the bed.'

He enjoyed it with her as he'd enjoyed it with the girls in France but when she crept out of the room after dark he made a half-hearted attempt not to feel relief and then gave in to it. She'd been exciting in bed but she talked incessantly and afterwards she'd frowned at him and slipped the insult in as smoothly as a thermometer: 'I wonder how different you'd be if you didn't have any money. I mean you're the sort who always takes it for granted. That whisky was lovely, mind you, but you've an obscene over-confidence for a seventeen-year-old.'

He felt disloyal in a strange fashion. He'd never made love to Patricia but she was the girl in his mind, all the while in France and now here with Anne: Patricia would probably laugh at him but he didn't feel promiscuity was his style; and now it wasn't so much that he felt any betrayal of Patricia as it was that he felt disloyal to Anne. He'd known her longer than any of the others, and while she probably didn't think of him more than once in six months there was, nevertheless, a way in which he felt Anne had been his first girlfriend.

But then, he thought, by now Patricia may have someone else, and may have forgotten me altogether. It is a feature of war that opportunities for starting relationships are abundant, but for establishing them rare.

It was three o'clock in the morning – Thursday, 4 December – the trivial fact ran obstinately through his mind as the staff car whipped him through the deserted streets of London. It delivered him to the St James's Park entrance to the Annexe. He produced his special pass and waited while it was checked against records by the Royal Marine corporal. He had the freedom of the place now — a red card. He went downstairs into the Hole in the Ground and glanced into the officers' wardroom, with its bar behind the tatty green curtain; seeing no-one there he went on to the duty officer's desk. 'Peter Hamilton. I've had a message to meet someone here.'

The duty officer shuffled his calendars. 'Sorry. Nothing here.'

Fuming, Christopher went back to the communications room. He got the use of a green phone and rang the SOE office, Room 60 upstairs in the Annexe.

'Christopher Robin. I'd a message to meet Owl but he's not here.'

'Sorry old boy, I don't know anything about that. You might try him at home.'

He dialled the Chelsea number and it was picked up on the first ring. Owl barked at him: 'Where the devil are you?'

'In the Hole. Where your driver brought me.'

'Christ. The bloody fool must have been asleep. I told him to bring you here straight away.' Owl swore a barrack-room oath. Christopher grinned, realizing that there'd be no telephone operator's ears to be blistered by that one; on the green phone all conversations were automatically fed through the scrambler.

'Listen to me,' Owl barked. 'Go back to the car. Tell the bloody fool to run you out to Paddington. I'll meet you there — there's no time to be lost. I've still got to finish setting things up but I should be there shortly behind you.'

'What's on?'

'Just pull your finger out and get there.'

He landed with a weary confused memory of having eaten several breakfasts at five-hour intervals, but there was still a great distance to go. He stretched his legs on the snow-crusted tarmac; the frozen surface crackled under his feet like eggshells. The Canadian forest came right down to the verges of the runway and the trees were coated with a delicate layer of ice. They looked as if they were made of glass, quite beautiful glittering in the sun.

The van was being unloaded by two men in Canadian parkas

and Wellington boots. Christopher didn't go near them; he didn't want a close look at their holdall – not yet.

They were on the ground less than twenty minutes and then Mallory was waving at him and shouting something – in the din of revving engines he couldn't hear Mallory at all but he understood the summons. His tunic whipped against him and ballooned when he walked into the propwash and climbed into the plane.

He pulled the hatch up after him and secured it and made his way up to what would normally have been the bomb aimer's seat. In the cockpit Mallory glanced back and Christopher gave him a nod and then Mallory was reaching up over his head to turn switches and inspect gauges and the fuel lorry was pulling away following the van. A man on the wing secured the fuel-tank cap and jumped down. Christopher climbed back into his electrically heated flying suit, plugged it in and hung the oxygen mask round his neck, ready to cup it over his face when they reached ten thousand feet.

He was used to the drill by now; it was their third landing since they'd taken off from a bomber station in Cornwall where he'd watched them wheel the plane out of a Mitchet hangar and been astonished by its great size – all that to carry one seventeen-year-old passenger? *It's the only craft we possess that has the range and speed for the job,* Owl had told him.

On the first long over-water leg Mallory had uncapped the coffee bottle and sat with him chatting about the plane, of which Mallory was very proud. It was one of the first six production Liberators to have come off the Consolidated assembly line; Mallory had been flying it since March – Prestwick to Newfoundland to Montreal. Two of the six had crashed in August and killed forty-four men. 'But we've got the bugs out now and these loves will outlast the war, I promise you. This ship and I plan to end up flying passengers together for a commercial airline.'

Mallory was a fund of technical information; the four-engine plane had been designed as a bomber but converted to an unarmed transport by riveting the bomb bays shut and plating over the gun turrets; the bomb bays were used for cargo and extra fuel while benches had been bolted in along the sides for passengers on the transatlantic ferry service; the transatlantic crossing took about nine hours and it was a great improvement over all predecessors.

They were skirting storms over the Atlantic then and Mallory had remarked that in this sort of weather they navigated by dead reckoning. The co-pilot had said drily, 'Why couldn't they have thought up a more cheerful name for it?' But they'd made landfall over Newfoundland within four miles of their charted anticipation and Mallory had said, 'You disappoint me, lad – four miles error, suppose we had a target to bomb?'

'Four miles out after two thousand odd, I'll not complain of that,' the co-pilot said complacently in his mild Scots burr.

There were moments with Owl when the abyss seemed to open. Christopher had trusted the men who'd trained him but now Owl had given him an order he couldn't understand and it was up to him to decide whether to obey it or not. He didn't like the responsibility. He had thought them incapable of serious error but now he suspected Owl had made a mistake and he felt betrayed.

Owl had got on the train with him and briefed him in the compartment with the door locked against chance intruders. When Christopher objected to the job Owl had replied, 'One has one's orders,' and Christopher had said that wasn't good enough. 'Look, this can't be right.'

'I know, Christopher. When you're seventeen there's no justice.' Owl's sarcasms infuriated him. 'Listen to me now – the priority is absolute. Do you understand me?'

A storm had met them in Cornwall. Christopher hoped they'd have to scrub the mission but it had passed and Owl had pushed him into the Liberator with a parting word: 'Christopher, listen to me now. Your successful execution of this job is more important than you can imagine.'

He tried to sleep and managed to doze fitfully; the monotonous drone of the engines broke time into fragments so that he lost his sense of its passage and became confused. They flew south and west until he was able to disconnect the electric suit. They landed in California, at San Diego; the job might have been hastily laid on but Owl's efficiency was impeccable when it came to paving the way for refuellings and inspections. Christopher recalled his bleak conversation in the train with Owl: 'Do you *always* win?'

'I always try to,' Owl had replied.

Sod Owl. At the aerodrome Christopher had asked for a telephone but Owl had vetoed it. 'There's no scrambler here.'

'I want to know that Tigger has reconfirmed these orders.'

'Do you think I'm lying to you?'

'I want your word on it, then.'

'You have it,' Owl had snapped.

Until he'd reached Canada he hadn't been sure what method they'd decided on. Owl had talked of the possibility of cyanide gas, easy to disperse through the ventilation system, but evidently he'd changed his mind about that – perhaps the risk of discovery of the cause of death afterwards was too great; in any case the bags did not contain gas cylinders.

Mallory shook him awake. 'Half an hour, old chap.'

'Right. Thanks.' He made his way to the toilet, cleaned himself up. He was now Peter Hamilton, Lieutenant RN, on special orders from Admiral Submarines. He undressed and fitted himself into the Sibi Gorman diving suit and clipped on the parachute and harness over that, plus an uninflated life-belt. And finally he strapped to his left thigh, almost like a Knight of the Garter, a band of shark repellant copper acetate. He attached the cargo parachute to the gear they'd picked up in Canada – it all fitted into one heavy watertight canister into which he had put one item from London – the uniform of a lieutenant RN and of course his personal gear and anything else he wanted to keep dry. Then he devoted his attention to checking every strap and buckle; Herndon and the chaps at the parachute school had impressed it indelibly on his mind that it only took one loose fitting to kill you when you were jumping from 3,000 feet.

It was barely dawn when he struggled to get the jump-door open. Wind rushed through the fuselage and made his eyes stream. It was 0540 hours, Sunday, 7 December, and Mallory circled the drop-zone until a white phosphorus flare came up from the dark surface below. Christopher didn't have time to search the sea for the source of the flare; Mallory shouted at him and he kicked the cargo chute out and followed close after it, pitching out of the doorway and hunching himself to roll away to avoid the aircraft's tailplanes.

He was out and free. The plane was moving fast away from

him. He floated spinning; he spread his arms and legs to get some control over the tumbling attitude of his body, catching the wind on the flats of his palms and using them for rudders to stabilize his fall. Wind rushed against his ears and he had a confused glimpse of the cargo canister's drogue chute popping open beneath him.

There wasn't much time; three thousand feet was a fast fall. He found the ring of the ripcord, gave it a yank and waited, counting seconds; ready to pull the emergency back-up cord but he didn't need it: the chute popped open and he ignored the vertigo and braced his muscles against the sudden wrenching tug. He felt bruised and crushed breathless when the harness brought him up short, squeezing his ribcage and tugging under his arms. Then he was swaying slightly, suspended under the life-supporting canopy of silk with that brief euphoric sense of spacelessness and motionlessness.

He saw the cargo canister splash down and he made blades of his feet, pressing his ankles together and aiming himself at the water like a lance. If you went in at the wrong angle you could break half the bones in your body; a water drop was always tricky because of the random surface-angles of the waves and the sea could be as hard as a rock.

He felt it whack against the toes of his rubber suit and then he was crashing through the surface, water up his nostrils, the harness grabbing him and not letting him plunge as deep as gravity demanded. He had to fight down the impulse to cough. Think fast and clearly now. The water was amazingly warm. His fingers groped for the quick-release clasp. His accoutrements weighed him down. Must get out of the harness fast because you could strangle on the shroud lines with the surface currents whipping the chute around. All it needed was a gust of wind to pick up the silk canopy. . .

His eyes were open underwater but there wasn't much to see except the tangle of straps and lines all about him like seaweed. Finally he was free of the harness and he let himself drop a few feet while the air went sour in his chest. Ignore that. Concentrate. He propelled himself away from the spaghetti, four or five powerful breast-strokes, then turned the vent knob of the compressed-air bottle. He heard the hiss and felt the lifebelt swell up round him. Then it was lifting him to the surface.

When his head broke surface he expelled the carbon dioxide from his lungs and gulped a great lungful of humid warm air. He drew it in as far as he could, held it a few seconds, expelled it and sucked again. The exercise cleared his lungs and his head stopped swimming. Then he turned a slow circle in the water to get his bearings. The wind was blowing his abandoned parachute slowly across the water. There wasn't much of a sea. Half the horizon was alight with graduated pastel shades of dawn and against that lovely horizon he saw the dark sinister outline of the submarine's conning tower: it was trimmed down, decks awash, to present a low silhouette and minimize discovery. Now he saw something else superimposed on the submarine — a smaller object bobbing on the waves, coming towards him. It was a rubber dinghy with two men rowing it. Once he caught the outlines of their heads against the dawn sky.

They knew where he was; he ignored them for a bit and continued his circle until he spotted the other chute. Then he kicked towards it, letting the life-belt support him, swimming with strong thrusts of arms and legs.

The wind was trying to inflate the collapsed chute but the canister was bobbing buoyantly. He got one hand on its shroud lines and rested there, floating in the life-belt, and waited for the dinghy to come and pick him up.

The log entry was written in Dutch and he asked the third officer to write out a translation for him in English.

SIGHTED FLEET 0535 DEC 2. . . . INTERMITTENT SIGHTINGS UNTIL 0750 FLEET ZIGZAGGING. MEAN COURSE 135°(T) SPEED APPROX 16 KNOTS. SIGHTED 6 AIRCRAFT CARRIERS 2 BATTLESHIPS 3 CRUISERS 6 DESTROYERS. IF PRESENT SPEED AND COURSE MAINTAINED DESTINATION OAHU ETA 0600 DEC 7. 0800 SURFACED TO RECHARGE BATTERIES. SENT SIGNAL CLASS 1 CIPHER TOP SECRET IMMEDIATE C-IN-C EASTERN FLEET REPEATED ADMIRALTY EYES COMMANDER IN CHIEF & FIRST SEA LORD ONLY. 1100 RECEIVED SIGNAL FROM C-IN-C EASTERN FLEET ORDERING ME TO KEEP RADIO SILENCE AND AWAIT

FURTHER SIGNAL WITH ORDERS FOR POSITION
TO PICK UP OFFICER WITH SEALED ORDERS. NO
CONTACT TO BE MADE WITH ANY SHIP OR PORT.
TOTAL SECURITY TO BE MAINTAINED.

Christopher said, 'All right. Thank you. I've got orders to
remove that page from the log.'

The Dutch captain – a lieutenant commander – and the first
lieutenant looked worried. The three of them were crowded
into the captain's small cabin. Christopher tore the page out of
the log book and folded it into the sheet on which the first
lieutenant had pencilled the English translation. Then he said,
'I'll want the copy of the signal forms – the signal to C-in-C
Eastern Fleet and his reply.'

'Get them, please.' The captain watched the first lieutenant
leave the cabin. He pulled the curtain shut and said, 'Is this
necessary?'

'They're my orders, Captain.'

'Bloody cloak-and-dagger.' The captain's English was col-
loquial.

The S-K submarine was running on the surface, diesels
thrumming. A sea breeze ruffled through the boat below decks,
coming down the open hatches, but it didn't dispel the stench.
The boat seemed clean and efficient; Christopher supposed all
submarines probably smelt like this.

Since the fall of the Low Countries their exiled navies had
served the Allies under British Admiralty operational control.
In the Western Pacific the only sizeable fleet of Allied submarines was the fifteen K and O boats of the Royal Netherlands
Navy with their headquarters in the Dutch East Indies; since
the summer of 1940 they had been keeping an eye on the
Japanese. Most of them were concentrated round the Dutch
areas of Java and Borneo but with increasing signs of Japanese
restlessness the Admiralty had scattered a dozen of them along
a thin watchful picket-line that stretched from New Zealand
north to the western Aleutians in the Bering Sea.

The first lieutenant brought the signals into the cabin and
Christopher shredded the papers into the captain's head.

There was a packet of small envelopes in Christopher's tunic
pocket. He handed one to the captain and watched him break

141

the seal. 'I'm expecting a signal from the Admiralty. When we've cleared the reefs we're to trim down with the aerials above water and Q tank flooded.'

The captain read the orders again and pressed his lips together and Christopher was enough of a sailor to understand his disquiet. The swell was now running to seven or eight feet on the surface and it was pointless in such seas to discharge the batteries for hours on end so close to the surface. A ten-foot trough might conceal, say, the hull of a wreck with a keel heavy enough to do a great deal of damage even to the armoured prow of the S-boat.

But it couldn't be helped because there was a chance the orders might be cancelled – the real orders, the ones that had never been committed to paper; they existed only in Christopher's memory of the icy ring of Owl's voice on the train. And if the signal to cancel was transmitted along the chain of cipher offices from Gibraltar to Cairo to Aden to Ceylon to Brisbane to Auckland, Christopher didn't want there to be any chance of missing it; a great many lives would depend on it.

The captain thrust the document into the first lieutenant's hand. The captain had a sandy spade beard and the pale unhealthy skin of a submariner. He was a bit older than most and perhaps he had his eye on a bigger ship; certainly he wasn't accustomed to taking unwelcome orders from junior officers aboard his boat – particularly foreign strangers.

Christopher had some trouble meeting his gaze. It was hard enough being in the same boat with the man, let alone the same small cabin. He didn't want any personal contact; he didn't want to know anything about him.

He said, 'If any signal comes through on that frequency please notify me immediately. That's vital – there may be a change in orders.'

'Yes, naturally.' The captain's impatience was transparent.

'These' – Christopher opened another envelope – 'are the orders for course and speed, to bring us to a prearranged position at dawn tomorrow.'

The captain took it and glanced down. 'The Fijis.'

'Yes. I'm to be put ashore on Viti Levu just along the coast from Suva.'

The captain wasn't ready to buy it right off the peg. 'There's an airfield at Suva – they could have flown you there.'

'I've a job to do here first, sir, and my arrival in the Fijis is not to be noticed.' Christopher kept his eyes fixed on the envelopes. 'Now I'll need access to the torpedoes and torpedo tubes for this alteration job and that will keep me out of your hair for a while. None of this was my idea, sir. You'll be rid of me by noon tomorrow.'

It was part of his cover as Lieutenant Peter Hamilton that he was an expert in warheads and explosives – a junior boffin of sorts.

Considering the haste with which the scheme had been laid on it was astonishingly ingenious – if it worked. The captain had been given to understand that Lieutenant Hamilton was on board to make alterations to his boat's torpedoes in an experiment that might safeguard the submarine during torpedo attacks.

'It's a magnetic fixation device,' he'd explained to the captain, 'coupled with a timing device that delays detonation for up to an hour.'

To Christopher it had seemed transparently implausible when they'd first explained the scheme to him and he wondered that the captain didn't refuse to cooperate; the captain must be wondering whether the Admiralty had taken leave of its senses – some fool of an engineer having a silly game and unaware of the difficulties it all made for the good Dutch boat and its crew. But the captain was a loyal officer and did not seem disinclined to obey the orders; he only asked the sort of question one might expect: 'How does it work?'

And Christopher explained it as he'd been told. 'The torpedoes are to be set to shallow depth and slow speed. When they're fired, the magnetic field is activated after the torpedo has travelled five hundred yards. The field is generated by batteries. We've adapted the magnets from shipyard loading equipment. When the torpedo strikes an enemy hull, it adheres to the hull by magnetic force. It clings to the ship until the delayed timing device detonates the warhead. By that time you can be well away, and safe from depth-charge attack. You'll still know when the torpedo explodes, of course – the new Asdic gear should pick it up even at considerable range.'

The first lieutenant had spoken drily in Dutch and the captain had grimaced; he'd said to Christopher, 'If we're that far away we'll have no way to confirm the damage.'

Christopher had no answer to that one. He fell back on an apologetic I've-got-my-orders-sir and made his way out of the captain's quarters.

Of course the gunnery officer and some of the ratings had to know what was being done to their torpedoes and there was no way to work on the fish without being observed; quarters were too cramped and in any case he couldn't very well order them out of their own duty stations. The job had to be done openly, right under their noses, and he wasn't at all sure he could bring it off without someone discovering what he was up to. Indeed, two of the officers had engineering degrees – not un-common in the submarine service – and he didn't see how it was possible to fool them at all; but he went to work, follow-ing the coded instructions in his envelopes and the torpedo design plans he'd collected in Canada.

The whole story about magnetic fields and delayed detonation was a monstrous lie, of course, but he had to insert the flat batteries and wires and metal plates in such a way as to make it look convincing to the officers and ratings – a neat trick, he thought wryly, if one could bring it off; these Dutchmen were no fools.

It was to his advantage that most of them spoke no English and those who did had a limited command of the language; the captain's English was good enough of course but he was not present, and the first officer's English was halting at best; the chief engineer and the torpedo officer had minimal English. Christopher explained his actions in rapid clipped speech, try-ing to sound like an efficient Royal Navy officer who was im-patient and somewhat bored with their questions; in that manner he managed to fudge his explanations and at the same time appear as if he knew what he was doing and had vast experience with torpedoes. Of course they had to believe they understood the installations – in case anything went wrong.

In actuality he was frightened half to death. His course in demolition in the Fens had hardly prepared him for this, and the instructions he carried were barely adequate to guide him through the tight-packed maze of mechanical and electrical devices under the smooth polished skins of the torpedoes.

He'd put it angrily to Owl: *For God's sake, I don't know the first thing about bloody torpedoes. Why me?*

Because we need someone who knows how to work completely alone, without support or organization or team members. And because you have an aptitude for mechanical things – you were born, seemingly, with an innate understanding of the way things work. And because you've demonstrated that you can be relied upon to carry out orders and keep your mouth shut. Good Heavens, man, I should think you'd be flattered to be so trusted!

Flattered! Bloody hell.

He worked slowly on the evil instruments, cautiously turning screws and lifting off plates, exposing the dread innards of the torpedoes. With time on their hands some of the crew volunteered to help him by opening up the other fish and he didn't think he could stand that – if only they knew what they were helping him do! – but it would have made them suspicious if he'd denied them so he left them to it.

The devices were as simple as they were dreadful to contemplate and the only way he got through it was to concentrate all his attentions upon the physical details of the job in hand. He had time, however, to wonder where Owl had found this answer during the twelve hours he'd spent in the Liberator on the hop between Prestwick and Ontario; somewhere Owl had found a specialist who'd laid the whole thing out in time for Owl to get specific coded instructions off to Canada for delivery to Christopher's plane. Then it had taken Christopher hours to translate the signals into plain English because Owl had sent them in the Milne code to insure against leakage; the code was unbreakable unless the interceptor knew which editions of which books were being used. In his holdall Christopher had carried a cheap edition of *The House at Pooh Corner* and the code referred – by page, line and character number – to letters of the alphabet in that book.

He had the real plans in his pocket and he consulted them as he needed; he left what appeared to be duplicate copies of them lying about so that the Dutchmen could glance at them – those were fakes, describing non-existent magnetic fields and the like. The fact was that no torpedo battery could pack enough electric power to create a magnetic field strong enough to make a heavy torpedo cling to the hull of a ship moving at speed through the water. But he'd been instructed to explain that one away by claiming that the scientists in England had developed a new alloy that provided unprecedented conduction and magnetic force. This 'new alloy' was the stuff of which the thin metal straps were made, the straps that came out of his holdall to be uncoiled and slipped into the topedoes across their detonators and under their metal skins. 'The whole torpedo becomes a single giant magnet,' he explained – only barely managing to get the lie out through his teeth.

In fact the 'new alloy' was ordinary steel-copper bonded straps and its real purpose was simply to carry a small electrical current from the timing device to the warhead detonator.

What he was doing, in actuality, was to turn each torpedo aboard the submarine into a time-bomb.

He was doing it right under their noses – at times they were actually huddled over him, their breath warm on his neck, watching his hands at work inside the torpedo mechanisms; and he kept waiting for the outcry of discovery.

It's no good trying to be stealthy, Owl had adjured. *If you look the least bit furtive they'll suspect you at once. Keep it friendly. Explain everything you do. Let them participate.*

Yes, he thought bitterly – but how do I look them in the eye?

The sweat ran down his face and there was another risk too, because the boat was running trimmed down almost on the surface and she rolled uncomfortably through the water and he had to be careful because if she lurched the wrong way he could strike a spark that would disintegrate himself and half the boat.

And he kept listening with one ear for the voice that would draw him away to the wireless – waiting for the order to cancel the job. It had to be cancelled. It *must* be cancelled. Because if it weren't he didn't think he could go through with it.

Attaching the timing devices and setting them was the most dicey part of all because that was when he was actually arming the devices and he had to do it in full view without letting any of the Dutchmen see what he was up to. The timers were soundless clocks without faces; once they were wired into the circuit it only took the turn of a key to set them running, but if anyone had asked him why he turned the key he wouldn't have had an answer that any of them would have believed. He went from torpedo to torpedo, fitting the deadly clocks in place, turning the keys and backing away, and nodding briskly to the ratings who happily took his place and screwed the nacelle plates back into position. Each time he felt relief when the plates took their places, concealing his evil handiwork inside; each time he turned away and breathed deeply and then bent to the next torpedo and felt the dread return.

When it was done the first lieutenant clapped him on the arm. 'Well I do not believe this thing will work at all, you know, but we'll be good sports, yes? And try it out for the Admiralty.'

Feeling weak and sick he only nodded and attempted a feeble smile; he didn't trust himself to speak. He hid in the head by the officers' wardroom – pressed his eyes shut and tightened his muscles against the spasms of nausea. Finally he washed, tried a meal in the the wardroom, couldn't eat, and accepted the captain's offer to rest in the first lieutenant's bunk while the first lieutenant was on watch.

Below decks the heat was like a fluid and the deck scorched his bare feet; he could not rest. Heaves of vomit kept filling his throat and nostrils; he clawed his way into the head barely in time. In the end he returned to the first lieutenant's cabin and pulled on his boots and went forward; he had difficulty finding his way in the dim glow of the red night-vision lights. He waited while a rating ran lightly up the conning tower ladder and then he followed, nearly tripping on the rungs. On the bridge the officer of the watch looked at him peevishly; his presence aboard, his occupation of space, made their lives even more uncomfortable than usual and he was a stranger whose presence disturbed the pattern of settled routine.

She was running on the surface now, charging batteries. A gust of wind came down the open hatch like a breath from an oven. It was high summer here below the Southern Cross. The air from outside didn't disguise the sickly sweet stench of oil and sea and sweat and steam and the lithium hydroxide that was used to purify and recirculate the oxygen throughout the ventilators.

By the ship's chronometer it was just past midnight; here on this side of the International Date Line it was Monday 8 December 1941. He felt as if he'd been aboard the boat for weeks; actually it was only eighteen hours.

He had no sleep at all. By 0330 he was prowling the boat again, unable to keep still. There had been no cancellation signal yet. *Wait – wait for it.* It wasn't yet dawn when the captain spoke – in Dutch so Christopher didn't get a word of it, but there was urgency in the captain's voice and then the wireless operator turned up his loudspeaker – an incoming broadcast and it was in plain English. A high-pitched voice with flat American inflections and a fevered pitch near panic: 'The *Arizona*'s on fire and I think they're beating up Hickham Field. . .'

He stood rooted, the deck lurching under his feet as the S-boat slammed through the waves, and listened to the surging and fading voice crying through the static, somehow conveying with terrible immediate reality the scale of the appalling destruction the Japanese surprise attack was inflicting on the United States Army and Navy bases at Pearl Harbor.

Listening to it he knew there would be no recall now, no countermand. The Japanese attack had taken place as Owl had said it would. It meant Christopher had to carry out his orders.

Sickened again, he went to leave the wireless table. The officers glanced at him in the weird red glow. The captain thrust his face close to Christopher's – a belligerent tense whisper: '*Why weren't the Americans warned?*'

Christopher only shook his head. Then he managed to speak: 'Please make my dinghy ready.'

'Not just yet,' the captain breathed. He was in a rage. He began to turn away. 'We'll have new orders now. We'll soon be at war with Japan. . .'

'Your orders stand,' Christopher said. His voice sounded dead in his own throat. 'They come from the very top and they take priority over everything else.'

'We'll soon check that.' The captain was swinging towards the wireless signals table again and Christopher moved quickly to interpose himself.

The captain's jaw worked and Christopher realized it must be going through his mind that Christopher was a junior officer in a foreign navy. The detonator timers were running and he knew if he didn't re-establish his authority *now* there was a risk that the captain would break radio silence. Christopher said in a falsely calm voice, 'Captain, I represent the Admiralty here. The boat is subject to Admiralty orders in the name of Queen Wilhelmina of the Netherlands. . .' He drew breath and tried to put everything else out of his head: 'The Admiralty knew this was coming, didn't they. They'd had your sighting report. And they laid on this operation *after* they'd had your report. Don't you see these orders were meant to be carried out only if the Japanese actually struck Pearl Harbor? There's no possibility of any change in the orders. But I can tell you this,' he lied. 'When you open that final sealed envelope you'll find your targets are Japanese.'

The captain's face changed, sagging in the eerie light. Christopher said, 'I'm sorry, sir.' *Dear God, Captain, accept my sorrow if you can.*

The first lieutenant spoke mildly in Dutch; he was pointing to the chronometer and the captain's eyes pulled away from Christopher. 'Very well,' the captain said. 'You may go ashore now, Mr Hamilton.'

In a turmoil of rage and blinding grief he pulled bitterly at the oars. The rubber dinghy plunged wildly through the surf. He had a wild impulse to broach it deliberately and let the currents suck him under but his arms kept pulling the oars and his Sea Scout training kept him stern-on to the surf. The dinghy had only a few inches of water in it when he crashed up on to the coral beach. He dragged it up above the waterline and looked out from the top of a low hill across the emerald waves. Sea glare hammered his eyes. He couldn't see the submarine but she'd be submerged by now, running at periscope depth again and heading out into the open sea. There, obeying his orders, the captain would stand her four miles offshore awaiting the signal he expected Christopher to flash at him from the mirrored lens of his miniature heliograph. This would tell him that he was to open the sealed orders giving him a new course.

Christopher checked his time. He had another twenty minutes and he did not think he could wait it out. A bird flew overhead and settled in the tall palms that ran along the coral coast; seagulls drifted on the air currents but nothing else in sight stirred except the waves. The air was sticky with humid tropical heat and he wasn't accustomed to it. It only reinforced his terrible depression and he was hardly able to drag his feet as far as the coast road a little way up the hill. It was a rough graded track paved with crushed seashells and there was no traffic on it. He examined the slopes above and the horizon to either side. Nothing stirring. To keep himself busy he returned to the rubber dinghy, selected the few things he'd need to keep, tossed everything else back into the boat, jabbed a few punctures into it and pushed it out into the surf. Then he shouldered his remaining bag and climbed back up to the road.

There was no way he could possibly see anything so small as the head of the periscope four miles away but he knew its approximate bearing and he only had to shift his eyes a few degrees when he saw the start of the eruption. From this distance it was nothing more than a small upheaval – a waterspout that geysered and died away; then another, and then still more.

The detonator clocks were exploding at intervals rather than all at once and it took time – perhaps a minute and a half – before the last of them blew up. By that time sea would have invaded the ship's batteries and filled the hull with chlorine gas where it wasn't already filled with water through the ruptures that the torpedoes had made through its riveted hull plates. Death, he thought, would have been virtually instantaneous for the fifty-six officers and men aboard.

The sounds of the explosion reached him very faintly: dull thumps. Blank-eyed, moving like a mechanism, he turned his footsteps eastwards along the coast road and began to walk towards Suva where Mallory was waiting for him with the Liberator.

Chapter Eight

They topped up the tanks at Perth and laid over at Mombasa. Then they were held up in Cairo because someone on Auchinleck's staff commandeered the Liberator to ferry drugs and medicos to, and wounded from, the 30th Corps which was fighting the Afrika Korps beyond Tobruk. None of it mattered very much; Christopher went round in a daze, and when new orders for Peter Hamilton came from London on 12 December he obediently climbed on board a Berwick flying boat at Alexandria. If he had been asked to describe Mombasa or Cairo he'd have been at a loss.

The Berwick set him down in the roads at Southampton and he was lightered ashore along with a boatload of walking wounded Anzacs whose limited vocabularies consisted mainly of 'mugs' and 'shits'. It was Pooh who collected him at the dock and Christopher managed to give him some sort of smile but it was not very convincing because Pooh gave him an odd look in return and hurried him along to the waiting staff car. 'Terribly sorry about the delay in Cairo. None of our doing, of course. We didn't even know about it until yesterday. Why didn't you signal us?'

'It didn't seem that important. They needed the plane.'

Something in the dull dead tone of his voice drew Pooh's face round. Christopher watched the back of the driver's neck. 'I've got one request if you don't mind.'

'Of course.'

'I should like to see Tigger straight away.'

'Well I'm sorry, old lad, but that won't be possible.'

Christopher breathed through his teeth, *'Make* it possible.'

'Not likely. He's left the country, you see. Yesterday, aboard *Duke of York.* He'll be in Washington next week.'

Christopher slumped in the seat. He closed his eyes. 'When he comes back then. First thing when he gets back.'

'I'm sure he'll be happy to see you. In the meantime Owl will want to debrief you.'

'How much do you know about this job?'

'Nothing at all, dear boy. I know you've been in the Far East, nothing more. It must have been rather exciting for you. You'd never been out to that part of the world before, had you?'

It was dark by the time they reached London. There'd been a raid and a block of flats was burning hot and bright along one of the main roads. They had to make a detour and crawled behind a convoy of lorries, everything murky in the blackout, reflections of firelight flickering red on the higher walls.

They drove up to Swiss Cottage and Pooh bundled him into Northways through the garage entrance. Owl had a two-room suite of offices there in the unmarked naval intelligence section behind Admiral Submarines; at one time Christopher had tried to count up the number of different offices Owl had in London. In a sense Owl ran a department that didn't exist; therefore he did not spend much time in any one place and there were no doors with his name on them.

Owl was there, alone, waiting for him; he rose to his feet eagerly and Christopher attempted to wither him with his hardest glance. 'When Roosevelt called it a day of infamy,' he said, 'he didn't know the half of it.'

'All right,' Owl replied, unflappable. 'Thank you, Colonel,' and Pooh withdrew after patting Christopher avuncularly on the arm. Owl pushed Christopher back into the private office and closed the door with a soft click. 'Restrain your outbursts if you don't mind. We've trained you better than that.'

There wasn't much in the room. A steel cabinet; a desk with three telephones, one of them green. Large maps on three easels – western Europe and the British Isles; North Africa; the Pacific. There was one spare chair but it was piled with books and documents. The wastepaper bin was one of those heavy metal ones with a wire basket inside it; you pushed it over near the window to set fire to its contents.

Christopher stared at Owl and said, 'I've just killed fifty-six Dutchmen and been responsible, one way or another, for the deaths of two thousand Americans at Pearl Harbor and God knows how many others on Guam and that other lot. I haven't killed a single German or Japanese on this job. Now perhaps you'd like to tell me just whose side I'm fighting on?'

Owl pulled out the chair behind the desk and pointed an imperious finger down towards its seat. 'Sit down and listen until I give you permission to speak.'

'Stuff it. I've finished taking orders from you. I've had time to think this out and I. . .'

'*Sit down.*'

'. . . and I don't. . .'

'Christopher, damn it all, will you sit down? I owe you an explanation and I'm going to give it to you if you'll shut your mouth long enough to listen to it. It won't take long and you're free to let off steam when I've finished. Fair enough?'

But he wasn't giving in that easily. 'You may think you have the right to order someone to die – you may actually have that right – but you don't. . .'

'I have the right. There is no limit to what you can be ordered to do. Our whole civilization is at stake.'

'You don't,' Christopher resumed stubbornly; and then the meaning of Owl's words struck him. He laughed cruelly. 'Don't talk to me about civilization,' he said.

Owl studied him coldly. Not a hair was out of place, Christopher noted. Owl might have just groomed himself for a magazine photographer. 'We are a small island,' Owl said, 'with limited resources and we are the last bastion of, yes, Christian civilization in the European hemisphere, discounting a handful of spineless neutrals. We're all that stands between Adolf Hitler and his thousand-year Reich. We hadn't got the forces or the equipment to go it alone, Christopher. Another six months, perhaps another year, and we'd have been finished. The only hope we had was to bring the United States into the war. With their industrial capacity and the size of their population we can win the war. Without it we'd lose; it's as simple as that.'

'I don't want to argue politics with you. Look – have you counted the number of loyal Dutchmen I murdered out there? They were our *friends*!'

'Casualties of war,' Owl said in his flat cool voice. 'They couldn't be depended upon to keep silent. All it needed was one man from the crew of that submarine, perhaps having a drink too many in a pub somewhere – allegations leading to inquiries leading to God knows what. A withdrawal of American support from the European theatre? We didn't *know*; we couldn't risk it.'

'But it's done now! They didn't have to die. All you had to do was keep them out at sea on wireless silence until after the Japanese attacked Pearl Harbor, if that was what you'd wanted. Once America's in the war she's not going to pull out of it. Now that Hitler's declared war on America she can't do anything about it.'

'Well we had no way of knowing he'd be such a bloody fool as to do that, did we?' Owl's smile meant nothing; it was a twitch, a tic of reassurance. 'If we'd forwarded the sighting report from Admiralty to Washington they'd have known the attack was coming and God knows how they might have handled it. Our best analysis was that they'd get highly indignant and call in the Japanese ambassador and demand to know what a Japanese battle fleet was doing in those waters. It would have forewarned Tojo and of course they'd have cancelled the attack and withdrawn the fleet. America might still have been tottering along the fence of neutrality when Hitler marched into London. The sentiment of the American people was firmly against war until last Sunday. This attack, or something like it, was the only thing that could do the job for us. Thank God for Tojo.'

'My God. You actually mean that.'

'Of course I do. And let me tell you another thing. If the Americans ever find out that we knew of the attack in advance but didn't warn them it was coming. . .'

Owl finished it with a barely perceptible shrug. Christopher never was able to penetrate that mask; he found himself wondering whether the job had made Owl ruthless or whether it was his innate ruthlessness that had drawn Owl to the job. He wished he knew which it was: it could make a difference.

Owl said, 'Those unfortunate Dutch sailors saw something they shouldn't have seen. Their destruction was a matter of policy. You were simply an instrument of that policy – it's nothing to make you wear sackcloth and ashes, Christopher. The blame isn't yours. Lay it squarely on me – I don't mind.'

'I want the whole picture then. There's a girl in Bletchley. Patricia Falkiner. She tried to pump me when I was in training. You put her up to that.'

'Not personally, no. But it was done under my directions. Standard vetting procedures, Christopher. Why must you always take things so bloody personally?'

'Then I was jumped,' he went on in the same monotone, 'by some rough types who put me into hospital. They wanted to know about Ireland. . .'

'And you told them nothing.' Owl smiled, more broadly this time. 'I was quite proud of you then.'

'So they were yours. Vetting me again.'

'Yes. Are you surprised? No, you knew it already; that's clear enough. So why feign indignation?'

'There's just one thing more. Roberts and I and four others who all turned out to be working for various sections of yours were taken off for separate training and they brought us six Germans to practise on. We were given stories about their crimes to get our blood stirred up and then we were turned loose on them. Ever since, I've had the feeling perhaps those Germans weren't war criminals at all. I've asked myself about that—what if they were just POWs, the poor guinea-pig bastards?'

'What if they were?'

'Tell me which it was.'

'I didn't hand-pick them, Christopher. As far as I know they were guilty of certain crimes.'

'But they hadn't actually had trials or convictions, had they?'

'Probably not. I don't really know. It was a long time ago, wasn't it?' Owl stood with his arms folded, one shoulder against the wall beside the window. Had it been daytime he might have been looking out of the window to impress his indifference on his visitor. 'Have you finished raking over the ashes?' he said.

'I believe in this war,' Christopher said, 'but aren't we supposed to be fighting it to prove there's some sort of difference between *us* and *them*?'

'For pity's sake spare me your schoolboy philosophizing. We're in it and we've got to go all-out to win it. If you believe in the war as you say you do, then that's got to be your guiding principle. In any case it's mine. I offer no other justification for my orders.'

Owl faced him, meeting his glance, and Christopher saw no guile in him at that moment. Owl said, 'I could have told you a good deal more before sending you out to the Pacific but it wouldn't have made the job easier and it would have cluttered your mind with complications you didn't need to concern yourself with. We don't keep you in the dark for sinister reasons when we send you on an operation, Christopher. We do it to give you the best chance to keep your mind clear for the job in hand.'

'There must have been some other way to do this one.'

'Perhaps. It had to be done very quickly and there wasn't time for subtle reasoning. A wiser man than I might have found some other answer for it.'

It was as near an apology as he'd ever heard Owl make. Then Owl said, 'You're getting the dirty jobs just now and that's unfortunate but someone's got to do them and you're the most reliable agent we've got, except for these occasional outbursts of conscience. I tolerate them, you know, because you're so good at the job, and because I know you've got no-one else to complain to, and everyone needs an escape valve now and then. I know it's difficult running alone, Christopher. The pressures mount up and there's no-one to share them with; it's not like being a Tommy under fire who's got a chum beside him in the trench. The rarest form of courage is the courage to face danger alone when you know no-one's observing your performance. You've exhibited that rare virtue and therefore we have made extraordinary use of it; circumstances have forced us to make use of every advantage we've got. I've used you and misused you, I grant it, and I'd be surprised if it weren't running through your mind that after the war's over you'd like to kill me.'

The accuracy of the guess was uncanny; it made Christopher flush. He was angered by the heat in his cheeks but Owl only smiled a bit and said, 'You must leave the responsibility for these decisions to me and not try to take the guilt upon yourself. If my orders are improper or incorrect then I'll be the one who must stand in the dock when this is over. In the meantime your value to me, and to yourself, will drop to nil unless you stop trying to shoulder impossible burdens. You're a servant of the King. Do as you're told. Leave the policies and the agonizing to your superiors. All right?'

Then Owl added in his dry-as-dust way, 'The job's not quite finished yet, as it happens.' He gave Christopher a sheet of notepaper with his own handwriting on it. 'The usual drill—commit it to memory because you can't take it out of this room with you.'

It was brief: three names. Two Royal Navy signals officers; a Wren second officer. The first two names were followed by the addresses of their offices and residences, the third only by an office address in Admiralty, Whitehall.

Peter Randall. Colin Cosgrave. A. V. Colquhoun.

Owl said in the same voice, 'Colquhoun decoded the signal from the submarine. Cosgrove delivered it to Randall, who delivered it to a signals officer at C-in-C Eastern Fleet. Another copy was brought to me but the chap who carried it is one of us.'

'Are you reserving the privilege of murdering everyone at Eastern Fleet to yourself, then?'

'It won't be necessary. Only one officer saw the signal. His car took a direct hit three nights ago. Providence, perhaps, or merely coincidence – who can say?'

Christopher put the sheet of paper down on the desk. His question was very soft but he was looking Owl in the eye. 'When I'm done with these,' he breathed, 'who murders me?'

'I had hoped,' said Owl with quiet menace, 'that, like the person who brought me the signal, you were reliable.'

They'd trained him well enough and he didn't make mistakes with the two men on the list. Lieutenant Randall died without a word under the wheels of a tube train and Lieutenant Colin Cosgrove, RNR, his neck broken by one blow, would be found sometime the next day burnt to cinders in a house already half wrecked by bomb damage; Christopher set the fire cautiously and watched from a mews until he was sure it had caught properly.

Wren second officer A. V. Colquhoun was tougher because he hadn't killed any women and didn't want to start, and because he didn't have her home address – he wondered why they wouldn't give it to him – where he could wait in the dark to accost her in an empty street unobserved. He had to hang around the Admiralty and there was a risk, despite his naval uniform, of drawing attention to himself. It took half a day and several oblique inquiries to learn there were several Wren signals officers in that particular section but it so happened only one of them was a second officer. That made it a bit easier; he was able to take a post unobtrusively near the lifts and he caught a glimpse of the back of her uniform. Then he ran down the stairs and was in time to see her walk out into the darkness and up the Mall. It was nearly Christmas and at this time of year it was completely dark by six.

She wasn't very tall and from the back she had an attractive bouncy walk and a well-turned ankle. He never got a look at her face; he didn't want to see it. Dismally he trailed along until she turned past Marlborough House and up St James's Street. She crossed Piccadilly by the Ritz and strolled up Old Bond Street. Reaching Oxford Street, she walked over and wandered along, attracted by some of the shop windows. Suddenly she disappeared, turning right into Gees Court. Christopher sprinted to the corner. He knew Gees Court was a small alleyway where hardly a soul ventured; even more vital, there were two or three blitzed buildings there. He moved up on his toes, silently. *Don't think about it.* Concentrate on the job, the mechanics. Then he was right behind her and he'd come up so soundlessly she didn't know he was there.

He made a silent promise: he would never kill again.

He knew he would not be the first to have made that kind of vow, nor would he be the first to break it.

He could do it without ever having to look at her face but he had to be sure she was the right one so he spoke her name: 'Colquhoun?'

'Yes?'

She began to turn, startled, and his bladed hand chopped down towards her; he didn't want to see her eyes. Something in the way she moved her head unsteadied him but he brought his hand down with desperate force; and then it was too late. The blow took her life – and he recognized her. His first girl, the girl from Harley Street – Anne.

He'd never known her surname.

The plan had been to bury the girl in the rubble of a half destroyed building and blow up the rest on top of her as if an unexploded bomb had finally detonated. In his knapsack he had the charges, fuse and detonator.

But there hadn't been anything to prepare him for this and after he'd made sure she was dead, he lifted her into the ruins and covered her with rubble. As he stumbled off, his eyes caught a plaque, spelling out in clear letters the name of the next street.

'ST CHRISTOPHER'S PLACE'

Christopher fled. He couldn't see where he was going because of his tears and he blundered right into a lamp post. That shook him enough to slow him down to a fast walk. He took back streets and passages wherever he could. Finally he was crossing under the trees in St James's Park, showing his pass to the Royal Marine corporal, going down the spiral stairs and continuing straight down past the first level down into Rat Alley, the third level below ground, where he opened the padlock of the trunk and got out an old Harris tweed suit that was a bit short for him at wrist and ankle. He closed the trunk and the padlock, spun the combination dial and sat down on the trunk. He covered his face in his hands and remembered that last glimpse of Anne alive, her nose tucked inside the upturned collar of her coat, surprised by his sudden voice but responding: 'Yes?' – not raising her voice, not expecting trouble really, because she wasn't the sort of girl to whom real trouble ever happened. A laughing attractive girl who had a serious job because there was a war on, but she'd never let it ruin her capacity for enjoying the casual pleasures. Even in bed at Harley Street she'd never stopped chattering and laughing.

He couldn't be sure whether in that last fragment of time before the chop of his hand had met her neck she'd recognized him or not. Now he'd never find out.

He dragged himself up the ladder – steel rungs imbedded in the concrete wall. He transferred everything out of the pockets of the naval uniform, burned it, and went out of the building empty-eyed.

Two days later Pooh met him when he emerged from jail and walked him along to the car and said, 'Thanks to your mother's connections we didn't have to lift a finger.'

'You'd have done better to let me rot in there.'

'We couldn't very well let you open your mouth in a magistrate's court, lad. Not that we don't trust you to be circumspect, but you'd have had an awkward time of it whatever you'd said – the police have methods of checking up on lies. The entire cover story might have been brought into question and then where might we have been? You understand, I hope, why we dropped a hint to your mother as to your whereabouts. She exercised her influence and *voilà*, the prosecution will offer no evidence. Much tidier all round, I should say.'

The car was running up towards Harley Street and Christopher said, 'Where are you taking me?'

'Home. You'll pack a few things and then disappear for a while. Stay on call and don't attract notice. Cool down, sort yourself out. That girl's at Bletchley—she's just got back from Bermuda.'

'Aren't you going to interrogate me?'

'Oh I think we've pieced it together fairly well for ourselves. You were upset, you've been driving yourself too hard, you had a few drinks in that pub and took offence at something someone said. A brawl started and the police tried to break it up. You refused to submit to their authority and you laid out three of them. With your training I suppose you could have killed all six of them. Is my analysis correct?'

'It's close enough.'

'You wanted a fight. You wanted to strike out and you wanted to be struck. You got what you wanted—I hope you're feeling a bit less aggressive?'

'Perhaps.'

'In any case it isn't anything that wants a debriefing, is it?'

'Put that way, I suppose not.' But it made him wonder how much Pooh really knew about the cause of his explosion. What did Pooh know about the Dutch submarine or the three murders he'd committed in London? Anything at all? Or everything? Pooh never seemed at all secretive but when you thought about it you realized how very little you really knew about him.

Stop it. You're suspecting everyone.

The car drew up at Harley Street and Christopher said, 'I want you to humour me if you don't mind. Would you send the driver up to gather a few of my things and pack a bag for me? I don't want to go in that house at the moment.'

'All right.'

It put Pooh right back in his good graces because he didn't ask any questions at all.

Pink from his bath, Winston ruminated on a tomato and cucumber sandwich. As was often the case, his floor was strewn with newspapers through which he had skimmed to find out what they were saying about him.

'We are making history,' he said to Owl. 'I had a whacking good session with Potus.' That was Franklin Roosevelt: POTUS – President of the United States.

Winston was drunk with triumph, Owl saw, and it was no time to try the facts on him; in times like these Winston was not a man to let facts get the better of him Just the same, *someone* had to try and bring him down to earth. Things were not going all that well. The Singapore débâcle – they were accusing him in the Commons of mismanaging the war and were preparing a motion to censure him. Nearly a year ago he'd been boasting in public utterances to Roosevelt, 'Give us the tools and we will finish the job,' and now not only the tools but the States were in the war and it didn't look any closer to being finished. Battles were still being lost, and the Americans were trying to decide between two policies, neither of which was attractive to Owl's view. Either they would concentrate their war effort in the Pacific against the Japanese – a choice that had to be discouraged at all costs – or they would come across the Atlantic in force, determined to invade the occupied Continent immediately and drive the Huns back to Germany. It was one of the few things on which Winston agreed with him; right from the start Winston was dubious about the American eagerness to assault Fortress Europe. 'I fear it may prove a ghastly disaster. We must persuade them to postpone such ambitions.'

An aide came in with the PM's black dispatch boxes and Winston sat down to deal with the documents. As always he was able to talk and read at the same time. Winston held up one document and Owl glimpsed the royal crest on it. Winston said, 'Remarkable, isn't it? Here I am, a servant of the King.' And he was, in truth, an unabashed royalist.

'If I might just mention the. . .'

'I've had some great trials in my life,' Winston went on. 'The desert – the wild charge of my 21st Lancers, the river war, Omdurman. I gave a patch of my own skin for grafting on a wounded man afterwards, you know.'

Trying to get word through to Winston was rather like trying to deliver a message by putting it in a bottle and throwing the bottle into the ocean.

Winston talked of pith helmets and the Boer War, his ox-wagon trek for the *Morning Post* and picnics on the veldt with delicacies from Fortnum & Mason. 'I went as a bicycle courier, of all things, trundling a signal from Ian Hamilton through the Boer lines at Ladysmith to C-in-C Lord Roberts.'

Winston's eyes popped in his excitement. 'It was a mighty relief to get through. That was in the days,' he lisped, 'before war became such a nasty business – modern war is not fun any more at the foot soldier's level, is it? We had great fun in those days – the mad gallops, the sporting risks.' He kept returning to Omdurman – that long-ago September in 1898 when the bugles sounded and the sun blasted the Nile plain and he'd faced the massed five-mile front of the waiting Dervish army. He spoke of Emirs, the Sirdar, Kerreri and Surgham Hill and all those other exotic names that rolled off his tongue with good-humoured memory until Owl, lulled off his guard, heard the musketry and felt the thunder and smelt the dust and tasted the blood and saw the destruction of the last great army of barbarians before the might of modern arms: ten thousand dead, the great Dervish armies destroyed for all time.

Abruptly Winston closed the boxes and struck the desk with his fist. 'We must flatten them,' he said. 'Flatten them out.' And for a moment Owl thought he meant the Dervishes until he realized that once again Winston's mind had returned to the present. 'But we must take care with the Americans,' he added. 'Franklin is a buccaneer. I admire buccaneers but my admiration can be coloured by caution when they are attempting their piracies against me. FDR wants nothing less, you know, than to take the empire away from Britain. The Americans have put a very high price – an extortionist's price – on the aid they've extended, and the price will go up still more when they allow us to persuade them to concentrate their efforts here in the European theatre rather than in the Pacific. The cost of that concentration will be unconscionably high as you know.'

'Yes, Prime Minister.' Singapore had fallen; that was the crux – it was the reason for the motion to censure Winston; it was the one defeat they couldn't afford.

'It's the gravest capitulation in our history. I am filled with anguish and self-reproach.'

'You'll get by this one in the Commons, Prime Minister. I

am not quite so certain about the next one. I'd hoped that when the Americans came into the war it would. . .'

'It will. It *shall*!' Winston fulminated. 'But we must not let them exact this bloody price! We're well on our way to mucking things up all round. Now I'm afraid I shall have to preside over yet another shuffle in war cabinet assignments, and we shall have to do something with that silly bastard in the Savoy' — he meant De Gaulle — 'and most important of all we must find a sensible and consistent policy for dealing with the Americans. It's not Franklin Roosevelt I'm worried about; he's a cheerful and transparent rogue. It's his war chief I'm afraid of — George Marshall. The man's brilliant but he's not on our side.'

Owl marvelled, not by any means for the first time, at Winston's heuristic mind: the genius he had for correlating disparate aspects and getting right to the core of things. It went with his tendency to jump to conclusions — to Winston a lack of disproof was taken to be proof and it might still be that General Marshall was waiting for a sign of British strength before committing himself; Winston might be mistaking neutrality for opposition; but in either case Marshall was indeed the key because he had Roosevelt's ear and would have a great deal to do with the shaping of American policy in the war.

Winston said, 'Marshall was taken completely by surprise by the Japanese attack on Hawaii, you know. He didn't believe they had the determination to carry out such a surprise manoeuvre. But Franklin Roosevelt — he's a devious clever fellow, John, don't underestimate the man. He didn't put it in so many words but I came away from Washington with the distinct feeling he'd known it was coming and he'd kept his mouth primly shut and allowed it to come.'

Owl stared at him. 'Roosevelt *knew*?'

'It seems his cipher people have been working terribly hard. They'd broken the Japanese purple diplomatic code — several weeks before the attack, I believe. Clever rascals. Whether the President knew the exact time and place of the attack is open to conjecture and I'm sure he'll never give anyone the satisfaction of full knowledge — his distaste for disclosure is notorious — but I believe he knew an attack was coming and, more, I believe he welcomed it.'

Christ, Owl thought, and wondered in awe at the irony of it.

Now he would never be able to tell the PM about the Dutch submarine.

Christopher knew that every Tuesday the Prime Minister lunched privately with the King at Buckingham Palace. Mr Churchill would not return from that meeting until mid-afternoon. Impatient with the need for delay Christopher went into Westminster Cathedral and sat, folded his hands, shut his eyes and tried to make his peace with God.

He went to a call box at half-past three and asked for the special Tigger number and heard the operator's sharp intake of breath before she demanded his priority authorization. He gave it to her and straight away he was put through: one of the special operators – a man's voice.

'Colonel Metcalf, please.'

There was a pause. 'About two minutes, sir.'

Then, almost to the second: 'Metcalf.'

'I want to see Tigger. It's important.'

'Yes, everything seems to be. Hang on, will you?' After a little while Pooh came back on the line: 'Half-past six this evening. I'll be there to let you in. In the Hole. All right?'

'Yes. Thank you.'

He used the interval to sort things in his mind and bring it all down to a few terse rehearsed sentences because he knew how easy it was to bore Tigger. He didn't leave the cathedral until it was time for the appointment. When he got to Storey's Gate Pooh shook his head – Tigger as usual was late with his appointments. Christopher wandered through corridors with Pooh following behind like a poor relation. They finally returned in time to see Commodore Mountbatten and Lord Beaverbrook emerge from the sanctum. Pooh let him in, then withdrew.

The Prime Minister sat in his cell – the room from which he made his wireless broadcasts to the world.

'It's very good to see you, my dear. Where've you been?'

'The Pacific, sir. Suva.'

'I didn't know we were at war with Suva.'

Christopher said between his teeth, 'Nor with Holland either.' But Mr Churchill didn't hear him.

'May I speak?'

'Pray be brief if you can.' The desk was littered with papers. Someone had marked up the cellophane overlay across the wall map of North Africa – great bold sweeps of chalk marks : movements of the desert armies, he supposed.

Christopher cleared his throat but there was a discreet buzz and Mr Churchill reached for his telephone. 'Yes? Ask him to wait a few moments.' Then he put it down and gave Christopher his eyes.

'Sir – I find this very difficult.'

'Be good enough to get it out all the same.'

'I'm sorry, sir. I feel a bit of a fool. It's quite possible you already know the things I feel I must tell you.'

'We shan't find that out, Christopher, until you stop beating about the bush and come to the ruddy point.' The Prime Minister's patience was vanishing at an alarming rate.

Christopher drew himself up. 'On 4 December last, a Dutch submarine in the Pacific sighted a Japanese battle fleet steaming towards Pearl Harbor. A signal report was sent to Admiralty.'

'I have fairly good contacts with the Admiralty,' the Prime Minister murmured. 'I know all this, Christopher.'

'The signal,' Christopher went on desperately, 'passed through several hands, and as far as I know every one of those people is now dead. It was I who killed them, sir, under orders, and it was also I who sank the Royal Netherlands Navy submarine. With all hands. Also on orders. If you already knew these things I apologize for having taken up your time. If you didn't know I felt you ought to.'

It had come out in a rush and he stood at attention with his hands trembling at his sides.

Mr Churchill sat with one hand half-clenched on the desk and Christopher thought he had never seen any living thing so still.

The Prime Minister, ashen, finally spoke in an unnaturally low slow tone.

'From whom did you receive these orders? Was it Uncle John?'

'Yes sir.'

'Direct? In person? Face to face?'

'Yes sir.'

'Was anyone else present?'

'No sir.'

The Prime Minister laid his smouldering cigar against his whisky glass. 'Who else was involved?'

'No-one, to my knowledge, sir.'

'Colonel Metcalf perhaps?'

'No sir. Not that I know of.'

Mr Churchill drew a very deep breath. 'You've been well trained, haven't you? If you're ordered to kill, you kill. No questions.'

'Yes sir.'

'And you didn't question these orders?'

'I did, sir, but I was told they came from you and I was told that the outcome of the war might depend on it.'

Mr Churchill's eyes lifted towards him. 'We are all fighting the same war, in our various ways. We are in a world civil war, my son, and it is the democracies against all the rest, and it is unthinkable that we should lose it. Yet in a way we must look upon ourselves as policemen whose duty is to protect the ideals of justice for which we stand. A policeman isn't merely expected to enforce the laws – he's expected to obey them as well. Sometimes one may lose sight of these principles on account of the strange solipsisms of military command. But if we have erred morally, Christopher, no-one is so much to blame as I. Responsibility lies with me, and not with Uncle John and certainly not with you. I have a feeling you came here to tell me these things to explain that you do not intend to do this sort of thing again. Ever. Is that your point?'

'It was my intention, sir.'

'Stout lad. Now I want you to take a holiday and report to me afterwards when you feel able to work again.'

'Thank you.'

'I'm glad you came forward, Christopher. Now pray be off with you.'

It occurred to him as he left Storey's Gate that the Prime Minister hadn't confirmed or denied any foreknowledge of the murders. It had seemed obvious from his reaction that he hadn't known a thing about them until Christopher had revealed them to him – but there'd been nothing in his actual words to prove it.

But then, he thought, that was Mr Churchill's way. The

Prime Minister wasn't likely to share his private thoughts with a boy at a time like this; nor was he likely to make any indiscreet display of disloyalty to his subordinates. All the same, it lifted Christopher's spirits a great deal to realize the fat man had been innocent of any knowledge of the crimes.

The PM's cabinet room in Downing Street was tidy, not because its occupant was a tidy man but because his servants knew it meant their jobs if they didn't clear up after him. Mrs Churchill was most particular about such things.

'I'm glad you could come,' the PM said, and it struck Owl how perversely polite Winston could be when he didn't have to be. 'Sit down, John.' Another glance and it became evident that the PM was exceptionally grumpy. Perhaps it was still the Singapore fiasco; or perhaps his insides were soured, at this late hour, by an excess of brandy and Havana tobacco.

As soon as Owl had taken a seat Winston perversely stood up. Glass in one hand and cigar in the other he walked backwards and forwards, chin sunk towards his chest, scowling. 'I deplore cold-blooded assassinations,' he said. 'I know full well that there is a binding necessity for ruthlessness in war. If a nation under attack is incapable of ruthlessness it probably cannot save itself.'

Then he turned, timing it nicely for punctuation, reaching the last pace on the last word and coming about with an actor's dramatic instinct to stand still on the punch line: facing Owl across the width of the room, his cheek illuminated by the flickering wood fire in the hearth, Winston planted his feet and said, 'But one must distinguish between the ruthlessness of necessity and the brutality of cynicism or madness. You have overstepped the line.'

He muttered it, perhaps deliberately so, to force his listener to lean forward and attend. Still, the mutter and the lisp made him hard to follow and it was a moment before Owl's mind was able to replay the sounds and make sense of them.

'I'm not quite sure what you're. . .'

'*Submarines*,' the PM roared. 'Dutch submarines and British signals officers. Did you you think these murders could be kept from me forever?'

'I did what needed to be done.'

'In secret – with stealth – like a cowardly cracksman! A murderer stalking the darkness!'

'Prime Minister, we simply could not take the risk of what might happen. When I reported the sighting to you, your exact words were, if I may recall them for you, "This secret must be kept the most inviolate of the war – because it will win it".'

'No-one but a madman could construe those words to contain an authorization to commit mass murder!' The firelight danced wickedly upon his profile.

Owl said, 'It was the crew. Shore leave – a rating goes into a pub. He doesn't mean to say anything but he has a few pints and the news goes round the world. . .'

In his rage Winston flung his brandy into the fire – it exploded like raw petrol. Owl braced himself for a bellowing row that would shake the room but Winston stood in quaking silence and then, when he spoke, his voice was carefully controlled. 'I am the representative of the mightiest Commonwealth the world has ever seen,' he growled, 'and I will not have this. I will not have our destiny sullied and betrayed by such vile and dastardly crimes!'

Owl sat with his hands on his thighs, not moving. He'd defended himself with cold reason but there was nothing useful to add and in any case Winston was not looking for an argument; he wasn't even looking for contrition or apology – he simply wanted to vent his spleen, Owl realized. The best thing was to let him get it all out and then he'd come to the point. It might be a request for Owl's resignation but Owl doubted that very much. In certain ways Winston was the reverse of ruthless: he always found it exceedingly difficult to fire people, even though he was impervious to the emotional needs of his friends; often he was much kinder to his enemies, once he'd defeated them. Winston was always ready to make concessions but only from strength. Threats, resistance and opposition only closed him up. His pattern was to fight first, establish his supremacy, win the fight, *then* conciliate. The thing to do now was simply to ride it out and let him have his own way; once he felt he'd battered Owl to a suitably chagrined and obeisant position he'd forgive him and get on to something else. But it would be a mistake to grovel or to agree with him too easily; Winston needed the sense of battle and the sense of victory.

So Owl maintained a stubborn silence while the Prime Minister railed at him about matters of morality and justice and all those other virtues which, in other moods, Winston himself was the first to admit were the sort of thing that went out of the window immediately war was declared. From the intensity of the PM's monologue Owl began to see that there was a very specific and climatic *dénouement* in Winston's mind. Listening stone-faced to the cascade of glistening prose Owl found himself excited by anticipation and the suspense of not knowing what great inspiration this was leading to — for it had become quite apparent that Winston had had one of his 'great ideas' and that the moralistic diatribe was simply the setting in which he intended to display the jewel.

At last he reached the penultimate moment, signalled quite plainly by his dramatic pause and his return to his seat, where he contrived an extended silence by slowly relighting his cigar. Then, watching Owl slyly across the top of the flame, he flicked the lighter shut and said, 'I am capable, if unwillingly, of making certain allowances where you are concerned — allowances that might not be made by a comrade who hadn't known you as long as I have. The strict course of morality would compel me to dismiss you, strip you of all rank and authority, even bring you up on capital charges. But this would be impractical, not to mention indiscreet, and furthermore I believe you are a talented man of incalculable value to our war effort and I believe you are malleable, in the sense that I am capable of restraining and controlling your most brutal instincts henceforth.'

Right. Now we're getting down to it.

Winston said, 'All I want from you this evening, after reasonable discussion of the points at issue, is compliance with my wishes. Compromise.' He extended his hands before him, one of them clutching the cigar between two fingers, the palms facing each other and the right hand about two feet above the left hand. 'The right hand is the Prime Minister and the left hand is you, John. And I expect you to compromise with me in this fashion.' Then Winston lowered his right hand about two inches and brought his left hand all the way up to meet it. 'Do you understand me?'

Owl dipped his head half an inch to acknowledge it.

'Very well.' The PM lowered his hands. 'Henceforth no-one —

no-one — is to be killed simply because he knows too much, or because he may have a loose tongue. In fact there will be no further killings of any kind, of any person, for any security reason whatever. Understood?'

Owl nodded again.

'Neither Englishmen nor Allies nor neutrals are to be murdered, *regardless of provocation.* The sole exceptions are, of course, cases of patent treason, and we must leave those to be dealt with by the courts.'

All sorts of retorts had entered Owl's mind but he held his tongue; the PM had not finished yet and an interruption at this point could throw him into another rage.

'Henceforth when there is evidence that we are endangered by the unreliability of any person who has too much knowledge, you will arrange the comfortable and secure isolation and confinement of that person for the duration of the war. I am ordering you, therefore, to establish immediately a detention centre for such persons. I think it might be wise to choose an offshore island as the site of such a camp.'

The idea had merit, Owl conceded. Turning such people loose at the end of the war might be tantamount to opening Pandora's Box, of course, but in the meantime the solution was sensible and even inspired. Winston's compassion lay generally towards principles rather than individuals; he could be quite Machiavellian in his dealings with this fellow or that, but on matters of policy and even strategy he was a paragon of honour.

The central truth about Winston, he thought – and you had to understand it clearly to get anywhere with him – was that he was quite out of his time and ought to have been born in the eighteenth, not the twentieth, century.

Assuming the PM was finished with him for the evening, and not wanting to overstay his fragile welcome, Owl uncrossed his legs and made as if to rise. Winston made him stay. 'There's one thing more. A question has come up in my mind regarding young Christopher.'

'I thought it might have. It was Christopher who put you on to this, wasn't it?'

Winston gave him a long scrutiny in which Owl saw very little warmth. Finally the PM said, 'Certain intimations came to my attention and I interviewed the boy, yes. I ordered him to tell me everything he knew about it.'

Winston was perfectly capable of lying through his teeth to protect someone. Owl knew that. He also knew Winston rarely took the trouble because there were very few people he wanted to protect. Yet his peculiarly avuncular feelings towards Christopher Creighton might well make an exception of him, and Owl knew he was no closer to the truth now than he had been before he'd asked the question. It was no good accusing the boy of treason simply because he'd spilt a few secrets to the Prime Minister, who was after all his ultimate commander.

'I am disturbed,' Winston said now, 'not only by the casual murders of those hapless Dutchmen and the signals officers but also by the cynical uses to which you've put that young man. He's a paragon of young English manhood – he's bold and daring, eager to go in harm's way and clever enough to get the job done. But there's no need to tear him apart by flinging every filthy job you've got on his plate. He'll be burnt out by the time he's reached his majority at the rate you're using him. And where these obscenely unsavoury matters were concerned, why in God's name of all people did you choose a seventeen-year-old boy to execute them? We've other men.'

'Because, like you, Prime Minister, I trust him,' Owl replied with simple candour.

Chapter Nine

'I always seeme to come to you when I want succour.' Christopher lifted her feet on to his lap and began to massage her calves and toes.

'Don't apologize. I don't mind.'

On the wireless a girl was singing *'I'm gonna get lit up when the lights go on in London'* with a bouncy accompaniment by Henry Hall's orchestra. They listened to it, not talking, and after a while Patricia sat up, sliding her legs across his lap. Her arms went round his neck; her voice was thick and sweet in his ear: 'Come on then.' Her nails dug into him.

It was dark when she woke him up. 'You've been having that dream again.' He didn't need her to tell him that; he was bathed in sweat. She switched on the light. 'The pubs haven't closed yet. Would you like to go out for a bit?'

'Yes.'

They went along the road and they'd nearly reached the pub when Patricia said gently, 'There is no-one behind you, Christopher.' He must have been looking over his shoulder too often. He saw her reflection in the dark window of Boots, the chemist, and smiled at bit queasily at it. Memories were running through him like tactile sensations and he wished he could feel what she felt when he was making love to her. He wanted to know how it was — what were the feelings in her nerve-ends? What was it like for her?

They left the pub at closing time. On the way home they passed a sweet-shop's window and Pat said, 'I spy with my little eye a box of marzipan,' and he said he'd buy it for her tomorrow if he'd got enough points left. She looked away and then finally, clutching his arm a bit tighter, she said, 'I shan't be here tomorrow I'm afraid. We're off to Bermuda again for a bit.'

'*Tomorrow?*'

'I didn't want to spoil it for us any sooner than I had to. I've known about it for several days.'

Back in her flat, Christopher sat forward on the sofa, fore-arms resting on his knees.

'Bloody hell.'

'It's only for a fortnight or so.'

'Who knows where I'll be by then?' He looked up. 'I put your face on every girl I see.'

Later she slept with her back to him in her usual position, legs bent and one hand under her cheek; he lay against her and they fitted like two spoons and he wished she didn't have to go, because he seemed to be frightened all the time now.

He visited his mother briefly. He couldn't reveal anything specific to her but with her staunch reasoned patriotism and clear manner of thought she managed to cut through some of the undergrowth of his confusion. Without anything being admitted she seemed to feel the force of his guilt and she managed, in her matter-of-fact way, to remind him there was a war on.

He was on the drift, checking in with Pooh at intervals by telephone to keep them informed of his whereabouts. One day he found himself at Chartwell in the Kentish countryside where he'd spent those crucial childhood times – the Weald, the beech forests and the lovely rolling lawns of Chartwell Manor. He walked through the grounds – a bit weedy now, becoming over-grown, remembering the long green-golden summer evenings here, remembering how his little sisters had sailed their toy boats on these ponds: now the ponds were stagnant with water lilies and silt. Out on the little island Mr Churchill had sat under his sombrero before his easels, liking the bright colours, disliking the browns and darker hues. And up there by the big windows Mr Churchill had enjoyed his occasional game of bezique – with great concentration – in the spacious drawing room before dinner.

A puff of cigar smoke drew his attention and, disbelieving, he turned past a tree to find the Prime Minister there, alone, in a sombre mood brooding across the Weald, so preoccupied he seemed unaware of Christopher's presence until Christopher cleared his throat.

The shock of surprise seemed to hold Mr Churchill speech-less for a bit. He was wrapped in overcoat and muffler, his hands deep in his coat pockets and his breath steaming before his face; his skin seemed unusually pink, even for him.

'I suppose,' Mr Churchill muttered, 'we were drawn here, both of us, to this lovely and peaceful place, to find strength. Both of us bent under the weight of this beastly war. Weary of playing the game that seems to have no end – and we must see it as a game because we can't face the terrible truths without ritualizing them. I pray you do not take your lot too hard, however. When one holds ministerial office, beleaguered by messengers and telephones – and especially when one is a man such as I who finds his only comfort in action – one can only envy the opportunities for youthful distraction that present themselves to a young man like you.'

'I'm sorry to have disturbed you.' And he began to withdraw but Mr Churchill bade him stay. They went to sit in the garden on one of the stone benches; night fell as they sat there in the chill. Mr Churchill for once had little to say and they spent most of that hour in silent communion. Then a flight of RAF fighters lifted off from nearby Biggin Hill to meet German bombers coming in across the Channel. The old man and the youth watched the air battle take shape in the crystalline sky. Chandelier flares came down from the German planes and hung motionless. 'If it were peacetime,' Mr Churchill said in a sort of awed tone, 'you'd have had to pay a good price to see that. They're quite beautiful, aren't they? Incredible. You could read a newspaper by it.'

It didn't take long – a few minutes – and the flares were extinguished, the battle gone somewhere else, the sky silent. Mr Churchill stirred and Christopher took his elbow to help him to his feet. Mr Churchill faced him briefly then. 'I must return to my war – and you, I think, to yours.'

He was making his way up George Street, feeling his way; two women went by and one of them called out cheerfully, 'Proper old pea-souper, innit?' Then he heard the air-raid siren but he didn't pay much attention at first; he wasn't far from Harley Street and he was determined to get there and make some sort of amends to the girls there. But then he heard the Dorniers. The sticks of bombs began to crash through the fog and one of them was near enough to send him reeling from the blast. Then he was running for shelter in the crypt of a church.

He wasn't the only one and by the time he fled into the church he was in a small crowd. It was St James's, Spanish Place. He followed the scurrying fugitives down the winding dripping stone stairs into a huge crypt that must have extended under the whole area of the church. The ceiling was supported by stone archways and the space was broken up by their pillars. Bombs whistled over, crashed down, shook the place; it wouldn't stand a direct hit but then there weren't many basements in London that would: the tube stations were the only safe shelters. The Luftwaffe was bombing blind, dropping them through the fog for sheer harassment, and there was no telling how long it might go on or how close they'd come.

People were still tumbling in through two or three stair entrances and there were paraffin stoves with boiling kettles; WVS ladies were handing out tea and cheerful talk and trying to look after everyone but it was becoming very crowded. The light came from storm lanterns. There was a hiatus of a few minutes and then everything quaked again.

Parents played games to keep the children occupied and the WVS volunteers were everywhere but there was an old woman in the shadows and no-one had noticed her. Christopher poured a cup of tea, carried it back across the crypt and knelt to support the old woman's head so that she could drink.

'That's kind.' Her voice was feeble, breaking into falsetto. In this light she seemed ghostly, as if all the colour had been bled out of her. A very old woman in a shabby black coat that had fallen open to expose a thin print dress inadequate against the chill. Christopher gently tipped the cup to her lips and she sucked at it.

'Hold me, lad, just hold me.' Her head came to rest on his shoulder. The floor shook with a nearby blast and the old woman trembled in his arms, skin and bone; her frightened eyes rolled up towards him, beseeching, and he sat back against the clammy stone pillar holding her in his embrace until her eyes closed and her tremors diminished: a faint smile lengthened her mouth and he realized she'd fallen asleep.

Cramped against the stone he sat drowsing with the old woman's fragile weight against him; he listened for the All Clear but he must have drifted off, for he didn't hear it and he only woke up when someone prodded him and he heard a man's voice: 'Sorry old chap but we'll take her with us now.'

He looked up and saw a pair of tired ambulance men, their faces chalky with plaster dust. One of them was lifting the old woman away from him and Christopher watched groggily, not understanding until the ambulance man said, 'Come on, that's a good lad, let her go now.' And he realized he still had his arms round her; he let them fall and saw then that the old woman was dead.

The ambulance men took her away and he sat alone in the crypt. *She must have died in my arms,* he thought. There must be some significance in it – and that it took place in a church. She hadn't spoken ten words to him and all she'd known of him was that he'd brought her tea and given comfort against her terror.

It was after midnight and he turned the corner into Harley Street but he didn't make it as far as the door. A wave of light-headedness made him put out an arm to reach for support but there was nothing to lean on and he only just managed to break his fall. Then he lay unable to breathe, his heart pounding, sweat pouring from his body and thinking with distant curiosity, *So that's what it feels like to die of a heart attack,* and then he tumbled into nothingness.

The face was kindly but remotely familiar. 'You're all right now.'

He was in a soft upholstered chair and he sat up slowly. 'Dr Philips, isn't it?'

'That's right. How did you know?' The wide face came closer. 'Do I know you? You do look rather familiar.'

'I used to live next door.'

'Of course! Christopher Creighton.'

'What happened to me?'

'I'd say it's straightforward enough. You came through the air raid, did you? Felt you couldn't breathe, your heart began banging about in your chest, pulse hammering in your head, outburst of perspiration – then you couldn't hold it any longer and you passed out. Is that about it?'

'Yes – exactly. Is it my heart then? Aren't I too young to be having –'

Dr Philips laughed. 'No, old boy, you're not having heart attacks. It's quite a simple anxiety syndrome. Has it ever happened before?'

'No.'

'Then I shouldn't worry about it a bit. It's the war, that's all. We're all frightened, aren't we, but our stiff-upper-lip code prevents us from admitting it so we bottle it up until finally it needs to find an outlet. Quite normal, actually. It's lucky you did it on my doorstep, though. Do the same thing in Soho and you'd be thrown in jail as a drunk.' The doctor laughed again. 'I shouldn't give it another thought unless it starts happening regularly – then it might be a good idea to consult a psychiatrist.'

It was the first time his splendid constitution had failed him and for an hour that morning he was troubled by it; he'd always taken his physical reliability for granted. But then he got caught up in the excitement of buying things and he forgot the incident. He'd never been very good at brooding. If a difficulty presented itself he was accustomed to resolving it; he didn't care for dilemmas and he didn't mind making quick decisions and sticking by them. It was no good worrying about things over which you had no control. He'd made one or two decisions in the past few days and he was on his way to carry them out, and that was that.

He spent most of the day using up his influence, his priority cards and the extra ration books they'd allowed him to take at Northways. By the middle of the afternoon he was exhausted and the sack over his shoulder heavy enough for Father Christmas. He carried it into a cinema and spent two hours watching *Sergeant York*, very impressed by Gary Cooper's reluctant heroism and the fine brave truth of the story of the backwoods American pacifist who ended up a hero in the Great War. He always enjoyed films with real heroes in them. He'd never had much patience with the *Hamlet* style of hero.

Along George Street the priest was repairing a bit of chipped cement on the church doorway and helmeted crews were going through rubble carefully prodding for delayed-action bombs. He shifted the weight on his shoulder and went up to the entrance of his father's house.

Lister answered his ring herself. 'Why hello, Christopher.' She was rather subdued; she hardly seemed to notice his burden. He carried it inside to the big hall table; behind him she was shutting the door and saying, 'I'm afraid we're going through a bad patch just now. We've lost young Anne Colquhoun.'

'I know. Someone told me. I'm very sorry. Look here, would you mind gathering the girls down here? I've something for them.'

Dubious but willing to humour him she went off. Christopher opened the sack on to the table and set the things out – a pillager's haul of booty: bottles of champagne, packets of cigarettes, chocolate, a baked ham, a roast duckling, a great slab of Stilton, sherry trifles.

They came in ones and twos: he heard their bursts of disbelief and delight.

'Oh, Christopher, how marvellous!'

When they were all there he got their attention. 'For just this one night,' he announced, 'we are going to forget the war. We're going to have a party.'

Once a day the King's brougham, with two liveried men, brought the King's notes and queries to Downing Street. It had the sort of quaint archaic touch that impressed the populace, Owl thought, without actually doing anyone any harm.

The brougham's horses clipped away, rubber shoes soft on the cobblestones in the July heat, and Owl made his way through the heaped sandbags with Metcalf. They showed their passes and were admitted and as always were kept waiting far beyond the appointed hour until finally they were granted an audience with the Prime Minister. Owl went smoothly into the cabinet war room; behind him Metcalf came crashing clumsily in as if to demonstrate that even if he did happen to be an intelligence executive he was not in the least furtive.

The PM exchanged scowls with Owl and granted Metcalf a momentary uninterested scrutiny, as if having to remind himself who Metcalf was.

The PM detested flying but he'd returned not long ago from a trip to Washington and Owl could see straight away that it hadn't done anything for his digestion or his temper. Owl hadn't seen him in past several weeks, during which Tobruk had fallen—an event hardly calculated to gladden Winston's heart. The Americans had looked like giving up on Britain altogether and going it alone; hence the PM's hasty attempt to patch things up. Then Roosevelt in his wonderful six syllables had turned it round: 'What can we do to help?' Still it wasn't that easy.

'We're in a spot of bother,' Winston said, putting it more mildly than Owl would have done. *What he means is, we're in a bloody mess.*

Winston went on: 'I've got to persuade the Americans somehow that they must postpone their "Sledgehammer" invasion of France and instead confirm "Gymnast" for North Africa. Only Franklin Roosevelt stands with me on this; it's contrary to the wishes of Marshall and his chiefs of staff. Marshall and Admiral King have told the President he must either invade France or transfer the American emphasis to the Pacific. Now of course the fall of Tobruk has succeeded to the extent of persuading them at least to postpone their plans for France. Nevertheless it's a terrible price to have paid for such a slender and ephemeral gain. And the fools still can't see how catastrophic a premature invasion of the Continent must be!'

Winston sat squat behind his desk, rather like the photographs of Mussolini in his office, Owl thought. He wore a dressing gown decorated with crimson dragons—fresh from his afternoon kip. It was widely known he slept bare-bottomed in a silk vest.

Winston went on, 'Apart from the President's there's precious little wisdom in Washington. The Americans are always too impatient—instant coffee, instant rice, instant warfare. They are temperamentally incapable of playing the waiting game. I am abysmally unable to show them that our objective must not be to rush to claw at the gates of the continental fortress—our objective, clearly, must be to make the war last. Hitler and Mussolini have limited resources. They are surrounded and blockaded for all practical purposes and their supplies of oil and other necessaries are dwindling steadily. In time they'll exhaust the raw materials and we shall have them. We must simply hold out. Hitler's only chance was to win the war quickly—when we withstood the early Blitz we showed we could win. Now he's committed two-thirds of his strength against the Soviet Union and he seems determined to exhaust everything at hand — his petroleum, his raw materials, and his people. We must encourage him to do just that, and at the same time invite him to meet us on ground of our own choosing where we may nibble at his underbelly and at the same time maintain the blockade round him. In the end the balance of the war will shift and it will be done with a minimum of casualties on our side. Against this strategy we have the suicidal impetuosity of the American generals who insist on storming the fortress immediately rather than starving it out first. Their memories are too short — one shudders to remember Haig and the senseless batterings of the 1914–18 war against the fortified German line.'

Furiously then Winston brandished a hand: 'At no one time since I assumed this office have I felt such feebleness and futility as I've felt in trying to deal sensibly with these imbecilically adventurous Americans. They have commendable boldness and execrable commonsense. And in their childish eagerness they are determined to have their way. If they are not dissuaded they'll lose the flower of American manhood against the guns of Hitler's *Festung Europa* and then of course they'll blame us for bringing them into it. I shall have nothing, in the end, beyond the hollow satisfaction of having told them so.'

In a grumbling afterthought he added, 'There is also the dreary but significant fact that for all their rattling of sabres the Americans have had no experience in mounting amphibious landings. Our best estimates are that nine out of ten soldiers would be dead before they got off the beaches. Yet we must not appear arrogant, for if our recalcitrance should offend them too much they would pick up their toys and go away to play at war with Japan.'

Winston glanced sepulchrally at Owl. He looked like the victim of a hangover but Owl knew the impression was false; Winston rarely if ever experienced hangovers.

It had not escaped Owl's attention that the very attributes Winston accused the American generals of possessing were those that he himself possessed in abundance. The only difference was that Winston had a higher degree of cleverness than they did and, despite his stubbornness, Winston was a man who benefited by the wisdom of his own mistakes and in that he had the experience that the Americans lacked. *Our salvation,* Owl thought drily, *may lie in the fact that Winston does not always get his way.* But the irony was that now, when Winston *ought* to get his way for once, it looked as if he was going to fail.

Winston was watching him through pale, motionless half-lidded eyes. 'I've put the problem before my staff. They've offered no sufficient solution. I now put it before you. I confess an abysmal inability to see my way through this. I seek ideas wherever I may find them. Pray let me have your thoughts.'

Owl saw Metcalf sit up astonished. It was utterly unlike Winston to solicit advice and it struck Owl that Winston, by including Metcalf in the invitation to this meeting, was acknowledging something Owl hadn't credited him with: an appreciation of the quality of Metcalf's mind.

But the plea had been addressed directly to Owl and it was upon Owl that the PM's eyes were fixed now. As they stared at each other, Owl felt they were closer than friends: they were, in a way, enemies – bound together by the knowledge of shared crimes. The bond between reluctant conspirators was as strong as welded steel.

Owl said slowly, 'You're asking for my inexpert opinion. For what it's worth, I've spoken with General Clark, and he believes with Eisenhower that when Harry Hopkins and General Marshall arrive here they'll bring written orders from the President to come to a speedy arrangement. It's my feeling that you've nearly convinced them of the rightness of your position – it's just that they haven't admitted it yet. Colonel?' He turned to Metcalf, yielding the floor.

Metcalf cleared his throat nervously and gave him an unfriendly look, as if he'd have preferred to remain neglected in the background. 'Well,' Metcalf began, and cleared his throat again. Owl nearly laughed aloud: the image had suddenly struck him of Winnie the Pooh fattened on too much stolen honey and stuck in the hole.

Finally Metcalf said, 'Perhaps it would help if we took into account the Americans' notorious tendency to believe only what they can see and touch. They're very fond of pragmatic evidence. Their generals may be bold and impetuous, as you say, Prime

Minister – but they're also the sort of people who quickly learn simple lessons from practical demonstrations.'

'Pray don't be roundabout, Colonel Metcalf. If you've got something to offer I await it eagerly – if not, don't obscure the issue.'

'I'm sorry. I haven't a plan to offer – only the thought that it might be useful to demonstrate to the Americans the impracticability of storming the French coast. I was thinking of operation "Rutter", sir.'

Winston scowled. 'We had to postpone it twice this month in deference to the weather. At the moment it's on the shelf, cancelled.'

'Yes sir. In the circumstances I thought it might be worth reactivating.' Metcalf smiled ingenuously.

'Pray continue,' Winston purred.

'The Americans have already approved the operation in principle, I believe. Quite frankly, sir, I've felt for quite a while that it was a mistake to cancel it in any case – there are sound reasons for carrying it out, even if the odds on success are poor. God knows we need better intelligence of the Germans' coastal defences.'

'The chiefs of staff felt it would be too costly,' Winston said.

'Well I suppose, with respect, Prime Minister, that the force would have to be an expendable one.'

'That's a cold-blooded view, Colonel.'

'But isn't it important that we mount such a rehearsal – to feel out the German defences and learn as much as we can about them? We've got to find out what they can throw against us. And if we do that now, Prime Minister, it will demonstrate the situation to the Americans in an obvious and practical way.'

Winston's frown was less argumentative than thoughtful. 'Montgomery's against remounting it. Security – the troops who were to be in it have all been dispersed ashore.'

Owl had put on what he belatedly realized was his foxy little smirk, in response to the cleverness with which Metcalf had been improvising; realizing it, Owl erased the smirk quickly and said, 'We could get round that. Leave Monty out of it. Have someone else – why not Mountbatten? – remount it in absolute secrecy. Keep no records. Change the code name of the operation.'

Winston said slowly, 'It would serve several purposes, wouldn't it. It conforms to our "set Europe ablaze" policy. We'd get our intelligence — we'd test the enemy's defences — we'd find out if it's possible to capture an enemy port for staging purposes — and we'd convince the Americans beyond a doubt that mounting a cross-Channel invasion is impractical at this time.'

Owl said, 'I suppose those Canadians are the ones. No-one's really expendable, but they haven't been tried in combat and that makes them somewhat less valuable than blooded veterans.'

Metcalf chimed in: 'The Canadians — of course! They've been smashing up Aldershot, making a complete nuisance of themselves, demanding combat — their officers have been pounding on every desk in London trying to get into action. They're perfect for it.'

Winston said abruptly, 'Will you two stop palavering? I want to think.'

Owl felt nearly reckless enough to reply, *We'll stop when we've finished!* but he held his tongue; you couldn't push Winston too far.

Winston flung his lighted cigar over his shoulder without looking behind him. It landed as it always did smack in the middle of a fire bucket strategically placed on the hearth. He said, 'We'd need to have the highest common factor.'

'Of what?' Owl asked, baffled.

'Of the defences. It's no earthly use five thousand men making a reconnaissance in force — trying to capture an enemy port as a rehearsal for invasion — unless the Germans are waiting with everything they've got. We can't learn anything if we catch them asleep. Colonel? What are the intelligence estimates?'

'Apparently the Germans have a battalion there — about fifteen hundred men. Low-ability troops.'

'Precisely. They won't test our assault, will they. No. We need the highest common factor — the worst possible conditions, so that we may test ourselves against the best the enemy can put up against us in a major assault.'

Owl felt an unfamiliar excitement. 'There's one way to insure that, you know.'

'Yes John?'

'Tell the Germans we're coming.'

It brought Metcalf's head round angrily: 'You can't mean that!'

'Of course I can. I do.'

'You're talking of plotting the premeditated betrayal and sacrifice of our own loyal soldiers!'

Owl said, 'Either we lose a few thousand now or we lose several hundred thousand – if we don't reconnoitre their defences or if the Americans invade prematurely.'

'Surely there are other means to the same end.' Metcalf glared at him.

Winston said, 'Confound it, John, be good enough to wipe that silly expression off your face. You've got the cynical smile of a man who's just discovered that nothing – not even depravity – is what it's cracked up to be.'

'You misinterpret my face.'

'Then what, pray, amuses you so?'

'The challenge. Letting the Germans in on it will be fraught with risk. There's so much liaison now between our intelligence people and the Americans that it will be incredibly difficult to keep word of it from reaching them – and of course if word of it ever got to the Americans we'd all be lynched.'

Winston's mind seemed to have moved elsewhere while Owl spoke; the PM's reply, when it came, seemed indirect. 'We shall have to change that wretched code name "Rutter", of course. That was enough to depress anyone – no wonder it brought us bad weather. "Jubilee", I think. Has a feeling of celebration about it.'

Owl looked away.

'Well it's better than bloody "Rutter",' said Winston.

Owl said quietly, 'Then the enemy is to know we are coming?'

When the PM looked away again, refusing to commit himself directly, Owl put the matter with blunt frankness. 'Prime Minister, do you wish me to provide German intelligence with secret information of our plans for "Jubilee"?'

It seemed an age before Winston looked at him. Then he said, 'Can you do it without letting the Americans know we've done it?'

'Yes.'

'Then we must do it,' the PM said with displeasure. 'When it comes, John – and it will come, for the Americans' patience is not without limit – the battle of France will have been won upon this "Jubilee" beach. For every man we lose here, we shall save a hundred in the subsequent great assault. But by God it tests my heart.'

Great fires lit the sky in a dozen places, outlining the craggy walls of half-destroyed buildings. Fire lorries were trying to get through the rubble. A pair of Home Guard pensioners carried someone on a litter towards a first-aid post. A dazed woman stared down at a dead baby, flames dancing behind her; a lorry lay overturned against a shattered house; an army tank was trying to push the lorry out of the way, its tracks slipping on the smooth paved surface, and a child with a bandaged hand lurched past the black Humber saloon, evidently aimless with shock. A sullen fat old woman pouted at the sky, her arms akimbo, as if to chase the bombers away with the heated force of her glance. Ambulances drew away, to be replaced by new ambulances; and rescue crews were clearing the rubble, searching for victims. This wasn't happening nearly so often now; but once or twice a month the Luftwaffe still came over to get its licks in.

Pooh recognized one of the rescue workers – a slender figure in the tattered remains of a naval officer's uniform. The man pitched great chunks of rock aside, clawed at something, then gently lifted a wailing child, covered in blood, from the debris. He carried it tenderly to one of the ambulances. Impulsively the nurse who took the child bent forward to kiss the rescue worker's grimy cheek.

The planes had gone but heavy flotsam still tumbled through the flames from a high rooftop and a house began to collapse. Pooh ducked; something bounced off the roof of the car. When things stopped coming down Pooh stepped out of the Humber and picked his way across the stones. He intercepted the rescue worker, who'd taken shelter behind the ambulance, shielding the nurse and the child with his body. The young man's eyes blinked at Pooh without recognition.

'Come along, Christopher.'

Christopher grinned at him. The lad undoubtedly had no idea what that did to his soot-masked face. 'What's on, then?'

Pooh took him by the arm towards the car. 'It's a different

sort of job,' he said. He added, 'Rather like running the gauntlet. You'll love it.'

It was a road in Dublin with red-brick Victorian houses and high trees. Dublin was not under blackout restrictions but neither was it altogether carefree; most of the street lamps were out – either blown out and left that way or deliberately extinguished – and the only ones left overhung the crossroads. Here and there lamplight showed round the edges of window curtains. Christopher went up one of the trees as surefootedly as he'd climbed the firs at Chartwell. He pulled out the Very pistol and aimed it a bit high because of the curved trajectory the missile would follow: second floor, second window from the left. The window was dimly lit; the room itself was dark but the corridor beyond it had a light that spilt through. They'd told him, *He doesn't sleep under the window so you're all right, you won't hit him with the blasted thing.*

He checked again to make doubly sure. Number 52 Northumberland Road: the German legation.

He squeezed the trigger and there was a hollow pop, like a champagne cork. The Very pistol bucked in his hand and he heard the missile sizzling across the road. The the smash and tinkle of glass and a thud when it hit something – a wall or the floor. By then Christopher was on his way quickly down the tree. He hit the ground and dashed into a passageway; there probably wouldn't be any pursuit but he'd been warned not to take chances.

The cartridge in the Very pistol was not the usual flare but a message pellet. It was designed to fit the pistol but had a reduced powder charge and nothing in the head that would ignite; simply a cap that you unscrewed to expose the hollow inside. You could put anything in there – gemstones, papers, photographs rolled up. In this case it was a sheet of notepaper with an invitation to a private meeting and enough clues to tantalize the German into keeping the rendezvous. *Come alone,* the note had insisted, but Christopher doubted the German would comply with that. For all they knew it was a trap, so he wasn't surprised when five of them entered the woods the next morning.

*

He'd discarded the Very pistol and waited unarmed, listening to them crash through the woods of Braye and thinking how easy it would be to ambush them; this surprised him as he'd never been given reason to doubt the vaunted cleverness and efficiency of German intelligence. These men were walking right into it, spread out a bit among the trees, but he could have finished all of them with a grenade and a Sten gun; then he remembered Pooh's remark as they'd left Northways: *You may have a dicey time. They can get rather rough when they're asking questions of someone they don't trust. The hardest thing about this job will be remembering that unless your life itself is in danger, you're not to fight back.*

Christopher stood in an open patch and listened to them thunder forward in the wood. He was wrapped in a cheap mackintosh he'd bought for the meeting so that if this didn't work out and he managed to get away, he'd drop the mac in a dustbin and they'd have trouble finding him in a crowd. But if it came to that it would mean everything had gone wrong and there'd be nothing left but to try to save his skin. The objective wasn't to escape from the Germans; quite the reverse.

We want you to turn traitor, Christopher.

He remembered the wry face he'd made. Then he'd flaunted his hard grin at Mr Churchill and replied, *That might be a pleasure, sir* — looking pointedly at Owl to show what he meant.

It was a grey Irish morning, a trifle misty and there was a hint of rain to come, but it was warm enough. They were right on top of him now. Finally two Germans appeared before him and one of them had his hand in his coat pocket and with the hand, Christopher knew, there had to be a pistol. The others weren't in sight but he could hear them getting into positions, surrounding him. He made a show of anxious unease — *Remember, you're purporting to be an amateur at this.* He flung both hands high in the air to show them he was unarmed. *Be snide but be scared. All right? They understand fear, it makes them feel at home. Don't overdo it but let them know they've put a fright into you.*

The two men were walking towards him: a thin man in a black leather coat down to his ankles and a dark slouch hat, American style, the brim turned down all round; and a stocky fellow with red hair and a grey tweed topcoat. The thin man had the cruel and furtive face of a criminal to whom safety had become dubious and every encounter a possible trap; the stocky red-haired one had the sort of easy-going calm that came from having seen nearly everything and been unimpressed by it. That one, he was sure, was the boss. Christopher didn't recognize the crest embroidered on the reddish tie but it looked regimental. If the Germans went in for that sort of thing.

He heard the others stirring in the wood behind him and to either side; he realized then that it was deliberate: they wanted him to know he was locked in.

The red-haired fellow said in a mild voice, 'We'll search you for weapons if you don't mind.' His English was good but his accent gave away his origins.

'Go ahead, old boy. I've a pen-knife in the left trouser pocket — don't let it throw you into a fit.' Christopher spoke in a languid public-school drawl, one eyebrow arched.

The thin man advanced and began to pat him all round, roughly sliding his hands along Christopher's clothing — there was something unpleasant about it, nearly perverted; he had the nasty feeling the German was enjoying it a bit too much. Finally he stood back and spoke to the other man, something brief in German.

The red-haired man had a high wheezy voice. 'Rudolf Breucher.'

'You can call me Smith.' *Don't make it too easy for them — make them think they're having to work for it. They trust things more if they have to find them out for themselves.*

Shaking the German's hand was like gripping a freshly caught trout.

'It's not my name, of course, but it's the name you'll know me by.' Christopher had practised the supercilious nasal drawl until Pooh had approved it. He wore a droop-lidded expression of bored upper-class arrogance. 'Before you consign me to the churchyard I suggest you listen to what I have to say.'

Breucher was amused. 'Very well, Mr Smith. Speak.'

'I'm a leading coder in the Royal Navy. Rather junior, obviously, but I'm in signals and I've got top security clearance.'

'I see. What is your SDO?'

'I'm at 9 Princes' Gate — Headquarters Combined Operations.'

Breucher had tried to trip him on that one. SDO: Signals Distributing Office.

He saw the significance of it register. Breucher was impressed. 'Are you on leave?'

'Yes. I've seven days.'

'Who told you to come to me?'

'Really, old boy, use your loaf. The address of your legation's hardly a secret. I fired a message through a dark window – I assumed someone would come. I didn't have your name, did I.'

Breucher's the one who'll respond, Pooh had told him. *They always send Breucher. That's why we're sending you out to Dublin rather than, say, Madrid or Lisbon. Breucher's the best of that lot – he never says a word about anything to anyone, got the tightest lip in the Abwehr.*

'Who provided you with the flare pistol?'

'Well actually they're flogging them in Piccadilly Circus. You know – brollies, the *Daily Mirror* and Very pistols?'

Breucher glared a bit and Christopher let his eyes wander away. *Remember – supercilious but not very brave; you crack easily when challenged.* 'Actually,' he said, 'we did a few hours' training on trinkets like that. I helped myself to a few of them from stores – thought they might come in handy. I do hope you won't turn me in for pilfering HM Government property.' He smiled, trying to make it a weak smile.

Breucher let the silence run on; it was supposed to unnerve him, he thought, and it was having that effect. Christopher cleared his throat. 'Look, I don't intend to tell you very much – I've got to protect myself, haven't I? It's no good prying into the sordid details of my motives and that sort of rot. Let's just say I've got the sort of tastes that one can hardly support on a leading coder's pay. If I don't tell you anything about myself it's better for both of us and anyway I'm not asking you to believe anything about me – it's the information I've got that you'll want to be interested in, and if it proves worthless you needn't pay for it. Fair enough?'

'What information?'

'Well now, old boy, that wants a bit of negotiation, doesn't it? What am I offered?'

It made Breucher smile. It wasn't a cruel smile; he was simply jaded – he'd seen it all before. 'Tell me, Mr Smith. Doesn't it trouble you to betray your country?'

'King and country – the Union Jack, Britannia rules the waves, the sun shall never set, etcetera etcetera. Right. I dare say I shall live with it. Money soothes the fevered conscience, don't you know.'

'I see.' Breucher was clever: he gave nothing away, he only smiled and let you talk on.

Christopher said, 'You think I may have been sent out by British intelligence to smoke you blokes out or to plant false information. Well I haven't, but there's nothing I can say that will prove it. The only way you're to know whether I'm genuine is to put me to the test.'

Be mysterious – remember you're a clever snot and you're trying to protect yourself. Don't play your trump card until late in the game.

'You could kill me here on the spot, I suppose, but I'm taking that risk because I credit you with good sense. You've nothing to lose by taking me on consignment, as it were. If my information proves false you can always murder me when I return to pick up my payment. If it proves true I shall want a good deal of money as an encouragement to take the risks again.'

'What information?'

'They're laying on a cross-Channel excursion. To one of the French ports.'

'An invasion of the Continent?'

'No. A raid on a port.'

'Parachutists?'

'No, it's to be amphibious.'

'What port?'

'I haven't got that yet.'

'Calais, perhaps?'

'Haven't the foggiest. It hasn't been sent through yet. I think they've changed the target once or twice. It was laid on originally for some time in July before I was brought up to Combined Operations but they've postponed it twice – unfavourable weather the first time, and then they were ready to go on with it but by chance a flight of your bombers went after some of the shipping. They had Montgomery in command but they've taken him off it. It was even cancelled a few weeks ago but then they started it up again.'

'Without something more concrete, Mr Smith, this information is worthless.'

'Once we've made a mutually satisfactory agreement I'll get the rest of the information to you.'

'What arrangement would you consider satisfactory?'

'Shall we say ten thousand pounds? Five-pound notes would do.'

'Payable after we've had time to judge the accuracy of the information?'

'Right.'

'You're trusting us, then?'

'If you don't pay for the first lot you won't get any more. If you want to call that trust, you're free to do so.' Christopher showed his teeth. 'When you chaps take over England I shall want a nice spot in the puppet government, of course.'

The thin chap in the black leather coat had been listening to it all but there was no way of telling whether he understood English. Abruptly he spoke to Breucher: a quick burst of words delivered in an emotionless rasp of a voice. Breucher replied in German and then said to Christopher, 'Herr Kinski doesn't seem to have been particularly charmed by your performance.'

Christopher glanced archly at Herr Kinski. 'Sod him.'

There'll be Black Shirts hanging about, Pooh had told him, *but you must leave it to Breucher to deal with them. You don't want to get mixed up in those ludicrous rivalries between the Abwehr and the SS.*

A flat pistol appeared in Kinski's hand. 'Come along, Mr Smith.' It was thick but it was English.

'Oh, I say, that's hardly sporting.'

'We are not on the playing fields.' Kinski flicked the pistol to one side. 'Move along.'

Christopher let his anxiety show when he turned quickly towards Breucher. 'Where's he taking me?'

'To see to your comfort while we await results of an inquiry. I'm afraid he's quite right. You'll have to resign yourself to it.'

'I say, old boy, I'm due back in London in a week's time.'

'You'll be back by then. If you're not you'll have had a road accident—delayed in hospital. We'll send the information along to London from a hospital in Ulster.'

'You can't do that. You don't know my name.'

'We'll know it by then,' Breucher said. 'Come along now.'

The bedroom was comfortable enough but they'd bolted the shutters closed across the windows. The house was some miles southwest of Dublin, a large late-Victorian house set back behind stone walls, farms all round.

They hadn't quite given him the run of it but he wasn't handcuffed and if he'd wanted to make a break for it he'd have had ample chances.

Breucher wasn't around much; neither was Kinski. His keepers were three Abwehr men, only one of whom spoke enough English for conversation. They wore mufti and seemed to have nothing against Christopher; several times they invited him to play cards in the drawing room. He wasn't very good at cards and as his German was almost non-existent he didn't understand most of their conversation, but he was happy enough for the company; he wasn't cut out for solitary confinement.

Breucher reappeared forty-eight hours after his incarceration. 'Are you comfortable here?'

'It's not Claridge's, is it.'

'But then neither is it Wormwood Scrubs.'

'I'm playing your ruddy game, aren't I? I don't have to like it. It's my first leave in a year—I could be in a feather bed with a warm companion now. A bit more of this and I'll start raising the price of things. You might tell that to your bloody superiors.'

'I won't keep you too much longer. The instructions went out yesterday and I should have the replies by tomorrow.'

'Where's your chum Kinski?'

'I've no idea.' By his tone Breucher didn't care to know. *They hate one another like cats and dogs*, Pooh had said, *the Abwehr and the SS. The Abwehr are gentlemen, you see. They're professionals. The SS are common thugs.* Breucher said. 'I'll try to ensure you don't see much of Herr Kinski.'

'Every silver lining has its cloud,' Christopher agreed.

It didn't amuse Breucher; perhaps his command of idiom

wasn't good enough. He said, 'We're going to find out who you are, you know. You might save me the trouble.'

'Sorry about that but I'd rather you had to find it out on your own. In case, you know, they become suspicious later on. No-one can give testimony that I told you my name. You may have come up with the wrong identification on me.'

'I doubt that.'

'A court might have to believe it. Reasonable doubt and all that.'

'You're an odd fish, Mr Smith.'

'All I want's me money.' He said it in a Cockney accent and grinned unpleasantly at Breucher.

Breucher disregarded it. 'A word of advice. Once we've learnt your identity we intend to keep it to ourselves. The intelligence service, I mean. It won't be bandied about the other services. Don't assume that because one German knows who you are, all Germans know it. Don't give your name to people like Kinski.'

'I'm not giving my name to anyone at all, am I?'

'Just keep it in mind,' Breucher adjured. Then he left.

Once you're in Abwehr custody you're all right because Canaris doesn't give the time of day to Himmler. But you must make sure that when Breucher learns your identity the SS doesn't learn it. It's those early moments that are the crucial ones. If there's an SS man in earshot and you think he's got your name from Breucher you'll have to find some way to kill him without the others knowing. The SS have no finesse. They'd spread your name all over Berlin and it wouldn't be long before it got back to London – then if one side didn't kill you the other would.

His jailers locked him in that night. He reviewed what else they'd told him about this job.

The Germans had a small network of spies throughout Britain, Pooh told him. Virtually all of them had been 'turned' – they were under control of British MI-5 supervisors who'd given them the choice of becoming double agents or being hanged for espionage. 'Breucher will send signals down the apparatus and someone in London will get instructions to pry through things and find out if there's a leading coder who fits your description in Combined Ops HQ. Given that clue they'll be able to root out your records and the report will go back to Breucher.'

Christopher had been a bit confused. 'I'm not in the Royal Navy, sir. Peter Hamilton is. What records are they going to find?'

'Don't worry — we cooked up suitable records for you. You're Leading Coder Creighton now.'

'I don't like letting them have my real name.'

'It can't be helped, Christopher. It won't be bandied about, I shouldn't think. With luck only Breucher and Canaris will know your name. But it's standard Abwehr practice to assign code-names to their agents. You'll go into the network under a code-name of their choosing. It's in their own best interests, isn't it — they don't want someone riffling through their files and finding out the real names of their agents in England. I don't suppose they realize we already know who all their agents are.'

Now he had them all suspicious but that was all right. There was no way to penetrate them without provoking scepticism. The idea was to play the game strictly according to the visible rules and not play tricks on them: *Don't resist them and don't try to confuse them. Act straightforward, even arrogant: you've got something to sell — they can buy it or not, it's up to them. Of course if they don't buy it that means they're on to you and then you'll have to get out as best you can.*

The interview with Mr Churchill had been very brief this time.

The Prime Minister had looked up from the desk and not risen to his feet. 'I thought it had better come from me personally, just to set you off, so that you can be certain it's not one of Uncle John's dastardly tricks.' Mr Churchill had glanced blandly towards Owl and then come back to Christopher: 'You're the spoilt child of a rich but miserly surgeon. You're disgusted with your trivial position and the few shillings of your naval pay — you're selling secrets to the Germans solely for the money. You're a traitor. Be good enough to play the part with conviction and dash. Now I've a good deal of work to do — Uncle John will fill in the lurid details.'

Then Mr Churchill had got up, come round, and put his arm on his shoulder. 'Christopher.'

'Sir?'

'Guard above all this new reputation of yours as a traitorous young man. For if anyone should become proud of you, you are lost.'

There was a strong wind but the plane had loud engines and he heard it before he saw it. Breucher took his elbow and they went running out across the field. He didn't like this at all but Kinski was back there with his hand in the pocket of the leather coat and his face made it clear that if Christopher tried to bolt he'd be shot down before he'd run ten feet.

They'd sprung the surprise without warning – collected him at the house, bundled him into a car and brought him here without any explanation; Breucher had been waiting and Kinski was half in the shadows, hovering. Christopher didn't know how much Kinski knew. And he had no chance to find out. As soon as he'd stepped out of the car, Breucher had gripped his arm. Breucher's thumb pinched the nerve just above the elbow and Christopher had shaken himself loose, letting his anger show, but Breucher had simply told him to come along and then the plane had appeared and now they were climbing into it – a twin-engine French job with civilian markings. Breucher pulled the ladder up, secured the cabin door and said, '*Allez*,' and in a moment they were bumping along the grass and Christopher had a glimpse of Kinski's black coat disappearing into the back seat of a car.

The engines went up to high throttle and the noise covered nearly everything. Breucher had to lean close and speak directly into Christopher's ear: 'You may as well relax. This will take time.'

'Where are we going?'

'At the moment our route is confidential.'

'You chat up a storm, don't you, Breucher?'

'Call me Rudi. We seem destined to be together for a while. What do your friends call you? Kit? Chris?'

'Never mind.'

He was curt because he wanted to think it out. It was Kinski he was concerned with. The only thing to do was to find out whether Kinski had found out things that could hurt him. And the only way to do that, he supposed, was to soften his arrogant attitude towards Breucher and try to find out whether Kinski had dropped any hints. Breucher wasn't offensive; he was merely the enemy. It shouldn't be hard to do, but when he looked at Breucher he thought of death. It made him wonder if he would spend the rest of his life hating Germans.

Breucher had called him by name, or near enough to it; they'd found the information in London, then. But precisely what information had they found? Pooh had been very confident that MI-5 had turned all the Abwehr people in London into double agents but the Germans weren't amateurs. Maybe the Abwehr merely wanted MI-5 to *think* they'd turned all the German agents.

They'd found his records all right; but had they also found out the records had been planted? That could be the reason for this flight, he thought. Maybe they wanted to get him to Germany for interrogation at the end of a hypodermic needle. Then he thought: if it was an arrest they'd have put him under restraint of some kind – handcuffs, drugs. There wasn't anyone else on the plane, just Breucher and the air crew; and apparently Breucher wasn't even armed.

Finally Christopher said, 'Look, you're right, we may as well be civil to each other. One gets a bit strung up, you know?'

'Yes. We've got a journey ahead of us and I thought it might be better all round not to make it unpleasant for ourselves.'

He learnt a bit about Breucher. He'd been a police detective in Wolfsburg, with a good record in the German navy in the 1914–18 war, and when Admiral Canaris had taken charge of the Abwehr in 1935 there'd been a drive to recruit ex-naval officers with police experience. Breucher spoke freely enough of himself, although without an excess of vanity; he was amiable and he gave away nothing significant. 'I'm sure it's all in the records in London in any case. You can't run a network under their noses for two and a half years and expect them not to have built up a dossier on you. They know who I am. If they were to order my assassination they'd have to start again from square one, not knowing who'd been sent in to take my place. That's what makes me reasonably confident they haven't sent you over merely to get me alone and garrotte me.' Breucher rolled his eyes towards Christopher to show his amusement.

Christopher said, ' "They" haven't sent me anywhere. If they even knew I was on this plane – '

'Never fear. Your secret is quite safe with me.'

'With you, perhaps. But what about the others? I don't trust your friend Kinski any further than I could throw Buckingham Palace.'

'Kinski knows nothing that could harm you.'

'I'd feel better if I could be sure of that.'

'If you knew a bit more about the structure of the German services you'd feel confident enough.'

It was as near a straight answer as he was going to get out of Breucher and it satisfied him. Pooh had explained with some care that the SS didn't have agents in England; espionage was the Abwehr's job. The Abwehr had its own codes, which MI-5 believed had not been broken by the SS or the Gestapo. Christopher deduced that if MI-5 had turned the Abwehr's agents, it must have obtained their individual codes.

Pooh had briefed him in detail on the Abwehr and its chief, Admiral Wilhelm Franz Canaris. *You'll do better if you know the chaps with whom you're dealing. Canaris is an odd bird and his eccentricities have communicated themselves to some of his subordinates. It helps to know how those people think.*

Right then. Canaris. He's about fifty-five but he looks older. Born in the Ruhr. When he was a child everyone called him Willy. I doubt anyone calls him that any more. Possibly even his wife calls him Admiral. Passed out of the naval academy in Kiel and made a lieutenant on the crusier 'Dresden' in time for the 1914–18 war.

The ship had fought in the Battle of the Falklands and been scuttled; its survivors had been interned in Chile according to the laws of neutrality but Canaris had escaped, swimming and then rowing from his island prison to the mainland. He'd obtained false papers and made his way back to Europe, bluffing his way through British border controls and slipping into neutral Holland. He'd arrived back in Hamburg in late 1915. That was when he'd been assigned to naval intelligence. He served as a spymaster in Madrid and Genoa. Legend had it that he became Mata Hari's lover, then recruited her, then had a quarrel with her and denounced her to the French, who shot her. *Probably apocryphal*, Pooh had said, *but it points up something about him. He's got a way of changing his mind.* The Italians had arrested him as a spy and put him in prison but once again he'd made a daring escape: he murdered the prison priest, donned his cassock and walked out.

He's got a ruthless imagination, you see. He doesn't do the expected things.

After the armistice he'd joined the staff of the Weimar ministry but as soon as he came to know the bureaucrats he became contemptuous of them and began to betray them to the navy – political conspiracies, secret re-armament, efforts to restore the Kaiser. He supplied the conspirators clandestinely from government stores and kept the rightists appraised of the secret doings of the Weimar cabinet. As a result he became a favourite of the admirals and involved himself deeply in virtually all the officer corps plots against the Weimar government, of which there were several.

He's not a Nazi. Not a party member, that is. He doesn't like the trappings of organization, you see. He never wears his decorations, for example, and wears his uniform only when protocol demands it. Otherwise one usually finds him dressed in something more appropriate to a tramp.

Then Pooh had said, *This may be important so remember it. Canaris is not a Nazi and we are not certain whether he is even loyal to Hitler. He's loyal to Germany, however, and that's what you need to remember about him.*

At the time, Christopher hadn't pondered a great deal on the significance of that distinction.

Canaris had been a captain when he'd been given command of the Abwehr in 1935. Grand Admiral Raeder, who was his commander in the navy, disliked and distrusted him; Canaris only got the appointment because Raeder had been instructed to give it to him. It seemed Canaris had flattered Hitler sycophantically in a magazine article he'd written. *Whether he meant any of it is open to question, of course, but if he was looking for favouritism from the chancellery he got it. Most of the top Nazis loathe and detest him – Ribbentrop, Himmler, that lot. He's only had two friends at court, really – Heydrich, who seemed to like him, and Field-Marshal Wilhelm Keitel, who was his direct superior in the old OKW High Command.*

Keitel was still on the General Staff, of course, and he served as a buffer for Canaris; Keitel was a Nazi but most of Canaris's friends were not, except the late Reinhard Heydrich, the Butcher, and that was mainly because of family connections by marriage; Canaris had cultivated him simply to keep a channel open to information from Hitler's headquarters.

One of these days his arrogance will displease the Führer and they'll be stringing Willy Canaris to a gallows but in the meantime he's the chap we must deal with over there.

Deal with – Pooh nearly made it sound as if Canaris were a British agent.

The plane was on a southeasterly heading – possibly to Lisbon. Somewhere on the Continent he was to be interrogated by someone too important to come to him. If they were taking Christopher that seriously then they were going to vet him with extreme care and he'd better play his trump card *now* to give Breucher time to get used to the idea.

He said, 'We're not going to Germany by any chance, are we?'

'Why?'

'I might look up an old friend there.'

'You have a friend in Germany?'

'In Berlin, I imagine, these days. He's quite important in the government.'

'Is that so.' Breucher was interested but determined not to show it.

'In point of fact, old chap, he's your foreign minister.'

Breucher's eyes crinkled a bit; he was ready to smile as soon as Christopher showed he was joking. But Christopher said, 'Herr von Ribbentrop and my father are old friends. They were at school together. I saw the foreign minister only two years ago, in fact, in Belgium. We had a nice chat.'

Breucher scratched his jaw. 'You are saying, then, that Herr Joachim von Ribbentrop can identify you and confirm your bona fides?'

'Well, of course, old chap. You know his reputation for never forgetting anyone. I'm sure he remembers me very well.'

'If this is a bluff it may be your last one. You understand that.'

It confirmed something he'd wanted to know. If Breucher

was prepared to call his bluff it meant they were going where Ribbentrop could expect to be found: Berlin.

Berlin, he thought. He felt excitement.

How many English boys your age do you suppose have this opportunity in the Year of Our Lord Nineteen Forty-two?

Chapter Ten

It was called the *Fuchsbau* – the Fox Lair – a massive grey building in the Turpitzufer. The car brought them along the Reichpietsch Ufer, between the Tiergarten and the canal; Breucher pointed out the sights to him, not without pride. Here and there he saw damage from British bombs.

There was a heavy double staircase but Breucher took him to a very small lift and they were detained for a while there by an officer who examined Breucher's papers. Christopher listened with some care to find out whether Breucher was going to mention his name. Breucher didn't. Score one for the old boy.

White-bloused women flitted through corridors, most of them carrying papers or folders. Then going up in the tiny creaking lift Breucher said, 'A rare privilege for an Englishman. You know where you are, don't you?'

'Abwehr headquarters, isn't it?'

Breucher showed him into a smallish room at the back of the top floor and pointed to an armchair. 'Wait here.'

There was a sleepy official at the desk and Breucher conferred with him; the man's eyes came around towards Christopher like the slow-swinging muzzles of naval gun turrets and rested upon him while Breucher knocked at a farther door and went through it. Christopher put both hands on the arms of the chair and kept them there; he tried a grin on the guard but it had no effect.

He always feels the cold – wears a hat and coat nearly all the time, even indoors in the summertime. A very odd bird our Willy. In strange ways a very strict moralist – nearly a mystic. How he's survived this long in that key job is a mystery. He could be purged any time. He's brilliant, talkative, a very good cook and he loves those bloody dogs of his. Got a reputation as a 'master' linguist – the legend is he speaks about eleven languages fluently – but actually the propaganda machine's been at work there. He encourages the legends, of course. That's why we don't know how much of the mythology is true – Mata

Hari, for example. But I can tell you this much – he's got a clever mind and fantastic intuition. He's a formidable bastard.

Breucher summoned him. Christopher went through the door. The office contained a black leather sofa, a huge wall map of the world and a large desk littered with porcelain and glass trinkets. The man behind the desk looked as if he might have been assembled out of mismatched parts rather like Dr Frankenstein's monster – small, flaccid, fragile, wrinkled. Stringy tendons held the collar of his shirt away from his neck. His hair sprouted in tufts, whitish-grey, and his face was ruddy. A crumpled felt hat adorned the corner of his desk. He was wearing a disreputable overcoat.

'Canaris,' the man said, and motioned Christopher to be seated. Then abruptly he said: 'Why do you want to do it? Why are you betraying your country?'

'That's my affair, isn't it?'

Canaris said something in German to Breucher after which Breucher withdrew from the room.

'I'm honoured,' Christopher said, 'by all this attention from on high.'

'Perhaps I ought to caution you that you're not in a country where sarcasm and an upper-class sneer will help you.' Canaris's voice was thin and catarrhal.

Canaris poked about the desk top, moving things aimlessly – a glass swan from here to there; as though it were a chess piece. He appeared vague, absent-minded, inattentive.

Eeyore.

The code names were only for cipher reports and he didn't think he'd have a chance to make any. Rabbit was Adolf Hitler. Rabbit's friends were the Abwehr; Rabbit's relations the SS; Ribbentrop was Small. Looking at Canaris he thought they'd got it right – Eeyore: his appearance was a good match for Milne's donkey.

It was as if Canaris were reading his mind: 'We're assigning you a code name.'

Christopher stared at him.

'We've decided on Aeneas. It's arbitrary. Do you object?'

'No. Why should I? So long as my name isn't bandied about.'

'You will go into the records as Aeneas and your designation is R-19. Do not write it – remember it.'

Aeneas. R-19.

Two dachshunds snuffled into the room, claws clicking as they scrambled for a purchase on the polished floor. Canaris had a fitful way of smiling; his eyes seemed oddly vulnerable and candid when he reached down to lift one of the dogs into his lap. He let his arm trail, scratching the other dog behind the ears.

Canaris said, 'Tell me about yourself.'

Most of it was the truth because it was easiest to remember and it could be checked. Mainly Canaris seemed interested in his relations with his father and Christopher stayed with the facts except for the lie about his father having cut off his allowance and disinherited him.

'They can have their ruddy wars,' he concluded. 'It's a "me-first" world, isn't it?'

Quietly, without hostility, Canaris said, 'I don't believe you.'

'I can't help that, can I?'

'If your information is false the money will be no good to you.'

'I know.'

Canaris was watching him obliquely. Christopher said, 'My terms are these. I want. . .'

'*Nein.*' Canaris lifted the dog from his lap and set it down beside its companion. 'It's not for you to make terms. It's for you to accept them. You've asked ten thousand pounds. That is acceptable but the time and method of payment will be determined by us. Now you will please give me the information about this reconnaissance in force.'

'As soon as I have it.'

'No. You have it now. You're a clever young man, and only a stupid one would have come forward prematurely before he had something to sell.'

The chair in which Christopher sat was right up against the map on the wall. He twisted his neck to look up at it. *When it's clear they're calling your bluff then give it to them. Until then, hold back because the longer you keep contact the more you can learn.*

They'd wound him up and set him running but now the decisions were his to make. He said, 'They're coming over the Channel.'

'Where?'

He put the tip of his finger on the map. 'Bang across the Channel. Dieppe.'

'The date?'

'19 August.'

The study in Ribbentrop's house was luxurious, reeking of plunder. The foreign minister stood in a smoking jacket beneath a Renaissance sculpture; he had acknowledged Breucher's presence with a stiff word or two but it was clear he considered Breucher beneath him, a servant of sorts, on a level with the armed man who'd accompanied them and who stood just behind Christopher's shoulder now with his hand on the Walther discreetly concealed in his pocket.

Ribbentrop studied Christopher's face and for a terrible moment Christopher thought he hadn't recognized him. He put on his most charming boyish smile. 'Foreign Minister.'

Evidently it was the smile that made contact with Ribbentrop's memory. His face changed. 'The young man who was so bold as to tease an ambassador. And how is your father?'

'Very well, I suppose, sir.'

'You suppose?'

'We've had a bit of a falling out. We don't quite see eye to eye regarding the outcome of the war.'

Ribbentrop nodded slowly to indicate his wisdom. 'Indeed. Well, fathers have been known to be in error at times, haven't they? I'm glad you've come to us. When the war is won you may find yourself in a position of some importance among the new English Hitler Youth Corps.'

'Thank you, sir. I look forward to it.'

Ribbentrop said, 'In 1937 Winston Churchill warned me not to underrate the English. He was quite right of course. They are one of the great Aryan peoples and you are a splendid example to us.' Then a quick glance towards Breucher. 'If you have any difficulty with our intelligence gentlemen I'm sure you'll let me know of it.'

It was addressed to Christopher but intended for Breucher. Ribbentrop hated Admiral Canaris but he knew the Führer still had faith in his intelligence chief; fearful of offending Hitler, he tolerated the Abwehr but he seldom let an opportunity pass to get a dig in.

Breucher said something in German and Ribbentrop snapped a reply to it; then the foreign minister turned and offered his hand to Christopher. 'I'm afraid I must dress for a dinner engagement. It's been very good to see you again. I hope you'll call on me in your subsequent visits to Berlin.'

In the car Christopher said to Breucher, 'What was that you said to him?'

'I reminded him of the security around you. You're a most valued agent – we don't want him dropping your name at diplomatic parties, do we?'

Christ. He hadn't even thought of that.

'I think he'll keep it to himself,' Breucher said. 'He takes a delight in conspiracies.'

Let us pray.

'It would seem you've passed the test. But you must not expect to be forgiven your trespasses because of your foreigner's ignorance. You are on trial here and if I were you I should put away your supercilious public-school ways and toe the line. Perhaps you will see the point if I mention that during my last trip to Berlin one of my colleagues, a man who had been a good friend of both mine and the admiral's, was brought up on civilian charges after he killed a man he knew to be an American agent. Perhaps he was merely being zealous but he'd had no orders to kill the man and when he was condemned by the criminal tribunal Admiral Canaris did not lift a finger to save him. The man had been convicted legally, you see, and was guilty of the crime. The admiral does not tolerate such things.'

Christopher found himself listening for inflections in Breucher's voice. When a man spoke a language other than his own you sometimes could not be certain of the subtleties of his meaning. Breucher had an ironic sense of humour; he seemed obliquely to be warning Christopher. It was as if they'd seen through the falsehood but they still wanted to find out what he was up to.

It was sticky; it had been, ever since the plane had collected him in Ireland. No-one had prepared him for that. Breucher and his people could make any number of mistakes, but if *he* made just one mistake he'd be dead.

But the real detonator might be something over which he had no control; the quality of the information he'd given the Germans. *You are to give them Dieppe*, Owl had said. *You're to tell them the date and the forces involved*, and he'd laid out the details for Christopher to memorize. *If anything goes wrong*, Pooh had added – by which, he now realized, Pooh had meant perhaps a false alarm at Dieppe or an amphibious Allied landing somewhere else on the French coast – *you'll have to rely on your own resources to get out*. Then Pooh had given him safe houses and contacts in Dublin, but he wasn't in Dublin now; he was in Berlin and none of them had counted on that.

It came down to the unhappy realization that they'd told him what to say to the Germans but they hadn't entirely persuaded him that it wasn't misinformation designed to mislead the Germans into defending the wrong target. If that was the case Christopher was in real trouble. Certainly both Pooh and Owl had assured him that the information was indeed accurate, but the reason for betraying it to the enemy baffled Christopher.

They'd shown him copies of the actual signals and orders he was to describe to the Germans. They'd shown him the table of organization for the raid: five thousand Canadian soldiers, one thousand British troops, fifty American Rangers. *Purpose of operation: reconnaissance in force with the aim of seizing and holding a Channel port suitable for the accommodation of incoming troops and supplies for a full-scale Second Front invasion of the Continent of Europe. Unit commanders will keep in mind that the incursion is designed not to hold the beach-head indefinitely, but rather to secure it only long enough to test the ability of new LCTs to land new model Vauxhall 'Churchill' battle tanks across beaches, to ascertain feasibility of capturing a major port by frontal assault, to test tactics and techniques of coordinating combined arms in amphibious landings, to determine efficacy of air forces for overhead support and cover, and to appraise naval systems for delivering and covering both the infantry and armoured forces and the invasion fleet itself. Second, raid is designed to test strength and effectiveness of enemy defences. Enemy strength and capability are to be*

studied carefully by unit commanders for subsequent use in pre-
paring Second Front invasion planning.

'The irony is,' Pooh had added, 'we laid this on at first to convince the Americans — but they've come round already. Still,
we'll carry it out.'

But it was possible they'd prepared the documents for his
benefit alone so that he could describe them under German
interrogation. It was possible they'd changed a vital element in
the copies they'd showed him: changed 'Calais' to 'Dieppe', for
instance. The two words had the same number of letters and it
would have been easy to lay in a strip of white paper, type six
letters on it and make a photocopy. Or they might have changed
'29 August' to '19 August'. Anything like that to throw the
Germans off and lull them away from the real target or the real
target date.

What was the date now? The fourteenth — Friday.

In five days' time, he thought, he'd find out. It might be the
last thing he ever found out. For it was clear that Canaris meant
to keep him here until the nineteenth.

Owl's room on the second floor at Storey's Gate was number
sixty; there was no label on the door. He was at his desk later
than usual; the building was silent; he awaited Pooh, who was
in his box in the Albert Hall listening to the London Philhar-
monic play Brahms under Muir Mathieson's baton.

A fortnight ago Owl had tried to put the problem before
Winston but the PM was preoccupied with his difficulties in the
Western Desert and had no interest in German radar. Then
Winston had taken off in a bomber to Gibraltar and sub-
sequently on to Cairo to visit the troops who were in the field
against Rommel. He'd met with Smuts and Alexander and had
waffled for several days trying to decide whether to remove
Auchinleck from command of the desert armies. No-one knew
when he'd return to London. When Winston went out to the
front he was drawn to the flash and stench of battle like a moth
to a flame. He'd finally torn himself away after relieving the
Auk and replacing him with Alexander, with Montgomery in
command of the 8th Army; now the PM had flown on to
Moscow in an LB-30 Liberator bomber to meet Stalin and
Molotov. In a day or two he would fly to Teheran and then back

to Cairo to visit Monty's 8th Army in the front lines. It might be another ten days or a fortnight before the PM returned to his job, and Owl was disgusted with him.

Winston's parting shot had been a killer; he'd ordered the RAF to stand down its planned heavy-bomber coverage at Dieppe the next week. 'The bombardment is cancelled,' he'd announced, arguing at length that it was ridiculous to bomb a city to rubble, blocking the streets with debris, and then land tanks that had to use those streets. It was all quite plausible but Owl had the feeling Winston was more interested in having the new Churchill tanks acquit themselves well than he was in putting on a proper show at Dieppe.

Winston hadn't budged. He was delighted at having the new machines named after him. It was only his due, he'd insisted, since he'd been responsible for the introduction of the tank into modern warfare in the Great War. The Churchill model had been introduced in 1939 and had proved a disastrous failure on nearly all counts. Winston had had them redesigned from the treads up and Vauxhall had been delivering them at a fast rate; now the PM was anxious to see it prove itself in combat. There was still uncertainty among the armoured commanders whether the Churchill was of any real use. It had been designed on the assumption that this war would be like the last one and that a tank's primary usefulness would be in crossing trenches and craters; it was built for crushing weight rather than speed or manoeuvrability. At best, downhill on smooth ground, the Churchill could make fifteen miles per hour, and there was some question as to its mechanical dependability. It weighed nearly forty tons and probably would collapse certain types of bridges if it tried to cross them.

Owl had seen a few trials and been unimpressed: the little two-pounder turret gun wasn't much good for anything except punching holes in plaster walls, and the three-inch howitzer mounted in the front plate had no traverse field of fire; you had to turn the entire tank to aim it.

You couldn't very well tell him to his face that he had an astoundingly superficial command of practicalities, or that his lofty disdain for details could be the cause of catastrophes. The tank, the standing-down of bomber cover – they both came to the same thing: Winston moving his pieces about the board, not even telling his commanders what he was up to, playfully experimenting with no thought to the personnel or equipment or transport or time scale or even the weather.

Conversely it was a matter of principle with Winston that a commander didn't sacrifice men unnecessarily because he might need them later. That had been the obstacle at the outset — 'Rutter' — in persuading him to give Dieppe a go and they'd only brought him round to it by impressing on him the tentative nature of the operation. It was to be a brief raid and the troops were to retire quickly before the enemy could chew them up too badly. But of course the outcome would depend on their pluck. It was to be hoped they would remember their orders and not try to be bloody heroes.

Metcalf came in. 'What's on?'

'The boffins are insisting on this radar rubbish. We've got to deal with it — there's not much time left.'

'How?'

'The man's a civilian, of course,' Owl said. 'They want him to get into Dieppe and examine the German coastal radar. It's risky because it means our lads will have to capture an installation intact and hold it long enough for the boffin to run through his drill. The best estimate they're able to give me is six or seven hours. He'll be laden with equipment and he's got to be an expert in British radar, which of course is a good deal superior to the German.'

'We can't afford to have our man fall into Jerry's hands.'

'Quite.'

'Provide him with a crack unit to guard him, then.'

Owl said, 'That's all very well but suppose they're overwhelmed by an enemy counter-attack?'

'I see what you mean.'

'I think we shall want Roberts for this one.'

'He's in Marseilles.'

'Bring him out then.'

'Not much time,' Pooh observed.

'Just do it. When he comes in tell him his orders are to kill our radar boffin if he looks like falling into Jerry's hands. Roberts will do it without fuss.'

'That's rather tough.'

'Can you suggest an alternative?'

'No.'

'You'd better nip round to Signals, then. And none of this is for Dickie Mountbatten's ears.'

Metcalf reached for his coat. He looked unhappy but there was nothing for it. He turned at the door. 'There's been no word from Christopher.'

'I know. It's possible they've wiped him off the board.'

'Blast.'

'Possible, I said, but not likely. The lad's got an astonishing talent for landing on his feet.'

'Perhaps – but the odds have to go against him sometime.'

Breucher studied him across the breakfast table and when Christopher looked up, Breucher smiled. 'Don't tell me you're alarmed.'

'Suppose there's bad weather and they have to postpone it?'

Breucher shook his head. 'Then I'll be sorry and you'll be dead. If the Allies don't come to Dieppe tomorrow then I can't save you. Nobody can. It's the Führer's order.'

They were talking in French because that was the cover they'd given him and he didn't speak German and they were in the crowded canteen of the Fuchsbau with Germans all round. Christopher's papers made him out to be Vichy French, a minor foreign office clerk; it would survive casual inquiry because he spoke French well enough and he could be passed off as an Abwehr agent who'd been spying on the Vichy government and brought to Berlin for debriefing.

'Finish your coffee,' Breucher said. 'We've a plane to catch.'

'Dieppe?'

'Naturally. We'll see for ourselves how reliable your information is. Obviously for your sake I hope it's authentic.'

In the car on the way to the aerodrome he tried again: 'Look, old boy, any invasion can be rescheduled at the last minute if something goes wrong.'

'Let us trust, then, that nothing does.'

It was still daylight at eight o'clock when they were collected off the plane by four men in leather greatcoats and driven round the back of the city in a heavy rattling Panzerwagen.

'You're important, you see,' Breucher said drily. 'We're giving you the best protection we can.'

'Against what?'

'Partisans, Resistance, whatever. Your life is too valuable to be risked casually.'

'Now that's a comfort.'

'How old are you?'

'You've had the reports.'

'I've forgotten.'

'I'm nineteen,' he lied. 'Why?'

'When I was nineteen,' and Breucher shook his head a bit sadly, 'I was facing Russian guns across the snows of Poland. Nothing seems to change very much, does it?'

'Am I to have these four blokes in leather for company for the rest of the trip?'

'I'm afraid so.' It was all Breucher said but the bleakness of his voice implied that the four SS men were both his guards and, if it became necessary, his executioners.

They wore the twin lightning-bolts of the Waffen SS; it meant Breucher had spoken the truth – the order had come down from Hitler or someone in the Führer's headquarters, and not from Canaris. Not that it mattered very much whose finger was on the trigger.

His mind worked on the chances of escape. No likelihood of jumping off the Panzerwagen; too many obstacles and they'd have him before he got out. But every instant now he had to keep alert to possible exits.

There was a Wehrmacht compound – they had to pass through a gate and their papers were examined. He tried to ascertain whether the high fence went all the way round. But there were buildings and trees in the way.

Then they were dismounting and the four men gathered round, Breucher leading the way into a day room that must have been evacuated in anticipation of his arrival; there were a billiard table, an old piano, sofas, magazines.

Then a small figure in a rumpled overcoat materialized in the shadowed corner of the room.

Canaris.

Breucher said something in German and one of the SS men argued with him until Canaris spoke with quiet authority and the SS men saluted and withdrew. Breucher shut the door on them and Canaris said, 'They will remain just outside. Their orders are to keep you in sight but I didn't think we needed their disagreeable presence in the room with us.'

'Thank you, sir.'

'Breucher, you'll find the lavatory just in there.'

Breucher, taking the hint, went directly through the door and shut it, leaving Christopher alone in the room with Admiral Canaris. *I could kill him now, with my hands.* But it wasn't in his brief and it would serve no purpose.

Canaris sat down on the piano stool and hooked his elbows over the piano lid. He crossed his legs, leaning back; he looked quite relaxed. 'Sit down.'

'Should I be flattered by this private audience with you?'

'No. But you needn't be boorish.'

'Sorry.'

'You play the role well enough but it doesn't convince me,' Canaris said. 'As a defence against revealing your fears it's fairly effective, but your eyes are rather too candid — they don't match the sneer or the foppish voice.'

'Think what you like,' Christopher said; but his heart had begun to pound.

'I fear you're relying too much on the foreign minister's identification. All he can tell us is that you are who you claim to be. He can't tell us whether you're a loyal Englishman or a traitor.'

'I prefer the word "opportunist" if you don't mind.'

'As you wish. I have no difficulty believing your information, you know. I'm sure it's quite true — there will be an amphibious landing here within the next eight hours. I believe that for the same reason that must have inspired Churchill to initiate it. Some day the Allies intend to invade the Continent in force and they must feel out the limits of Germany's defences. They must know the sort of fight Germany is capable of joining if the worst possible circumstances apply and we are forewarned and prepared for the assault. Such an exercise would be of little use to Churchill if it were unopposed or under-opposed. The last thing he would wish to do would be to take us by surprise with this little venture. Therefore he must make sure that we Germans are prepared.'

Christopher did not trust himself to speak.

'You may well be a double agent working for Britain,' Canaris murmured, 'but I shall keep such suspicions to myself so long as your information proves useful to me. Do you understand?'

'I really don't know what you're talking about, sir.'

'Of course. Circumstances force both of us to be circumspect.' Canaris uncrossed his legs and rubbed his cheeks with both hands, covering his eyes momentarily; he looked very tired. When he lowered his hands he gave Christopher a bloodshot glance and then got to his feet and went round drawing the blackout curtains. 'This town is a seething nest of Allied spies and French Resistance patriots. They would report to London and Washington if they saw any sign that we were preparing to meet an anticipated attack. We don't want that to happen, of course, because if such intelligence reached the Allied field commanders they might decide to cancel the raid, and in any case such reports would alert the Allies to the fact that someone had betrayed the plan to us; it could put you in jeopardy and we prefer to keep our agents free of suspicion when we can. We've been careful to give an impression that no defences are being strengthened here. We haven't cancelled any leaves or passes. For the past four days our pilots and soldiers have been going off their posts in uniform and then creeping back in – by the back door so to speak, and mainly at night – in mufti so that they will be on duty without their presence being known to the Resistance. We are ready, you see, but we don't *look* ready. If the attack fails to materialize, of course, the armed forces will be very unhappy with me. I certainly hope your information proves to have been correct – for your sake of course, but also for mine.'

'If it comes to that I'm afraid I shan't bleed for you on my way to my execution.'

'The point I wish you to recognize, young man, is that I'm taking quite a risk in acting on your information. It's a measure of my belief in your value as an agent. You see, even when one knows that the enemy is deliberately placing certain information in one's hands, one can learn a great deal from such information.'

Canaris, he thought, was nearly as talkative as Mr Churchill himself. While he prattled on, delving into the intricacies of espionage, Christopher listened with half his attention and studied his immediate prospects. The day room had two doors, one of which apparently led into the lavatory where Rudi Breucher was. There were four windows, two front and two back; he had no doubt that the SS men had them all covered. It looked rather bleak for an escape. The ceiling looked solid and the floorboards didn't look easy to lift. Even if he silenced Canaris he didn't see a practical way out of the box.

He heard the gnash of some heavy tracked vehicle outside. Canaris was saying, '. . . doesn't really matter in the end, of course. All that matters is the result. Do they attack or do they not?' And then Canaris went across to the lavatory door and rapped on it. When Breucher emerged, rubbing sleep out of his eyes, Canaris said, 'It's nearly midnight. Time we went to our observation station.'

It was a pillbox bunker under the Bismarck Battery on the eastern headland overlooking the harbour of Dieppe. The low ceiling was a mass of reinforced concrete and he found himself thinking bleakly that a direct hit from a naval gun could bring it all right down on his head.

There were long slits in the thick walls, designed for the traversing of machine-gun muzzles; but there were ten of them along the seaward face of the bunker and, of those, five were weaponless, given over, he supposed, to observation and command. The five guns looked vaguely like Maxims but probably weren't; they were manned by Wehrmacht crews who made a point of ignoring the visitors – Admiral Canaris, Breucher, Christopher and the unwanted escort of four Blacks in leather. 'The Blacks' was what everyone seemed to call the SS. Of the four men, indistinguishable by their faces, one wore an officer's epaulets. That was the one whose eyes never left Christopher's back. He could feel them – a sensation as tangible as the pressure of a knife point.

A signals lieutenant came by handing out ear-protectors and Christopher followed Breucher's lead by hooking them round his neck where they would be close at hand when needed. The enclosure was illuminated by dim red lamps; it was partly blackout protection but mainly assurance against night-blindness. Canaris and the rest looked weirdly Mephistophelean, dim figures in a deep red.

Breucher said in a voice calculated to reach no further than Christopher's ears, 'When you return to London and you have more information you'll want to know how to reach me again. Put some rubbish on a postcard and sign it "Aeneas". On the second day after the card is posted I'll meet you at the same spot in the woods of Braye at ten hours in the morning. Yes?' Breucher was trying to reassure him that there'd be a next time. Christopher nodded, more grateful than he dared admit.

Through the observation slits he had a faint impression of a pale line of beach under the white cliffs that bracketed the town. A silver mist curled off the water. There were no lights; Dieppe was within point-blank range of the RAF. When he ducked his head for a glimpse of the sky he saw stars in profusion. The weather appeared excellent and there'd be no excuses on that account if the attack failed to materialize.

He thought he could feel the minutes of his life ticking away. The SS Sturmführer's eyes drilled into him and the man actually had his finger curled round the trigger of his machine-pistol; there wasn't a prayer of escape from this dismal place.

He said to Breucher, 'What's his name?' He rolled his eyes towards the Sturmführer.

'I don't know. Does it matter?'

'If I meet him in Hell I shall want to know who to ask for.'

Breucher asked the Black his name.

The reply was accompanied by a stiff clicking-together of heels: 'Leeb. Albert Leeb.' Christopher thought he'd never seen such brutal eyes. Albert Leeb was short and there was an effeminate delicacy about his mouth; he had brown hair and a moustache in emulation of Reichsführer Himmler's. He looked as if he took his pleasure from cruelties.

Albert Leeb, he thought. *I shan't have trouble remembering it.*

A corporal went round pouring coffee from an insulated bottle. Christopher sucked gratefully from his cup and wondered if it would be the last thing he'd taste. It was *ersatz* coffee, horrible stuff.

Canaris stood nearby. He peeled back the rumpled sleeve of his overcoat to look at his watch. Breucher murmured, 'If they're coming they're quiet about it. We've sent a convoy straight up the Channel right across the path your landing craft will have to take – if they're coming. The idea's to give the impression we're not expecting an attack. Also of course this is the best time to get a convoy through because your navy won't care to expose itself by opening fire prematurely.'

'Clever bastard, aren't you?'

'I can hardly take credit for it,' Breucher said. 'I believe it was Admiral Doenitz's idea.'

Christopher remembered his own little war against Doenitz — back in Ireland along the cliffs. It seemed a lifetime ago, a different lifetime. He'd known who his enemies were then, and who his friends were.

It was warm; the air was still and damp. The SS had long since stripped off their leather coats. Only Canaris remained bundled in heavy clothing; the man never seemed to get warm. Christopher kept wiping the sweat off his palms. It was clammy on his brow and the back of his neck. He was so tense he felt he might burst at any moment.

It took them by surprise when it started because it didn't come the way they'd expected: they heard gunfire but it was somewhere off in the distance — at least five miles away by the sound of it. A field telephone buzzed and there was a good deal of quick movement around the bunker, Canaris pushing someone aside and taking up the phone, talking and listening, his eyes coming round icily towards Christopher. He spoke roughly to Breucher, who hurried over to Christopher. 'Vastrival and Quiberville to the east — Belville and Berneval to the west — they are landing commandoes there.'

'I told you they'd start with diversions to either side.'

'If it's a trick —'

The sudden noise obliterated the rest of Breucher's words: a great whistling whoosh of incoming shells, the *whump* of a heavy naval bombardment pounding the beaches. Breucher was at the observation slit and Christopher saw him stiffen. He was lifting the Zeiss glasses to his eyes, bracing his elbows on the concrete. Canaris shambled forward and had a look; Breucher was turning and his smile was genuine. 'You have your reprieve, Aeneas. They are here.'

He crowded to the slit and heard the sawing of Canaris's breath; Canaris had the night glasses now. It was dawn and in the faint light he saw the massive shapes emerging from the mists — transports, warships, escorts. Their silent materialization was quite eerie. Smaller craft crept in formations towards the beach. The guns kept thundering. RAF Blenheims dived, laying billows of smoke; Hurricanes pounded the Bismarck Battery above them. *Fighters*, he thought. *Where are the bombers?*

Canaris was watching him with what seemed to be an ironic expression, and in that moment with his dim red-washed face before him Christopher had the sudden feeling that Canaris was looking straight into him and knew the whole truth; also that he found it somehow amusing.

The landing craft were nearly on the beach when the guns resumed. He wasn't sure whether it was the German shore batteries that began it or whether there'd been a salvo from the navy; when he returned his gaze to the sea there were geysers from German shells and flashes from British naval guns and he had plenty of time to wonder where the hell the RAF bombers were.

The floor rattled and he felt the vibration right through his bones. The gunners manned their machine-guns but they had nothing to shoot at and they simply kept watch on the long-range duelling; the bunker pounded and shook from the recoil of the howitzers implanted all round. Once or twice there was an exceptionally heavy thump that shook the pillbox -- a chip came down from a corner of the ceiling — and he thought perhaps those were British shells seeking the range but he couldn't be certain because the slit observation ports restricted the view. He did see it when a navy shell fell short and made a great white puff against the face of one of the cliffs. There was a tremendous avalanche of chalk that seemed to fall ever so slowly until it struck the sea and sent up a vast cloud of water, foam and steam.

He didn't want to see any more. He turned towards the steps at the back, thinking it was time to go; he'd made his grisly point. But Canaris blocked his way and began to speak. Christopher couldn't hear him. He lifted one edge of an earmuff and Canaris was shouting: 'You will stay until it is done. I want you to watch the consequences of your act.'

And Canaris dragged him back to the slit port.

The smoke cleared; Messerschmidts wheeled, diving to the attack. In the strengthening dawn he saw the landing craft struggle in the shallows.

The racket was terrible, even through the heavy ear-mufflers, and everything down there seemed chaotic. A landing craft was blown right out of the water. A few of the LSTs had made it as far as the beach; their ramps slammed down and the tanks began to inch towards shore. He saw the archery of German machine-gun tracers curving towards the beach while infantrymen threw themselves flat and then lifted themselves from the sand and tried to run forward.

German planes wheeled overhead, beating up the landing craft with cannon and machine-gun. Spitfires and Hurricanes sped among them, trying to drive them off. British armour rolled up on to the beaches into point-blank shellfire and he didn't see a single tank get off the beach.

He saw little groups of men run into the edges of the town, taking shelter in streets and buildings; the sky kept brightening, exposing what had formerly been pockets of shadow.

A tank blew up – a hit in the fuel tank – and there were objects in flames all along the crescent beach. They'd landed the first wave in the northeast not far beneath the bunker and he was looking nearly straight down at them as they tried to run or crawl towards the town to the southwest. One sizeable tight-packed unit of men was making a determined run up towards a bunker on top of which a radar scanner revolved. They were maintaining discipline and making good progress, firing mortar and automatic rifles and hurling grenades to clear a path ahead of them. Nothing else seemed to be advancing at all: the Canadians were pouring ashore and being cut to ribbons. The din was continuous and his ears rang; he knew he'd be half deaf for a week.

The gunner beside Christopher was pouring tracer towards the fast-running platoon that was climbing towards the radar emplacement but the range was too great and he saw the tracers fall short. A landing craft out in the harbour was sinking and men were all over her sides like insects. Men lurched blindly round on the beach, unguided and in tatters. Anti-tank shells and artillery and mortar were smashing up the armour faster than it could be landed; shelled LSTs blocked the waterline and men were dying everywhere.

Yet another wave was coming in, trying to find space to land; the soldiers were caught in the crossfire from shore batteries. When the sun came up through the mist the slaughter intensified and men were jumping into boats from harbour piers, over-filling the boats and capsizing them or being blown to pieces. Across the beaches the German machine-guns sent a raking enfilade and Christopher saw blurred figures spinning away.

Some part of that tightly organized little unit of commandoes had reached the radar emplacement and taken refuge inside it. There were German infantry assaults but British guns from the pillbox held them back.

Canaris would stare out of the slit port for a while, then turn with his hands rammed into his coat pockets and pace round the bunker with his head down. Once he stood for a long time motionless with his arms folded, hunched over a bit, simply staring at the bare concrete floor.

Breucher proffered the field glasses and Christopher reluctantly accepted them. He didn't want to see any of it but he felt obliged to. He was already composing in his head the icy report he was going to make to the Prime Minister.

Some of them were probing the streets of the city, running from house to house but taking their losses and never really securing anything; they kept falling back towards the beaches and now the navy was trying to get them off but the Germans had no shortage of ammunition.

The RAF was overhead – fighters in a frenzy to drive off the Luftwaffe – but one of the Germans, jettisoning his bombs, seemed by accident to drop one of them right down the funnel of a British destroyer out there: she blew up with a stunning roar and sank swiftly, men leaping over the side like insects. Then a flight of Hurricanes made a pass at the Bismarck guns and Christopher ducked below the lip of the slit port while their bullets chewed up the headland.

The fight had commenced at first light and now, by mid-morning, it was already breaking up. The navy had its hands full with German raiding ships and submarines; the men on the beaches were on their own. A few of the LSTs were still seaworthy and men were crowded into them like matches in a matchbox and a direct hit on one of them meant an entire company wiped out at a stroke. The Canadians were trying to use every skiff and lighter and fishing boat in the port but the Germans were sinking them nearly as fast as the invaders could get aboard them. Wounded men flopped about the beaches, stumbling over the dead; mainly the beach seemed cluttered with the dead – the carcasses of tanks and abandoned guns and men. So far as Christopher could see, only a handful of the elephantine tanks had made it off the beach.

At some point Breucher handed him the glasses again and he focused them on the radar pillbox and saw an ant-chain of men descending from it, covering their own fighting retreat with an efficient mobile rear guard of mortarmen and automatic-riflemen. Some of them were ramming their rifle butts against the earth to launch rifle grenades. A Wehrmacht platoon was pushing them back towards the beach but taking heavy punishment to do it. The figures in the midst of the retreat drew Christopher's attention; one of them was slight and elderly, the other had a curiously familiar way of moving, shoulders rolling, head swaying. *I know that man*; but the face was partly concealed under a commando beret.

Smoke still rolled heavy and black from the gutted destroyer that had sunk in waters too shallow to cover her over. Spitfires swooped through the smoke to line up on the headlands and race along at treetop altitude raking the German positions. It wasn't doing much good; the positions were fortified. He saw black bursts of flak in the sky. Lean high subchasers were carving angry tight-curving wakes through the harbour and behind them the waters erupted from their depth charges. A warship of some kind – cruiser or destroyer, he couldn't tell from this distance – stood off and loosed heavy salvoes of HE shells and incendiaries at hotels and boarding houses; here and there houses erupted into flame.

Canaris sat back in a corner now, on the floor with his rounded shoulders wedged between the walls, arms folded over his upbent knees, looking at nothing in particular. With the ear-muffs over his crushed hat he looked like a beggar drunk in a doorway.

Christopher lifted the glasses again and focused on the unit of commandos who'd come down from the radar emplacement. They'd fought their way right down to the beach now. It was about half past ten and they'd been inside the radar fort six hours or more; they'd taken heavy losses and there weren't more than eight or nine of them left. He saw the frail elderly man again, and right beside him the muscular figure who'd seemed familiar; he was helping the old man into the last LST on the beach. Its screw churned up the water, holding the ramp against the beach with a foot or so of water flowing across it; the old man stumbled for footing in the wet sand and the big fellow virtually manhandled him aboard the ramp. Then the big fellow turned to look back and a bullet struck him; he fell back, arms windmilling, and the beret fell off his head and Christopher recognized him immediately through the Zeiss lenses.

Roberts. He'd last seen Roberts in occupied France. What was he doing *here*?

Roberts fell away from the ramp and went face down into the water and did not lift his head again. The ramp winched up on its chains and German tracers ricocheted off its metal, leaving white smears where they'd struck; the engine reversed and the LST pulled away. Somewhere the guns were trying to get its range; he heard the firing and presently the water began to spout all round but the LST growled away, zigzagging.

Roberts lay floating in the water, the current drifting him lazily. It wasn't exactly that Roberts had been a friend. They hadn't particularly liked each other; but he knew the man and that made the whole tragic mess personal. He dropped the field glasses on to the concrete ledge and turned bleakly to look at Admiral Canaris. Canaris took no notice.

The shelling trailed off and stopped. In the unfamiliar silence Albert Leeb was watching him. After all these hours, the finger was still curled round the trigger of the machine-pistol and Leeb was still waiting.

Breucher said something; Christopher didn't catch it and didn't care. Then Breucher tugged at his sleeve. 'It's over. We may as well go.'

Breucher wheeled to speak sharply to Albert Leeb, who seemed disappointed; he slung his Mauser and used his hands to light a cigarette. He said something in a rasping voice and turned away. Breucher turned to Christopher to translate Leeb's remark. 'Captain Leeb observes that there seemed to be a certain lack of coordination among the Allied services here. I must say if that's your war ministry's idea of how to implement a combined operation, we here in *Festung Europa* haven't much to worry about.'

Christopher said nothing. Canaris was climbing slowly out of the bunker and they followed him out amid the big guns to the parapet of the headland. A few Spitfires were still evident and there was an occasional heavy artillery bang out at sea somewhere but a stillness had settled upon the beaches and the harbour; it was all corpses down there and now the stink of death began to drift up into Christopher's nostrils. It all struck him as terribly familiar; he remembered the last day at Dunkirk.

Canaris simply walked away.

Christopher felt Breucher's grasp and shook it off but Breucher pointed him forward and they walked back away from the cliff. Behind him he had a glimpse of Albert Leeb, who looked weary and reluctant to relinquish the sight of his prisoner. But he stayed where he was while Christopher and Breucher walked away from the battery.

Chapter Eleven

He tried smoking a cigarette but couldn't stand the taste of it and half stubbed it out, leaving a noxious smoking ember. He poured something very carefully from the bottle into the glass and drank it back, feeling as if he must have swallowed an octopus the night before.

Patricia was putting her things on: the uniform blouse over the bra, the skirt over the slip, black practical shoes over the nylons. Then he took another measure from the bottle and, red-eyed, looked up at her while she stood tapping her foot; the flesh under the stocking quivered and then she buttoned up the skirt. 'You've grown quite tall, you know. You can't hide in a fourteen-inch bottle.'

'Let it never be said,' he replied, 'that Christopher Creighton couldn't hold his drink.' His speech told him he was drunk again, or drunk still.

When he kissed her she kept her lips tightly compressed. She turned away quickly. 'You're in a perfectly brutal mood, aren't you?'

'Quite horrid,' he agreed. 'But do we have to go on being polite to each other in cool voices?'

'Perhaps we'll try again when you're sober. That was the most appalling night I've ever spent.'

She was gathering up her things on the way to the door and he wheeled violently, kicking the door shut with a deafening slam.

She said mildly, 'That won't help.'

'You're wrong. It helps.'

She pulled it open again and glanced at him as if to see whether he intended to bar her way. He stood back, feeling petulant, and Patricia gave him a grave parting glance, no smile. Then she was gone and he flung himself into the armchair reaching for the bottle, making a melodrama of it and then laughing at himself: *Are you trying to impress someone?*

But her curtness, her unwillingness to forgive, made him wonder whether their careless spontaneous affection could possibly survive the war. Up to now she'd loved him with a blind partiality, but now. . .

Then he realized what an abysmally selfish thought that was. *What right had he to expect her forgiveness?*

'Are you all right?' Owl looked genuinely concerned.

'Quite all right. Perhaps a little concussion. From the noise you know. It was quite a show the Jerries put on.'

Christopher dropped the sack on the desk; it made a faint thud and he tore at the drawstring until the notes spilt out on to the desk. 'Ten thousand in fivers. Care to count it?'

Owl examined one of them by the light of the window and dropped it back to the desk; he said, as if without interest, 'They're quite good but they're counterfeit of course.'

Then Owl sneered, 'What – no rage, no tantrum, no outcry of honourable protest?'

Christopher bared his teeth. 'You wanted to know how good their defences are. You found out. That was my job.'

'You did it extraordinarily well.'

'I wonder whether the dead will take comfort in that.'

'Christopher, we are at war. That's the sum of the answer I can give you.'

'I keep wondering if Roberts recognized me there at the last. He was looking right at me.' Christopher drew a deep breath and closed his eyes. When he opened them, Owl was still there: sleek, unrufflable. Christopher said, 'Who do I betray to them next?'

'Next time you'll sell information that's false. Now they'll believe it.'

The debriefing took days: they wanted everything. He had to remember every detail about Breucher, Kinski, the flight to Lisbon, Switzerland and Berlin; about Canaris, Ribbentrop, all he could remember of the Abwehr building – the architecture, floorplans, personnel; about the flight to France, the military compound, Albert Leeb and the observation bunker, his close-up view of the debacle.

Afterwards Pooh fed him tea and scones. 'We've got the official casualty figures if it matters. Of the six thousand one hundred troops embarked for Dieppe, about two thousand five hundred have returned, including a fair number of wounded and including one thousand men who never landed. Our losses were something short of four thousand, killed or captured – and a great deal of matériel.' Pooh watched him obliquely. 'It will serve as a lesson to our friends who clamoured for a premature invasion of France, and it has provided an object lesson for the planners who must lay on the eventual Second Front. When we achieve victory over there, it will have started here.'

Christopher set the cup down, swallowed the last mouthful of scone and bolted towards the door. On his way he said, 'Tell that to Roberts.'

The Prime Minister was still somewhere in Egypt visiting Montgomery's front lines and Christopher returned to Patricia's flat; now he felt a grim matter-of-factness and a lightheaded determination to have a good time. But his forced cheer seemed to alarm Patricia much more than his earlier moroseness had: he seemed powerless to control himself – he went jolly, raucous, wild, wilful, strident. Finally she said, 'You're like a Hurricane pilot knowing at any moment you're to be sent up on your last mission.'

'Don't you like me better without the long face?'

'No. I think I liked you better before.'

'On the tenth of November we intend to invade Norway in force. There will be four amphibious landings scattered among the fjords – these are the beach-heads.' Owl put four pins in the map and Christopher's eyes followed the movements of his spidery fingers.

Pooh occupied the chair beside Owl's desk. He pushed a thin sheaf of typewritten papers towards Christopher. 'You'd better have a few hours to memorize these.'

'Why don't I photograph them and give them the pictures?'

'You don't want to be caught going over the Irish border with incriminating photographs, do you? Besides, if they want photographs let them ask for them. You don't want to look too professional.'

Christopher turned, catching Owl's eye. 'It's false this time, isn't it? We're not invading Norway at all.'

Owl made no discernible reply.

Pooh said, 'Have a look at those letter-orders. Do they seem false to you?'

Christopher went through them, once over lightly; he'd buckle down in a moment. 'They look all right,' he admitted.

'If they're looking for confirmation ahead of the event,' Pooh said, 'you might suggest they keep an eye on our fleet movements out of Scapa Flow.'

'They do that anyway,' Owl remarked, 'but your suggesting it may soothe their fevered suspicions.'

Pooh said, 'Hitler suspects we intend an invasion in Norway. I'm not sure why he expects it – perhaps his ruddy astrologer. In any case he's already got a big show laid on for us up there. Fortifications, coastal guns, the lot. They've shifted a good part of Raeder's navy to Norway – capital ships of the line.'

Christopher studied the map. 'Then they won't have to move to cover this assault – they're already in place. What's the point?'

'Yours not to reason why, old boy.'

Owl said, 'Just memorize the information and take it across to Breucher for us, that's a good lad.'

In Dublin he left the train and gave up his ticket at the gate and melted into the flow: he wore a sailor's pea jacket and an old hat and his shoes were scuffed. He took a room in a bed-and-breakfast place, showing his false identity papers, and remained in the room all afternoon and night, reading the newspapers, playing patience and listening to the BBC news. He wasn't any good at waiting but the Resistance jobs in France had taught him how to pass the time without going up the wall.

The postcard he'd dropped in the box in London would have reached Breucher this morning and with luck Breucher would make the rendezvous tomorrow; if Breucher didn't turn up he'd have to come back the following day. It should be an easy job, this one, but he felt nervous. It was on the easy ones that you made the mistake of relaxing your guard. He remembered how Roberts had made it right to the end and then turned back for a last look and they'd put a bullet right in his heart; he'd actually got one hand on the chain to pull himself aboard.

He didn't often indulge in retrospection, but he'd be eighteen soon and it felt like a good moment to take stock. Two and a half years ago they'd taken him out of school and made a spy out of him in Belgium and Ireland. Then they'd turned the spy into a hatchet-man, sent him out to sink a Dutch submarine and murder a few English service people; then they'd turned his coat and sent him over to the enemy to betray a few thousand Canadians.

With or without the intent, he thought, they'd done nearly everything you could do to a boy to break him and it was a wonder he wasn't a raving lunatic. *You must stop feeling sorry for yourself now*, he thought. But he felt utterly trapped.

He wasn't the type of cold-blooded heartless bastard that Owl set up as the ideal agent. Someone like Roberts had been far better cut out for this work than Christopher was. What they needed for jobs like this was a surgical procedure to remove the conscience. It was harder if you were the sort who tended to worry about the poor beggars whose lives you were tossing under the wheels.

Pooh had been quite paternal about Dieppe. *If it hadn't been you it would have been someone else. We'd have got the information over to Canaris one way or another, you know. You were simply a messenger, that's all. Don't blame the messenger for the bad news.*

And Owl with his sepulchral enthusiasm had been offensively oblivious: *They were told when they went in that it wasn't going to be an easy landing. They were soldiers, taking soldiers' risks.* Right, he'd thought, but I'm glad I'm not the one who has to tell their mothers that they're dead.

He was aware that anger was building up inside him and that a moment of climax loomed somewhere ahead of him because nobody could live with this kind of dilemma for ever. But it was still a nebulous thing and he wasn't even certain what the choices were, let alone what the decision might be. Sometimes he thought the answer lay in taking Owl by the throat and squeezing the life out of the bastard, but then the cooler second thought always came and he knew that wouldn't solve anything at all. Owl hadn't made the war.

Back in England his age group were being called up. They went dutifully or with enthusiasm but in any case with hope: the war couldn't go on for ever and they expected to survive it — they had to carry on as if they were immortal. He'd never really thought about it—it surprised him when he realized he hadn't a clue as to what might come afterwards. He'd been behaving as if he'd never get any older and the war would go on for ever—a bleak sense that his life would end before the war did, so what was the point in making plans? But now he thought for the first time that perhaps he lived a charmed life, as Pooh insisted, and this being the case he might survive the horrors and the adventures. If it happened he could see himself hanging about the victory celebrations trying to return the beaming smiles but wanting privately to weep because they'd taken him out of real life at fifteen and turned him into a war machine the way you turned a half-grown puppy into a guard dog: you weren't likely to have too much success turning the animal back into a pet afterwards.

It was something he needed to watch. He knew one thing: when the war ended he wasn't going to stay on in the secret service. He would have to find something else to do; perhaps if he thought about it long enough an idea would come to him.

Breucher was alone in the wood. 'Kinski wanted to come along. I managed to leave him behind.'

'I'm glad of that, he's a nasty piece of work.'

'Herr Himmler likes to keep his watchdogs on us,' Breucher replied. 'You have something to sell again?'

'Of course. But the price is higher.'

'Naturally.'

'I've been thinking in terms of twenty-five thousand quid.'

'Are you sure you don't want to make it guineas?'

'Why not?'

'If the information is satisfactory I'm sure there'll be no difficulty about the price.'

He'd known there wouldn't be; it would be counterfeit anyway. He wondered how much bad money they'd managed to filter into the British economy.

With a straight face and his bored smarmy air Christopher gave him the information about the planned Norway landings. Breucher took it all down carefully in shorthand, asking him to repeat things now and then, interjecting questions, some of which Christopher had answers to, finally closing the notebook and putting the pencil away. 'Excellent. The high command will be delighted with this.'

He waited in the Northways office and, dead on time, Owl hooted his way in: he seemed in excellent spirits and actually smiled when he welcomed Christopher with a brief handshake. He hung his umbrella over the hat-rack, peeled off his mac and went round to sit down under the window, the panes of which were streaming with rain.

'It seems they've bought it. We've been monitoring Jerry's movements round the Norway perimeter. Hitler's been convinced for some time that we mean to strike there, of course, and your information to Dublin put the icing on the cake. They've reinforced their defences and the German fleet has remained there on station, just where we want it.'

'And where *don't* we want it, then?'

'In the Med. We simply wanted to insure that we didn't get major interference from the German navy while we were putting the troops ashore. It's one of the lessons Dieppe taught us.'

Then Owl tapped his desk calendar. 'Today is the fifth of November. I want you to send another of those postcards across to Herr Breucher and indicate in it, if you can, that the matter is most urgent. Then you're to go across and meet him again. We want you,' he explained, 'to mend your fences with them.'

'It's North Africa.' Christopher told Breucher. 'What Churchill calls the soft underbelly. They had fantastic security. I was taken in. They put out a barrage of false orders – they've even equipped the forces with cold-weather gear and maps of Norway. But it's all been a smokescreen. I only stumbled across the truth by accident. They're invading North Africa.'

'On the tenth?'

'No. The eighth.'

'Tomorrow!'

'Yes. I've only just found out myself.'

'Where in North Africa?'

'I'm not sure. It looks like Tobruk and Casablanca. Possibly Tripoli as well. But they've code named all the landing beaches and I haven't been able to connect up the code names.'

229

'Give me what you've got.' Breucher fumbled for his notebook. 'I'll have to get off a signal immediately, though I doubt there's time for it to do any good.'

None whatever, Christopher thought; the short-wave channels would be jammed ferociously for the next twenty-four hours by British transmitters.

He had to try and look devastated but it wasn't easy. 'It's a major invasion, three Allied task forces under Eisenhower. One British, two American. All three landings synchronized to begin at dawn.'

Tobruk, Casablanca and Tripoli were not the main targets of course but they were the targets he gave Breucher and he saw Breucher write them down; if the message did somehow get through to Berlin it would mean the enemy might draw forces away from the real targets – Algiers, Oran and the north Moroccan coast.

'The operation's code named "Torch". They're already on the way in.'

You can give them that much because they'll see it for themselves and we'll have air cover off carriers and the Rock. They haven't a prayer of getting German or Italian ships into those waters that quickly. You may as well make it look good – give them everything we've got, so long as it's too late for them to act on it. Everything except the actual target beaches.

'Our fleet is impotent. Stranded in Norway.' Then the German pride in Breucher asserted itself. 'It will be all right. We have pulled many a rabbit out of the hat before.'

They haven't been up against this lot, Christopher thought – Eisenhower, Cunningham, a mass of Allied armour and air cover and naval strength. And at this moment Montgomery was beating up Rommel at El Alamein.

He watched Breucher dash off through the woods and went back to his hired bicycle, pedalled slowly out towards the lane, and found himself whistling a jaunty tune.

One of Winston's typists was still tapping away on the Remington Noiseless but the war rooms were quiet and it was getting on for most people's bedtime. Most of Owl's encounters with Winston took place at night nowadays. The PM slept till just before noon every day, then slept again for an hour in the afternoon, then worked until about three in the morning, often dictating notes in bed. 'Nothing happens in the morning,' he'd explained to Owl on one occasion. 'Or if it does, it's afternoon by the time the news reaches me.'

'Early to bed, early to rise,' Owl had replied, 'and you never meet anyone interesting.'

'Quite.'

Nevertheless Owl did not share the PM's nocturnal metabolism and he found lately that he needed to fortify himself with strong coffee before entering Winston's chamber to endure the evening haranguing.

Winston was still dressed in the waistcoated suit he must have worn to dinner. He advanced smiling. 'Good evening.' And then brushed vigorously past Owl to shut the door. They were alone – that was unusual; normally at this hour the PM tended to review the day's events and issue last-minute orders for the next day; that meant surrounding himself with his circle.

'I lament that I must bear a cross,' Winston said. 'The Cross of Lorraine.'

'De Gaulle?'

With great intensity Winston said, 'Sometimes the man makes me spit. He's a pompous giraffe.'

'I thought you rather liked him.'

'Sometimes. But this – it's a squalid nuisance.'

'Darlan?'

Winston growled, 'Will nobody rid me of this turbulent admiral?'

Henry to his barons, Owl thought automatically, *about Thomas à Becket*. The PM liked a nice phrase and seldom minded where he lifted it from.

'This dirty Darlan,' Winston concluded acidly. Morose and pale, he proceeded to launch into a lofty monologue on the subject; Owl paid very little attention to it because he knew it all anyway.

The intricacies of the relationships among the Free French, Vichy and the Allies were impossible to unravel; Darlan seemed to acknowledge loyalty to no-one and kept threatening to turn towards the Nazis or the Vichy government or the Allies, depending on who offended him; apparently he wanted the Allies to mollify him by making him, in effect, the high commissioner of all North Africa. But his Vichy forces had actually been shooting at Allied troops, killing quite a few British and American men and sinking warships, and everyone was disgusted with him.

'We've trouble enough with the Germans and the Italians,' Winston concluded, 'without needing to trouble ourselves further with this renegade Vichy guttersnipe at our backs. Ike only gave him the job on impulse. Darlan has been appealing to Franklin Roosevelt and the President has had to back him and, of course, De Gaulle considers that the last straw. I concur with De Gaulle in this matter. Darlan must be replaced with a high commissioner who can be relied upon to obey orders. But I do not concur with Charles's scheme for effecting that end. Have the French confided their plan to you?'

'No.'

'They have done, to me. It was in the yellow box last night.'

'And?'

'It's imbecilic. I realize one must take risks in war but can't a man be dismissed without such Balkan machinations?'

Owl said, 'Well I suppose there's some question as to who, if anyone, is empowered to dismiss Darlan. He claims allegiance to the government of France but he chooses not to recognize De Gaulle's lot. Who's left?'

'Eisenhower perhaps. As commander of the Combined Allied Forces.'

'It's sticky,' Owl said. 'Darlan has been adept at refusing to acknowledge Eisenhower's jurisdiction over him.'

'How does the confounded fool keep his men so loyal to him?'

'Personality,' Owl said.

'The men around Charles want to kill Darlan and replace him with Giraud.'

'Well it's not our problem, is it?'

'It may very well become ours. Especially if this French scheme goes awry. I do wish they'd stop dropping things like this in my bloody box. It puts me in an impossible position. Suppose the attempt fails? If it's laid at De Gaulle's door, what prevents him from implicating me in the plot? The Americans would want to know why, if I'd had foreknowledge of it, I had sat on my hands.'

'Then we must see to it that the French plot does not fail, mustn't we —' Owl smiled.

'One boy like you is worth two thousand French field-marshals.' Thus growled Mr Churchill at the boy.

Then Owl had taken him round to Northways for briefing. Owl was thinking that perhaps he had underestimated Winston's comprehension of psychology. No-one could resist high praise when he had earned it; young Christopher certainly had earned the PM's encomiums but the important thing was that it gave Christopher in his own mind a reputation he now had to live up to. It was the best way of seeing to it that he remained reliable.

The boy was gone now, winging south, and Pooh wandered about the office like a stray mongrel in search of familiar scents. Owl said, 'Must you?'

'What?'

'Pace about.'

'I'm just asking myself how the boy is wearing. He's only just turned eighteen, hasn't he?'

'Seems healthy enough to me. This one will be the next thing to a holiday for him — all he needs to do is hold someone's coat.'

'It could turn nasty.'

'That's why we chose Christopher, isn't it? He knows how to get out of things.'

'It's hard on him.'

'I do wish you wouldn't *bleed* so much.'

It brought Pooh up short; he glanced angrily at Owl and then, in an abrupt change of subject, said, 'I met Darlan a few years ago in Cairo.'

'And?'

Pooh said, 'At last for once the enemy turns out to be someone I can really hate — you know, the villain of all my prejudices.'

The plane brought Christopher in from Gibraltar to Blida airport on the plateau. It decanted him into a bright sun which was not very hot. The air was cool but thick, like glue.

A man in a French subaltern's uniform came out of the Nissen hangar and saluted with colonial violence. 'Lieutenant Hamilton?'

There was an American jeep with a French driver. It took

them down into the town: Bedouins, Arabs, soldiers in various costumes, beggars, pariah dogs. The place was very white and he noticed the absence of women from the streets.

Little grey birds flitted soundlessly from roof to roof. There was a hedge of oleander and another, zealously watered, of bougainvillaea; then they were in the courtyard of a white Moorish building and the subaltern was carrying his luggage inside for him.

He showed his papers at the desk. The subaltern waved back the barefoot bellman and preceded Christopher up a flight of chipped stairs and along a verandah off which doors opened into bedrooms; the subaltern stopped at one and knocked.

There were two of them: a middle-aged man in a uniform that Christopher didn't immediately recognize and a frail young man with fevered eyes who stood with his back pressed against the stucco wall.

The subaltern dropped Christopher's bags on the luggage rack, saluted and left the room without a word, pulling the door shut.

'Henri d'Astier,' the Frenchman said. From his briefings Christopher knew who he was: Henri d'Astier de la Vigerie, Commissaire de la Police of Algiers and closely associated with the clandestine Corps Franc d'Afrique, a secret organization of Free French partisans that had worked within the Vichy structure. D'Astier was about forty. He had jowls and pouched tired eyes. It was his brother François, De Gaulle's chief of staff in London, who had briefed Christopher on the situation in Algiers and provided him with the letter of introduction which Christopher now presented to the Commissaire.

D'Astier read it without hurrying; then he pocketed the letter, examined Christopher's documents and finally, as if an afterthought, indicated the nervous young man who stood against the wall: 'Monsieur Bonnier — Lieutenant Hamilton.'

Fernand Bonnier de la Chapelle. They hadn't known much about him in London: only that he was the instrument of the scheme, having volunteered for hazardous duty and having been recommended by someone to someone. It all sounded rather unprofessional, and now when he went across to shake Bonnier's hand he was disturbed by the nervousness that came off him like a vibration.

Bonnier seemed fragile and terribly young, though in fact he was a few years older than Christopher. A great mass of blondish hair added two inches to his height. His smile was tentative; he was ready to cringe, Christopher thought.

D'Astier said, 'Please sit down, Lieutenant. Have you any thoughts to offer before I begin?'

'I'd rather have all the information first.'

'Your French is excellent.'

'Thank you.'

'I suppose it's one reason why you were selected?'

'Yes.'

'And of course you've been trained for this sort of thing.'

'Yes.'

'You seem very young.'

Christopher glanced toward Bonnier. 'So does he.'

'Well he's a fanatic. But he's proved himself before.' D'Astier was talking as if Bonnier wasn't in the room. With a slight laugh Bonnier slipped his glance away and ran nervous fingers through his hair. Christopher was trying not to mark him for weakness but the signs were all there.

Abruptly Christopher said to Bonnier, 'Have you ever killed a man?'

'No.'

Score one in his favour: at least he hadn't hedged.

Then Bonnier said: 'Have you?'

'Yes.'

He had an uneasy feeling about all this. When he'd worked with the Resistance in France, he might not have known his comrades but he knew he could depend on them.

A cigarette smouldered in the corner of d'Astier's mouth. 'Admiral Sir Andrew Cunningham is in command of the Allied naval forces here. I suppose you've some pretext for being present? At some point you must report to him.'

'Naval intelligence. I've answers to questions if they're asked.'

'Very good. Now I shall not be able to be seen with you very often. I shall turn Monsieur Bonnier over to you for final preparation.'

That was Christopher's job here: to make sure Bonnier was trained for it, to get him in and set him up. Owl had been quite specific: *You're going out to Algiers to hold his coat. He's had experience but not quite in this class. He'll want your guidance but he's the one in the line of fire. You ought not to be at risk — you're the tutor on this one, that's all.*

It's got to be seen to have been a French operation, Owl had added. *That's why he'll be identified and arrested afterwards. You've got to be out of the picture by then. But the job's got to be done properly — that's your concern.* Christopher understood: it was an order. He also understood it had loopholes: if the French botched it, the French must be *seen* to have botched it. Owl didn't want any blame falling on London.

D'Astier was saying, 'We'll provide you with all the necessary information. Monsieur Bonnier already has most of it. He can tell you where Darlan sleeps, eats, works. How he's guarded. What tooth powder he uses. His office is in the Palais d'Eté and you'll probably choose to strike there because that's where the security is lightest — the chauffeur and bodyguards are left behind once he enters the palace. There are only the four men of the security guard on the front gate and a few guards patrolling the corridors. Darlan's aides and secretaries take long lunch breaks, normally two hours or more, and his office is empty then.'

'Doing it shouldn't be hard,' Christopher said. 'Getting away — that's another thing.' He said it because he wanted to see how much Bonnier knew about what was planned for him afterwards.

'That's for you to work out,' d'Astier replied. 'You've only to worry about getting yourself out, of course.' So that answered that. 'I must leave now. *Bonne chance, messieurs.*' The Commissaire shook each of them by the hand and went.

Bonnier said, 'He doesn't wish to know any of the details, you see. If he doesn't know my plan he can be genuinely surprised by the event. I hope you didn't think him rude.'

'No — but this whole thing smacks of under-preparedness. We've got to be careful. How many others know about this plot?'

'I don't know.'

Marvellous, he thought, *bloody marvellous.*

It turned out Bonnier was a good marksman. Christopher's first job was to get him fitted out in a French officer's uniform and bring him round to the Allied firing range but he didn't need much training in that respect; he was capable, though somewhat careless through absentmindedness. Mainly what Bonnier had going for him was enthusiasm. Christopher didn't want to learn much about him because he didn't want the relationship to get personal; but he felt he ought to know why Bonnier wanted to do the job and why the French had selected him for it – both facts might have a bearing on the outcome. He wasn't able to find completely satisfactory answers to either question but he'd never altogether understood the French mentality and he attributed it to that. There were complex machinations involved. Exactly who was behind the plot was not clear. It had received the blessing of De Gaulle's headquarters in London but it hadn't originated with De Gaulle. Whether d'Astier's brother in London was behind it was something Bonnier professed not to know.

If Darlan were murdered by an Englishman the repercussions would thunder round the world, Owl had explained. *The assassin must be French. To that extent we and the Free French are agreed. Nevertheless the young man they've chosen is an emotional chap, I'm told, competent but perhaps not likely to remain cool under stress. Quite bluntly I do not trust a hot-blooded young zealot to bring it off properly – and if it's botched it will put us all at risk. You are to see he doesn't botch it.*

Bonnier was descended from a family now impoverished to whom pride and dignity were nearly the only things left. He believed France had been sold out by Quislings and cowards; he seemed determined to show the world that all Frenchmen were not like that. When Christopher asked him, 'Why didn't you join the Free French Army then?' Bonnier only replied that it wasn't *important* enough. Evidently he wanted to get his name in the history books. There was something about his determination and vulnerability that made him most likeable. He seemed to feel a compulsion to prove his courage and he kept talking metaphysically of heroics: how, by taking frightful risks that brought one closer to death, one therefore came closer to life.

Christopher knew those feelings but when Bonnier spoke of them he sounded as if he'd got them out of books. Mainly it looked as if Bonnier simply wanted to make a name for himself. He was the sort who'd boast about it afterwards. That was one reason why they'd sent Peter Hamilton to Algiers: Peter

Hamilton didn't exist and if Bonnier began to spread any tales then London could righteously deny everything.

They did most of their work in a room in the rue Lafayette in the old quarter. At the outset Christopher had said, 'The best way to do it is to use explosives. You go in during the lunch hour, set the bombs and you're miles away when they detonate. You plant two bombs, perhaps three, to cover the entire room — that's the advantage of working in a confined space.'

But Bonnier was having none of it. It was a matter of honour; he must face the villain. There was no budging him. So they were armed with 7.65mm pistols of Belgian manufacture loaded with jacketed hollow-point bullets.

They were on the balcony. Long evening shadows lay across the courtyard. 'Let's run through it once more, then. We'll do the job tomorrow, right?'

Somewhere the muezzins wailed, calling out the sunset prayer to Allah. A cloud scudded across the sky and it began to drizzle. Bonnier poked a cigarette into his mouth and stooped to light it. He had to hold both hands over the match, cupping them together against the rain, but the cigarette was too wet and finally he gave it up and went inside. Christopher said, 'You'll be all right. Everyone's nervous before a job like this.'

Bonnier cast an eye at him ruefully. 'I resent being afraid. It's undignified.'

Christopher knocked the flies off a loaf of bread, pulled it open, wrapped it round a length of cheese and tore it in half to share it with the Frenchman. 'We've covered everything a hundred times but let's go through it just once more, all right?'

'Must we? It's not that complicated, is it? You go in first, preparing the way for me, and when you've cleared everything I come in and shoot him.'

'Let's just go through it a step at a time if you don't mind.'

Admiral Cunningham's headquarters was in the Hôtel St George but a chief petty officer there directed him to the signals office halfway across the town and it was from there that he sent the

Milne-coded signal to Owl. Two hours later, some time after midnight, he had the reply:

CONCUR YOUR SIGNAL. EVERY STEP WILL BE TAKEN TO PROTECT SUBJECT AFTER EXECUTION OF MISSION.

He'd wanted to know that they weren't going to throw Bonnier to the wolves. Reassured, he went back to his digs and turned in. Before he fell asleep he had time to wonder how much Bonnier really knew about all this. It seemed obvious he didn't recognize the extent to which he was being used: the French had managed to convince Bonnier that assassinating Darlan was his own idea and that they were simply offering support to his initiative. They intended Bonnier to be caught. No-one would believe his rantings afterwards; naturally he'd try to implicate the Commissaire, who arrested him, and the Free French – he'd name anybody if it would get him off. That was how it would look. He'd have to be caught, however; otherwise how would the world know it had been a French plot rather than an English or American one?

Bonnier would be arrested and named as the killer. Afterwards, however, he'd be kept safe from execution or retribution. That was the understanding. Apparently he felt that in the end he'd be lionized as a hero of France. There was no point disabusing him. Christopher wondered what would become of him in the end, after he realized the disappointment he faced.

Admiral of the Fleet Jean François Darlan was a tiny man. They watched him drive out of the palace in the back of his car, convoyed by the bodyguard car. Bonnier reached for the door handle but Christopher stopped him. 'Not yet.'

They waited in the parked car a while longer; at one o'clock a knot of people emerged from the palace, most of them in uniform, and Christopher said, 'That's the staff from his office. All right.' He got out of the car, locked the big envelope under his arm like a swagger stick, walked out to the corner, waited for a gap in the traffic and went across to the palace annexe gate.

The security men were French, of course, but they were backed up by two Spahis, native cavalrymen, huge men with ferocious faces. When the job went into its last stage he was going to have to run that gauntlet; he sized them up with quick glances and wondered how good they were as sharpshooters.

The envelope and his papers got him through the gate into the palace. The envelope was mocked up as an official sealed dispatch 'for eyes only of Captain B. Charbonneau.' When he was inside the gate he walked, not hurrying, up the wide steps. In a corner of his vision he could see the mouth of the narrow passage that had been designed for use by servants and now seemed to function as the junior staff's exit; several bicycles were parked in there, along with the motorcycle Christopher intended to use later. If you came out of the window of Darlan's office and crossed the garden you were at the point where that passage opened into it.

He went through another security examination just inside the palace annexe and then he was crossing towards the stairs. A French officer marched smartly towards the main doors, his heels clicking on the tile floor, and at the top of the stairs a two-man patrol walked across his line of sight. He went upstairs briskly, taking them two at a time – a young British naval officer knowing where he was going.

They'd reconnoitred the palace for four days; he'd been in and out a dozen times on various pretexts and the security people were used to his face by now. The whole thing was complicated by the distrust in which everyone held everyone else. The palace revealed a great variety of uniforms – French, British, American, Dutch, Polish, Bedouin, Berber, Arab. The Free French were particularly xenophobic towards the British and Americans because they hadn't been allowed in on 'Torch': London and Washington had kept them completely in the dark about the invasion until the landings took place. There was also the fact that De Gaulle was 'Churchill's Frenchman' and was not trusted by the Vichy French in North Africa, mainly because he had defied Pétain on every occasion and had supported various Churchillian machinations against Madagascar, Syria and Dakar. At the moment very few of these French would accept De Gaulle as a replacement for Darlan; the only suitable candidate who was acceptable to both sides was General Henri Giraud, who had escaped from a German prisoner-of-war camp six months earlier and had been raising hell against Germany ever since. His rallying cry, disdaining the Gaullists, was *We don't want to be freed by the Allies. We want them to help us free ourselves.* He'd made few bones about the fact that he wanted to be high commissioner and thought he could do a better job than Darlan was doing. That shouldn't be very hard, of course. Darlan's idea of dealing diplomatically with his allies had been summed up in one of his tantrums: *'Merde! Les anglais!'*

There was a lavatory halfway along the hall and he waited in there, taking out his service revolver and shaking it by his ear – listening to the rattle of cartridges – and then putting it away and checking the clip of the 7.65 Bubi under his tunic. Then he waited, pulling the window open to look down into the passage where the bikes were parked.

Bonnier arrived in the black Peugeot 402 at the annexe gate and emerged wearing a brown overcoat with the collar turned up conspiratorially, and Christopher made a face; then Bonnier disappeared into the side door below and Christopher had nothing to occupy him except concern.

Christopher went along to Darlan's outer door, took a breath and pushed it open, rapping on the panel with his knuckles. The excuse was ready on his tongue but there was no-one in the anteroom and he went inside, locking the door behind him and then doing a quick search through the four rooms of the suite. Owl had been precise about that: *No witnesses. Either eliminate the witnesses or walk out and try again later.* Owl probably would have preferred that he wipe out any witnesses and go ahead and get Bonnier to the objective but he'd left Christopher the opening and Christopher was prepared to back out and have another go later. But there was no-one in the suite so it was on.

He checked behind the blackout curtains and inside the wardrobes and he looked behind the curtain in Darlan's private shower. No-one. When he re-entered the anteroom he heard Bonnier's nervous code knock and unlocked the door; Bonnier edged his way inside sweating and leant back against the wall, closing his eyes. Then the first thing he tried to do was light a cigarette but Christopher batted it out of his mouth and Bonnier's face flooded with colour.

'That's all they need to smell when they walk in here.' Christopher picked up the cigarette, pocketed it and hauled Bonnier along to the main office. The clock made it ten minutes to two and he had a look at Darlan's desk calendar. The admiral had an appointment at a quarter past three so the job had to be done before then and it was to be hoped that Darlan didn't dawdle over lunch today. Christopher opened the latch of the double doors that gave on to the courtyard; he peered through to the gardens – a patrol of spahis walking across the lawn, two officers in the shade conversing, a pigeon ducking its head for crumbs.

'You look like a spy in a German film. Pull your collar down. Relax.'

There were photographs on the wall: Admiral Darlan shaking hands with dignitaries and smiling for the cameras. Darlan had little pig eyes and looked as if he might enjoy screwing twelve-year-old Arab girls. It was said he'd offered his services to Hitler at Berchtesgarten earlier in the year.

A door latch; footsteps. Bonnier stared wide-eyed, rooted to the spot by fear. Christopher pushed him behind the curtain, went in beside him and held his hands ready to gag Bonnier. The glass on the photographs served as mirrors and he watched a junior officer come in, lay a folder of documents on the desk and withdraw. When the outer door clicked Christopher began to breathe again.

'You'll have to do better than that.'

Bonnier came out from behind the curtain. His Adam's apple rode up and down with spasmodic swallowing. He nodded his head vigorously. 'I know – I know.' But he nearly dropped his pistol and Christopher told him to put it away until it was needed.

They went back into the anteroom. The spahis were still in the garden. Bonnier looked as if he were going to pieces.

'Anywhere in the trunk,' Christopher counselled, keeping his voice right down. 'The heart if you can but any torso shot will do the job.' The dum-dums were cut in quarters to fragment upon impact; they would carom around, tearing up organs. 'One shot – that will be enough. They may mistake a single shot for something else and that's in our favour. Understand?'

'Yes – yes.'

Closer to death, he thought, *and therefore closer to life*. What utter rot. Bonnier was close to catatonia.

Christopher heard it first – footsteps in the corridor. Bonnier moved without needing a prod this time and that was encouraging. He flattened himself against the wall by a filing cabinet. Then someone was in the room.

There was the click of heels, the squeak of shoes – Darlan walked across to his office. The pistol came up in Bonnier's hand. He walked from the filling cabinet and Darlan said something – more of a grunt than a word.

Darlan stood halfway across the room, staring at Bonnier's pistol; he hadn't seen Christopher.

Darlan's eyes lifted and met Bonnier's and that was when Bonnier froze.

Bonnier stood limp with the pistol in his hand. Darlan's eyes did not move from Bonnier's face and Bonnier did nothing at all, just stood there with horror frozen on his face and then Christopher saw that his finger was dead white on the trigger – the bloody fool had forgotten to push the safety catch.

There was no need for Christopher to take aim. His gun had been levelled at Darlan's stomach all the time. He squeezed the trigger as if it were a target range exercise. But the admiral had turned to tackle Bonnier and the shot went by him. Christopher fired again and saw the impact push Darlan back against the wall clutching his stomach.

There was a knock at the outer door. Christopher crossed the room with two long strides and pressed his pistol into Bonnier's hand. 'Give me yours – quickly!'

Christopher tugged and Bonnier relinquished the pistol. There was another knock. The door started to open and Christopher was gone – through the window and into the garden. Those were the orders. He mustn't be found in there.

Two shots rang out from the office as he landed with knees flexed, down on the palms of his hands. He came up and walked slowly across the gardens. If the spahis had seen him it was too bad. After a moment he turned off into the narrow passage.

The motorcycle was where he had placed it. He climbed on and rolled it forward, not starting the engine, pushing it along with his feet – taking his time and not wanting to alarm anyone with a racket. He made it as far as the mouth of the passage and waited there. He could hear voices shouting from behind him – but he didn't hear any more shooting and that was a good sign.

The motorcycle had been laid into the plan in case there was pursuit and he sat ready to kick it into life and make a run through the gate but the confusion that followed wasn't a panic; after five minutes a soldier came out of the palace, ran to the gate and talked briefly to the guards. Darlan was dying; a car had been summoned. They were shocked but it was obvious they thought they'd caught the assassin. They used the word 'injured' but he'd seen it go in and he knew Darlan didn't have half an hour left in him. So he left the motorcycle where it was and walked to the gate where he allowed the guards to tell him about the terrible thing that had happened. He was appropriately shocked and outraged. Then he made his excuses and walked away.

Christopher walked briskly through the corridors on the balls of his feet like a man expecting a fight.

Signals office. The armed marine guards knew his face by now but they wanted his papers anyway. Identity documents and his special pass. Supreme Command were changing passes every few hours in a futile attempt at security – it was a tedious instance of locking the barn door; the assassination had taken place two days ago. An hour ago he'd carried a green pass; now he carried a yellow one and he only had it because of blind luck: he'd come straight here from Admiral Cunningham's headquarters in the Hôtel St George and the flag lieutenant had called him back to the reception desk on his way out of the lobby to remind him to collect the new yellow card. Otherwise he'd have been subject to arrest and what a lovely irony that would have been – go about committing murder in their midst and end up arrested for bearing the wrong coloured paper.

The marine guards glanced at the yellow pass and gave the papers back to him. One of them smiled in deference to the officer's insignia he wore. Christopher again endured the tedium of establishing credentials at the checkpoint outside the cipher room. None of the half a dozen Wren officers and ratings there looked at him until he grinned with a certain wickedness and dropped his canvas bag on the desk; then the officer behind the desk, without looking up, said ruefully, 'Ah, Mr Hamilton,' and went on scribbling in a crabbed hand on the margin of a typed document. As if as an afterthought the man said, 'There's been a reply to your signal.' The man pawed swiftly through the message slips. Finally Christopher signed for it and had the signal in his hand.

He put the card away with his other identity papers, picked up the signal and canvas bag and found space at one of the tables. He glanced at the clock above the door — twenty-five past seven in the morning and, unless this signal held a reprieve, Bonnier would be shot in twenty minutes' time. He'd spent the night – Christmas – fruitlessly pleading for Bonnier's life and sending coded signals, 'Christopher Robin to Tigger,' seeking reprieve. This was the first reply.

A window was open and the room was chilly but Christopher felt sweat burst out in beads on his forehead. He took the A. A. Milne book out of the canvas bag and went through the pages rapidly, his thumb peeling them back like that of a bank clerk counting money. The message took shape under his jabbing pencil:

TOP SECRET IMMEDIATE. CEASE PLAYING POLITICS RETURN FORTHWITH OWL.

That was all. A flash of anger. When he pushed the books back into the canvas bag he thought with cool precision: *Very well. It's up to me to get him out of there alone.*

There was a window at the end of a third-floor corridor that overlooked the compound. He took the stairs three at a time. From this elevation he could see down past the pale ancient wall that ran round this part of the Champ de Tir de Hussein Dey. Its tall gates stood open to admit a lorry that rumbled through — metal hoops but no canvas; a squad of French soldiers waiting to jump down when the lorry stopped. The firing squad.

They hadn't brought Bonnier out yet. A quarter of a mile away, beyond the corner of the casbah, the body of Admiral Darlan would soon lie in state in the rotunda and those who would salute it this morning would include Giraud and Eisenhower and Cunningham: the hypocrisy of it appalled him.

Attired in the hideous panoply of state ritual a small group of French officers arrived at the gate and entered the compound. The distance was too great for identification; he wondered if one of them was Giraud, who now commanded in Darlan's place and who had wasted no time in convening the court-martial on Christmas Day and sentencing young Bonnier to die on Boxing Day. The wheels of injustice spun with unseemly haste.

Christopher had no choice but to walk in boldly, relying on such identification as he had to get him past the sentries at the gate; then cut Bonnier loose and make a run for it, straight through the gate opening. Suicide run. But what alternative was there?

A diversion would help: a handkerchief in the spout of the lorry's fuel tank; a sulphur match, explosion, fire.

The rudimentary plan was forming in his mind. He turned from the window and made for the head of the stairs, moving swiftly. Bonnier was scheduled to be executed in less than ten minutes.

He walked right into it, blindly, at the first-floor landing. They had begun to spread out along the corridors to search for him but he blundered unaware into their view; one of them gave the alarm and instantly he was surrounded by men in police uniforms and d'Astier, the Commissaire, was before him. 'I'll have your revolver, please.'

Christopher understood well enough. 'There's to be no reprieve, then?'

'None. We've orders from London to see you safely on your way home.' D'Astier's fingers beckoned gently and Christopher undid the holster flap. His mind sorted and discarded the possibilities of escape. He counted eight policemen in the squad – all of them armed. The Commissaire was too polite to voice threats but they'd shoot him quickly enough if he forced the issue. Christopher proffered the revolver butt first and d'Astier took it, handed it to an aide and took Christopher's elbow.

When they emerged into the sunlight d'Astier said, 'They're bringing him out,' and through the tall gates across the boulevard Christopher saw the zouaves marching Bonnier to the wall. The firing squad was not in Christopher's line of sight. A detachment of spahis took position before the gates, burnooses rippling in the cool wind, their long rifles across their chests. An officer's call rang distantly across the air – 'Load'. Christopher heard distinctly the harsh clack of rifle bolts slugging home.

Against the wall, lashed to the post, the slender young man

246

trembled but kept his chin high. The sun was on his face; his eyes were shut.

D'Astier guided Christopher down the steps and into the waiting Renault. They handcuffed him to the looped hand-strap and the aide in the front seat sat twisted round with the muzzle of his Le Mat propped on top of the upholstered seam, trained on Christopher's throat: they were taking no chances with him, they knew his skills.

D'Astier settled in beside him and the door clunked shut; the driver put the car in gear and when it drew away from the kerb Christopher heard the crash of the executioners' gunfire.

He shut his eyes and bowed his head, blind with sudden tears. 'Bastards.'

D'Astier's voice was gentle: 'I agree, the haste is rather indecent.'

Christopher wiped his eyes on his sleeve. The car lurched round a turning. They were driving, he saw, not towards police headquarters but towards the harbour.

D'Astier said, 'I spoke with Bonnier in his cell last night. He said he was ready to die for the glory of Free France. He said he had shot Darlan for the honour of his country.'

Christopher fixed him with a disbelieving stare. 'He confessed? He told them he shot Darlan?'

'It's hardly a secret, is it?'

'Why did you stop me?'

'We didn't need an incident. You'd have accomplished nothing—only your own death. Questions would have been raised. That would have served no purpose. You must understand, monsieur—supreme command wanted him out of the way. He'll reveal nothing to anyone now, will he?'

D'Astier's complacency sickened Christopher. 'You could have saved him,' he said angrily.

'No. Like you, I could have made a vain attempt to influence the outcome. I'd have sacrificed myself to no purpose. Don't you see it yet? His execution was ordered.' D'Astier glanced up towards the roof of the car. His meaning was clear enough. Did the order come from London, Washington, or the Free French?

The Renault chugged on to a pier and stopped. His hands were freed and d'Astier walked him to the end of the pier. A

ladder led down to a small open outboard motorboat, two harbour policemen in it. Christopher said, 'Listen to me,
d'Astier. . .'

'Don't make trouble, my friend. It would accomplish nothing
other than your own destruction.'

Acidly Christopher said, 'I don't suppose you intend to admit
your part in the plot.'

'No more than you plan to admit yours.' D'Astier beckoned,
an over-the-shoulder gesture, very casual. The aide walked
forward from the car.

'Your aircraft is waiting.' D'Astier held his hand palm-up
over his shoulder and behind him the aide pressed Christopher's
revolver into it. D'Astier slipped the revolver into Christopher's
holster and buttoned the flap down over it. 'It is unloaded, of
course.'

'Perhaps we'll meet again.' Christopher snarled.

'I imagine not. Bon voyage, monsieur.'

Christopher started down the ladder. D'Astier said, 'Tell me
—how long have you been at this sort of business?'

'Three years.'

'And how old are you?'

'Eighteen.'

D'Astier said, 'I shall never understand the English.'

Chapter Twelve

It was an innocuous office in the Ministry of Pensions. Approaching the door, Winnie the Pooh stabbed a finger towards it and said to Christopher, 'Abandon hope,' and pushed it open.

The girl at the desk was plump, new to Christopher. 'He's expecting us,' said Pooh, and the girl nodded them through. Christopher did not know how much Pooh knew of the affair and therefore he had not spoken of it in the train from Portsmouth. Pooh had kept up a running monologue – the North African successes, Monty's push, the difficulties the Germans were having at Stalingrad, something about naval battles in the Pacific – Christopher hadn't listened with any care; he hadn't slept on the plane because the anger had kept him keyed up and he'd been rehearsing what he intended to say in the confrontation with Owl.

Pooh ushered him into the rear office.

'Thanks for delivering him intact,' Owl said, dismissing Pooh, who smiled slightly towards Christopher as he withdrew. Christopher stood before him and said in a flat calm voice, full of enforced control. 'You gave your *word*.'

'There simply wasn't time, old lad. No-one expected Giraud to run Bonnier through the steeplechase so quickly. And after all they did arrest him with the smoking gun in his hand. I am sorry, Christopher. Please believe me. But there simply wasn't time to push a reprieve through the clumsy machinery of combined Allied command. One can't really expect everything to go according to plan, can one?'

'Who stopped the reprieve, then? You?'

'Giraud, I believe.'

'No. It came from higher than that.'

'Perhaps someone with De Gaulle, then? I know as much about that as you do. Sit down, won't you? There's no sense in standing about.'

Dry and dispassionate, Owl went on, 'I should like you to know that Tigger and I did everything possible. We didn't fail for want of trying.'

Christopher was not mollified. 'I signalled to you that Bonnier didn't kill Darlan. You could have acted on that – through the Prime Minister and General Eisenhower if need be.'

'No.'

'He didn't have to die!'

Owl raised a warning finger. 'Ease off, Christopher. I won't stand for tantrums. You don't understand the politics of it.'

'Sod politics! It's all right for you – you didn't have to sit handcuffed in d'Astier's car listening to them blast him.'

'I should have looked a proper fool if I had.'

'I might as well have shot Bonnier myself.' He suddenly felt very tired.

Owl only watched him with a schoolmasterish scowl.

Christopher deliberately kept his voice down. 'Before I went out on this one I told you I'd done with killing innocents for you. You gave your word Bonnier would be brought out safe.'

'I did my utmost to keep that pledge. I failed.'

'You bastards think all you need do is. . .'

'Sit down.'

It was fatigue, more than the tone of command in Owl's voice, that made him comply. Owl pulled his own chair forward. He tapped Christopher on the knee, cool and menacing. 'It's time you put away childish things,' he said. 'Bonnier was a casualty of war. Nothing more. He knew what he was about – he undertook the risk with his eyes open. For certain things men have always been ready to kill, and ready to die. This isn't a matter for schoolboys sniggering in the lavatories and arguing points of philosophical morality. It's a bit late now for you to turn your collar round, don't you think?'

Christopher blinked. He made a stubborn effort to recall the speech he'd rehearsed. Betrayed by weariness he spoke with artless directness. 'I've been murdering people for you and Tigger since I was fifteen years old. It's finished. No more. You've broken your word to me once too often. I'm sick of being the Prime Minister's private hatchet-man.'

'That's your final word, is it?' Owl seemed bemused. 'Then I'd better bring you round to tell that to Tigger.'

In the war rooms the little wooden sign that had been slipped into the 'Weather above' slot bore the word 'Sunny' for the benefit of those who spent weeks down here without surfacing.

Owl took him down the tunnel and left him in Mr Churchill's chamber. He leant against the wall and waited. A childish piping voice, familiar from half-waking dreams, echoed through his head alarmingly. *How many did you kill today?* He stood half-awake without reckoning time. Then suddenly Mr Churchill was in the room with him, and the room was made different by his presence.

'Well, my dear.'

A Royal Marine entered, handed the PM a whisky and soda, and withdrew. There was ice in the glass. Tigger growled, dipped his hand in and threw a handful of ice into the dustbin. 'You shot Darlan, then?'

'I did.'

Christopher pushed himself away from the wall, standing loosely to attention. It did not escape him that Mr Churchill did not offer him a drink; he was oblivious to the comforts of others.

'Afterwards you placed the smoking pistol in the Frenchman's hand?'

'It was what he wanted.'

'For the glory of France,' Churchill murmured in French in his atrocious accent; then back to English. 'You liked the youth, I take it?'

'Yes.'

'Uncle John rang through to me, of course. I am forearmed. You've had enough slaughter, have you? You've come to show me the error of my ways. Perhaps you expect this to be one of those 'Let us forget you're a soldier and I am your commander' talks? I'm sorry but I must disappoint your expectations. You liked Bonnier just as I rather like you, but I sent you out there all the same. Because our allies needed it, because the circumstances required it, and because strategy compelled it. Christopher, it is not the first time I shall have said this, and I am quite sure it is not to be the last, but I trust you will listen now. Without victory there is no survival. That's the nature of the war we must wage against this monstrous Nazi tyranny. The immediate issue before us is neither freedom nor human welfare, neither morality nor justice for the innocent. It is the raw issue of power. Warfare, whatever it may not prove, does decide the disposition of power – military, and also political and economic power. Power, of course, is amoral; hence the issues of war are not susceptible to moral examination. And as you certainly must know by now, in war individual morality is always the first casualty. Every casualty is immoral – Bonnier's no more so than that of any soldier in the line. But the issue is power and the elimination of Darlan was necessary to its exercise.'

Mr Churchill's eyes were not twinkling, as they sometimes did; they were glittering. Christopher wished he would get over his harangue but he knew there was no interrupting him. When the monologue ran down and he remembered the whisky in his hand, the PM gave Christopher a reproachful look as though the young man were taking up too much of his valuable time. Abruptly the old man said, 'What do you want?'

It took him aback and he found himself thinking, *Want? I want to be fifteen again – I want none of it to have happened.* But what he said, rather stiffly, was, 'I should like release from my present duties, sir.'

'And what will you do if it's granted?'

'Join the Royal Navy and get a real commission – not this.' He indicated the uniform he was wearing – Peter Hamilton's uniform.

'I see. You want to get back your honour. You want to fight a clean fight.'

Christopher had never felt so tired. 'I've earned it,' he said. 'At least I've earned that much.'

Unaccountably the old man wasn't annoyed. 'You've got hubris – do you know the word?'

'No.'

'From the Greek. Freely translated it can be taken to mean insolence in the face of the gods – a cheeky willingness to offend one's betters.' Then at last the twinkle: 'It's a trait they've often accused me of possessing. Whoever my betters may be.'

'Yes sir. Am I to get my release?' He pushed it hard because it might be his only chance; Mr Churchill was in an unusual mood. It wasn't often one got his attention, not in any personal way.

Head thrust forward on his short neck the old man scowled

towards the sleeping cat on the bed. 'You've grown up. You can't very well pass for a boy on a bicycle any longer.'

'No.'

'On the other hand you must realize we've invested a great deal in your training and apprenticeship. Are we to waste that?'

'I should think,' Christopher said with muted rage, 'I've paid that back by now.' He took a pace forward and hesitated. It occurred to him, not for the first time, that Mr Churchill was peculiarly vulnerable: he was the Prime Minister of a great nation and had placed himself alone in a room with a young man who had been trained to kill in a hundred ways.

If the same thought had occurred to Mr Churchill he made no show of it. He glowered at Christopher. 'You're very angry, aren't you?'

'I bloody well am. Sir.'

'An angry man makes mistakes. If I sent you into the field again, feeling as you feel, you might make a mistake – the sort that could go heavily against us. You make me vulnerable, old son, and I don't like it, but what am I to do about it?'

'I suppose you could have me killed.'

'You say that with such indifference. Is life that painful for you?' Then he muttered, 'You've faced danger and death with brash cheer – you're a buccaneer and a brigand after my own heart. I shan't ever forget the demonic audacity with which you crashed into my life the first time – you were eleven years old, weren't you? But then we've both grown older. Perhaps we've even grown up a bit. I believe the salve of time will heal your wounds. You've been of great value to England and to me but I suspect it would diminish if we remained together. You've changed and the war has changed; it's not the same adventure for either of us now.'

Christopher stood erect with an effort. 'Am I released then?' He pressed it with truculent stubbornness.

'Yes.'

It so startled him he was uncertain he'd heard it right.

The PM went round the desk. 'Go on – go and fight your honourable fight.' He reached for a telephone. His eyes came up, a faint and fading smile; an abrupt preoccupation and the pale eyes slid away as he put the receiver to his face.

Christopher went to the door and glanced back. The old man was muttering into the mouthpiece, glowering at one of the wall maps; he'd already forgotten Christopher.

At midnight Owl presented himself at 10 Downing Street and one of the secretaries took him through to Winston's cabinet room.

The PM said, 'I've just come from a conversation with Mr Roosevelt from the loo.' The 'loo' was one of Winston's private jests: a cubicle in the underground war corridors which contained a portable lavatory and his private direct telephone line to the White House. Everyone knew about it and everyone except Winston found it ludicrous. It amused the PM to conduct affairs of the mighty alliance from that particular throne.

'We'll be meeting in North Africa in about a fortnight. Marrakesh or possibly Casablanca – I'm leaving the specific arrangements to Cunningham and Bedell Smith. Mr Roosevelt will be there, and Eisenhower. I suppose Giraud will be there. I want you to invite De Gaulle. Do it in such a way that he'll be pleased to come. He's a nuisance but he's France and we must have him there.'

Owl understood. The invitation must be carefully arranged; De Gaulle would resent it if he felt he were being summoned.

'With reference to General De Gaulle,' Owl said in his dry way, 'he might have made things difficult over the Darlan affair. Fortunately it came off, in the end, but no thanks to the French. *Le grand Charles* has an unhappy tendency to believe that whatever he orders will perforce be done. It seems never to occur to him that an instruction from him might be botched by some fool down the line. The entire plan for using Bonnier was addled from the start. Only young Christopher saved us this time. Without him we'd have had a mess on our hands. It may be a mistake to invite De Gaulle to participate in the meeting.'

'The French need a hero,' the PM replied. 'There's no-one else but Charles. He's got the presence for it, the voice, the magnetism and the flair. When France is liberated he must be there to hold them together against the Bolsheviks. Get him to Morocco,' he concluded imperiously; but he softened it by appending 'John'. It was odd, Owl reflected, in view of their long friendship, how seldom Winston addressed him by that name.

In a characteristically abrupt change of subject Winston said, 'I want you to give young Christopher leave to join the Royal Navy.'

'He's played on your sympathy then.'

'He's earned it.'

'What did he do? Fill you with feelings of guilt? Children are such moralists,' Owl complained.

'He's no longer a child.'

'He's hardly eighteen. But then I suppose one has one's principles, doesn't one?'

'Don't mock me,' the Prime Minister chided. Owl proffered a deprecating smile; he took note of Winston's pouting lips, the drooping right eyelid, the signs of fatigue. Owl thought, *No man has ever spared himself less,* and felt an unaccustomed compassion towards his friend.

'We've worn him out,' the PM went on. 'He needs time to recover his bearings. I believe he'll be all right because he's extraordinarily resilient but I want you to let him go.'

Owl reflected on Winston's odd attachment to Christopher, not for the first time; Winston's distorted heroic memories of his own youth had found new life in the boy.

Owl said, 'I don't think it's wise.'

'Nonsense.'

'Leave aside the fact I'd be distressed to lose so valuable an agent. Let's concern ourselves with the release to normal naval duty of a youth who for three years has been involved in work so sensitive that any leak could cause terrible consequences. Suppose he should reveal what he knows? It might be conscience, it might be resentment or spite – no matter. He might speak out.'

'No.'

'It's a risk,' Owl insisted. 'No matter how you may minimize it. Such revelations could bring about nothing less than your downfall as head of this government. I must ask you to reconsider the decision.'

'No. He won't betray me.'

'If nothing else, suppose he's captured and questioned by the Germans?'

'He's been questioned by the Germans before, hasn't he.' Winston grinned, relishing the scoring of a point. Then he became animated and, as always, lapsed into his lisp; he stuttered a bit as well, so that Owl had trouble following some of it. A slave to his own rotund and thundering words, Winston went on at inordinate length, generally to the effect that the plucky lad had earned an honourable retirement from the wild and dangerous and distasteful operations of the past three years; that Christopher deserved to have what remained of his childhood and youth returned to him; that Winston knew the boy like a son of his own and trusted him; and – in several neatly punctuated paragraphs – that this was all he intended to say on the matter.

It was an astonishing performance, not because of the raillery – which was customary – but because it was a very personal speech and came from a man to whom the faces, not to mention the names, of many of his most steadfast and worshipping servants often remained unfamiliar.

The PM had one further surprise for him. At the end of his discourse he peered pugnaciously into Owl's face and said accusingly, 'You're thinking of the possibility of arranging a fatal accident for him, aren't you? Don't. I should be very cross.'

It was unlike Winston ever to know what was going through another's head; he was not, in that sense, an observant man. But he was not altogether off the mark. Owl said, 'That would be putting it rather strongly. I do think, however, that if you insist on his being turned loose then at least we must arrange to keep a close eye on him.'

'You'll find that will prove an utterly unnecessary precaution.'

'Nevertheless.'

'Very well. If you insist on making a fool of yourself.'

'It will give me comfort,' Owl said drily. Winston's moods, he knew, were subject to fitful change; it was possible this conversation would soon be forgotten; but Christopher, so long as he remained outside, would remain a threat. No matter how remote, the threat must be countered.

At a quarter to four on New Year's eve he let himself into Patricia's flat with the key she'd given him, carrying a bottle of champagne and a bunch of flowers. In the street an attractive girl in uniform had pedalled by on a squeaking bicycle and when she'd looked his way she'd averted her face quickly. He knew the thing that must have alarmed her was his face.

'Patricia?'

There was no reply. He went through to the little sitting room. She'd taken the flat furnished; the room had the usual faded clutter of lower-middle-class digs, print upholsteries and yellowed antimacassars and heavy curtains over the blackout curtains. She hadn't bothered to change it because she wasn't particularly domesticated. He opened the kitchen window to set the champagne bottle on the still to keep cool. He dropped his bag in the bedroom and went back to the telephone. He rang the usual number. Finally Pooh's avuncular voice came on and Christopher said, 'Tigger's given me a release. I'm in the navy.'

'Yes, I know. How on earth did you bring him round to it?'

'No idea,' Christopher said. 'He must have been in one of his soft-hearted moods.'

'Capital,' said Pooh.

'I just rang to say — I shan't forget you. You're the only one who. . .'

'Stuff it,' said Pooh in gruff embarrassment. '*Bon voyage* in the senior service.'

'Thank you.'

'Are you all right, then?'

'I suppose so.' Christopher said something polite and rang off.

Are you all right, then? He wondered what sort of answer he could possibly give to that question if he were to be honest. Physically everything seemed to be in proper working order; his mental capacities seemed unimpaired; but he remembered the girl on the bicycle who'd been frightened by what she'd seen in his face. He sat down before Patricia's dressing table and tried to see in the mirror what might have alarmed the girl.

It told him nothing. You couldn't see your face as others saw it. It looked unremarkable enough to him — a good square face on a well-shaped head, fair hair cut militarily short; people told him he was good-looking and he did not disbelieve them — and he looked away after a moment because there seemed something unmanly about examining one's own image. From what he could see there were no obvious indications of demons hidden there. The eyes were simply blue eyes—perhaps a bit less revealing than most but nothing remarkable.

Fitfully he went into the kitchen. He found a bottle of lemon squash, opened it and walked restlessly through the flat with a glass in his hand. The girl on the bicycle kept coming back to him. A girl in uniform—afraid of him—inevitably it forced him to think of Anne.

Christopher Robin—How many have you killed today?

He'd no idea how long he had been sitting there when Patricia's voice shocked him awake: 'Hello there.' When he looked up she was dropping her tin helmet and respirator on the side table. He hadn't heard the door at all.

She swept off her cap and shook out her hair and crinkled her nose at him. Christopher stood up, awkward; he'd had his elbows on his knees and he'd got pins and needles.

'Cat got your tongue?'

'They've given me ten days' leave before I report to Lochailort. I'm in the Andrew now.'

'I know. What's wrong with you, then?'

'You *know*?'

'Your colonel rang. He told me I might expect you on the doorstep—like a wet kitten. That's how he put it.'

Pooh. 'The sod knows everything, doesn't he.' He hobbled towards the kitchen, feeling disconnected from reality, as if the objects around him were further away than they should have been; he retrieved the bottle from the sill and turned to find her in the doorway watching him. He lifted the bottle at arm's length. 'Happy New Year.'

'What sort of greeting is that?'

He put the bottle down and she came to him; her hands went up behind his neck and he felt the slump of her soft body against him; he felt through the cotton the warmth of her skin. All the pent-up rage seemed to pour out of him as if a drainplug had been pulled. 'Oh Patricia. . .'

She tipped her face up for his kiss. Then she went into the bedroom to change out of her uniform. He followed her into the room; she was nudging his kit bag on the floor with her toe as she went by. 'I suppose you've washing to be done.'

'You and Pooh—you make a right pair.' Christopher made a face. 'He'd make a smashing mother-in-law.'

'He's terribly fond of you.'

He said, 'Can you get any time off?'

'I'm afraid I can't before Sunday. They keep telling me there's a war on.' She kicked her shoes off and padded to the wardrobe in her slip.

'Shoulders back,' he muttered, and as usual she ignored him. She had magnificent breasts but she had a way of hunching her shoulders forward as if to minimize them.

'I wish we could go off somewhere,' she said.

'Can I hang about anyway?'

'I'd be crushed if you didn't. But what will you do with the days?'

'I don't know. Pull myself together.'

'Poor Christopher. They've put you through the mill, haven't they? I think you need to talk about it.'

When he worked the cork out of the bottle it popped to the ceiling. She watched him stand there stupidly with champagne dripping down his fist. Looking at it she said, 'If you keep it bottled inside you long enough. . .'

'Did Pooh tell you to say that?'

'No.' Flash of angry green: 'Credit me with a few thoughts of my own.'

'I'm sorry.' It occurred to him that he hadn't brought glasses. He went into the kitchen to get them. When he emerged he found her in the sitting room; she said, 'What shall we have to eat?'

'I'm not very hungry.'

'Shall I make scones and honey?'

'All right.' He followed her back into the kitchen, raised his glass, and said lamely, 'Happy New Year again.' He watched her take things out of cupboards and begin to mix the dough. 'They've released me. But they're afraid when I go back to a normal sort of life I'll start to relax and I'll forget to keep their bloody secrets. I've got to spend the rest of my life not talking about it, haven't I? I want to put everything behind me and start again. I don't know if I can but I want to try. I'm not sure how to set about it. What would you do in my shoes?'

Patricia smiled. 'Wear them.'

'Bloody great help you are.'

'I can't live your life for you.' She put the scones under the grill. 'You don't want me to tell you what to do – you want me to help to take your mind off it, right?' She reached for his hand; her voice went throaty, her grin sexy: 'Let's just celebrate the New Year.'

'You ought to have had a date tonight.'

'I've got one.'

'But you didn't know that.'

'There's a party at Bletchley. I begged off it after your colonel rang. I haven't been out with other men in a long while, you know.'

'You should do. I shan't be in London much after my leave's up.'

She lifted his hand to her lips. 'Don't you understand? There's no-one else I want to go out with just now.'

'A remark that should earn you a kiss.'

'I should think so,' she agreed, and tipped her face smiling to meet his lips.

In the sitting room he put a coin into the meter and turned up the gas fire. A siren wavered eerily in the far distance and he heard faintly the thump of bombs. They went about the room tucking in the edges of the blackout curtains. With an explosive burst of feeling Christopher said, 'I hope to God we're still the same with each other after the war ends.'

'We'll take what comes, shall we?'

There had been a time, he reflected, when he too had been able to take things a moment at a time without thought for the future. At that time everything had been an adventure and the only threat had been boredom. But he had been a child then.

Chapter Thirteen

The officers' training at HMS *Lochailort* in the Highlands was rugged. Up before dawn for a swim in the freezing river wearing only a singlet and shorts, carrying a rifle and pack up out of the water. There were Wren stewards serving in the wardroom. His friend Nigel Anderson chided him for not pursuing them but then Nigel didn't have Patricia.

Nigel had a carefree approach to life. His father was a prominent barrister, rumoured to be on the point of taking silk. It turned out that he and Christopher knew some of the same people. Nigel's sister had been a pupil at Madame Vacani's. 'I may have danced with her,' Christopher said.

One Saturday night they waited in the local for the Fort William train; there was a dance on. Nigel looked at the clock. 'Give us a couple of pints, love.'

'I don't know as you deserve them, I'm sure.' The girl drew two bitters and caught the gleam in Nigel's glance: 'We'll have none of that, you randy octopus.'

The place was full of tobacco smoke; Christopher could hardly see the people at the far end of the bar.

Nigel affected a silk scarf tucked under the collar of his coat. 'I'm thinking of applying for COPP when we've passed out.'

'What's that?'

'Combined Ops Pilotage Party,' he whispered. 'Submarine reconnaissance commando unit – lots of derring-do, going in under Jerry's nose, blowing up U-boat pens on the French coast, that sort of thing. Midget submarines and diving suits.'

'That's new to me.'

'I've a friend there. It's secret work, you know, but I'll put your name in if you like.'

A half minute's thought; then a grin. 'All right – yes.'

'You wait, Christopher. We'll win the bloody war on our own. Bottoms up.'

A week later he received a message to ring a number in London. He recognized the number and ignored the message.

The next day the chief called him in. 'You've got orders to ring this number.'

Now it was an order. Fuming, he placed the call. Pooh said, 'We'd like you to come down to London for a little chat.'

'It's not on. I'm out of all that for good.'

'Just a chat, Christopher. No commitment. We can arrange a day's leave.'

'The answer will be no. Why bring me all the way down to London to hear me say that?'

'Christopher. . .'

'Is it a job?'

'In a way. Of sorts. Look – you might even like this one.'

'Don't bother to ring back.' He replaced the receiver and left the call box.

Bloody leeches.

The past haunted him at intervals but sometimes days went by when he was able to forget it; days at sea when the fine spray drifted against his face carrying the tang of salt and freedom. He was looking forward to the end of the course and getting his commission. In the meantime on shore leave he went off with Nigel and raised merry hell.

The Allies were fighting in Italy but the Luftwaffe had virtually disappeared from the skies and the war seemed a bit distant most of the time now. Everyone awaited the Second Front; American troops were beginning to appear in the towns in large numbers and the general feeling was one of impending victory. It was no longer *will we win*, but *when*?

Relieved, restored and revived, Christopher felt healed and happy.

Owl had taken Pooh to dinner at the Savoy Grill and hadn't talked a word of shop during the entire meal. Pooh was uneasy when they returned to Storey's Gate; he'd have preferred to be on his way home but Owl wanted to discuss something. They went up to Room 60 and Owl said, 'Let's keep our voices down, shall we?' He pointed to the floor. There'd been a bomb hit near Downing Street some time ago and the Prime Minister and his wife had moved into the Storey's Gate building – to a flat just above the steps leading down to the Hole in the Ground. Owl said, 'The floors have ears,' and poured out two measures of Rémy Martin. No wartime belt-tightening for Owl.

'How much do you know about "Overlord"?'

'Very little. It's hardly my area.'

'It soon will be,' Owl said. 'Winston and FDR settled it at Quebec. They've targeted "Overlord" for May.'

Pooh lifted the grass wryly. 'I thought the PM was doing everything in his power to discourage the landings in France.'

'He's been reluctant. He didn't want to see the beaches carpeted with the bodies of British soldiers. But he's been fighting a rear-guard action for two years and the Americans have never taken off the pressure. I think Roosevelt convinced him — Roosevelt and Hitler's boffins.'

'Oh?'

'Roosevelt because Winston's really quite fond of him. The President seems convinced he can't survive the next elections unless he can present his voters with a big victory over here. That's enough to influence Winston, isn't it — he'd much rather go on dealing with Franklin Roosevelt than with some devil he doesn't know.'

Pooh regarded the cognac in the bottom of his glass. Owl said, 'The German boffins plan to deploy a variety of new ironmongery. Hitler's rather mad for secret weapons and apparently some of them actually work. Pilotless aircraft, jet-powered planes, flying bombs, and so forth. Within another year they'll have all those things operational. We can't afford to sit still any longer and wait for Hitler to starve. At the moment the only thing preventing the Nazis from winning the war is the Russians and we can't have the Russians winning it by themselves, can we. That's Winston's view and I share it.'

Owl refilled their glasses and settled into his seat. It was a large comfortable leather chair. 'At this point Hitler isn't merely waiting for an Allied invasion — he's praying for it. He sees it as his last chance of a decisive victory in the West so that he can give his undivided attention to the Soviets. He may be right — the pessimists in Combined Operations are predicting casualties as high as ninety per cent if the Germans know we're coming.'

'As bad as that?'

'They've built the bloody Atlantic Wall, haven't they. *Festung*

Europa. One can't help remembering Dieppe. Multiply that hundredfold. . .'

'I see.'

'Our job's obvious then — find the means of persuading Hitler that the invasion will take place at point X, while in fact it takes place at point Y.'

'Do we know which points X and Y are?'

'No. It hasn't been decided yet. But we've got to start laying the groundwork. All the intelligence services are involved — the intention is to inundate Berlin with deceptions — a thousand lies, all designed to convey the same information.'

'Then we'll need to muster everyone we've got.'

'Yes.' Owl's voice was quite low and grave. 'Even Ike's chief of staff gives "Overlord" only a fifty per cent chance of success as things stand now. We've got to improve those chances, haven't we.'

'Indeed we have.'

'The trouble with Winston is he never does things by halves. Now that he's decided to capitulate to the Americans he's become "Overlord's" staunchest advocate. It won't be long before he's straining in the traces to be off — and we know his disregard for practicalities, don't we. We've got to keep him from going off wildly in the wrong direction.'

'What do you mean?'

'I mean that given his head he may plunge in too deep and too fast. He's ordered "C" and Intrepid and the rest, all of us in concert, to lay on this vast web of deception. Well it may be too much. It may strike the Germans as being too convenient and too deliberate. A big red herring is much easier to detect than a small one, isn't it?'

'What do you suggest we do, then?'

'I'm only thinking out loud. But it might be a good idea to explore the idea of offering Hitler alternatives. Put our eggs in more than one basket.'

'Perhaps,' Pooh said, 'but in the end, whatever the PM's faults, I think we must trust his fighting instincts.'

'I trust his instincts,' Owl replied. 'It's Hitler's instincts I'm worried about.'

Christopher marched smartly into the captain's office and

saluted. This moment was one to which he had been looking forward with keen anticipation and he couldn't keep the smile off his face when he came to attention and awaited the blessing of the navy.

When the captain spoke it was like a shower of ice crystals. 'The Admiralty has sent orders to return you to Portsmouth Barracks as a rating. I'm afraid you're not getting your commission, Creighton.'

He stood stunned. Nothing in his exemplary performance during training could have caused the denial. He had passed out third in his class. He'd had no black marks at all. His arms hung at his sides and he felt powerless to move.

'I'm frightfully sorry about this.'

'Did – did they give any reason, sir?'

'No. I'm sorry, Creighton, but it's no good arguing the point with me. I'd nothing to do with it, had I.'

Christopher stumbled furiously out of the office.

An eager autumn sun brightened the day but it might have been midnight. So much for youthful idealism and his determination to set things right. It seemed that he'd blotted his copybook irrevocably and there was no redemption after all...

Then the penny dropped.

Owl. The bizarre bastard.

Owl laughed at him. 'It got you here quickly enough, didn't it. Sit down, won't you?'

'You're inhuman.'

'Come now. I haven't the time to be human.'

'Bugger time – and you.' He pounded the desk with his fist. 'If I don't get that bloody commission all your commando bastards with arms locked won't stop me from...'

'You'll have your commission by this evening if you'll sit down and discuss things in a rational way.'

It took the wind right out of his sails and he frowned at Owl. 'Do you mean that? About the commission?'

'Yes, with an appointment to COPP. That's what you want, isn't it?'

Christopher was still suspicious. 'What's the price?'

'Sit down.'

He sank into the chair.

Owl said, 'We knew the refusal of a commission would be the last straw. It was a device to provoke a reaction. We needed to know how you'd take it, you see. If you'd gone storming about, laying waste to pubs and blurting out your spite against me in front of whores and policemen, we should have had to send you away into detention for the duration. As it is, by keeping things to yourself and coming directly to me you've passed the test and —'

'I'm not interested in passing your bloody tests!'

'Nonetheless you've passed this one with flying colours.'

'Hurrah.'

'You will be commissioned immediately upon your agreement to perform one final mission for us.'

'You bastard.'

'It won't take place for some months and it will interfere very little with your naval duties. You're simply to place yourself on call, ready to act for us when called upon.'

The choice was clear enough and there was a tug of loyalties but it didn't take him long to respond; he'd made the decision months ago and told them then and nothing had changed except for their foul blackmail. 'I'm not killing for you. You can keep your ruddy commission if it's. . .'

'It's nothing like that. You won't even carry a weapon.'

Christopher thought, I'll make him sweat a bit. 'I think I've heard that one before,' he said.

'This time it's quite true. No assassinations, no executions. You'll be making contact with Breucheur again and sending some information across to the other side. That's the sum of it.'

He was quite certain that wasn't anything near the sum of it because if it was a simple matter of delivering misinformation they could use anyone — one of Breucher's own agents perhaps.

'As I say, it'll be several months before it comes up, if it ever does,' Owl said. 'In the meantime you'll report to HMS *Dolphin* — 5th Submarine Flotilla, Portsmouth — and occupy yourself with reconnaissance missions on enemy beaches. Do look after yourself. We don't want the Jerries depth-charging you to the bottom of the Channel.'

Christopher was a Snotty now — a midshipman RNVR. It was real, not something they'd tricked up in the printing presses in the cellars at Northways. Owl hadn't understood. *It's beyond me how you can set so much store by it. You've achieved a record of valour that puts that of any admiral in the fleet in the shade – if the work hadn't been clandestine you'd have won the Victoria Cross ten times over if it were possible.*

He pedalled in through the imposing fortress gate. The sentry saluted him. He went past several outbuildings and racked the bike beside twenty others and went inside. Nigel was waiting. 'You're two days late. What happened?'

'There were some red-tape difficulties about my commission. I had to go to London to sort it out.'

'But it's all right, is it?'

'Yes. Everything's fine.'

'Thank God for that. We'd heard rumours you'd got the sack.'

Christopher grinned. 'Never fear.' He'd fought too hard for this: if necessary he'd have gone to the Prime Minister and demanded reinstatement.

Nigel looked at his watch. 'We've still got forty minutes. Let's have a pint.' He steered Christopher towards the ward-room.

'Forty minutes till what?'

'COPP briefing. They're saying we've got some sort of big show laid on. You and I are just coming aboard in time for it.'

'Good. I can do with some action.'

They filed into the big room and took their seats in rows like worshippers arriving for the Sunday service. Nigel nudged Christopher and pointed towards the map easels on the stage at the front of the room. Cloths were draped over the maps to conceal them and Nigel said, 'I can't wait for the strip-tease.'

The hubbub dwindled when a knot of senior officers marched in from the rear and everyone came to attention. There was a burly captain at the head of the group and he climbed on to the stage and took the podium, a long stick under his arm. 'Be seated – be at ease. Smoke if you wish.'

Nigel whispered in Christopher's ear: 'That's Urquhart. Big reputation in the boats.'

The captain took time to light up a pipe; soon the room was thick with smoke.

'If you'd be so kind as to let me have your attention. . . Right. We're here to talk about D-day. The invasion of the Continent. I can't tell you when or where it will be because I don't know myself, but we do know it's got to be somewhere between Den Helden in Holland and Brest on the Brittany peninsula. We know it and the Jerries know it. Somewhere along those six hundred miles of coastline the D-day landings will take place, probably within the next six or eight months. It's a matter of logistics and support — we've got to deliver the force across the Channel and we've got to be within fighter range of the RAF airfields. I'm not telling you anything Jerry hasn't already discovered for himself, but I'm about to' — Urquhart made it 'aboot' and you could still hear the Scottish lilts — 'and you are to keep quiet about everything that's said here this morning.'

The captain put his pipe down in a glass tray, extracted the stick and nodded to one of his officers, who tossed the cloth back over one of the easels to expose a map of the European coast from Denmark to Spain.

'Jerry knows we're coming.' The stick slid along the beach lines. 'Hitler has given the job to Field Marshal Erwin Rommel, a gentleman I'm sure we all remember. Rommel is nobody's fool. He's been given the job of making the Atlantic Wall impregnable against us. You can be assured of two things: that he's done his best to carry out those orders, and that his best is very good indeed.

'Now then,' Urquhart went on, 'we've had quite a bit of information coming in from Resistance movements across the Channel which indicates that the Atlantic Wall is intended eventually to stretch along the entire coast as you see it on this map — from the Jutland peninsula to the Spanish border. As yet the fortification is incomplete but Rommel has concentrated his construction along the Channel where he knows we are most likely to strike. The German defences are numerous and strong. Millions of hidden undersea mines and other obstacles have been laid off the shore. Onshore there are blockhouses, trenches, anti-tank walls, barbed-wire entanglements, minefields several hundred yards deep, pillboxes and bunkers, gun positions, infantry revetments, Luftwaffe airfields, the lot. Forests of stakes, mines, wires and booby-traps have been stretched along many of the most likely landing beaches. In short, as I said, Rommel is doing his job.

'Now it's our turn to do ours.' Another puff of the pipe, a canny good-humoured look round the room from face to face. 'When Ike and Monty and the rest of them go ashore they'll want to know what they're up against. It's our job to provide them with that information

'Between now and D-day, whether it's six weeks or six months from now, the objective of COPP will be to reconnoitre every inch of likely beach between Den Helden and Brest. And when we've covered it all once we're to go back and start again and keep updating our intelligence until the flag goes up.'

Another cloth came off another easel. This one was a schematic drawing, a profile of a beach: waterline, and under it a sloping sea floor, and then the slope of the beach and the dunes above and the dry land above that. 'Your job will be to gather every scrap of information you can obtain. Offshore defences, both floating and underwater, including the charting of shoals if any. Onshore defences – mines, obstacles, gun emplacements, concertina wire, whatever. Everything is to be mapped with precision to the inch. Ike wants reports on everything from beach gradients to the type of sand – he must know whether a given beach is suitable for wheeled vehicles or tracked vehicles or no vehicles at all.

'So far as I know, the site for the D-day landings has not yet been decided. Whether the decision has been made or will be made soon is beside the point. Our assignment is to continue to reconnoitre *all* possible beaches – and we'll have orders now and then to leave evidence that we've been there. The purpose, of course, is to confuse the Jerries as to our real target. Also if any of you are captured you won't be able to tell Jerry anything useful. I'm sorry about that but that's how it's got to be.

'Individual commanders will receive specific orders to cover their own sectors. This briefing is intended to put you gentlemen in the over-all picture. Are there any questions?'

Fog rolled over the ship and enveloped her in a chill silence. The skipper had posted lookouts at bow and masthead; she proceeded at dead-slow revolutions, deadlights screwed down over all the portholes. On the bridge he saw the muffled officer of the watch pacing—a bulky figure barely discernible in the thick dark. There was the sound of creaking ropes and Nigel came along cheerfully, glistening in his Sibi Gorman blacksuit, flippers dangling from his fingers.

It was risky navigating because they were on dead-reckoning and if the ship got in too close there might be mines in the water but Nigel didn't seem aware of the dangers. Nigel seldom noticed anything that didn't have wheels, wings, potable alcohol or well-turned legs and breasts. He'd driven racing cars before joining the navy and he'd wanted to get into the Fleet Air Arm but he had a peculiarity of vision: not colour-blind but colour-confused—he had trouble with blues and greens. It was enough to keep him out of cockpits but he wasn't the sort who got crushed by that sort of thing. He was brash but seldom intense. Put an obstacle before him and he wouldn't batter it; he'd find another way round.

It hadn't escaped Christopher's notice that perhaps he'd become Nigel's friend because he was very much what Christopher would have been like if he hadn't been steadied by experience.

The sound of someone's approach came drumming against his ears and the CPO was there, amiable: 'Right, sir. Your turn now.'

'Thank you, Chief.' Christopher went along to the rail and they climbed over, down the Jacob's ladders. The kayak had been lowered and they got into it with care to maintain its balance. Then they cast off the lines and pushed the kayak away.

This was a one-way job for the ship and it disappeared into the fog. Christopher said, 'All right,' and they began to paddle.

Christopher's outfit was a Sladen Shallow Water Diving Suit. There wasn't much uniformity in COPP because the unit had been expanded too rapidly and they'd had to make use of everything available: that was why they were doing this recce by kayak off a surface ship rather than coming in from a midget submarine. There weren't enough five-man submarines to go round.

They made slow progress, alert to the danger of floating mines. Magnetic mines wouldn't be affected by the wooden frame or skin of the kayaks and that, along with its shallow draught and silence, was a principal reason for its selection; but there might be floating contact-detonator explosives.

The fog began to break up as they got closer inshore; there was an unusual east wind and it was driving the weather off. That was bad luck but it couldn't be helped.

He could hear waves lapping gently – it was a long sloping beach and there weren't any shoals to chop the water up. Nigel went over the side, eeling cleverly into the water, and after a moment his hand came up and gripped the gunwale and when his head broke surface he said, 'About two fathoms here,' in a dead-low voice and Christopher took up the paddle and pushed the kayak further inshore, Nigel swimming alongside towing the gunwale.

'Right.'

Christopher put up the paddle and handed the light anchor over the side and Nigel placed it in the water and let it sink to prevent the sound of a splash. Christopher let the line grow taut and then secured it to a crosspiece. He lowered one waterproof equipment sack to his partner and slipped his arms through the harness of his own and then he straddled the bow and flipped himself face-down into the water so that she wouldn't capsize.

They prowled about underwater for a while, swimming through the shallows, playing their lights. The RG battery lamps were not very bright and cast a reddish light through their lenses; watchers on the shore wouldn't see the glow. You had to use a green face-mask lens. The sea bed here had a shallow slope to it and the tide-line was a hundred feet or more away from them even though they were swimming in ten feet or less.

Because of the shallows the Jerries didn't seem to have mined the water. They switched off the lamps and swam towards the shore, reaching the five-foot point and standing up with their heads above water to steady their breathing.

A sentry was walking the beach, silhouetted against the pale sand. Nigel paddled closer to Christopher. 'Bloody hell.'

'Wait a while. He may move on.'

But it was trouble because the beach was as open and unsheltered as Salisbury Plain. There had to be lookout posts somewhere above it and without the fog it was too exposed, sentry or no sentry.

They went back underwater. Scooping up sand samples into screw-top containers and making sure they kept the containers in the right order because that was how they'd label them when they got back on board. You used a pocketed cartridge-belt for that and started with the first pocket to the left of the buckle and worked your way all round. This sand would be the same as the stuff on the beach because at low tide it would be exposed just like the other. But they had to sample it at twenty-yard intervals just to make sure: Ike's tanks wouldn't want to be running into sudden patches of quicksand.

They had no breathing apparatus; it was a skin-diving job and the blacksuits were more for camouflage and insulation than for pressure protection, since they rarely dived deeper than twelve feet on these coastal shots. But the Channel was *bloody* cold in April — and if it weren't for the wet suits they'd have perished from exposure.

Christopher carried a waterproof writing tablet with perforated lines and he used the special pencil to write in depths and gradients and negatives on mines, shoals and underwater obstacles. It would all go dutifully into the reports but he doubted they'd ever be used for anything; this coast was too far north for it and everyone knew the landings would take place around Calais anyway but there were outside chances of which the Germans had to be aware and part of the job was to keep the Germans uncertain.

Nigel surfaced, teeth chattering. They looked shoreward: the sentry was gone, either inland or round the headland. 'Want to chance it?'

'It's what we're here for,' Christopher said.

'Well it's warmer than bloody *Varbel*.' They'd been sent up to Scotland the previous month for a two-week tour of duty in rotation with the other crews; that was the roughest sector, not because of Germans but because of the water temperature. The base up there was HMS *Varbel* II at the inside tip of Loch Striven where COPP had its X-craft midget submarine bases and the depot ship, HMS *Cyclops*, lying just offshore. It had been nobody's idea of desirable duty and most of the chat in the locals of Rothesay and Dunoon had to do with how soon the crews could get back to the 'fleshpots' of Portsmouth. Well they were back now but it seemed just as bloody cold and the waters were mined like pincushions.

There was a broad-bladed windmill standing high in silhouette and almost certainly there'd be German spotters in it; and there were low humps just above the beach that might be hummocks and boulders but then again they might be pillboxes. Christopher went ashore on his belly and Nigel was right beside him: 'What if it's mined?'

Christopher said patiently, 'Do you think that sentry would have been walking up and down on it if it were mined?'

'All right.' Nigel was nervous, that was all. Christopher knew the feeling well enough.

The lumps were bunkers. Crawling closer he could see that much. There were coils of wire between them but all that was up above the beach and there didn't seem to be much of anything in the way of defences on the sand itself. He did spot a number of steel tank-traps up above the high-water mark and he sketched them in the notepad. They were moving an inch at a time and they spent a good three hours working from one end to the other, crawling under the overhang where they couldn't be seen from the bunkers above.

The sentry came back twice – the same sentry or a different one – but Christopher and Nigel lay in their black suits in the deepest shadows under the overhang and as long as you didn't move you weren't likely to be spotted. But then they were making their way back out to the water at three in the morning and they'd crossed half the distance when someone came in sight at the far end and they lay flat and Christopher heard the scrape when Nigel unclipped his commando knife and slipped it out of the scabbard.

It was clouding over again and there was hardly any light. The sentry was more of a suggestion than a figure; as he came nearer Christopher began to hear the crunch of his footsteps in the sand. He was walking along near the top of the beach where the sand was hardest packed and made for the easiest footing. On that course he'd pass twenty or thirty feet inland of them and there was a good chance he wouldn't see them.

Christopher had his hand on the hilt of his knife but he didn't draw it out. Nigel was holding his knife right down against his leg with the blade underneath so that it wouldn't show. The sentry came along, not hurrying, scanning the waterline because they'd been told to look out for British reconnaissance commandos. His rifle was balanced across his shoulder and it would take him time to manoeuvre it into the right position; that was in their favour but if the sentry got a shot off it would alert every machine-gun along the crest.

Then the sentry stiffened. His face was turned towards them and he stopped, one foot ahead of the other, peering into the gloom with his head thrust forward as if to burn it away: the rifle began to come down off his shoulder. Seeing in the dark wasn't easy: it was something that had to be learnt. The sentry still wasn't certain what he saw but the next thing he'd do would be to walk straight over to them and there were only a few feet between them now.

Christopher heard the rustle of movement beside him and saw Nigel had sat up. His knife was pulled right back; he was about to stab the sentry head on. With no more than an instant to spare Christopher grabbed his wrist and pulled Nigel down to him. He whispered urgently in his ear: 'No. Let him come to me.'

Direct knife stabbing was never any good; he'd had that driven home by his instructor agents. Nigel wouldn't have known this because COPP and commando courses didn't cover even ten per cent of the killer courses Christopher had taken. Killing anyone with a direct stab was twenty to one against: the rib cage hung protectively and through a uniform and greatcoat it would be almost impossible to penetrate.

The sentry came nearer, his footsteps drowned by the waves breaking on the beach. His foot came down and Christopher struck. His flipper cracked the rifle away, his left arm encircled the sentry's throat and wrenched the neck right back, and the fighting knife flashed upwards, the fingers of Christopher's left hand guiding the steel point under the man's ear and the right hand ramming it into the German's brain.

Christopher lowered him silently. It had taken six seconds. Average, thought Christopher. I've done it a bloody sight faster than that.

Now he sprawled flat beside the dead man and waited for it:

if the machine-guns were going to open up it would happen now.

Nothing. The sea had masked all sound.

He turned and crawled away, leaving the fighting knife in the body: the Germans would find it there and know they'd been hit again. That was what Supreme Command had ordered on this one. 'Leave a clue or two.'

They slithered into the water and Nigel said, 'Thanks.'

'All in a night's work.'

They swam out to the anchored kayak and managed to get into it without overturning it. That was an art and it had taken them a week's training to learn it. They pulled in the anchor and paddled out through easy swells and now the adrenalin began to drain down and they felt the real misery of the bone-chilling cold.

They had to paddle out nearly half a mile and Christopher dropped a hand grenade over the side into the water. There was a muffled thud and some bubbling from the pressure; then almost instantly the submarine surfaced fifty yards away, alerted by the signal grenade – and they de-activated the buoy, dived out of the canoe and left it to float in to shore on the current: another clue to let the Germans know they were under surveillance.

The hatch was open and they went down the ladder, their teeth chattering; the conning tower was darkened inside and someone handed them cups of hot tea and Christopher had to hold his in both hands, but all the same he shook most of it out of the cup before he could get it to his mouth.

He still had five days of the fortnight's tour of duty but he was ordered to report to Captain Urquhart. The officer at the door kept him waiting ten minutes and then sent him in; Christopher stood before the big captain's desk, at attention and puzzled because the orders to report here had been for him alone and not for the unit.

'Sit down, Creighton. You needn't look so tense – I'm not going to tear a strip off you. Quite the reverse, actually. You've had a commendation from your commander – you've done excellent work.'

'Thank you sir.'

The desk was covered by a long strip of photographs that had been taped together end to end – aerial pictures, taken from quite high up. There was a pale coastline towards the top, running irregularly along the length of the strip, and the rest was water, nearly featureless except for dots here and there that were ships and boats.

The captain followed Christopher's glance and explained: 'We do these aerial film strips at fifteen-minute intervals to get a picture of the movement patterns of ships entering and leaving the area. It helps us plot the enemy's minefields. This particular area's just off Calais and you can see how narrow the channels are that their ships keep to.'

'Yes sir. It's clogged with mines just round there.'

'That's right, you've reconnoitred that sector once or twice, haven't you?'

And nearly strangled on mine cables underwater more than once. But that wasn't the sort of thing you complained of.

'Have you got any impressions you'd like to pass on, Creighton?'

'Impressions of what, sir?'

'The Atlantic Wall. Ideas for breaching it. Our superiors are considering all suggestions.'

'Well there's one thing that's struck me, sir.'

'Go ahead.'

'Everything's directed outwards towards the sea, sir. Once you penetrate behind it they're defenceless – those guns can't be turned inland. There are no gun ports in the back sides of the bunkers. It might suggest, sir, that either those positions could be attacked from behind by paratroops, or we could land from the sea along very narrow spearheads so as to drive through a narrow opening and sweep out round behind them. I'm sure the same idea's occurred to a thousand others, sir, but I'm afraid it's the best I can offer.'

'It's worth passing upstairs. Well done.' It was said of Urquhart that he made a terrible enemy and a superb friend; he believed strongly in loyalty down as well as loyalty up. They said he'd go to the ends of the earth for those who'd earned his respect. But words like 'satisfactory' and 'adequate' were terms of opprobrium in the burly Scot's vocabulary; if you weren't outstanding you weren't good enough. There were junior officers who fought to get into his command — and others who fought equally hard to get out of it.

Therefore it meant something more than it might otherwise have meant when the captain said, 'You're not doing a bad job, Creighton, and I don't want the trouble of replacing you.'

'Replacing me, sir?'

'There's a colonel waiting to meet you downstairs. Army intelligence chap. It seems you've been singled out for some sort of cloak-and-dagger work. I've had instructions from Admiralty and they came from a desk so high I can't even see over it, so I'm not in a position to argue the point with them. But it's probably a volunteer job — these things usually are — and I want you to know that I won't consider it a black mark against you if you decline to volunteer for whatever they've got laid on for you. Without knowing anything about it, I'm inclined to the verdict that you're more valuable to me than you can be to them.'

Now it was definitely conspiratorial, right down to the wink. 'They've given us a ruddy impossible job here and I couldn't do it at all without chaps like you who've got the initiative and the intelligence to go beyond their training. Of course the trouble comes because as soon as you start parading your excellences they come to the attention of these bloody thieves in MI-6 and that lot. I made the mistake of forwarding your commander's commendations to Admiralty and I'm afraid that's all it's taken; now they've sent this bloody colonel down here to flog the romance of the secret service and pinch you from under my nose. I can't be seen to be objecting to it, but I wanted you to know my feelings.'

It had to be Pooh, of course. He couldn't tell the captain that he was mistaken, that they hadn't singled Christopher out because of his COPP record but rather they'd had a previous hold on him that the captain knew nothing about. It made him feel like a rotter but he did his best to make up for it:

'I shan't desert the fold, sir.' He said it with his old saucy grin. 'I'll do my best to convince him I'm a snivelling coward.'

'Right — that's the spirit. Off with you now. Room twelve.'

Christopher stood up to attention. 'Thanks, sir, for the vote of confidence.'

'Aagh,' the captain said, dismissing it. 'I'll say just one thing.

What Britain needs now is a few more snivelling cowards of your type.'

Pooh looked a bit embarrassed, as well he might. Christopher pulled out a chair and sat down without a word and let Pooh have the benefit of his cold stare.

Pooh shook his head backwards and forwards to express dismay. 'Ah, Christopher. You're a man too early – old before your time. I feel wretchedly responsible for it.'

He didn't reply; he was angry and let the silence work on Pooh's nerves.

'You're needed, old son.'

'Well I'm very popular. I'm needed all over the place.'

'You're having quite another war, aren't you.'

'Another war from yours, yes.'

'Christopher, you want to realize that what we are asking of you is a bit more important than thrashing about in a diving suit along with twenty other young men.' Pooh tugged at the tips of his moustache. 'The main German force opposing the Allied invasion will be Runstedt's ten armoured divisions. His Tigers and Panthers are superior to our tanks in nearly every respects. The Sherman tank's shells cannot even penetrate the German Tiger's seven-inch plate.'

'What of it?'

'It's vital that German armour is lured away from the "Overlord" invasion beaches. Otherwise we've no chance at all. You saw what happened to our tanks at Dieppe. Look here: the "Overlord" troops will soon be sealed into their staging areas to wait for D-day. The Germans know all about that. They don't know where or when, precisely, but they know it's to be somewhere on the French coast. We've got hundreds of thousands of men spread through camps throughout the south of England – you've seen it yourself. All roads and railway lines have been cleared for "Overlord" traffic and no-one can move from one sector to another without these bloody transit passes and we've got trains, lorries, vans, jeeps, everything that has wheels carrying millions of tons south, always south. Jerry can hardly fail to have been informed of this vast concentration of men and materials. Do you want figures? Believe me I've got them implanted on my eyeballs. . . The size of the force is spectacular but there's a weight of apprehension and the morale among the "Overlord" troops is very low. Even the Combined chiefs expect to lose eight or nine out of ten in the first assault on the beaches. And that will happen unless we can distract Hitler, Rommel and Runstedt away from the true target of the invasion. That's why we have called upon every agent within reach to help bombard Berlin with confusion and misinformation. And that's why you're being called.'

Pooh stopped then, to let him absorb it, and Christopher looked down. He discovered his fist – the knuckles had gone a bit white – and stared at it as if it were an unfamiliar object. Then he deliberately opened the fingers and forced his hand to relax; it required an act of will.

Pooh said, 'Your job will be to re-establish contact with the Abwehr in Dublin and keep the line open so that we can feed information down it as the time approaches.'

Without looking up Christopher said, 'If the chances are that poor why risk the invasion at all?'

Pooh said, not ungently, 'It's not for you to make those decisions, is it.'

'And it's not for you to give me orders. I'm not under your command.'

'When it comes to that we're all under the same command. Do you want us to go through the tedium of obtaining written orders from the Admiralty?'

Pooh looked a great deal older than he had when Christopher had first met him only four years ago. His face had gone pasty from all the sunless hours underground; his hands were mottled with cyanotic age spots; flesh hung in loose turkey folds under his chin.

Pooh said, 'We're all under the direction of the Prime Minister, aren't we? Listen – I don't enjoy this. But in the circumstances it can't be helped and Owl did warn you. We need *every* agent.'

'Next you'll tell me, like he did, that I won't have to murder anyone this time.'

'That's perfectly true. The intention is to save lives – not the enemy's of course. . .'

'There have been times when I haven't been that sure who the enemy is.'

'I'm beginning to lose patience with. . .'

'With broken promises and sacrificing four thousand men on the theory it may save forty thousand later? With murdering your girlfriend in the dark and sinking a submarine full of unsuspecting loyal allies? With murdering one French tyrant so another one can take his place? Is that what you're losing patience with, Colonel? Because it's what I've already lost patience with.'

'Oh, lad, I am sorry.'

In a softer tone he said, 'I know you are. They're not your schemes. You've been dragged round through the thistles the same way I have. But that doesn't change anything. I don't want this bloody job. This time let some other stupid hero have it.'

'It's hardly very profound,' Pooh said, 'but war makes murderers of us all.'

'It's not the same and you know it.'

'Christopher, Christopher. . .'

'I got out of it. I'm not going back in. You can tell that to Uncle John.'

Pooh said, 'You think I've come down to pull the rug out. Well I haven't. You like it in COPP and you don't want to give it up but this job won't mean having to give it up. A short break, that's all. I'm sorry. Perhaps I should have explained that at the beginning.'

Christopher shook his head. 'Do you think that makes any difference?'

'I thought it might. You'd only have to nip over to Dublin a few times and sell bits of information to Breucher. He'll buy it from you, I think, where he'd suspect it if it came from anyone else.'

'It wouldn't be that simple. These jobs never are. I'd end up kicking over the china shop. Look, go back and tell Uncle John that you've tried hard but this one's just not on.'

Pooh only fumbled with his moustache. Finally Christopher said, 'I look like a selfish bastard, don't I? Perhaps I am. But I've been told too many times that this job or that job can determine the outcome of the war. I just don't believe it any longer. I don't believe I'm making any less of a contribution to the war effort where I am than if I went back to work for you. You'll get the job done just as well without me.'

Pooh let the silence extend a bit before he said reluctantly, 'Your refusal is firm, then.'

'Too bloody right it is.'

'Then I've no choice but to instruct you to report to the Prime Minister. Friday evening at ten, Storey's Gate. Your orders can be taken to come from the Admiralty. Please be punctual.' Pooh went towards the door but then turned and put his hand on Christopher's shoulder. 'I'm sorry, lad, but it's too important for personal feelings.'

Office of Works. The Hole in the Ground. He hadn't been in it for a whole year. It struck him now, going down the spiral stairs, that the place was not dissimilar to the description they'd had of Hitler's underground bunker in Berlin.

The steel doors stood open and when Pooh took him through he was Peter Hamilton once more. He went past the 'loo' where the PM's private red telephone to the White House was concealed and it reminded him, oddly, of a time in 1941 when he'd been ordered to report to Mr Churchill there and he'd knocked and entered to find King George VI sitting there in his uniform telling the Prime Minister one of his navy jokes. On another occasion Christopher had glimpsed the King hurrying through the corridors in pyjamas and dressing gown. Cabbages and kings, he thought; the Hole in the Ground was a unique place, nearly a fairytale sort of place where kings in pyjamas mingled with cipher clerks and teenage paladins, crown ministers and faceless assassins, field-marshals and ordinary seamen. It was surprising how much laughter rang through the echoing concrete passages. It must be quite different, after all, from Hitler's bunker.

One of the staff told Pooh that the PM was expecting them and was in the War Room. They went round to it.

The war headquarters of the British Empire, but it was an astonishingly small room; the last man in always had to squeeze his way between occupied chairs and the wall to get to his seat.

It had nothing to mark its door except the numerals '69'. A Royal Marine pensioner stood on guard and Pooh looked through the small square window in the inside door. Then he pushed it open but someone inside was talking and Pooh waited for him to finish. 'But he is to be brought back out alive, whatever the cost. That is imperative. Do you understand? I shall tolerate no failure on that score.'

Christopher had difficulty in recognizing Mr Churchill's voice; it was weak and rather hoarse.

'Lieutenant Hamilton, sir,' said Pooh.

'Send him in. Thank you'

Christopher entered. Pooh backed away and closed the door behind him.

The PM sat in his customary chair. A man in a trilby hat and a dark overcoat sat at the table with his back to Christopher and did not look round.

Mr Churchill sat hunched and scowling, perspiring freely. His face had a grey tired look and there were unhealthy blisters under his eyes. He'd had pneumonia badly the past winter in North Africa and he'd only just survived it. He said to Christopher, 'Are you taking care of yourself?'

Unaccountably it made Christopher's eyes fill with tears. 'Yes sir, thank you.'

He began to circle round the trilby-hatted man but Mr Churchill's white hands flashed. 'Pray stay where you are a moment.' Then he addressed himself to the man in the hat: 'Hamilton is a *nom de guerre*. You will know this young man as Christopher Robin.' Then back once more to Christopher: 'The gentleman with his back to you is here at great personal risk to himself, and you are not to look at his face. It is possible you'll never have contact with him again. If you do, however, he will identify himself to you by giving you an order in which he will incorporate the phrase "valiant enterprise". Will you remember that?'

'Yes sir.'

'If you ever receive such an order from this man, you will obey it as if it came directly from me – instantly and without question or hesitation. Now be good enough to stand easy and shut your eyes and keep them shut until I speak again.'

Mystified, Christopher closed his eyes. He heard the man in the chair swivel round to look at him – *studying my face so that he'll know it when he sees it again.* Then the scrape of the chair and he felt the man brush past him; he caught the scent of harsh tobacco smoke from the man's clothes. Knuckles struck the door behind him; footsteps; then the door clicked shut.

'You may open your eyes. Sit down.'

He took the proffered seat. 'Sir — are you quite all right?'

'Pray don't ask such indiscreet questions. My health is good enough, I suppose. But these hours are bleak and sombre. I am dispirited and low of heart.' He'd been sitting up, bent forward with elbows on the table; now he flopped wearily back. 'I cannot help reflecting,' he growled in his preternaturally tired voice, 'upon an unfinished brick wall and a cheeky ill-behaved young man and the cataclysmic tumble that brought us first together.'

His puckish smile was not the sort that could be ignored; Christopher found himself responding in kind.

Mr Churchill said, 'Now I'm given to understand you've lost none of your cheek. You've refused an order from Uncle John, is that it?'

'Yes sir.' There was no point in denying it.

The Prime Minister looked as if he hadn't had any sleep for weeks. He'd lost nearly the last of the wispy bits of red hair on top of his head; his pink skin had gone sallow. He still had cherubic features and there weren't many creases or lines but his eyes had a pale watery film on them and his hands weren't steady. He was, Christopher realized, just about seventy years old now. He was still rotund but he seemed to have begun to shrink a bit, for the dark coat hung on him loosely in folds.

'I shall not attempt to sway you with moral arguments; there probably aren't any. You've been over-used, misused, and on occasion ill-used — I refer particularly to the incident of the Dutch submarine, for which no excuse is possible and no apology adequate.'

The Prime Minister then levered himself to his feet with visible effort, using both hands on the arms of the chair, and began to walk round the perimeter of the room, grave but animated, looking very old but striding vigorously as if to belie it.

'The matter is important,' he said, 'otherwise I should not have accorded you the time for this discussion. I can tell you the weight of the world is upon my shoulders just now, and I say that not in a silly effort to solicit your sympathy but simply in an attempt to state facts, so that you may understand the gravity

283

of the situation and the importance that I place on your participation.'

He stopped before the map of the Channel coasts and Christopher watched him examine it; Mr Churchill had a love of maps and would often gaze, his eyes roving caressingly, from point to point. Finally he jabbed a finger at the centre of the map. 'We have selected five beaches along a fifty-mile section of the French shore. Beginning at the western extremity, the two beach-heads code named "Utah" and "Omaha" will be assaulted by the Americans, while "Gold", "Juno", and "Sword" to the east will be taken by combined British–Canadian armies. The landings will take place along this shore to the east of Cherbourg on the penisula.'

Then his arm dropped and he examined Christopher's face across the length of the room. 'The date is tentatively scheduled for the beginning of June. About six weeks from now.'

He came down past the backs of the chairs along the table, head thrust forward bullishly. 'Our preparations have been made on a scale unprecedented in enormity, and the deceptions are equally grand in scale. A fictitious army group of huge proportions, under the command of General Patton, has been mocked up in Kent complete with dummy transports and landing craft. The initial beach-head landings in Normandy will appear to the Germans to be a diversionary strike, and we intend Rommel to hold his main forces in Calais against the threat of a major invasion by Patton's army group across the Channel narrows. In this manner, and only in this manner, can we hope to breach the defences of Corporal Hitler's Fortress Europe, by deceiving the enemy into waiting for us where we do not intend to arrive. In the meantime we shall drop three airborne divisions behind the beach-heads to interdict bridges and railways and roads by which Rommel might otherwise move his armies south to meet us.'

The fat man was describing a plan for victory but his voice and his manner were cheerless and pained. He said, 'I've told you the general outlines of the actual plan and I trus you will keep it to yourself. Now I intend to tell you what you're to tell the Germans. You're to help persuade them that our real target for the invasion is the Pas de Calais. Patton attacking from Dover.'

Mr Churchill returned to his chair but did not sit down; he came on round it, walked past the back of Christopher's seat and began another circuit of the room, only to halt a few paces away and turn back. 'I shan't ask this of you on grounds of moral principle and I shan't command you in the name of King and country. I simply ask it of you as a favour to me personally. Will you do it?'

It was as if Christopher had spilt something and was sitting there stupidly agape watching its dark stain fissure across a carpet before him. He felt himself drawn back into the darkness against his will but he had no power to refuse the fat man, none at all, and in that moment there was an instant flash in which he could see, as if in the brief illumination of a thunderbolt, the endless chain of cruel choices and equally cruel decisions that were the Prime Minister's lot.

Humbled, he felt incapable of speech.

'Were the situation less grave,' Mr Churchill said, 'I should not have the heart to ask you to serve in our dark little secret army ever again. But I must ask it of you, this one final time.'

'If you ask it, sir, of course I will.'

The PM advanced to face him at arm's length. 'I asked you once before to guard above all your reputation as a traitorous young man of no character. I can only repeat that stricture. If the Germans should ever suspect you are a man of honour. . .'

Then the PM, who was not a man easily given to physical expressions of affection outside his immediate family, awkwardly placed both hands on Christopher's arms. 'I hope – indeed, I pray – we are not consigning you to your death.'

Chapter Fourteen

On the way up to Patricia's digs he stopped at Northways and bought a packet of twenty Players. He added the packet to his parcel of daffodils and blackmarket whisky and went up the steps whistling. He felt quite good, as if he'd passed through a dilemma and shed his load. The decision was made and that was always better than having it hanging over one. All he had to do was follow the drill.

So he greeted her with a smile and she seemed happy to see him but she looked tired. 'The place was bung full of German ciphers all day and I'm run off my feet.' She'd changed into a rustling silk blouse for him; her breasts caressed the cloth fondly. 'Thank you for the flowers – I love them so.' He remembered how she'd cried the first time he'd given her flowers.

They switched on the radio and spent a while dancing to soft music, not really dancing so much as standing there in each others' arms, swaying a bit but hardly moving their feet. The good smell of her hair was rich in his nostrils. When the news came on they sat down on the floor and leant against each other, back to back, listening to the world's events.

President Roosevelt was having his chest X-rayed in Bethesda Hospital for bronchitis, though he refused to stop smoking through his long cigarette holder. Letters had been released to the American press revealing the possibility of General Douglas MacArthur's standing for the presidency in the autumn electtions. There was the drily rendered information that since 1939 the British army, navy, and air force had given out a total of 27,151 medals. The United States, having been in the war only since the end of 1941, had passed out more than 175,000 medals to its armed servicemen, and now there was an announcement from Moscow that the Soviet Union had decorated more than two million heroes. Russian Air Force Major Pokryshkin had shot down his fifty-ninth German plane today over Romania, and in the Pacific an American air ace with the singular name of Richard Bong had knocked down his twenty-seventh Japanese aeroplane, earning a case of Scotch whisky from

Captain Eddie Rickenbacker—a reward of dubious value to Bong, who was a teetotaller. The British Major General Orde Charles Wingate, leader of the Burma Raiders, was reported dead in a plane crash on a Burmese mountain peak. 'And today in Algiers, General Henri Giraud, who last week refused General Charles de Gaulle's request to resign as commander-in-chief of French forces in North Africa, was given the sack. The Gaullist provisional government has announced that General Giraud has been retired on full pay to the reserve command list.'

Christopher stood up and switched it off.

'What's on earth's the matter? Have you seen a ghost?'

'One just walked over my grave, that's all.' Then he relaxed. 'Ghosts are dead things, aren't they. I don't want to think about the past any more. Why don't we nip down to the pub?'

'There'll be a mob. It's Saturday. Let's stay in. Do you mind awfully?'

She was giving him her up-from-under look, very grave. He said, 'You're acting as if it's our last night together. What's on?'

'You've been to the Hole in the Ground, haven't you.'

'You know I can't talk about that.'

'With the invasion coming they're asking more than they've ever asked of everyone. The risks have gone up for us all, haven't they. They're bound to be sending you out somewhere. No, I shan't ask what it is and I don't expect you to tell me anything, but I feel as though this is one of those bittersweet moments in the cinema when the boy and the girl become very shy with each other and start making all sorts of promises. Making a date for the day after the war. I suppose I'm a foolish sentimentalist—I've always burst into tears at the drop of a hat. Don't pay any attention.'

'I've been rotten all round, haven't I. Here one day, gone the next. Not the sort you can depend on, am I.'

She said, 'That's all right. That's what love is, isn't it? A willingness to be exploited.' She gathered her shapely legs and stood; she swayed towards him and he caught her in his embrace. She said, 'You're not a bad lot.'

'No,' he replied, 'I'm not, really.' It was a discovery he was making about himself.

'But there's one thing that gives me goose-pimples. I can't

stand the light of glory I see in your eye,' she said. 'Try not to be too much of a bloody hero, Christopher.'

'No. I should be careful in my old age,' he agreed.

'I wish you good luck – all the best of it – because I want you to come back. Not just for the day after the war.'

'You're all the luck I'd dare ask for.'

'Oh,' she said, 'you can do better than that.' And she tipped her face up, smiling, for his kiss.

The map of the southern half of England was blotched with bits of sickly salmon pink like a skin disease and the legend underneath identified that colour as 'Restricted Areas'. They extended from Land's End to Yarmouth, from Wolverhampton to Brighton. There were huge pink stains round Torquay and Rye and Colchester in regions where a year ago there'd been nothing much but farms and woods. Every town with a harbour had a pink ring round it.

Owl was saying, 'Nearly everything in Suffolk and Essex and Kent is counterfeit. Dummy encampments, airfields full of plywood planes that look good enough to fool Jerry's aerial recce cameras. The real concentration is right down in the south getting ready to jump off for Normandy – the rest's a smokescreen. We've managed to convince them we've got three times the force we've actually got. Or we think we've convinced them.'

If it was working, Christopher thought, it was the most monumental deception since the Trojan Horse.

Owl had a one-foot wooden ruler. He drew it across the map from the Dover–Folkestone coast to Calais. 'That's where we want them to think it's coming. They're prepared to believe it, which is a great help to us. They can't imagine us taking the long way round. Why would we steam eighty miles to Cherbourg when we can get to Calais across less than a third of the distance? Our fighters would have that much more time over the target at Calais and, of course, it's a far larger port than anything in Normandy.'

'You're making it sound as if we're doing the wrong thing – we ought to be attacking at Calais.'

Owl said, 'Well certainly that's what we want the Germans to think. Actually with the Mulberry equipment we've no need of a natural harbour – in fact it would be a handicap. We learnt at Dieppe that you can't capture a well-defended port without bombarding it – which of course renders it useless until you've had time to rebuild it.

'And the terrain in Normandy will be better for combat operations, not to mention the fact that it's far less heavily defended than Calais. The Resistance chaps have been doing a bang-up job for us in Normandy, as it happens. They've had people working as forced labour on the construction of the Atlantic Wall in that sector and they've had a chance to muck it up nicely without the Germans knowing. They've deliberately mixed far too much sand into the concrete, for example, so that some of the blockhouses and bunkers will crumble like sand castles at the first shell hit. No, Normandy's where we're going. But oddly enough Hitler's the only German who believes it. The entire officer corps stands against him. They all believe it'll be Calais. And they've begun to persuade him. Rommel's been a big help to us there; he's always believed in straight lines, the shortest distance between two points. He doesn't credit us with deviousness, I suppose; it's not commonly thought to be an English or American trait.' Owl smiled.

It was a cruel smile and didn't reach his eyes. Christopher felt uneasy; it was a smile Owl used only when he had something particularly nasty in mind.

Owl was getting down his brolly and mac. 'Come along.'

'Where?'

'Wimpole Street. You've an appointment with the dentist.'

'The *dentist*?'

They had the waiting room to themselves and Owl said, 'It's a standard device. Actually it's a German invention from before the war. We call our version the "L" pill.' More popularly known as the suicide capsule. Implanted in a hollowed false tooth and easily accessible – you can work the tooth loose with your tongue and roll the capsule into your mouth. Then all you need to do is bite down on the capsule to break it inside your mouth, and swallow the liquid contents.'

'What contents?'

'Cyanide. It's not painless but it's very quick. You'll be dead in a matter of seconds and there's no way they can torture information out of you in that time.'

First it was Mr Churchill: *I hope we are not consigning you to your death.* Now this. They kept telling him it was a humdrum job of going to Dublin and selling false information, then they filled him with intimations of mortal jeopardy. Cyanide!

He shot to his feet. 'Forget it.'

'Sit down.'

'I'm not having any bloody suicide pills.'

'Yes you are, and I'll tell you why. The chances are a hundred to one you'll have no use for it, and as soon as you're back from Dublin you can spit it out and flush it down the lavatory; but it's a standard precaution we must take when we send any agent into the field who's got information in his head that we don't want the enemy to have. Hitler's mad-Frankenstein boffins have had years to practise their techniques on the poor buggers they use for test animals in their concentration camps. They've invented a thousand methods for extracting information from people. It's just not possible for any human being to hold out against those techniques. We don't expect our agents to be superhuman. If by some terrible mischance you're taken prisoner by the SS or the Gestapo and they start attaching electrodes to your genitals or injecting chemicals into your arteries, you won't stand a chance of holding out, and in any case if that happens you'll know you can't get out of it alive. They never leave them alive after they've squeezed them dry. The "L" pill won't save your life, Christopher, but it will give you the choice between an excruciating prolonged death and a quick merciful one.'

Christopher stood with his hands in his pockets not bothering to conceal his anger. 'When I went out on the Dieppe party you gave me information to sell to the Germans but you never told me if it was true or false. I had to find out by standing in a bunker on the Dieppe cliffs. Then I went back to Dublin and sold them the plans for a phoney Norway invasion that I didn't know was phoney for sure until afterwards. You kept me well in the dark both times. This time suddenly you've gone out of your way to tell me the truth about the biggest operation of all — and then you tell me I'm expected to kill myself if it looks as though the Germans are going to get the plans out of me. I don't pretend I understand any of it, but it's not consistent and it smells like something that's gone way, way off.'

'I'm afraid the blame for it must be placed on the PM's doorstep. He felt the only way to bring you round was to explain the facts to you and impress the importance of this job upon you. Once he let the cat out of the bag I had no choice but to tell you the truth. I'd have much preferred to have handled this the way we've always handled such matters in the past. I've never believed in telling the agent in the field any more than he needs to know to get the job done.'

The Owl did his awkwardly unconvincing best to look reassuring. 'The chances are you'll never even have to think about it. When you come home you'll spit it out and that's that. In the meantime I'd suggest you take it out of your mouth before you go to sleep — you don't want to bite it accidentally, do you? There's one more thing — it's no good just popping the capsule out of your tooth and swallowing it whole. If it remains intact it will simply go through your system and you'll defecate it. It's got to be bitten, hard. It's made of a substance rather like glass. It must be fractured to spill out the poison — the only way to fracture it is to bite down on it quite hard. You do understand?'

'Too bloody well.'

The car was a non-descript Austin Seven, black and a little battered, bearing an ordinary civilian number plate; Owl had developed a passion for anonymity in everything except his personal dress. He drove the car himself. On the way to Paddington Station he said to Christopher, 'There's one more fact you must know.'

'I can hardly wait.'

'Yes, well I'm afraid it's a spot of bother. You've an annoying habit, Christopher, of picking things up the way one might pick up a dead rat, but in this case you may well be right. It's information we haven't been able to evaluate properly but it may have a strong bearing on your success or failure and in fairness I think you must know about it. Your friend Admiral Canaris has been sacked.'

Christopher said, 'I'm surprised they took so long about it.'

'So am I. But it's happened at an awkward time for us. Actually it took place more than two months ago.'

'Was he arrested?'

'No. Eased out. Taken away from the Abwehr and given a

transfer to the Department of Economic Welfare in Potsdam. Ribbentrop wanted him thrown into a death camp but Hitler saved him. But since Canaris's departure there's been a vast shake-up in the German intelligence services and it may mean a great deal of trouble for us. They've formed a central combined intelligence service to take over not only the Abwehr but half a dozen other agencies, and it's all been placed under the command of Walter Schellenberg. Schellenberg's a nasty piece of work. He's a young SS officer and a protégé of Ribbentrop's.'

Owl had been keeping his eyes on the driving but now he glanced at Christopher beside him. 'What it means, you see, is that all German intelligence is now combined under Himmler's SS. Your friend Breucher is no longer autonomous in Dublin.'

'I see.'

'That fellow Kinski is still there; now he's got authority over Breucher. The SS have never trusted Canaris's people – with good reason, I might add. We haven't time for a discourse on the history of German intelligence operations but suffice it to say that one of our most powerful allies, unwittingly or otherwise, has been the Abwehr, and Ribbentrop has always suspected as much. That's why there is a chance you may be held and questioned when you go to Dublin. Don't be surprised if it happens. I'm relying on your uncanny genius for getting out of tight spots. The "L" pill is only a last resort and I trust you won't be tempted to use it prematurely. It's a ticket out, but very much a one-way ticket.'

'You needn't worry yourself sick over that.'

'I thought not,' Owl said complacently, pretending Christopher's sarcasm had been lost on him.

Christopher reached over into the back seat for his canvas bag; they'd reached Paddington. The sooty monolith of the station was suitably depressing for the hour, he thought.

Owl turned to look at him, unblinking. 'Good luck, then.' And put out his hand.

Christopher looked at it before he took it; to the best of his recollection it was the first time Owl had ever offered to shake his hand.

Driving back alone into the West End, Owl wondered whether it would have made any difference if he'd put Christopher in the picture more clearly. Perhaps not; but as a matter of principle you never told them more than they needed to know.

For exposing Christopher to hazards Owl had put the blame on Winston, but actually they'd planned it together and the only thing that had surprised him was the agony the PM displayed in coming to the decision. It was, of course, the only conclusion they could have reached but that didn't seem to make it any easier for Winston. He really was quite fond of the boy.

The Germans had thrown the spanner well and truly into the works when they'd sacked Canaris. It put the entire double-cross system at risk. Now the SS had taken charge and for the first time since the outbreak of war it was becoming necessary to regard the enemy's intelligence service as just that: the enemy.

It had been more of a friend than an enemy until recently. Canaris had been a traitor since 1939 – if not to Germany then at least to Hitler and the Nazis. Oh, there'd been no direct contact between Canaris and anyone in the West; Canaris wasn't that big a fool – he hadn't come over to England and said, 'I want to work for you chaps,' or anything like that, but his actions made his sympathies obvious enough.

Apparently it had been what Canaris saw in Poland in 1939 that had turned his loyalties firmly against the Nazis. He'd been present at the executions when the murder squads of the SS and Gestapo had massacred civilians in mass graves they had dug themselves. Stunned, Canaris had made it his business to find out whether Hitler himself knew about these atrocities. He'd found out that Hitler not only knew about them but had ordered them.

He'd contrived to make the Abwehr acceptable to the Nazis and at the same time he'd polished it as a weapon against them. He'd arranged for the 'accidental' crash of that plane in Belgium with the complete German plans for the secret invasion of that country; the pilot – under instructions – made such a poor job of destroying the papers that they were easily restored by his captors, and the leak had forced Hitler to postpone his invasion plans nearly six months.

Canaris's office had managed to leak to London the plans for the invasion of Russia in June 1941. Canaris forewarned a

British envoy in Switzerland so that the man had time to get out before Heydrich's assassins could find him; he betrayed Hitler's plan to sabotage the French fleet in Toulon by having his men bungle the job; he countermanded Gestapo plans to execute five captured French generals and deliberately botched the attempted assassinations of Weygand and Giraud; he provided Hitler with faulty intelligence of all kinds – that Japan would be America's principal target; that Russia's strength was not very formidable; that British radar would be of no importance in the Battle of Britain.

His downfall had been expected and the only surprise was that it had taken this long.

Now Himmler and Schellenberg were collecting evidence that would crucify Canaris and his followers – and that meant discrediting the Abwehr networks. They wouldn't buy anything right off the peg if it came from Canaris favourites like Rudolf Breucher, or Christopher Creighton.

Owl had told Christopher there was a slender chance he might be detained for questioning by the SS in Dublin.

It wasn't a slender chance at all. It was virtually a certainty.

He heard them coming through the wood and they hadn't learnt anything about covering their sound; it was like the first time and he remembered that very clearly now while he waited for them. By the sound there must be at least three men.

Rudi Breucher appeared, looking a little older and he'd put on weight. And Kinski was there too. He didn't see the third one but there were three; he'd known it from the sound, and that meant the third was creeping up somewhere in the trees.

It was a tightrope, this one, and it kept fraying and unravelling under him. It had started out looking like a straightforward job of selling phoney plans to the enemy but every time Owl had opened his mouth another high-explosive shell had flown out. But there was no turning back. He'd given his word to the Prime Minister.

Breucher's glance kept flicking towards Kinski, who stood a bit to one side with a hand in his coat pocket and eyes hooded like a lizard's, not saying anything, just lending a sinister presence. And there was the menace of knowing that the third one was prowling unseen behind him somewhere.

There was only one way to play this — as if he'd got total control of it. Christopher turned towards Kinski and said coldly. 'Tell him to come out where I can see him.'

'What? Who?'

'The sod crashing about back there. Tell him to show himself.'

Kinski's face went red and he looked like turning stubborn so Christopher said, 'I came over here to sell the plans for D-day and I'm not likely to do it with a bloody Luger aimed at my spine.'

Breucher said drily to Kinski, 'I think you'd better do it,' in English, and Kinski chewed his lip a bit before he turned his head and let his call sing out through the wood. After a moment a bull-necked oaf plodded out of the trees. It wasn't a Luger, it was a Walther; but the oaf didn't even have the sense to hide it in his pocket until Kinski barked at him in German and the oaf put it away. He came round and stood beside Kinski and looked on with bovine indifference.

Christopher had both hands in the pockets of his mac and he said, 'I'm not unarmed this time.'

Kinski's face reddened again but he said nothing.

'Let's talk alone,' Christopher said to Breucher. He didn't turn his back on Kinski, though. He backed up, one step at a time, feeling his way cautiously because he couldn't afford to stumble. Breucher came along and Kinski stood rooted, uncertain how to handle this because it hadn't been covered in his brief. The oaf didn't matter of course; as long as he was in sight he didn't matter because he wouldn't do anything until Kinski pushed a button.

Breucher seemed to be enjoying himself. He walked on past Christopher and began to talk — inconsequential things, the death of his mother-in-law, the nice weather. He was just keeping it running so that Christopher could steer by the sound of his voice; once, without altering his tone, Breucher said, 'To your left a bit now, there's a tree in your path.'

Finally they stood forty feet away from Kinski and the oaf. Christopher dropped his voice right down. 'This will do.'

'It won't serve much purpose, really. I'll have to report to him whatever you tell me. We've got a new structure I'm afraid; the admiral's been removed and the services are combined now.'

'Canaris is out?'

'Yes, I'm sorry to say.'

'And I'm sorry to hear it.' He had to pretend he hadn't known. Christopher kept his eyes on Kinski, not on Breucher; Breucher was beside him and they talked in low voices so that Kinski couldn't hear. 'That's up to you. But I won't deal with Kinski. Look, I've got the whole show, it's taken me months to get hold of it and I expect to be set up for life by the price of this one. It's going to cost you a quarter of a million quid.'

'Is anything in the world worth that much?'

'This is. I've got the lot. The date, the time, the place – the beaches they'll hit, the forces involved, right down to the last landing craft and Spitfire and airborne squad behind the lines and glider drop. This is the big show – D-day. They'll pay for it all right. And one more thing; I won't take Monopoly notes this time. I want it in Swiss bank credits, Swiss francs, and the bankbook to prove it.'

'I told them it was a mistake pawning that counterfeit off on you. That's why you stopped selling information to us, isn't it.'

'Too right. I nearly got pinched half a dozen times trying to pass that stuff. Finally I had to sell it for a tenth its value to a shabby piece of work in Soho.' He watched Kinski and the oaf sit down on the ground, Kinski making a face; he'd made up his mind to wait it out because it wasn't going to do him any harm. If Christopher was going to give information to Breucher voluntarily that was easier than torturing it out of him.

Christopher glanced at Breucher. 'This time I'll have two-thirds in advance and I'll have proof of it from Switzerland before I tell you a thing.'

'They won't go for it, old man.'

'I'll give you a sample to help persuade them of my bona fides. Tomorrow night two of our men will recce the beaches below Bayeux. Now your chaps can observe but they're not to touch them – you don't want London knowing you're on to them, do you. But tell your coastal watch chaps to keep an eye out and they'll see the recce take place. The point is, I'm giving you a secret that can easily be proved to be accurate. I'm giving it to you to demonstrate my access to information.'

'And what about the D-day plans?'

'You'll get them when I see proof the money's been deposited in my name. It's got to be one of those numbered accounts and no-one's to have authority to withdraw from it except me.'

'It takes time to. . .'

'There's time. Not much, but enough. If you tell them to get a move on.' Christopher made as if to turn away; then he said, as if as an afterthought, 'I'll meet you here again in forty-eight hours. That should give you time to authenticate the Bayeux information and have the bank account opened.'

'I'm afraid that won't do,' Breucher said. 'Kinski won't accept it.'

'Then it'll have to be your job to *make* him accept it, old boy, won't it. I mean, let's think back to something your pet admiral said to me once. The shoe's on the other foot now – it's not for you to make terms, but to accept them. You know my terms. If you want the D-day plans you'll have to do it my way.' He jerked his head towards the two men who sat on the ground forty feet away. 'And you can tell that to the Master Race over there. I don't care how you convince them. You'll think of something, I have every confidence in you.' He kept his voice cold. Inside, he was thinking, it wasn't as if Breucher'd had a choice in picking the wrong side. Breucher had been born on that side just as Christopher'd been born on his.

'At least give me some of the information now,' Breucher said. 'I need to give them something to justify the expenditure. Something more than a two-man reconnaissance on a beach.'

'I'll give you this much then – Patton's in command of the principal assault force. And the date of the invasion is less than four weeks from now. How much less – well that's something you'll get when you've paid for it.'

'Patton? That confirms what we already suspected. It's Calais, then, isn't it?' He wheeled round in front of Christopher. '*Isn't it?*'

'Sorry, old boy, but if you don't buy the ticket you don't get to see the show.'

Over Breucher's shoulder he could see Kinski and the oaf get to their feet, hands jabbing into their pockets; Breucher's sudden movement had alerted them. Christopher without hurry lifted the Webley .380 out and held it in plain sight, not aiming at anyone in particular but just letting them know he hadn't lied about it. Then he said, 'Forty-eight hours, and come alone next time.' He backed away into the woods.

Actually he made it forty-six. He wanted to get there in time to make sure they weren't preparing an ambush for him.

So he was there two hours early and used the first hour of it for a careful prowl. He didn't find anything at all. It didn't mean they didn't plan to jump him, of course, but at least he'd know where it wasn't coming from.

That preliminary meeting hadn't been particularly dangerous because the D-day information was such a vital matter for them that they wouldn't dare make a single move, no matter how minor, without instructions. Today, however, they'd have had their instructions.

Finally Breucher came and he appeared to be alone; at least there weren't any crashings back there in the trees.

'It is all agreed,' the German said by way of greeting. But he didn't seem pleased to report it.

Then Christopher understood why because Breucher added, 'There's just one stipulation. They insist the money cannot be paid unless you are willing to go to France and remain there until the invasion is over. Like Dieppe.'

With a pained little smile and a faint shake of his head Christopher thrust his hands into his coat pockets and considered the man's face. Breucher wore worry like an identifying scar on his forehead.

'Then we seem to be at an impasse. It's too bad. I really could have used that money.'

'You can have it, just as you prescribed. All you have to do is give them security. You'll be safe enough if your information's right – it will be the same as last time.'

'No. Last time there was Canaris and I could trust him. Kinski and that lot, they're a different thing. They'd run me through the torture chambers just for practice. I like money, old boy, but I like having myself intact even more.'

'If I gave you my personal. . .'

'Don't make promises you can't keep.' Christopher turned away and started walking. 'I'm afraid it's just not on.'

'Wait.'

He turned inquiringly. 'What for?'

'There must be a way we can settle this. It's too important —
I can't just let you walk away. Don't you see I've got my orders?'

'Then you haven't got anything to bargain with, have you.
I'm sure you've got instructions to say anything at all if it will
make me cooperate. It's no good, don't you see that? Either they
accept my terms or it's off.'

'Let's at least talk about it.'

Christopher scowled at him. 'What is it?' He stepped closer
to peer into Breucher's frightened eyes. 'Either you deliver me
or they'll have your head on a plate, is that it?'

'We've got to have those plans.'

'Then buy them. Pay for them. They're up for sale; you know
the terms.'

'You must understand. You've got to understand — this came
from the Führer himself. He said, how are we to know the
information is real unless we hold this agent hostage to the
truth? Look, we've prepared the transport, everything. I've got
the Swiss bankbook here in my pocket. Can you imagine what
we had to go through to get it here this quickly? But they've
got to have this reassurance, can't you see that? Otherwise you
might be selling us false information and we wouldn't know
which it was until perhaps it got too late.'

'I've only offered to sell you the plans. I haven't presumed
to tell you what to do with them. Hitler can believe them or not,
that's his privilege. You take the same chance when you buy
any information from anyone. Mine's the real goods, as it happens, but I'm not going to let them dab burning cigarettes all
over me just to prove it. Now you'd better come up with something else or we've nothing left to talk about.'

'You've grown old and hard since last time.'

'I've developed a healthy respect for survival if that's what
you mean. Don't you think we hear what goes on in those concentration camps on your side of the water?'

'The concentration camp was a British invention,' Breucher
replied fatuously. 'In South Africa during the Boer War the
English. . .'

It was Christopher's sudden movement that cut him off.
Christopher slammed himself back against the bole of a beech
and lifted the .380 out of his pocket; his eyes went quickly
round the wood.

He suddenly realized what Breucher was doing: stalling — holding Christopher here — and there could be only one reason for that.

Breucher said, 'What on earth are you. . . ?'

'*Shut up.*' He wanted silence; he wanted to listen. If they were creeping up round him. . .

'Come over here.'

Breucher stared. 'What?'

'*Come here.*'

Breucher hesitated and fear erupted from his eyes and Christopher knew he'd been right. He leapt out away from the tree and gathered Breucher's collar in his fist, whirled him round and locked his arm round Breucher's windpipe, jamming the .380 in his back. Through clenched teeth he rasped in Breucher's ear, 'Call out to them. Tell them to clear a path. We're walking out of here.'

The hairs on the back of his neck were tingling and he broke into a cold sweat everywhere but he couldn't see any movement in the woods; all the same, he tightened his arm round Breucher's throat. 'Tell them.'

'But there's no-one. . .'

'Then I'll look a fool, won't I? Just tell them. *Now.*'

Breucher struggled, not violently and not trying to break away but simply trying to get room within the crook of Christopher's arm to breathe. Christopher relaxed his hold a little. Breucher took a deep breath and began to yell in German, his voice ringing out among the trees. Afterwards there was silence and Breucher said, 'You see, there's no-one there.'

But then Kinski appeared.

Kinski was some distance away in the trees and he had something in both hands; it looked like a Schmeisser but it was hard to tell in the flickering shadows. Then there were other shapes moving in the wood. After six he lost count.

'Tell them to keep their distance. We're backing out.'

Breucher called out to Kinski, the cords of his throat vibrating against Christopher's arm, and then Christopher began to back away, pulling Breucher along with him, the .380 coming out and swaying backwards and forwards.

Kinski walked forward. 'You may as well let him go. We will shoot through him to hit you, if we must.'

Christopher made no reply to that. They weren't going to shoot. He knew that for an absolute certainty. He kept dragging Breucher back with him. Kinski kept plodding forward, keeping pace, and he saw shadows converging round him in the trees.

'Tell them to keep their distance or I start shooting. *Tell them.*'

He held a trump card in this and Kinski knew that Christopher knew it. They weren't under any circumstances going to kill him, so he could afford to shoot but they couldn't. It made them hesitant because if they closed in too tight and made him panic he'd start shooting them and they weren't likely to put up with much of that, Master Race or not.

The thing to do was get out of this one and then set up something else with Breucher. Next time they'd play it Christopher's way because he'd have shown them they had no choice. And they'd play along because they needed the plans more than they needed anything.

'Stand still, Kinski. You've come far enough.'

Kinski smiled a little and stopped obediently. He spoke in German and the shadowy figures stopped moving too. Christopher backed away with Breucher in front of him as a shield: otherwise they might try a snap-shot at his kneecap or his gun hand.

He had a motorcycle concealed a hundred yards further; he turned complete circles round Breucher as he went, surveying every corner of the wood.

Kinski was coming forward again, but more slowly and keeping his distance. That was all right; they wouldn't risk any long shots. Just the same his nerves were on edge and he had to blink the sweat out of his eyes. There was the old dry taste of fear on his tongue.

He'd learnt one thing anyway. They were capable of sneaking up silently when they wanted to. But that was all right because he'd been trained well and he'd been born with the right instincts.

More to steady his own nerves than anything else he said calmly to Breucher, 'Christ I'm disappointed in you. You rotten bastard.'

'I had no choice, you know that. My neck's in the noose too. They've got my wife. . .'

'It's a lovely lot you're working for these days, Breucher. Bear up now, we're nearly there. I hope your chums don't go round the bend and try to kill the goose that's going to lay Germany's golden egg. Next time you'll really come alone. It won't be here in the wood. And you'll come prepared to agree to my terms. Give me a telephone number where I can reach you.'

'Just call the legation.'

'No good. Those lines are tapped by half a dozen different groups, I'm sure.'

'There's a call box we sometimes use.'

'Number?'

'Ah – Dean 342.'

'Dublin number?'

'Yes.'

'Be there tonight at nine.'

The motorcycle. He glanced at the machine and was glad he'd had the foresight to leave it tipped against the tree with its kick-stand up and pointed away from the rendezvous spot.

He withdrew his arm from round Breucher's neck but held on to the back of his collar and kept close against him, the .380 up and roving just to keep them at bay. He could see two or three of them back in the tree but they weren't close; fifty feet or more away. Kinski was on the move again but only to bring himself to a point from which he could see clearly; he stopped too, and then everything went still, a momentary tableau.

'Right. Do you know how to start one of these things?'

'Yes.'

'Climb on, then, and kick the starter until she's running. Then climb off the far side and I'll take your place. You'll want to step back quickly to keep the wheel from running over your feet. Go on – do it.' It would give him added time to keep an eye on the Blacks.

He let go of Breucher's collar and Breucher obediently lifted his leg to straddle the machine. Christopher rested his left hand on the handlebar ready to grip the throttle after getting it started. He held the .380 up in plain sight, keeping it close to Breucher's ear although that was more of an act than a threat; Breucher wasn't a useful hostage in the normal sense because they'd be perfectly willing to sacrifice him if it meant getting their hands on Christopher.

Breucher kicked two or three times before the engine caught. Then Christopher had to reach across with his free hand to hold the turn-handle throttle up against its spring to prevent the thing from stalling. Breucher climbed off the far side of the machine and it left a little gap between them. That was when something massive plummeted out of the tree overhead and Christopher only had time to begin to raise his eyes and his gun before the oaf was upon him, crashing him to the earth — the shock of brutal pain, the .380 tumbling away, the oaf holding him down with grunting effort, Christopher's head spinning and men running forward through the trees from every direction. . .

Then the oaf climbed off him and he lay dazed by the blow. Kinski was grinning down at him across the muzzle of his Schmeisser. 'The game is over. Get up and come along.'

Chapter Fifteen

A knee in his back: a rough thrust and he pitched to the floor. The door crashed shut behind him.

He was not alone; it wasn't a cell. Someone stood in front of him and he twisted his face to drag his eyes up from the jackboots. Green uniform, black trim – the Waffen SS uniform – and then he recognized vaguely the face of the man who loomed above him. Christopher stubbornly got to his knees, reached to the wall for support and felt the room tilt when he climbed up the wall to stand erect. Pain throbbed mercilessly round his skull and there was a bloodshot red wash across his vision and he thought it probably had to be concussion; Kinski had knocked him around quite badly on the boat. First it had been fists but then when he'd dropped to the deck Kinski had got in a kick or two before someone had hauled him off.

The Black didn't say anything at all. He just stood watching Christopher, letting the silence work at him.

He didn't know where they were now because he'd been out of it part of the time and didn't know how long that might have been. He remembered a few things. They'd taken him down the coast in a van and they'd gone on board the fishing boat in the night and run out to sea without lights, Kinski bashing at him while the oaf held him down, and he'd been half-conscious when the U-boat had surfaced and they'd carried him below. He remembered the smell of it, not much more. A glimpse or two of pale bearded officers in ragged uniforms with grease smudges on their hands – a sense of resentment there, with submariners disliking the business of being pulled off patrol to ferry passengers. Drifting in and out of wakefulness, never really alert. Then he remembered the dock again, before they'd put him on the fishing boat, before they'd begun to bash him about. Rudi Breucher standing there on the little weathered dock, having been tense before but afraid now – Christopher remembered the rank acid smell of it – and then Kinski had said something in German and relief had washed across Breucher's face like sun after a storm. Christopher had said, 'Goodbye,

Breucher,' and Breucher had nodded vigorously and hurried away, afraid to speak. Christopher felt sorry for him because it was obvious they'd stop his clock sooner or later.

He remembered the smell of the sea, the rough hands lowering him into the conning tower, the smell of the U-boat — something new added to the usual familiar odour — the smell of the stale sweat of garlic eaters.

No recollection at all of the end of that voyage. They must have brought him ashore in a lighter, or perhaps the U-boat had berthed openly at a pen or dock. Next memory: sensation of movement, hands manacled painfully behind him while he sat in a vehicle of some kind, coarse hands gripping his shoulders to keep him from flipping over when the car took the bends. He supposed it was France somewhere. The car ride hadn't been a long one so this place was near the coast. A prison, prison camp, concentration camp, forced-labour camp, death camp — it was an old building, medieval perhaps; dank and bleak, thick stone walls. Electric lights hanging low with exposed black-insulated wires running along under the stone ceilings. Mortar crumbling between the stones.

When he looked at the Black it was like being at the wrong end of a lens. Then he knew why the Black looked familiar. Dieppe: the Himmlerian moustache, the soft mouth, the brutal eyes. Albert Leeb. A captain then; a colonel now, by his insignia.

He remembered the reluctance with which Leeb had let him go, at Dieppe; Leeb had wanted to kill him then. The burning eyes of a man who got his fun from inflicting cruelty.

Everything was too bright. It wasn't the lights; it was his eyes, the pain; he couldn't keep his eyes open. Somehow the too-brightness of everything brought pictures back from his memory: Mr Churchill's paintings on the easel, the little man-made island in the pond at Chartwell. Paintings noticeable for their colour more than for their draftsmanship — as luminous as the fat man's pale bright eyes.

Things kept swimming in and out like that: disjointed images, no connections among them, no logic to it. Leeb seemed to sway forward like a distorted reflection in an imperfect mirror, growing wildly larger, then shrinking away. 'Can you hear me?'

Christopher's eyes rolled up in his head. He tried to clutch the wall for support but his legs gave way and he toppled.

He awoke briefly and felt them carrying him out.

It was better now, his mind was tracking and he felt composed. But he didn't open his eyes just yet because he didn't want them to know he'd come to. He heard voices – one of them Leeb's and he understood a few of the German words, 'arrest' and 'execution' and 'Kinski', and he thought savagely, *Serve the stupid bastard right*. Kinski had tried to beat information out of him and at least there was the satisfaction of knowing he'd told Kinski nothing.

But then Kinski'd been crude, nothing but fists and boots and that wasn't the way you got information out of a trained man; all Kinski had done was half kill Christopher and that was why Leeb was sending out the order now to arrest Kinski and execute him. Because Kinski had all but killed Christopher and hadn't got any information out of him.

He couldn't stir without letting them know he was awake but he tried to do an inventory, working his way up from the feet a joint at a time, and there were bruises on hip and thigh where he'd been smitten by a jackboot on the deck of the boat; possibly a cracked rib, or that might be only a bruise too; kidney pain but not bad enough to be a rupture. He knew about ruptured kidneys, his father'd cut enough of them open. Stomach muscles hurt. He'd kept them tense while Kinski had pummelled him there and it could be a torn muscle but it didn't feel inoperative. The tendon across the left shoulder hurt like the devil where a fist had come down in it; but mainly the agony was in his head, like a red-hot band of steel being squeezed round his forehead and skull. He'd been kicked in the head, not once but several times, and the toes of Kinski's jackboots had been metal. No question there was concussion: blood vessels ruptured in there, bleeding into the eyes and the sinuses and the brain, building up pressure. It if was bad enough it could kill him, some time in the next hour or day or week; sometimes it took that long, even a month if it was the sort of slow arterial leak that didn't heal itself.

Then again he might be fully recovered in forty-eight hours.

Of course there was the hollow tooth. But that was a last resort and there were a lot of options before it.

They'd have to try to keep him alive until they got the information out of him and found out whether it was true; and that would give him time to see if there might be a way to get out. It wasn't the first time he'd been inside a German prison set-up in occupied France. He'd done four different jobs in three different camps, breaking people out. This time the only difference was he had to start the job from inside.

But it was his speciality – getting out of places – and if he handled everything right he might still have a fair chance; assuming he didn't bleed to death, and Leeb restrained his natural cruelty, and a few other things.

Well you had to have something to brighten the dreary hours somehow, didn't you?

He was feeling reckless, lightheaded, with a go-to-hell brashness. He opened his eyes.

His vision was better now. He was on something low and upholstered. A hospital bed? A stretcher? Then he realized it was simply an office couch. They'd stretched him out on it and they were waiting for him to come round. He wondered casually how many heads would have rolled if he *hadn't* come round.

On the table were clues to the fact that he'd had medical attention. A puff of damp cotton wool. So they'd injected him with something, possibly adrenalin, and possibly some clotting substance to thicken the blood and stop the leaking in his head. There was a cloth, neatly folded but also damp, and the smell of rubbing alcohol. They'd bathed him, then. He realized he wasn't wearing his clothes any longer; it was a coarse bathrobe tied round him. They'd probably examined him from head to toe for injuries. He wondered what they'd found and if his own earlier diagnosis had been accurate.

They didn't seem to have noticed yet that his eyes were open.

The ceiling was plaster and so he was in a different place from the cell where Leeb had waited unsuccessfully to interrogate him. This might be a commandant's office or perhaps the doctor's waiting-room. There was a desk across one corner of the room and if he dipped his eyes he could see three men, one seated behind it and two others standing round talking; one of the two was Colonel Leeb.

307

He closed his eyes again. If they were going to allow him this uninterrupted time then he'd better take advantage of it: try to think things out, put things in perspective, devise some sort of plan.

It was no good feeling resentful. Tigger and Owl had both known this might happen and Owl hadn't concealed it from him. It was his own bloody fault, actually, for not having had the sense to think they might spot the motorcycle and plant a man in the branches above it — stupid fool, it hadn't even occurred to him to look *up*.

Now he was in it, and the odds on survival were something like the odds on a legless man's winning the Olympic sprint but you couldn't always go by that. You had to keep alert to such slender threads of opportunity as might present themselves at unexpected moments. Like this one: they were leaving him alone just now because they thought he was still unconscious and there might be a chance to bolt off the couch and make a run for the door. But he might faint if he tried that and in any case he didn't know the first thing about the layout and you didn't go blundering round blind, wearing nothing but bare feet and a bathrobe, when you didn't even know where the bloody exits were. There was also the fact that he'd been briefed to sell them a pack of lies and he intended to keep his promise to Tigger.

I hope — indeed, I pray — we are not consigning you to your death.

If it had been an act it had been an awfully good one. He believed it then and he'd had no reason to change his mind. And the fat man had put his finger right on it: it wasn't just for King and country; what tipped the balance in the end was his personal loyalty to the PM. He'd do it; he'd see this right through to the end, not because of orders or blind unthinking courageous obedience or any other rot like that but because Tigger had asked it.

You're my paladin, the fat man had said that to him on several occasions. At first it had been a sort of joke between them, like the blasted bike. But after a while it began to feel like a proper fit. Churchill's paladin — that was something to be proud of and if it was all you had left then it was enough.

He wondered how different things might have been if he'd

ever been able to love his own father the way he loved Mr Churchill.

He kept his eyes shut but after a while someone came across the room and it was no good shamming; he looked up into the unfamiliar face and the man – a doctor, apparently – took his wrist to feel for the pulse, measured it against his watch and then spoke over his shoulder in a careless indifferent voice. The smell of drink came off him vaguely. Well if you were a doctor forced to work in a place like this you'd drink too.

Albert Leeb appeared above him. 'How do you feel?'

'I've felt better.'

'Your injuries are not as bad as they may feel. Nothing's broken. Steps have been taken to discipline Herr Kinski – this was not in his brief.'

Trying it on for size, Christopher thought. *He'll butter me first, of course.*

It was true about disciplining Kinski – he'd overheard something earlier – but they weren't doing it because of Kinski's brutality; they were only doing it because the fool had nearly let the plans slip through their fingers. Now Leeb was trying to make it look as if they were contrite.

He remembered Kinski and Breucher on the dock in Ireland.

Kinksi: *I'll take the prisoner from here.*

Breucher: *He is not a prisoner.*

Kinski: *He is now. Goodbye, Breucher.*

Leeb said, 'You needn't sit up just yet. You've had a bit of a concussion.' His efforts to be solicitous were nearly comical; he was miscast for the role.

Play his silly game.

'I told Breucher and Kinski, and I'll tell you. All I want is that Swiss bankbook. Then I'll sell you the information. You don't need to torture it out of me – all you've got to do is pay for it.'

'Yes, of course. I understand that. This whole unfortunate idiocy is Kinski's doing. Here.' And Leeb proffered something. Christopher lifted his hand and was surprised how weak it was; the little thing nearly fell from his nerveless grip.

Banque du Crédit Suisse. . .

He let it drop on to his chest. 'It's on deposit, then?'

'Of course. None of this was intended to happen. A grisly mistake.'

The U-boat laid on, the whole charade. Quite a mistake.

Christopher said, 'That's fine, then. If you'd like to bring someone over here who can transcribe dictation in English. . .'

Leeb seemed almost disappointed. Probably he'd been looking forward to extracting it a sentence at a time through pain-gritted teeth.

Anybody can print up a bankbook, he thought; but he had to make it look as if he believed them. He held it up and examined it very carefully, studying the signatures as if they meant something, showing he was impressed by the stamped seals (anyone can make up a rubber stamp for God's sake), smiling when he opened it to the accounts page and saw the sum written out twice, under 'deposits' and then under 'balance': SF 3,612,000.00. The rate of exchange was about twenty-one Swiss francs to the pound.

Then he went back to the front page and made a show of memorizing the account number, moving his lips as he did so.

Leeb had spoken to the third man, the one who'd remained across the room by the desk, a short chap with peculiar expressionless eyes that looked dead. Gestapo, possibly. That one had picked up a telephone and said something in German, and now a woman came in, thick-waisted and buxom with a hard handsome face but bad teeth when she smiled. Christopher looked her snidely up and down. 'How's your English then, ducks?'

'Quite good, *mein Herr*. I worked in your embassy in Berlin for five years.'

A bloody Nazi in the British embassy. Marvellous. He wondered how many dustbins she'd gone through.

He said, 'Right then. Take this down and don't make mistakes. I'll try to remember to talk slowly. You ready?'

She sat down with her notepad and pencil. 'Quite ready.'

The bloke across the room by the phone had a Schmeisser. He was bald on top with a dark monk's fringe that ran round the back of his head above his ears; a dark civilian suit and a broken nose. Christopher took him for Gestapo because they usually wore plain clothes. The machine-pistol was slung by its strap for comfort but his right hand was on the pistol grip and his finger through the trigger guard. Christopher understood that he was staying across the room so that Christopher couldn't jump him before he could start shooting. So they weren't at all lax, even though they were trying to make it look so casual.

He let his eyes wander away and began to talk.

'The main invasion will be spearheaded by the 1st United States Army Group under the command of General George S. Patton. It will assemble in several Channel ports – Dover, Folkestone, and so on, I'll get into the details in a bit – and its target is code named Beach Red, just north of Calais. The target area has a width of about forty miles and has been subdivided into beaches code named "Scarlet", "Maroon", "Pink", "Orange", and "Crimson". If you bring me a decent map I can pinpoint them for you but let's get on with the general picture first. D-day for Calais will be the seventh or eighth of June unless the weather turns bad, in which case they'll wait till the twenty-second because they want to hit the beach at high tide because they know about Rommel's underwater booby traps and they need high water to float across them. The Pas de Calais is about twenty miles wide at that point so they plan to assemble off Dover at twenty hundred hours on the night of June the sixth or seventh, and of course there'll be intensive RAF air cover all the way so you needn't count on the Luftwaffe doing much good. Now there are dummy armies – skeleton units and mocked-up equipment – assembled all over the south coast of England, partly to fool your aerial recce boys but also to provide enough men and weapons to put on a good show when they make the diversion landings in Normandy, which will take place a couple of days earlier. The idea is to draw all the German strength south into the Normandy peninsula, then make the real landings at Calais after the Normandy trick has drained off the defences there.'

'The Pas de Calais,' Leeb said. 'It confirms what we already suspected.'

'Right. But the first landings will be in Normandy, to draw you off.'

'Go on then.'

He went on.

It took a long time. He was hoarse and dry and hungry. Finally the woman got up and went out. While she was passing through the door and had it open he heard from somewhere in the building a cry – the kind of cry that would never again be uttered by that voice.

He didn't know if it was day or night; the room had no windows. The doctor came in, had a look at him, said something to Leeb and went out again, stumbling slightly. That doctor probably was never quite drunk and never quite sober.

The Gestapo man with the Schmeisser was sitting in a chair now, smoking, and two others had entered and ranged themselves along the far wall of the room – bruisers, muscle boys.

Leeb said, 'Now you want food and drink and sleep, don't you.'

'I shouldn't mind.'

'You shall have them all – as soon as you tell us the truth.'

He gave Leeb a bored look. 'I've just told you the truth. Why should I lie about it? I'd have a fat chance of living to collect the money if I were lying, wouldn't I.'

Leeb's smile was slow and terrible. 'I'll tell you how it is, Aeneas. You've told us the plans – if those are in fact the plans – so we've got what we brought you here for, and it doesn't matter what happens to you any longer. So just to be sporting about it we're going to apply pressure now and see if the answers still come out the same.'

'You bloody bastard. I thought it was too easy. Look – it'll come out the same no matter what you do to me. I've told you the truth.'

'We'll see.' Then Leeb glanced over his shoulder and with a little jerk of his head summoned the two muscle lads forward.

And now he was cursing them all at the top of his voice, screaming with agony: cursing Kinski and Leeb, cursing the bastard Owl as well because Owl had given him the out and he had the bleeding 'L' pill there and it meant he could take himself right out of this whenever he wanted to. That meant Owl had robbed him of his will to fight back by giving him the alternative and he hated Owl for that, hated what it was doing to him because everything in him shrieked for release and Owl had given it to him to use whenever he chose and he couldn't stand an instant more of this *pain, my God the pain*, he didn't even know what they were doing to him any more because if they went under a fingernail again it felt as though it was coming from anywhere at all, it might be the genitals again or the soles of the feet or the fingernails and *he couldn't even tell the difference any more* it was all one bloody great blaze and existence was nothing except the consciousness of pain.

The pill – the capsule – now was the time for it because if he let this go on one instant longer he'd lose the ability to reason at all and his mind would blot out the knowledge of the pill and he wouldn't be able to kill himself. Killing himself was the only way to end this pain now. The faces – Leeb, the muscle lads, the woman – they were all there, all prodding at him, needles and matchsticks in their hands and they weren't breaking his bones or even inflicting bruises. They weren't even burning his flesh because they didn't need to do anything like that; they'd got it worked out to a science. Some mad Hun doctor in a death camp had tried a thousand techniques on a thousand Jews and found out exactly how to hit the pain centres. You didn't have to do any real damage to the body to hit the nerve ends. It was better not to do any damage because you were trying to torture information out of the victim, not kill him, and the less real damage you did the longer he'd last. The only dangers were that his heart might give out – or his mind.

So they didn't use the matchsticks on the fingernails. They used the matchstick on the needle and then the *needle* under the fingernail, hot enough for excruiating pain but not enough actually to scorch the skin because you didn't want the bastard bleeding all over your neat grey–green SS uniform, did you. No, you didn't draw any blood at all; you didn't need to. The exact temperatures for maximum pain and minimum damage had been worked out by trial and error and were now being used on you.

By the time they'd started putting the hot needles up his nostrils he was too far gone with pain to know what they were doing to him and it only startled him the first time. After that it just blended into the general nightmare of agony.

The pill – *now*.
There wasn't any feeling left in his tongue or anywhere else

313

because he'd been desensitized to any sensation short of the extreme fire of agony and he wasn't certain he could even find the bloody thing with his tongue, but certainly if he put it off any longer it wouldn't work. *It had to be now.*

Something was happening outside his nightmare: someone's face was being slapped, not terribly hard, just rhythmic slaps to get someone's attention, and then he realized they'd withdrawn the blunt-topped needles and there weren't any fires, just the throbbing agony continuing from what they'd already done to him. He didn't know how long it had been since they'd stopped. He didn't hear his own screaming any more and he supposed that was a good sign.

A good sign of what?

It was the woman and it was *his* face she was slapping and his eyes must have opened or something because she stopped. His vision was down to a very narrow cone and when she withdrew her face from straight in front of him he couldn't see her any more. Then Albert Leeb's stubbled face replaced the woman's and Leeb said, *'Wasser'* and then someone was pouring water down him and he nearly choked on it when it went down the wrong pipe. The doctor was there, slapping his back hard, and he heard himself coughing, great harsh wheezing gulps of air; but he couldn't feel it and it seemed to be happening to someone else.

The Gestapo ghoul sat there smoking, watching him, no expression at all.

It was too ludicrous: he was sitting up on the bloody couch as if he were a guest at a party and he'd got too durnk and they were trying to sober him up.

An ordinary couch, a nondescript office. Torture chamber.

Albert Leeb: 'You have thirty seconds to tell us about the invasion. Then we'll resume if you don't tell the truth.'

It took him most of the thirty seconds to analyse the sounds in his memory and to bring himself to understand that the sounds had emanated from Leeb's vocal cords, that the sounds were English words, that the words could be broken up into entities of separate meaning, and that Leeb was telling him the torture would be resumed if he didn't talk.

It was truly amazing. They hadn't put a mark on him. Not a single mark that would indicate to anybody that he'd been tortured. In a few seconds more they'd start again and this time everything would break up in his mind into random fragments and he wouldn't be able to do anything about the 'L' pill because his mind would be gone.

But it was respite enough and he managed to find the hollowed tooth with his tongue by prodding everywhere, just exercising the muscles inside his closed mouth and making it keep moving even though he couldn't feel much of anything. It was as if he were in the dentist's chair and they'd given him something for the pain, only this was just the reverse. they'd given him the pain and that was the anaesthetic because it ruled out all other sensations. Now he distinctly *felt* the tooth come loose and there was the sense, more from memory and probabilities than from any actual tangible feeling, of the smooth pellet coming free and he got it centred by gripping it on all four sides: upper teeth, cheek, lower teeth, tongue – and he bit down with all his strength and felt something crunch between his teeth, and he forced the muscles to go into the spasms of swallowing.

The he waited for death.

But he didn't die.

They'd caught on, of course, and they'd leapt on him, hard hands prying his jaws apart, the doctor peering inside, everybody bleating in German and he heard it all but none of it made sense and it wouldn't have made sense in English either. He wasn't equipped for following anything coherently any longer.

They'd dragged him forward until they had him on all fours. Then the muscle lads or somebody had his feet right up in the air and the doctor was tickling his throat with something, prodding the back of his tongue while the others forced his jaws wide open and obediently his body provided the expected reaction. He vomited.

That didn't bother him. The poison was supposed to be instantaneous and once it touched the tissues of his mouth and throat it would do its work. What troubled him was that he'd been sure it would burn. At least there should be the sensation of liquid breaking free of the capsule. There'd been nothing. The thing seemed to have felt hollow and empty when he'd crushed it, although he was so far gone he couldn't be sure. The one thing he did know was that the pain didn't change in any way from what he'd had before. He kept waiting for death and it didn't come.

They dropped him on the floor and he supposed they were crouching round him, watching. He heard the anxiety in their voices and he believed he could faintly smell the stink of his own vomit.

Where was death?

'It seems they've given you a faulty suicide pill,' Leeb said. 'Too bad.'

Christopher blinked very slowly and tried to focus.

'An imperfection in the manufacture, I suppose. What was it, cyanide?'

Christopher closed his eyes. The pain had begun to subside but there still wasn't room for much else in his consciousness. It was an effort to understand what Leeb was saying.

He watched the woman light a match.

Leeb said, 'Let us try again, then.'

And the pain returned.

He heard himself babbling, on and on, not screaming any more because all he could do now was whisper, grating the words out through the interstices between his teeth because his jaw was locked tight with the pain and he hadn't the strength, the will or the presence of mind to open it.

What was he saying to them?

He began to listen to his own croakings and was appalled.

They'd stopped the torture again, that must be it. They'd given him time to regroup, regather his consciousness, recover a semblance of his wits.

He'd expected torture. He'd tried to be ready for it. He'd held out the 'L' pill as his escape hatch but the hatch had jammed and pain had gone beyond expectation and beyond endurance. Now he heard himself spilling it all.

'Normandy. The fifth or sixth, the weather. "Juno", "Sword", "Omaha". . . The whole bloody show. Patton's got no army. Nothing. I saw the plan; they told me. . . Tell them Pas de Calais, you *must* make them believe Normandy's a feint — if

316

they're waiting for us in Normandy we're lost... It's Normandy, *Oh God forgive me it's Normandy...*

'Who are you?'
  'Christopher Creighton.'
  'Your cover name?'
  'Christopher Robin... Peter Hamilton.'
  'How long have you been a British double agent?'
  'Nineteen-forty – Belgium.'
  'When is D-day?'
  'June the fifth. June the sixth.'
  'Where were you born?'
  'London.'
  'Who is Winnie the Pooh?'
  'Metcalf, Colonel Metcalf.'
  'Where will D-day take place?'
  'East of Cherbourg. Normandy...'

He was floating, as upon a cloud. Must be drugged, he thought. He did not feel discomfort; he felt very little of anything. A sense of buoyancy and warmth.

The woman. Absurd: he was embarrassed to have her there while his private parts floated in the warm water before her.

She was soaping his chest, her hands running round under his arms, lathering him, then letting him sink back into the water.

Then they were lifting him out of the tub. Must have been in it quite a while: something oily about the water, not just soap; perhaps a salve to anaesthetize his burns.

He'd been soaking a while, that was obvious; the flesh was puckered on his thumbs and fingers.

Clean clothes. They dressed him like a mannequin, one limb at a time, pulling his arms and legs around like a puppet limbs.

'Come along. You must be hungry.'

Mystified. They carried him along a corridor, the lights too bright for his eyes; he had to squint them nearly shut. They had him upright between them, the two muscle lads, and the woman walked along in front of them. Behind him he'd had a glimpse of the bald Gestapo man bringing up the rear.

'The curious thing about pain,' the woman was saying with

clinical detachment, 'is how temporary it can be. You'll feel quite all right after you've had another twelve hours' sleep. You'll be able to walk to your own execution. But first let's feed you up – there are a few more questions and they don't want you to faint from hunger.'

Some sort of gruel; he nearly choked on it. She was spoonfeeding him and the Gestapo man watched; he never seemed to blink. The Schmeisser hung off his shoulder like an appendage.

He kept shifting his hands in his lap trying to find a way to hold them so that they wouldn't hurt, but there wasn't any such position. He had to breathe through his mouth because they'd burnt the insides of his nostrils; and his bare feet were curled tight under the chair, nothing touching the floor but his heels. The pain had fragmented and localized now: toes, genitals, fingers, nostrils. He could separate out his agonies. Everything throbbed, as if the blood vessels had floated too near the surface and threatened to burst with each pulsebeat. Still it wasn't the entirety of existence any more. She'd been right; it was receding. There were chips of clarity in the corners of his mind and he was capable of concentrating for a few seconds at a time on things other than his pain.

The Gestapo man said something in German and the woman replied without looking at him; her tone was too guarded to reveal anything and he didn't understand German. She was afraid of the Gestapo man, that much was evident, and apparently he was a stranger; he must have been sent in to observe this interrogation but he wasn't part of the staff here. His presence was tolerated but not welcomed, that much was clear.

Christopher moved one hand and anguish stabbed through him, all the way up the nerves of his arm. Abruptly he realized the Gestapo man was speaking to him in English:

'Churchill – what is he like?'

It was very good English: he didn't sound like a foreigner trying on a strange tongue. It might have been a Londoner's accent. A trace of Cockney perhaps.

Christopher said, 'He's a warrior. Good enough to beat your Corporal Hitler.' It sounded limp but he was filled with shame and felt obliged to put some gesture of defiance on the record.

'They say he's a drunk.'

'Do they?'

'Have you ever seen him drunk?'

'No. But I don't know him that well.'

'You're lying.'

'Believe what you want.'

Albert Leeb came into the office and the muscle lads got up on their feet. Leeb nodded to them and the two lads went out, shutting the door after them but he had the feeling they'd stationed themselves just outside. The woman said something in German and it made Leeb shoot a sideways glance towards the Gestapo man, who met Leeb's eyes until Leeb turned away to reach for a chair. The Gestapo man was in SS uniform this time: grey–green fabric and a Hauptmann's epaulets.

Leeb pulled the chair forward and sat down uncomfortably close to Christopher. The woman put down the spoon and took the plate away. Leeb said, 'Have you anything else to tell us?'

'Bugger off.'

'It's a bit late for that kind of hostility, isn't it? Don't behave like a girl who wants her virginity back.'

'You broke me. I've told you everything you wanted to know.'

'No. You've only told us the answers to specific questions. Now you're going to give us the rest.'

'The rest of what?'

'Everything you know. Answers to the questions we haven't thought of asking. How much do you know about Churchill's spies operating behind our lines? Who are they? What are their covers? What other information can you give us about this special warfare directorate of theirs? What other plans do you know about?' Leeb stood up and pushed the chair out of the way. 'Start talking – we'll tell you when you can stop.'

Christopher felt lances in his toes and he closed his eyes and croaked reluctantly, 'You'll have to get it out of me the hard way,' knowing he couldn't withstand more torture but hoping it might snap his mind and turn him into a babbling lunatic before he betrayed anything else to them – knowing, too, that under torture they'd get less information from him because his mind would be too fractured to initiate voluntary information. They'd have to ask specific questions to get specific data, and if they didn't know what questions to ask then they wouldn't get as much.

Leeb's sigh of resignation was almost comically theatrical; Christopher managed to laugh at him — a hoarse hiccoughing sound. 'Very well,' Leeb said, 'if that's the way you wish it.' He said to the woman, 'Get the doctor in here; we'll want to make sure he stays alive and awake.'

'*Zu Befehl.*' With bovine obedience the woman turned towards the telephone and that was when the Gestapo man stabbed her in both eyes with spread rigid fingers and, as part of the same swinging movement, slammed the breech of the Schmeisser against Leeb's face.

The blow catapulted Leeb against the couch and the Gestapo man was already throttling the woman, cutting off her scream before it could begin. He went to his knees, bearing her down, the web of his hand crushing off her wind while thumb and fingers cut off the flow of the carotoid arteries. It was a hold that only worked on someone with a small neck and head where you could span the arteries with one hand; one of the many methods Christopher had been taught — the Gestapo man had been trained brilliantly. There hadn't been a sound from either of them except for the soft thud of Leeb's fall against the couch but Leeb wasn't dead and the ragged slow sound of his breathing was loud in the room. He'd been rendered unconscious by the blow, most of which had been delivered against the hinge of his jaw and the ear and the temple. It hadn't broken the skin but he'd almost instantly begun to turn purple, the broken capillaries spreading blood under the skin.

The Gestapo man had made all the right choices: the hard disabling blow to the *man* because men were less likely to react by screaming; the hand throttling the *woman* because she wouldn't be as likely to fight back by instinct or training and would be more susceptible to surprise and shock.

Christopher on his chair tried to get his feet under him. He didn't know what was going on or why, but shock flooded his system with adrenalin and he had a strength he hadn't owned five seconds before. He was upright, if wobbling, when the Gestapo man came up off the limp corpse of the woman and said in a swift low voice, 'Can you walk?'

'What?'

'No, I suppose not. Not fast enough at any rate. Bloody hell — I'd wanted them to give you more time to recuperate. Well it can't be helped, let's get on with it. Your shoes – over there. Put them on and be quick about it.'

When Christopher didn't move instantly the Gestapo man said, 'Oh, Christ's sake, *valiant enterprise – valiant enterprise.* I'm on your side, you bloody fool; now get your bleeding shoes on. .'

He stared stupidly but then it crept back into his memory: Mr Churchill in the war cabinet room: *He will identify himself to you by giving you an order in which he will incorporate the phrase 'valiant enterprise'. . . If you ever receive an order from this man, you will obey it as if it came directly from me. Instantly and without question or hesitation.*

The Gestapo man hurled the shoes at him. '*Get* on with *it*!'

The Gestapo man moved towards the door. 'We've got to keep talking – those two guards would get suspicious if the voices stopped; they're just outside the door. You may have to help me get through them. Are you good for anything?'

'I can try. Look, who are . . . ?'

'I'm here to get you out and that's all you've time for now. *Come* on, will you?' In great agitation the Gestapo man wheeled back to the couch and tugged the Luger out of Leeb's holster. 'Can you hold on to this thing?'

'I think I can.'

'Cover me, then.' He was pressing it into Christopher's hand. The pain shot through him like swords and he all but dropped it but he closed his fingers round it by an effort of will that squeezed tears from him. Then the Gestapo man was giving him a hand, half-carrying him across to the door, whispering now: 'You know the drill.'

It wasn't in him to utter any reply or question; his feet were like fire from the brief crossing of the room and it wasn't until the Gestapo man began to twist the knob that Christopher said, 'Wait,' and leaning against the wall for support summoned his breath and said, 'I can't walk, I'm sorry. I'm no good to you. Listen – kill me and get out.'

'Kill you? I'd love to. But my job's to bring you out alive. Now stop worrying about your feet; we'll handle this one thing at a time. Give me cover now.'

And the Gestapo man was opening the door and Christopher

saw the muscle men turning, lifting their weapons casually to show they were alert, then the surprise widening their eyes when they saw Christopher and the Luger in his hand. Then the Gestapo man burst out through the door wrapping one hand round the back of each man's head and slamming their skulls together before they had time to tighten up against it. One man's eyes rolled up and his knees gave way but the other one was dazed but not out and the Gestapo man went for him with the blade of his hand. The muscle man knew that one and turned his shoulder; it struck and bounced, must have hurt terribly but didn't incapacitate him. The muscle man was bringing his pistol up and filling his lungs to yell. In a blinding agony he tried to disregard, Christopher launched himself, clubbing the Luger down on top of the man's head with desperate haste.

The Gestapo man chopped again and this one went home. Then he thrust Christopher back inside the room, looked both ways along the hall, shoved the collapsing muscle man inside and dragged the other one in through the door. He pushed the door shut and leant against it with his mouth open and sweat all over his features. 'Christ. Thanks. If he'd got a shot off it wouldn't have mattered much whether he'd hit one of us or not. The whole building would've been alerted. That was fast work. Are you all right?'

The pain was excruciating. 'That's the silliest question I've heard all day.' He gasped it out.

The Gestapo man turned the key, locking the door. 'Look, getting you out is number two on my list. Number one's to get myself out — get a signal off to London letting them know exactly what information Leeb prised out of you. Leeb's reported everything up the line to Berlin by now, you know.' The Gestapo man climbed across two bodies to the desk and barked into the phone in German.

One of the muscle men was dead; the other was breathing. Leeb on the couch was alive, too, and the Gestapo man glanced at both of them while he talked into the telephone. Both men looked as if they'd be out for a while yet.

The Gestapo man rang off and said, 'I've summoned that shabby excuse for a doctor. Told him to bring his kit. He must have some sort of pain killer he can give you that won't put you to sleep. I need you walking — I can't very well carry you out of here.' Then he set about stripping the uniform off the dead muscle man. 'He's a bit bigger than you but it'll have to do. Get into his uniform.'

'What's the plan?'

'I've got access to a Resistance wireless. We make for that.'

'Right.' Christopher steeled himself and reached for the stripe-legged trousers. Through clenched teeth he said, 'I'll make it.'

The Gestapo man's reply was a harsh laugh.

When the doctor arrived in an alcoholic haze the Gestapo man showed him the Luger. The doctor wanted to minister to the four victims of the Gestapo man's silent assaults but the Luger convinced him and he opened his bag and selected a syringe and a phial. The Gestapo man spoke a warning and the doctor nodded regretfully. The needle went in and Christopher hardly felt it; it was nothing to the pain he already endured.

The Gestapo man shot questions and the doctor answered reluctantly, after which the Gestapo man rendered him unconscious with a timed squeeze on the carotids and started to fill his pockets with the items the doctor had pointed out in his kit: a syringe, several needles, two phials.

'This stuff should keep you going a while. Some sort of narcotic – you may feel lightheaded.'

He could already feel it coursing through him.

'We'll give it another few minutes – can't wait longer than that. Look, I'd better explain the layout. We're on the second floor.'

'Are there lifts?'

'Two cages at the north end but we'd better forget those. There are fire stairs at the south end. Locked and guarded of course but we'll take the guards out and use their keys. That's not a worry.'

'The trouble starts at the ground floor, then.'

'Right. Only one way out of this bloody place – right past the security checkpoint and out of the main door and it's always swarming with Jerries down there, inside and out.'

'Do we talk our way out or blast our way out?'

'We'll try to talk it through – you're in no shape for a fight. We're both in uniform – that will help. If they want papers you've got the man's but if they start asking you questions we're dashed — we'll just have to try and shoot our way out. There'll be vehicles in the courtyard. If you get out and I don't, grab the heaviest lorry you can find and try to crash it out through the gate — it's the best I can offer. Incidentally, my name's Heinz Gruber but they call me Harry — born in England but my parents had the misfortune to be Germans. I actually am in the Gestapo, you know.'

'What is this place?'

'SS headquarters, Cherbourg. We're right in the middle of the bloody city.'

'How do we get out, then?'

'Crash out. Look, it's crude but I do have a plan. One step at a time. Come on then.'

He had the one Walther in his holster and the other in his pocket with his hand on it; Harry carried the Schmeisser on its sling and they went along the corridor at a slow pace because the drug was working but nothing short of the bliss of unconsciousness was going to subdue the pain altogether. He had to concentrate on trying to walk normally and it hurt like the devil every time his weight came forward towards the toes of either foot. His steps were much shorter than usual. The cloth of the pocket rubbing against his fingers was enough to push the lid off his head. But the drug seemed to distance it all, as if he were a spectator to his own movements, and as long as he kept his teeth clenched he managed.

There was just one man at the locked door at the fire stairs, an SS corporal with a rifle and a ring of keys. He stood to attention when they walked up to him, Harry talking arrogantly in German and glancing behind to make sure no-one was in the hall — then abruptly Harry drove four stiff fingers into the corporal's solar plexus to punch the wind out of him so that he couldn't shout. The corporal folded over and his nose met the heel of Harry's palm coming up. He dropped like a stone and Harry went through the key ring muttering under his breath until he found the right one.

Then they were on the stairs and that was agony. The only way he could do it was to slide the heel of his hand along the iron-pipe banister, much of his weight on the hand. Harry blasphemed softly, dragged the unconscious corporal on to the landing, and locked the door to hide him, got a hand under Christopher's elbow and helped him along; he went down from tread to tread, keeping his weight on his heels but the shoes felt like hot coals against his toenails, and by the time they reached the first-floor landing he was reeling. On top of that was the necessity to keep quiet because there'd be another guard just the other side of the door.

'Rest a minute, then,' Harry whispered in his ear, 'but remember we haven't got long – somebody could knock on that locked door upstairs any time.'

Christopher was now certain that there was no possibility of getting out of this – out of the building, let alone Cherbourg. He was going to die. Well that was all right. He didn't mind. Death was what he deserved.

He blinked slowly. It was all passing him by, dreamlike; nothing really mattered because nothing was real. Memory was all he had to go by. He'd betrayed Churchill, given the secret up to them; they knew about Normandy now because he'd given it to them and he couldn't live with that.

Still – you're a professional. Act like one.

'All right,' he said, 'let's get it over with,' and heaved himself down the stairs.

But halfway down he stumbled and fell the rest of the way, tumbling, bashing himself up and Harry wasn't quick enough to catch him before he rolled to the bottom. Harry crouched beside him: 'Are you all right?'

'Fine.' He stood up, faster than he should have: blood drained from his head and he'd have fallen again if Harry hadn't propped him up. The drug was making him reckless.

Then he heard a racket. It seemed to be coming from up above and that was confirmed when he heard a door slam open and voices grow suddenly louder.

Harry cursed. 'They've found the bloody corporal. Come on, we've got to move now.' Harry pulled the door open, hooked his finger through the trigger guard of the Schmeisser and half-dragged Christopher through.

They were in the blind end of a corridor and at the opposite end it opened out into a vast space; as they approached and their angle of view grew wider Christopher saw that it was crawling with Germans, all of them armed. It was busy with cross-traffic but several men were jogging towards the lifts in the corridor with their weapons at the ready. That meant the alarm must have been given – by telephone from two storeys above, probably. Probably they'd also found Leeb and that lot by now. This corridor wasn't the place to be because anyone who emerged from it could be assumed to have come down the stairs. That must have been in Harry's mind because he pushed open the first door they came to and Christopher went in right behind him, pistol up at the ready; he and Harry were partners now and it was a tandem act and he did his part, covering Harry's back.

It surprised the sergeant at the desk. He didn't have time to do more than show his alarm. Harry's Schmeisser, swinging crosswise, nearly took his head off his shoulders.

An anteroom, no windows; there'd be some officer's room behind it through that next door. There was an intercom on the sergeant's desk and Harry pressed a switch to see if he could hear anything but nothing came through because the 'send' switch on the other end wasn't on. Harry glanced at him and Christopher nodded and then Harry turned the knob and yanked the door open; but there was nobody in the main office and he waved Christopher through, going back out past him to take the dead sergeant under the arm and drag him inside. He shut the door and bolted it. Christopher, covering the door, watched him cross directly to the window.

It was a courtyard, stone walls all the way round it and iron gates standing open. Harry'd been right: there were several vehicles parked neatly in a row – carryalls, armoured cars, a couple of Volkswagens, a black Fiat saloon and several slab-sided grey vans.

But the window had bars set into the stone.

Harry opened the casement and pushed experimentally at the vertical bars but they were well anchored and they weren't going to budge.

'Blast.'

Christopher sagged against the desk, supporting himself on one palm and a hip. He couldn't even feel the bruises from his fall down the fire stairs. He tried to gather strength because it would need both of them to get out of here: he'd done it before, training and exercise and SOE in France, and it was just a matter of not letting his body fail him.

Harry turned his back to the window and glared at the locked door. 'We'll wait till the corridor fills up with chaps blundering to and fro. Then we'll march out there and demand to know what's going on. Just follow my lead, right?'

Christopher's brain wasn't working particularly clearly but something had been knocking for attention and finally he had it. 'You could at least have had the decency to kill me before I spilt everything on them.'

'That wasn't part of the scheme.'

'Would you mind then just telling me what's on?'

'My job's to get you out alive.'

'You should have thought of that before they squeezed the whole bloody plan out of me.'

'I just do as I'm told.' Then Harry shushed him and put his ear to the door. After a moment he unlocked it and peered through, beckoning Christopher to follow. They went across the anteroom one at a time, swift strides, and Harry listened a while. When boots went tramping by he jerked the door open and thrust himself into the corridor. He began shouting — imperious, demanding.

A squad of men ran past towards the door to the fire stairs. A corporal had stopped to answer Harry's questions; the answers came out in short breathless bursts and Harry barked something at him. The corporal marched away and Harry walked straight up the corridor, not looking back. Christopher followed him.

He tried to look purposeful — as if he had proper business here. He watched everything at once. Harry went striding out into the vast lobby and then stopped until Christopher caught him up. He didn't say anything. Their uniforms gave them anonymity. The place was swarming with men, running about like chickens in a farmyard.

Then Harry moved out, obliquely making for the main door. It was shut and four guards stood ranged across it with their rifles at port-arms across their chests; quite obviously someone had given the order that no-one was to leave the building until things were sorted out.

Harry was walking not directly towards the door but towards the checkpoint where papers were examined. It was manned by an SS lieutenant and a staff sergeant. The sergeant was fiddling with a card file. The lieutenant sat back in his chair with his hands laced behind his head, looking amused by all the confusion.

Harry started barking while he was still six paces away and kept it up until he reached the desk. You didn't have to know much German to understand what he was on about. He had urgent business and they damn well better open the bloody doors and let him through. Christopher contrived to look impatient and businesslike.

The lieutenant lowered his hands; the smile dropped away and he said something coolly that prompted Harry to take out his papers and slam them down on the desk. Obviously the lieutenant knew him by sight from his previous passages through here. There was no suspicion in the way he glanced at the papers and handed them back, but the lieutenant spoke in a negative tone and sat back again, turning his palms up as if to say, *What can I do?* Harry launched into a fit of blustering but the lieutenant only kept shaking his head in polite apologetic denial.

Harry flicked a glance at Christopher. He recognized it as a signal and he was ready to follow Harry's lead. It would be better to get cut down in a fusillade than to be dragged back up to Leeb's office.

The lieutenant had turned to answer someone else's inquiry. Most of the Germans in the place were concentrated towards the rear of the lobby. An officer came out of the corridor, shouting orders. This broke up the mob; suddenly men were dispersing as if they had somewhere to go and Christopher assumed the officer had given orders to search the building.

In a minute, he realized, they'd search the office round the corner and find the dead sergeant. Then they'd know the fugitives were down here somewhere. It didn't leave much time to get free.

Harry turned away from the desk as if fuming. Because of the swing of his body he was obliged to hold on to the Schmeisser to keep it from swinging out and hitting someone; that gave him the excuse to hold it in both hands and as he was wheeling round his finger closed on the trigger and the Schmeisser began to stutter, shockingly loud in the confinement of the echoing high-ceilinged chamber. Christopher had pistols in both hands. The bullets raked straight across the doorway, hitting all four guards, and they were still falling when Harry yelled, 'Run for it!' He broke straight towards the door. It was a double door with glass panes and as his shoulder hit it Christopher saw a Volkswagen just drawing up at the foot of the steps. People behind him began to shout. There was a gunshot and then he was through the door, Harry ahead of him going down the steps, the door flapping shut behind him on its springs and then the rattle of automatic fire from within, bullets smashing up the glass panes but he was stumbling down the steps now and the gunfire whacked by overhead.

The passenger – a Wehrmacht infantry Hauptmann in battle dress – was halfway out of the muddy Volkswagen and scowling up at the noise of shooting when Harry yanked him by the wrist. He hauled the Hauptmann right out of the car and pitched him across the steps on his face. The driver was on his feet with the door open on the far side of the car and Christopher saw him reach for his service pistol. Christopher lifted the Walther from his pocket and felt the pain in his fingers when he squeezed off the single shot that knocked the driver away. Then Harry was shoving him into the passenger seat and running round to the other side of the car, pausing in front of the bonnet to spray the door of the building with his Schmeisser – that would drive them back, force them to keep their heads down for a moment longer. Harry leapt over the fallen driver and crammed himself into the seat under the wheel, punched the ignition and savagely thrust it gnashing into gear. The car pitched and bucked, the doors flapped as it accelerated.

It had taken them a while at the main gate to get the idea but belatedly they'd caught on. Now they were trying to swing the heavy iron gates shut – four men, two on either side, putting their shoulders into it. The gap was narrowing and there wasn't a prayer this little car could bash through those. Christopher thrust his arm out of the window and began shooting. The car was bumping on cobblestones and he hadn't a chance of hitting them but it might make them duck or flinch away.

It did better than that. Two of them stopped pushing the gates and turned to whip up their machine-pistols but Harry had the accelerator on the floor, changing from second into third, and the Volkswagen was right on top of them before they could bring their weapons into play. It shot through the opening like a seed squeezed from an orange, an inch to spare on either side, and Christopher would have lost his arm if he hadn't pulled it inside in time.

Through the window he had just a glimpse of a figure on a balcony above the courtyard – Albert Leeb, wheeling back into the building. Christ, that meant their identities would be broadcast everywhere. The others had perhaps seen an SS Hauptmann and a soldier – but Leeb knew who they were.

Machine-pistols and rifles were blazing at them from the gate and the walls. Harry was steering with maniacal frenzy, zigzagging, the tyres slithering up on to the pavement and back down. It was some sort of commercial area, warehouses and shabby old office blocks, vans and lorries and cyclists in the street.

Then it was a wide avenue. Harry twisted the wheel frantically and the Volkswagen nearly went over on its side making the turn. They veered into a side street with the protective walls of buildings on both sides and Harry slowed it down so they wouldn't bash into the walls. Christopher prayed the passage wasn't a blind one.

The passage seemed to end against a dark wall. Christopher thought bleakly this would be the end of it – all that trouble for nothing. But there was a turning to the left this side of the wall and Harry went into it, scraping paint off the car, and there was daylight at the far end. Harry knew where he was going.

Chapter Sixteen

They emerged into a little twisting street and Harry swung out into it without looking. There was a screech of brakes behind them, an indignant hoot, a little bump when something ploughed into them, but then Harry had it going again and they pulled away. They overtook a horse-drawn wagon, forcing an oncoming van over against the wall and there was more horn-hooting and the van driver's enraged shouts but it got them into the open and Harry had his foot on the floor again. The car didn't really work up much speed – like everything then it had a petrol governor on the engine and it wouldn't do more than forty-five, and already Christopher could hear the klaxons behind them.

Harry said, 'Listen now. We may get separated. Memorize this. Doctor Henri Ferté, 17 rue Foche, Octeville. Right?'

'Ferté, 17 rue Foche, Octeville.'

'That's two towns south of here. He's got the wireless. And he can do something for your injuries; he's a medical doctor. Now pay attention.' The car slithered on a grease patch and banged off a parked lorry, going far too fast for these streets. Bicyclists fled and pedestrians stood agape when they flew by. The klaxons were gaining.

'They believe Churchill and your controller put on an elaborate charade for your benefit – the maps, the plans, Normandy, "Utah", "Omaha", the lot. A deception designed to mislead *you*. Follow me? They know you're a British agent, a professional, because nobody issues suicide capsules to amateurs, and they know the controllers don't tell agents anything the agents don't need to know, so they believe you were told about this Normandy plan so that it could be tortured out of you. Don't ask questions, there isn't time – let me finish. Rommel's certain the invasion must take place across the Straits of Dover to Calais. He's concentrated his defences there, covering the Pas de Calais. I don't know where the bloody thing's laid on for; I'm too confused and nobody tells me those things anyway. It's not my job to plan the bloody invasion, is it. *But if the invasion is actually planned for Calais* they're going to get wiped out.

Annihilated. We'll lose the bloody war. I've just come down from Calais; they're pouring in from the reserve areas. Panzers, artillery, SS battalions, the lot. We've got to warn Churchill.'

Harry flung the car into a covered passage between a *pâtisserie* and a closed petrol garage. It was an apron into the car park behind the garage; no other exit from there but Harry seemed to know what he was doing. He squeezed the Volkswagen past a high red van and had the door open before she'd truly stopped. 'Out.'

There were several cars and vans parked haphazardly. Christopher thrust his door open. When he pulled himself out of the Volkswagen he saw gashes in the bodywork where several bullets had struck; the back window was starred.

The klaxons were close and Harry said, 'Get in,' waving him to a car but trotting away from it towards the turning in the passage.

It was an old high-powered Fiat and looked as if it had a lot of speed in it. The key was in the ignition.

Walking wasn't getting any easier; he leant against the car to ease his feet. He heard the klaxons go by in the main road outside – the hiss of car tyres and then, shortly thereafter, the jingle and chatter of treads that must belong to an armoured Panzerwagen, one of those open-topped versions with a slim 37mm Spandau mounted aft. Then Harry came back running. 'Right. Get in. We'll double back now.'

The Fiat didn't want to start right away but Harry pulled the choke and it began to growl – it had the big engine from the sound of it, one of the old Hispano-Suizas possibly. It was exactly the sort of car an arrogant SS turd would have commandeered from some wealthy luckless Frenchman.

They were a bit east of the city and when Harry drove it out of the concealed passage he turned left, back the way they'd come for a bit and then left again, running south at a good clip through cobbled residential streets on the hillsides. Some big houses up here – high garden wall, ivy-covered and flowering with spring blossoms. In one driveway he saw a parked Mercedes with Nazi flags – some high-ranking official sleeping in late. The Germans would have taken over a lot of these houses; they were the best digs in town. Over the rooftops of the grimy city you could see all the way out to the harbour and the sea.

Christopher said, 'One stupid question, if you don't mind. What day is it?'

It made Harry laugh without mirth. 'The fourth. It's the fourth of June.'

The houses were fewer now. Estates, then dairy farms and country cottages and nurseries with fruit and vegetable stalls by the road; green hills, trees, countryside, and here Harry batted along at a good speed but he kept one eye on the driving mirror because any car on a road like this would draw attention to itself and there was always the chance of a German checkpoint. Obviously Harry knew the country round here. There'd be armed roadblocks at all the major crossroads but these were side roads and Harry twice turned off into narrow rutted unpaved paths hardly wide enough for the car, branches scraping the paintwork until they emerged past some hidden farmhouses into another lane.

There were flowers here and there, putting fragrance in the air, and the sun was trying to break through but there were dark squalls in the west.

Harry said, 'Look, if anything goes wrong or we get separated, I've got only one other contact in the area. Do you know the rue Boel-Meslin?'

'In Cherbourg? I know where it is.' He'd been in Cherbourg twice with Roberts, two years ago on Resistance jobs.

'The place is called the Café des Pêcheurs. The Maquis leader's a girl, as many of them are – Nicole Lapautre. Her grandfather works in the café as a barman. He was a fisherman before he wrecked a boat in the Alderney Race and smashed up his legs.'

'They're right in Cherbourg? Why didn't we go there?'

'Because they haven't got a wireless.'

'A Maquis cell without a wireless?'

'They had one until last week.' Harry drove into the village. It was a cluster of very plain old sagging buildings with their front walls right up to the edge of the road. It would make a good trap and Christopher's hackles lifted with unease. He slid the pistol out – fire in his fingers – and held it in his lap.

'It's just along here on the left.' Harry was changing down for the turn.

They went through the main *place,* a statue of somebody on a horse out in the middle and park benches all round. There wasn't a single pedestrian in sight and that alerted Christopher because he'd seen villages like this before. Clearly Harry had seen them too because he said, 'We'll do a recce first, right past the house. It's the third one on your left up here. If it looks all right we'll swing round at the end and come back.'

Left turn into the street, off the square. This was a newer street and the houses were little bungalows set back behind garden fences. The third one had a bit more ground than the others: a gravel drive led past the house on one side into an open garage and Christopher saw the snout of a Peugeot parked inside. They gave doctors special petrol rations, of course. There was a sign above the low picket gate – serpents wrapped round a staff – and the lawn needed cutting but there was no suggestion of anything amiss. Harry went on as far as the end of the street where chickens ran about clucking between a dilapidated house and well-kept barn; he had to make a three-point turn because the car was too long and didn't have the lock it needed to get round the farmyard in one swing. Then they growled slowly back into the street and Harry pulled up on the opposite side some distance past the gate. There was a wooden plaque on the gate below the surgery emblem: *17 – Ferté.*

'Just wait here a mo.' Harry walked back along the verge and must have been studying the house across the street out of the corner of his eye; he crossed over, sauntered back, and finally went through the gate and up the path. Christopher gripped the pistol and noted that Harry hadn't switched the engine off; he'd left it idling in neutral.

Harry knocked and glanced over his shoulder. Someone peered out a window – Christopher glimpsed a pale face – and then the door opened. There was a brief low-voiced conversation in the doorway; Christopher couldn't see the other man very well. Then something caught Christopher's eyes and he bent down for better look. If he held his head just right he could see into the front window of the bungalow and right through to the side window. Beyond that, in the sunlight, something glinted.

He looked away, then looked again and it was still there but it moved, winking at him with bright shards of light.

He couldn't be sure but it might be a man with a rifle. And the greenish-grey contours behind it *might* be some sort of a German military vehicle. Christopher straightened up in the seat and opened his mouth to warn Harry but that was when someone inside the house flung Dr Ferté aside – if indeed that was Ferté – and suddenly the gunfire started, erupting everywhere at once.

There were shots inside the house, Harry was swinging the Schmeisser, a soldier was smashing the glass to shoot through the window. *Christ he's shooting at me!* and Christopher slid down in the seat and tried to take aim with the Walther.

Harry was stumbling back down the path, blazing furiously from the hip and someone pitched through the doorway. Christopher glimpsed a German uniform – and Dr Ferté was diving across the lawn trying to get down below the line of fire. Helmeted heads appearing in both front windows, Harry spraying them to keep them back. Christopher thrust the car door open for him and Harry reached for it grunting, 'Christ, a bloody set-up,' and then there was a fusillade from the window and Harry's spine arched back and he fell forward gaping.

But his last act of valiant enterprise was to toss the Schmeisser forward through the air and Christopher managed to catch it – livid flame in his fingers – and he dragged Harry into the back seat of the car. Then he was able to ignore the pain long enough to put a burst across the front of the house, driving them back for a moment, their heads ducking below the sills, and he had time to slide over the seat and engage the clutch.

He put another burst into the house and dropped the Schmeisser on the seat beside him – the magazine was empty. He rammed the lever into gear and let the clutch out, too fast, and she bucked but he had his foot on the accelerator and the engine roaring so she didn't stall. She lurched forward, throwing him backwards, and possibly that saved him because bullets were smashing the windscreen to bits now and glass was falling across his hands and into his lap. He screeched towards the square, gathering speed.

A bullet ricocheted off the tonneau. Ferté was dead on the lawn out there and they swarmed out of the house, four of them, dropping to one knee to fire at him over the little white fence. He ducked low in the seat and drove weaving from side to side. Hailstorm of bullets. He wrenched the wheel going into the town square and his last glimpse of Ferté's house in the mirror showed him an armoured car bursting out past the house through the shrubs where it had been concealed. The four men in the garden were running towards the armoured car to jump aboard. Then he was squealing round the equestrian statue and ramming the Fiat full-out into the farther street. Behind him he could hear the roar of the armoured car.

He had a slight lead on them and the powerful Fiat increased it. Two miles of curving farm roads; he took some of the bends on two wheels and ignored the possibility that anything might be coming the other way round the blind turnings.

He braked to a quick stop and whipped round in the seat. 'Harry?'

Harry, he'd assumed, was dead; but there was just a chance that he wasn't.

In the back seat Harry was crumpled akwardly where Christopher had heaved him in that moment of unthinking superhuman strength. Harry's eyes stared at him. With the engine throbbing there was no way of picking up a pulse but it was obvious from the way he lay that he was dead. The bullet must have cracked the spinal column and reached the heart because from the look in his eyes Harry'd been dead while he was still falling. His last flickering moment of life had given him the strength to toss the Schmeisser to Christopher.

He could hear the armoured car again and he put his foot down, turning left at a T-junction and praying it wasn't going to turn into a blind farm road; he rolled fast down a narrow impacted dirt track overhung by trees that had been planted in neat rows on either verge.

Ferté had betrayed Harry, that was the only explanation for it. The Germans had been waiting for them; it was a trap, and the only one who could have known they were coming there was Ferté. He'd given that information to the Germans and God knows what else he might have given them. When he got home Christopher would have to pass it on to SOE because Ferté

336

might have jeopardized anyone with whom he'd had contact in the Resistance.

When he got home. Christ, he was back into the old habits, thinking like an SOE agent again, as if this were still the fun and games of 1941. He brought his mind back to the present, glancing into the driving mirror, studying the road for turn-offs. He had to half-close his eyes because the wind hit him hard in the face at this speed; the windscreen had been blown out and now one of the tyres was beginning to flatten – one of the spent bullets must have got lodged in the outer casing and worked its way through. Fortunately it was a back wheel and he still had steering control. He wondered how long the wheel rim would hold out.

He was moving roughly southwest and Carentan would be somewhere to the east of him. This was fairly rugged country when you were on foot and when every step was painful; mainly farms but they were sprawled and terraced across hillsides and there was a good deal of climbing up and down to be done. He'd only been on foot an hour or so but already he was wondering whether he could go on much further. There was also the interesting question of just where the devil did he think he was going?

He'd driven the crippled Fiat off the road at the first opportunity and left it concealed in a copse. He hoped they'd be going too fast in the armoured car to notice the wheel tracks where he'd left the road. He'd left Harry's body in the car, starting to walk away before he'd summoned the presence of mind to go back and relieve it of a few possessions; Harry's money and papers, a single remaining loaded magazine for the Schmeisser, which he slung over his own shoulder to carry, and the syringes and phials Harry had taken from the SS doctor's kit. Christopher was going to need that stuff to keep going.

Keep going. . . At first the immediate objective had been simply to get away but now he had other things to think about. No time to grieve for Harry now, and no time to feel sorry for himself: he had to go on a while longer ignoring the bloody pain because there was a good deal of thinking to do. And finally – gruesomely, grotesquely, ghoulishly – he'd exchanged clothing with Harry, putting on Harry's uniform and hurrying away.

After nearly an hour's climbing he glimpsed the sea and he knew where he was now: the hills behind Cap de Flamanville and the waters he overlooked lapped up on Sark directly to the west. They were dangerous waters, he recalled, leading to the overfalls of the Banc de la Schôle. He was therefore about nine miles west-southwest of Cherbourg.

He was trapped on three sides by the sea here. He needed an alarming number of things: he needed escape, he needed food and medical attention and he needed to get his hands on a wireless. After that he needed a great deal of rest but he couldn't afford to think about that now; let it creep into his mind and he'd fall right off into healing sleep.

By the time he'd left the Fiat he'd heard the roar of an armoured car again. Soon these hills would be crawling with Germans. Apart from wanting him back for more questioning they'd want to make bloody sure he didn't get back to England to tell everyone that he'd spilt the plan to the enemy.

The first objective, then, had to be a wireless but that had implications too: he'd broken, he'd given the enemy everything they'd wanted, and if he reported that to London he'd be confessing his shame.

The realization gripped him in a paralysis from which he seemed unable to emerge: his mind flapped around it and he nearly cried out in anguish. He'd betrayed their trust and everything he'd been trained for. He'd caved in. It was too much to have to admit.

But he had to admit it because London had to be told that the Germans believed the invasion was set for Calais. Nothing else mattered.

A transmitter. Where?

If it were the other side of Paris he could hunt up the Resistance people from the old days but he didn't know the organization here. He'd worked the area twice with Roberts and he knew the geography well enough but they'd been running independent assignments down here and they hadn't had to make any local contacts. The girl Harry had mentioned — what was here name again? Nicole, yes. Nicole Lapautre, Café des Pêcheurs — well that wasn't much help because her group didn't have a wireless.

Still, wasn't it possible they might have access to a boat?

Perhaps it was too much to hope for. Cherbourg was the most massively guarded harbour on the French coast. COPP had reconnoitred it a dozen times and everyone agreed there was no way that Cherbourg could be attacked. Half a dozen immense forts overlooked the harbour and a fly couldn't move through it unobserved. For a single man, half crippled, to go back into that city and try to get out by boat would be insanity enough; but on top of that was the nature of the waters – the rocks and shoals off Ile Pelée, the bloody awful winds, the juggernaut tides rolling down the Channel past the tip of the Cotentin peninsula – the dreaded Alderney Race, its vast surge of water compressed into a narrow channel and lifted by the shallow sea bed into a smashing great overfall pocked with whirlpools and foam. Big ships had the power to steam into the wind away from it but even the bigger fishing boats and yachts had to wait for dead-calm weather before crossing the Race and any small boat would be overwhelmed without a chance.

There was all that and then there was the German navy to think about.

He was moving now, nonetheless, trudging northeast away from his previous course so that if they'd put dogs on his track he wouldn't be intercepted too quickly. He paid careful attention to his feet, taking each step with elaborate care and walking on until the pain became too terrible to bear any longer, and going on a while after that.

Think. Barneville-sur-Mer was down the coast somewhere, overlooking the Gulf of St Malo. Steal a small boat there? Make a run up the Channel?

Right, he thought drily – make a run up the Channel right under the guns of the German-occupied Channel Islands. Try another.

Find a German aerodrome, he thought wildly – kidnap a Luftwaffe pilot at gunpoint and force him to fly you to England.

Right, right, and parachute in like Rudolph Hess. *Stop fantasizing. Don't panic.* Think back: the lessons of training days. The first lesson of all: simplicity is always the answer.

But there was no simple answer. There was no answer at all.

It was impossible to think clearly. The pain was driving him mad.

He had to lie down, resting on one elbow. He took out the

phials and tried to read their German labels. That proved beyond him so he opened one of them and sniffed its contents. The clear liquid didn't have much discernible odour, so he tried the other one and that settled it; the second one contained pure alcohol. He swabbed a patch on his left arm, broke the seal round one of the needles and fixed it to the syringe, drew a half-inch of liquid into it from the first phial as he'd seen the SS doctor do – one cubic centimetre was what the doctor had given him before. A good thing you grew up in a surgery, lad, because at least you know enough to squeeze a drop out of the syringe before you go digging it into the vein.

He lay back throbbing with pain, waiting for the drug to take effect. Finally he rolled over and fumbled the phials and syringe back into his pockets, brought the Schmeisser up in his hands and looked all about him.

He was looking up at the hilltop he'd just crossed. Silly place to stop, he realized now; he should have stopped back there at the top under the trees where he could see his backtrail. From here he wouldn't see anything until it came over the top and that was point-blank. There could be a hundred men tracking him up the other side of the hill for all he knew: the wind came from the north and the sound would not carry this way.

He knew then that he'd been making one stupid blunder after another and it was amazing he'd got away with it this far. Unless he sorted himself out quickly he wouldn't last much longer: it took only one mistake to die. It was the torture, of course, the torture and the guilt and the confusion of this whole nightmare – but somehow he had to disregard all that; he must clear his head and survive – and that meant every sense had to be at the peak of alertness.

Right, then. What to do?

Don't stay here, you bloody fool. Get on with it.

He winced when he put his weight on his feet but he walked and that was what counted. *You've been trained to get out of things. Get out of this one.* Of course his training was based on the assumption that he had full use of his faculties...

Into a wood, stumbling a bit but still moving. An insect whined about his ear and when the noise stopped he reached up and crushed it and pain shot through him: he'd forgotten about his fingers.

He kept remembering Harry's face at the end. He'd known nothing about the man but Harry's death had hurt him, as if he'd been a lifelong friend.

Friends, he thought — his family, Patricia, the chaps in COPP and the men of the 5th Submarine Flotilla with whom they shared their quarters: he could see their faces. Never likely to see them again, he thought.

Submarine flotilla. . . The odd thought glanced off his memory again, nudging. Then abruptly he knew why.

The submarines had been keeping constant patrol two or three miles north of Cherbourg for weeks now — hanging about, spying on German shipping, watching for movements that would indicate German defence plans.

Right now one of the submarines of the 5th Flotilla would be lying just off Cherbourg — men he knew personally; so close — almost as if waiting for him, with food and medicines and wireless transmitters. . .

I'm not dead yet. By Christ I'm not!

He stumbled on, seeking some landmark.

Chapter Seventeen

He pedalled silently on the bumpy country lanes, trees dripping on him when he went under them, the road hard to see but he wasn't moving fast anyway because his muscles barely obeyed him.

He'd commandeered the bike by standing in the middle of the road, wearing the SS officer's uniform he'd stripped off Harry and thrusting his Schmeisser in the face of the aged post-man. He'd said something in harsh German-accented French about priorities and the Fatherland needing the postman's bicycle and he'd left the grumpy old man standing there with a resigned scowl on his face. It had been all Christopher could do to make his hands and feet work on the bike. As soon as he'd gone out of the postman's sight he'd turned off into a side lane and taken the bike back through the hedgerow and collapsed to wait out the daylight and try to get his brain functioning properly.

After he'd parked himself in the hedgerow for the afternoon he'd thought about giving himself another shot of pain-killer but he'd vetoed it because it would have relaxed him and he might have fallen asleep and he couldn't be sure when he might wake up again. So he let the drug wear off, and the pain kept him awake through the afternoon while he did his thinking. Now it was raining and the chill helped revive him.

The only means of contact he had with the Resistance was that café in Cherbourg and, risks or no risks, he was going to have to go there. He couldn't move about by daylight because the blood stains and holes in the ill-fitting tunic were too ob-vious. By night he might be able to get by.

He would move into Cherbourg as soon after dark as possible.

He'd retraced his movements in his mind and knew roughly where he was now. He'd come up inland parallel to the coast, north past Port de Dielette to Siouville, along the coast to Bivelle, thence northwest, climbing the 600 feet or so to Sainte Croix. Down the hills then, almost due east to Tonneville—

through Hainville – and now, pedalling through the early darkness, he was at the western approaches to Cherbourg itself.

Earlier in the day it had seemed the essence of simplicity to make his way to the British submarine off Cherbourg. He knew it would be there; it was always there. The realization had come to him as a stunning solution to his dilemma. But now he was seeing all the imponderables in it. How was he going to find the submarine? How was he going to get near it? Even if he found it, how could he make himself known to the submarine and persuade it to come to the surface?

The Germans had taken over the old French naval hospital on the western outskirts of Cherbourg and he rode the bicycle past it with his heart in his mouth, drawing the attention of the guards but no challenges; they saluted and he breathed again, pedalling past the Basilique into the centre of Cherbourg, then south to the rue Tour Carré – keeping to the middle of the street. The thing to avoid was any suggestion of furtiveness; boldness was the key. But he was watching every shadow and listening to every sound. An open car went past him, four Germans in uniform – he met the glance of the Leutnant in the back seat and contrived a smile. The car's slitted blackout headlamps disappeared round a bend. He was in the rue au Blé now; a left turn and he was in the rue Boel-Meslin. The café had to be somewhere just along here. He got off and walked the bike, seeking the right door, blinding pain shooting through him again.

The rain began again – it had been drizzling intermittently for hours and the German uniform had a rank smell. He'd reached the end of his endurance; he felt lightheaded, near collapse.

There – just a few doors ahead. He propped the bike in a side passage and emerged from it just as a foot patrol of three German soldiers appeared from a turning beyond the café. He fought the instinct to retreat into the passage; they might have seen him by now. Brazen it out – he walked forward slowly and hoped they would take his gingerly steps and disreputable appearance for mild drunkenness.

Keep moving now: he'd reach the café ahead of them as long as he didn't hesitate.

They carried their rifles slung across their shoulders and one of them flung his arm up in the Nazi salute and spoke – something in German, a short sentence. Panic fluttered Christopher's breath but he flipped up his arm in an approximation of the salute and muttered, 'Heil', and turned, reaching for the door latch. Something was posted on the door: a rain-drenched placard and he assumed it was an out-of-bounds notice but he had to trust his SS uniform to get him past the soldiers' scrutiny and he ignored the soldier's words, squeezing the latch and praying it wasn't locked.

The soldiers had broken stride and one of them was scowling but the door came open and Christopher stuck out his chin and strode through it, pulling it shut firmly after him.

He was in a box of blackout curtains and he stood there, hardly breathing, facing the door with his hands on the Schmeisser but the soldiers didn't follow him inside. After a moment when his breathing calmed down he turned and thrust the curtain aside and had a look at the place.

There were half a dozen small tables, a short counter with stools, a few photogrphs on the walls: a couple of Gothic cathedrals and the official portrait of Hitler.

There were only two people in the place. Both of them stared at him, all expression withheld from their faces. The girl wore a simple dress with the wide shoulders and frilly hem of her age; she had short-cropped dark hair and a not particularly pretty face. The man was old enough to be her grandfather. This had to be played with great care. He hoped he had his wits sufficiently about him to bring it off.

The old man's narrow-eyed stare was guarded and suspicious.

Christopher spoke in French to the girl. 'Is he your grandfather?'

'Is he under arrest?'

'No.' A wave of dizziness made him reach for the rim of the counter. 'Don't answer a question with a question.'

She said, 'Yes, he is my grandfather,' without heat but her eyes were defiant.

Christopher said, 'You could be shot for treason, both of you,' and waited to see how they'd take it because if they were the wrong ones or if they'd turned their coats he needed to know it.

The girl stared at his SS uniform and the old man said in a

gravelly whisper, 'If you think we need to be shot then I suppose you'll have us shot. What do you wish us to say? That we don't know what you are talking about? We don't, of course, but if someone has given false evidence against us there's little we can say that will change your mind.'

Christopher laid the Schmeisser down and sagged against the counter. 'Look, I'm English. Harry told me to come here. Heinz Gruber.'

The girl moved along behind the counter to stand beside the old man and he put his hand on her shoulder.

Christopher was having trouble getting his tongue properly around the words. 'I haven't had contact with any Maquis for more than two years. If there are passwords and countersigns I've got no idea what they are. I don't know what to say that will convince you – but I'm English and I need your help.'

They weren't buying it straight off the peg. Christopher lurched, nearly capsizing; he'd pumped up his strength to get this far but he hadn't anything left in reserve and he had to brace both elbows on the counter to keep from going over. He hung his head down and tried to fight the drain of blood from his head.

The old man's eyes had dropped. He was looking at Christopher's hand. The girl's glance followed the old man's – and her face changed. She said, 'They've been at his fingernails.' She clutched her fingers against her palms, memory of the agony reflected in her face.

The old man said, 'Who did that?'

'A pig named Albert Leeb.'

'I know that one,' the girl said. But still the old man reserved confidence.

Christopher said, 'Listen – you must believe me, it's vital.'

'Yes, it always is.'

'I've got to make contact with London.'

'We've no wireless here.'

'I know, Harry told me. But there's another way.'

He didn't know what the ointment was or where the girl had found it but it gave some relief and he didn't cry out when she fitted the plasters to his fingertips. She'd done an expert job of cleaning out the bullet-burn on his wrist with alcohol and wrapping it in gauze and tape.

They were in a small windowless room behind the café, the entrance to which was concealed behind the lavatory; he suspected this might have served as a secret meeting room for members of the Cherbourg Resistance. It contained nothing visibly incriminating; only a half dozen straight chairs, a table and an unshaded electric bulb dangling from the ceiling. In that unflattering light the girl seemed peculiarly flat-featured, nearly oriental. Perhaps she was Eurasian.

She caught his glance and smiled, and the smile changed her completely: it made her quite beautiful.

The old man came back into the room with a chunk of precious sausage, a quarter of a loaf of bread and a teacup filled with raw red wine. He said, 'After the Boche began to use mobile direction-finder devices we had to abandon the wireless – the risk was too great.'

Christopher grasped the bread gingerly in his tender bandaged fingers and despite himself felt a keen pleasure at the taste of the food and wine. 'You know there's to be an invasion.'

'Everyone knows – even the Germans know. It's why we are alone tonight. The members of our group are setting half of Normandy ablaze tonight. We've waited years for this.'

'We've dropped tons of supplies to you for sabotage and intelligence,' Christopher said; it didn't hurt to remind the old man of his debts. 'A great many grenades, among other things, thirty-six to the case. I'll want a few of them back tonight. Six will do.'

'Grenades are more valuable than gold,' the old man replied.

'American ones. British ones. I agree. But you must have captured a few German ones. They'd do just as well for me.' Guerilla groups didn't like German hand grenades because their long handles made them difficult to conceal in one's clothes.

The girl had set his boots aside. She was treating his toes. His feet were horrible swollen apparitions but she went about the job with matter-of-fact competence.

The old man inclined his head. 'Perhaps we can find a few German grenades,' he conceded, 'but why do I feel that's only the beginning of your list of requests?'

'There's only one other thing I need. A boat.'

The old man's laugh was a harsh cackle. 'A boat? Perhaps an ocean liner!'

'There are no words to explain how important it is that I get my message to London.'

'Young man – young fool – we've tried three times to help people escape from Cherbourg by sea in small boats. None of them survived.'

'None of them knew there was a British submarine within just a few miles of here. If I can get that far they'll pick me up.'

There hadn't been much wine in the cup but it was already making him dizzy; fatigue and shock and his injuries had caught up with him; drinking the wine had been a mistake and he had to tighten his muscles against a reeling wave of disequilibrium.

The girl said in her soft kind voice, 'You are in no condition for boating in the Alderney Race, you know.'

'Look – I know it sounds absurd but thousands of lives – French, British, American – may depend on my reaching that submarine.'

The old man watched him without blinking; and finally said, 'Just what was it you told to the Boche, then?'

'I told them too much.' He met the old man's eyes.

They lurched across the Quai Caligny to the small bridge across the lock gate; they had to get across it and of course it was guarded – a checkpoint and one sentry visible, probably others within earshot. Guile, rather than violence, was the main weapon in their arsenal. The old man behaved very drunkenly; the girl supported him on one side and Christopher, in his SS officer's uniform, on the other. Half-carrying the old man between them they struggled straight up to the bar-gate and Christopher scowled at the sentry until he brought his hand up across his rifle in a salute, to which Christopher responded with a quivering rigid Nazi salute, nearly slamming his stiff fingers into the sentry's helmet. The sentry would have noticed the plasters on his fingers anyway and thrusting them right in the sentry's face would prove Christopher had nothing to hide. Then, letting his face soften a bit, Christopher inclined his head slightly towards the girl and winked at the sentry while she said something in German, presumably about getting the old man home before curfew. The sentry thought for a moment, visibly, and then let them through, smiling a bit.

After that it was a long trudge and his feet felt like giving out at any moment. Once they were out of sight of the checkpoint, moving southwest past the church of St Clément, the old man straightened up and walked along with a severe limp.

The river Trottebec was narrow, a stream really; they followed its footpath as far as La Bagatelle and then turned northwest. Time slipped by and it was past curfew now; they crept carefully past the heavily guarded checkpoints on the approaches to the port fortifications, sliding through shadows and finally dipping their boots into the muck and sludge at the base of the wall of the old naval fortress. There was a jetty with a guard on it and they climbed over it one at a time, slithering on their bellies; there was a thin drizzle and no moon tonight — even without clouds there'd have been no moon; that was one reason why the invasion had been laid on for this weekend.

They were past the corner of the inner fortress now, moving northwest along the edge of a jetty, under the guns of the high Fort des Flamandes — they were at the lip of the Grande Rade, the outer harbour of Cherbourg. It was a vast area of water, four miles in width and there were only two usable exits for shipping. Both of them were guarded by massive fortifications. The trick wasn't so much to lay hands on a boat; the trick was to get the boat past those forts.

Christopher shifted the military pack on his shoulders. It contained six German mallet-grenades and one of them kept digging uncomfortably into his spine.

The night was wet and pitch black: good for security but bad for pilotage. He didn't think much of his chances of reaching open water and making contact with 5th Flotilla's submarine; but he hadn't seen any choice in the matter and now the girl and the old man were in it too.

The craft was a gaff-rigged twenty-five-foot fishing boat and it was hidden nearly under the guns of the Fort des Flamandes, in the Grande Rade, so that it only had to navigate one open passage to reach the sea. The hiding place in the old stone breakwater was so close under the walls of the fort that it was impossible to see it from the watchtowers.

His fingers were clumsy and painful even though he'd dosed

himself with the last measure of narcotic from the German doctor's phial; after a moment the old man shooed him away from the line he'd been trying to cast off, told him to go and sit under the boom and whispered a curt instruction to Nicole, who unfastened the line and drew it aboard.

Christopher heard water sloshing in the bilge and wondered how seaworthy the little craft was. It had the smells of age and the feel of hard treatment.

The old man murmured, 'We cannot escape from the harbour through either of the main passes. But there is a third, you know. Very small. The Passe Cabart Danneville. It lies about a mile from here. Forty metres wide.'

'I thought the Germans had blocked that one.'

'They have. But we have attended to the blockage—for occasions like this one.'

It was all the old man said. The girl, however, remarked that the passage up the east of Ile Pelée would be very hazardous and it was a good thing they had high tide on account of the rocks and shoals. She sounded a bit sarcastic but it was evident she had some seamanship and he got the feeling, from the brisk way she moved about the boat making fast line and hoisting sail, that she enjoyed the challenge.

The wind was northeast, not bad here but once beyond the protection of the fortress wall it would be high: probably Force 6, something short of a gale but not easy for a small boat under sail. They'd have to tack into it right under the noses of the German sentry-gunners on the lookout towers. The water was choppy; the boat bounced around fiercely.

They moved out under the smallest possible amount of canvas, the boat hardly making headway at all; they couldn't risk any noise because they were less than two hundred yards west of the sentry at the corner of the German naval base beyond the fort.

The old man had the tiller and seemed happy enough but Christopher was thinking what madness this scheme was: Cherbourg must be the most heavily guarded port of all and it was inconceivable they'd escape unseen. But the blackout helped—that and the fact that the Germans' radar wouldn't pick up this wooden hull.

The rain pelted his back. Heavy swells pitched the boat about;

he made his way towards the tiller to offer his help but the old man gave him a contemptuous glance and told him to stay out of the way. Christopher found a section of rail to wedge himself against, jammed his heels against a deck cleat and tried to grip the stanchion with his elbow because he didn't trust his hands.

With the wind from east-northeast the old man had no choice but to tack on a north-northeast course straight towards the top of Ile Pelée; they'd have to sail quite close under its guns before allowing the wind to turn the boat southeast towards the narrow pass. Christopher realized that the east-northeast wind was exactly what they did not need tonight: once beyond the Grande Rade they would be unprotected from its full force and its western six-knot tidal drift would tend to drive them straight towards the maelstrom of the Alderney Race.

The girl went nimbly off the bow on to the black rocks of the blockage that the Germans had dumped into the channel to choke off the Passe Cabart Danneville. It seemed an impossible tangle of debris and he was amazed when he saw her unfasten a couple of lines and walk forward, crouching, with an entire section of the rubbish-pile blockage sliding alongside her. It took him a while to realize they must have cleared out a section of the channel and then piled the rubbish on top of a raft or small barge and secured it in place so that it looked exactly as it must have looked before.

The old man remained on board, holding a line fast to the rocks; his crippled legs wouldn't have permitted him to go clambering about as the girl was doing. She was quickly out of sight in the darkness. At the moment it wasn't raining but that was only a temporary respite; it was a stormy night all round and Christopher knew that if the weather didn't clear soon there'd be no invasion this weekend. He thought of the hundreds of thousands of men massed and waiting.

They'd used this route three times before, the old man had told him, but they hadn't got away with it. Twice they'd had to turn back because of heavy seas beyond the harbour. The third time the boat had been carried into the Alderney Race; the boat had been lost and the old man had smashed up both his legs. He'd been saved only by the good fortune of a Kapok life-jacket and a passing freighter.

Christopher could hardly remember a darker night. But his mind suddenly seemed to clear — as if responding to the challenge of the elements. Too many people had been killed or betrayed by him; he wasn't going to allow these two to risk their lives on his account. Why should he? After all, he was a qualified naval officer; he had sailed since he was a boy; navigation and seamanship were in his blood.

He didn't know the girl was back until she was at the bow reaching for the headrope. Then she was pulling the little gaff-rigged boat forward into the passage and the old man was thrusting at the rocks with an oar to keep the gunwales from scraping.

It took ten minutes to tow the boat through the heaving passage of water. Then the girl disappeared again to push the rubbish barge back into place, closing the gap. As she did so, Christopher moved quietly to the old man. He had to summon all his strength: he got his arms round him, lifted him off the deck, swung him over the side and swiftly let him go on to the mud close to the girl.

Christopher pulled the headrope out of her hand. Only then did she turn in surprise and see the old man.

'God bless you, *mademoiselle, grandpère.*'

Then Christopher heaved on the gaff halyard, made fast and took the tiller, heading almost north by east.

He was north of Ile Pelée and it was about four in the morning and he was past high tide, fighting the current and the wind; he was heading her in as close as he could to the wind, trying to get well out to the north so as to avoid the Race. But the seas came crashing in and the little boat didn't seem to have much more than a prayer of surviving the passage. With every roll and pitch the deck was awash. The spray was higher than the mast; even in the darkness he had glimpses of a wicked sheen on the sail canvas: she was soaked up to the masthead and she pitched blindly now, yawing, plunging hard into the troughs, tipping half on to her beam; when the bow broke through the surface her timbers whined and creaked alarmingly. The blustering sea broke over Christopher and he clung to the tiller, an elbow locked round the after-stay but the waves kept picking him off the deck and he wasn't sure he had the strength in him for much more of this.

The wind was backing to the north and that was bad; it was a good two hours since high water at Cherbourg and that was even worse. The wind and the tidal drift were carrying him towards the west and there was nothing to be done about it. He was drifting towards Cap de la Hague and the Alderney Race.

He had the dismal thought that he'd come through everything the Germans could fling against him: SS, Gestapo, Wehrmacht, navy — only to lose a battle with this non-combatant ocean.

The boat was responding sluggishly to the helm and the pitch and roll were ominously angled. He knew at once the boat was wallowing. Christopher looked about him and had a vague impression of something metal in the cockpit — the bilge pump. He sat to lee putting his foot on the tiller and cried out when his fingers came into contact with the cold metal of the handle but he began to heave it up and down. The effort was almost more than he could bear but there wasn't any other choice because the boat was listing badly now. With one turn of the main sheet round a cleat, both hands pumping and his foot on the tiller, he lay awkwardly stretched across the boat and it was in the back of his mind as he gasped and pumped that if the sea became even a fraction stronger than it was now, the boat would broach. Christ, he thought, I'm falling off the end of the world...

His arms knotted with cramp. The boat gave all she had to give, faltering and clawing, her fragile bow breaking the sea but not taming it, and Christopher waited endlessly for the sudden snap of mast or the whiplash crack of a broken stay. Unaccountably he found himself speaking aloud: 'Christ — I must be on the west side of Hell itself.' He was almost enjoying the knives of pain in his fingers now; they assured him that he was still alive.

Spray on the wind lashed at his feet like a cat-o'-nine-tails but he hardly felt that. Black sleet pummelled his shoulders. The boat plunged nose first into a trough and a high roller broke across her; wood crackled and growled throughout the boat. For a moment he thought she'd go straight on down into the sea then but finally the foam rolled back and the bow began to lift, juddering at first, then swinging aloft as her stern plunged into the trough. She rode the sea hard, blasting through the crests, and Christopher's body ached as he fought to maintain the wind angle. When the swell lifted her and she began to swing he corrected with instinctive turns; he could hear the change in the squeaking scrape of her timbers as torsion twisted her in new directions. Then a cap loomed on her quarter and the crest caught her before he could meet it: it slammed her hard, tons of water cascading over the boat, and Christopher clung desperately to the tiller while the sea whacked him against the cockpit coaming and lifted him off the deck. Then it slammed him down again and he thought he'd cracked half his ribs. Her stern lifted free and for a moment the rudder had no grip and the sea shoved her round in an arc until the bows struggled up from the thunderfall: he put her helm hard up to the wind and she rolled steeply, the deck awash but the water running off now and she was righted until torsion twisted her in new directions. Then a cap loomed on her helm, got hold of the pump handle and heaved up and down upon it. Salt water had matted his uniform to him like mud.

The sea ran in striated phosphor-white streaks against its own black depth. She was too small, too light, too lively; she did not take it well and in the wake of each roller she showed every inclination to swerve and wallow but she was a tough Norman boat and if she steered badly at least she steered. She was taking enough solid water across her bow to destroy a more fragile vessel but her timbers must be heavy and solid below decks.

The wind nearly tore the hair from his head. Raw spray whipped his face and he did not know if he could take another half minute of this.

Then by the grace of the heavens he was out of the squall.

The seas continued to run high, the wind gusting to Force 7 in its erratic puffs, but he was outside the storm itself and there was time to pump her out properly, time to estimate bearings, time to breathe.

By day, or given moonlight, it would have been a fair job navigating these waters; in this pitch blackness there was no doubt at all he'd be forced into the Alderney Race within an hour. Christopher slipped the knapsack off his shoulders and cursed at the pain and clumsiness with which he had to attack its sodden buckles. Finally, one foot on the tiller, he had one strap unfastened and he got his hand inside. He removed three of the six grenades and pulled the arming pins one at a time and tossed the grenades over the side.

The explosions were muffled, barely audible up here, but if the submarine were anywhere within six or seven miles it would hear them underwater. He'd thrown two close together, then a pause, then the third.

Two and one wouldn't be the current operational signal; those were changed at frequent intervals. But it would only need one officer aboard the submarine to recognize the blasts as being an old COPP surfacing signal. But even if it were recognized that way, the submariners would be aware that it could be a trick. German E-boats prowled these waters frequently, carrying both depth charges and torpedoes, seeking out Allied spy vessels.

He had to count on the fact that a well-trained submarine captain would come to periscope depth and make a sweep. But the submarine would have to be able to see him. . .

Were there any flares aboard? Or a lamp? He lashed the helm with the inboard end of the mainsheet and stumbled forward.

He found the storm lantern in the locker: an oil lamp with a waterproof packet of matches taped to it. He had trouble getting it lighted in the wind; crouching over it, sheltering it with his body, he expended five matches before the sixth ignited the wick. Then he clamped the storm-chimney down to protect the flame, hooked the lantern over his elbow and made his way forward to the mast. *What if a German sees it first?* But you had to take those risks and he hoisted the lantern up the mast and it shone up there, a beacon for anything within five miles.

He hadn't reckoned the passage of time; the first streaks of breaking dawn took him completely by surprise. He had been tacking close to the wind trying to keep her away from the Race but it was a losing battle against the tide and it was far too late to turn back towards the shore. Any moment now he'd be caught up in the swirling currents. There wasn't much time left. The sea had drifted him to the west – perhaps too far west to reach the submarine with the grenade signals.

354

Too much time had gone by. If the submarine had heard the signal it would have appeared by now.

Perhaps it would be better to resign himself to failure and die. Better to fade into the anonymous indignity of death than to make contact with London and trumpet his shame to them all – Churchill, Owl, Pooh.

But this was one of those games which, once started, had to be played through to the finish. He knew that. There was no backing out now.

He pulled the pins and sent his last three grenades over the side.

The swells had dropped and the boat was bobbing with less violence; the muffled *wham-wham . . . wham* was quite audible this time. Christopher got his feet and began to search the horizons. The light was strengthening steadily, heavy grey clouds notwithstanding, and the wind had driven the mists off – he could see quite a fair distance. Cap de la Hague and Alderney were clearly in sight as he swept south with the Race nearly astern. . .

Then he saw it: the little fast wake of something breaking the surface – the periscope he realized, and then the sea was turning white and spilling off the sides of the conning tower as she surfaced. She was running head-on towards him, coming from the northeast, and Christopher saw her sleek upper casing emerge from the sea. The hatch came open and the captain emerged, followed by the gunnery officer and guns crew, men running fast towards the three-inch gun and that made Christopher whip his head around to look behind.

It was coming up fast in the distance throwing a high wake: it had to be an E-boat.

They must have spotted the lantern from inshore.

Christ.

Christopher made fast the sheet and tiller, stumbling on numb legs. He whipped off his coat, tore the shirt from underneath and stumbled forward into the bow, braced himself against the swell and began to signal: D–O–L–P–H–I–N . . . D–O–L–P–H–I–N. . .

He got the word off twice and then his arms had no more strength in them and he collapsed, kneeling, head down, eyes awash.

He heard the diesels roar: the submarine converting from electric motors to surface engines. Now she came thrumming forward at a high speed and the E-boat behind was coming up fast out of Alderney. The thought struck Christopher that the reason the submarine hadn't heard his first grenade signal was that it had been quite dark then and – you bloody imbecile – she'd have been running on the surface to charge her batteries. Of course she wouldn't have heard any underwater bangs, not with her own diesels making all that din.

He measured the distance to the speeding E-boat and estimated it at two miles. Not long before she'd heave into gun range. *There's time*. The submarine closed fast, her gun beginning to swivel towards the E-boat. The captain talked into the pipe, giving orders to the coxswain. The black boat loomed beside the Norman fishing boat; she was doomed, one way or another. The E-boat would sink her or she would sweep down the Race and eventually be smashed to pieces on Les Minquiers, and would be found hard by Mont St Michel.

He only had enough energy to throw his headrope to a petty officer on the submarine's casing; then he fainted.

FLAG OFFICER SUBMARINES REPEATED DOLPHIN FROM CAPTAIN SEAHORSE MOST SECRET IMMEDIATE EYES OF PRIME MINISTER ONLY XHTVI MIGPW BASZN PFJUL. . .

Chapter Eighteen

The PM did not have a study as such at 10 Downing Street; he used the cabinet room. Christopher had never seen it before. There was only one painting in the room. It hung over the Prime Minister's chair, which was the only armchair. It was a portrait of Robert Walpole.

Mr Churchill said by way of greeting, 'I'm told you required transfusions of five pints of blood. How are you feeling?'

'Quite well, sir. Ready for duty.'

It was nearly three months since he'd passed out alongside the submarine *Seahorse*. They'd told him later about the duel they'd fought with the E-boat – surface gunnery and then the emergency dive and the waiting game amid the depth charges.

'Of course the COPP unit's nearly outlived its usefulness,' the PM said mildly. 'The men may go out to the Far East.'

'Yes sir. I've asked for destroyer duty.'

'I know. The report came across Uncle John's desk.' The PM removed the cigar from his mouth. 'Losses on the Normandy beach-heads on the first day were expected to be seven men out of ten. You're aware, I trust, that the actual losses in the event were only one man out of fifteen. We achieved a magnificent tactical surprise.'

Christopher, standing to attention before the fat man, dipped his head to indicate he'd known that fact.

Mr Churchill said, 'Dunkirk and Dieppe have been avenged, Christoper.' His eyes seemed buried deep in their sockets as though he hadn't slept in months; his fatigue looked painful. 'For a week after the landings,' he said, 'Hitler persisted in believing them to be a feint. He waited too long, expecting a massed invasion at the Pas de Calais. By the time he realized he'd been hoodwinked it was too late.'

'You shopped me, sir.'

'Yes, we did. Chastise me if you wish.'

He'd been the icing on the cake, the last bit of flummery to convince the Germans the landings must be planned for Calais. Christ, he'd come to believe it himself towards the end.

357

The PM said, 'We couldn't tell you the truth beforehand. Your evidence only worked if you believed the lie.'

'But you did tell me the truth.'

'In such a way as to convince the Germans it was the lie.' Mr Churchill still carried his large gold watch in the pocket of his waistcoat. He took it out and looked at it. Without looking up he said, 'Christopher – if it's of any use, perhaps by forgiving me you may achieve a form of revenge.'

'Are you asking my forgiveness, sir?'

'It would make it easier for me to carry on. Yes.' The PM lifted his eyes then. 'We had good times at Chartwell, didn't we?'

'Yes – we did.' And he remembered them now. Pestering the fat old man who sat under the broad-brimmed hat before his easel. Thinking then that he disliked the old man.

The troubled eyes searched his face. 'It's the mark of the best class of warrior – and you are of that class, Christopher – that he lets nothing of his feelings show. But I wish you could be a bit less reticent with me. I wish I knew your feelings just now. It is important to me.'

Christopher opened his mouth to speak but Mr Churchill went on: 'You broke under intolerable pressure and you must feel great shame and guilt for that. I can only tell you that the shame and the guilt are mine. You betrayed no-one. We knew you would break. We depended on it. No man ever born on this planet could have withstood more than you withstood. If it's any comfort, you were selected for it because we felt you, of all the agents, had the best chance of surviving it afterwards. Your resilience is one of your remarkable qualities. By standing here in this room today you are fulfilling my faith in you. Can you understand that?'

Mr Churchill was looking at him again. Christopher tried to summon the right words to mind; he knew what he wanted to say but it had to be put just right.

The PM said, 'It's not finished yet, you know. They're on their knees but they're not defeated. To finish it we've got to go into their home ground and they'll fight for every foot of it, as we'd have fought for our own soil had we been invaded. We've still got dangerous work to do.'

Christopher found himself smiling.

The PM saw that, and replied with one of his own rare smiles. 'Are you still with me, then?'

'What's the job?'

'It's a rescue assignment. An errand of mercy this time. Uncle John has the details.'

'And you still trust me to bring it off?'

'Of course I trust you.'

'I'm still with you, sir.'

'Am I forgiven, then?'

'Not if it's a form of revenge. I prefer to think there's nothing to forgive. You do your job, sir, and I do mine. It's occurred to me that I do it rather well, all things considered.'

'Rather well? You're *bloody* good at it, Christopher.'

'Yes sir, I bloody well am.' And he grinned at the fat man: he gave it all the cheeky brashness of his childhood.

Mr Churchill got up from his chair and came towards him; he lifted one hand and let it fall upon Christopher's shoulder and Christopher felt the squeeze of his fingers. He wasn't sure if it was a trick of the light or if he saw the glisten of a tear in the fat man's eye. Mr Churchill said, 'When you're an old man I hope you'll be able to look back with pride upon the dark days when you and I and a fragile handful of men and women stood alone in the world against Hitler. Pray remember it, Christopher, whenever you feel tempted by remorse or shame. We've done dire deeds, you and I, God forgive us.'

And then he was gone, leaving Christopher alone in the cabinet room, and it occurred to him that it was the first time he had not gone out and left the fat man. Looking at the doorway through which Mr Churchill had made his exit Christopher, feeling a rush of love, smiled again.

Selected Bestsellers

☐	**The Amityville Horror**	Jay Anson	£1.25p
☐	**The Health Food Guide**	Michael Balfour and Ruby Rae	£1.95p
☐	**The Island**	Peter Benchley	£1.25p
☐	**Options**	Freda Bright	£1.50p
☐	**The Entity**	Frank De Felitta	£1.75p
☐	**Whip Hand**	Dick Francis	£1.50p
☐	**Secrets**	Unity Hall	£1.50p
☐	**Solo**	Jack Higgins	£1.50p
☐	**The Rich are Different**	Susan Howatch	£2.75p
☐	**Moviola**	Garson Kanin	£1.50p
☐	**Spike Island**	James McClure	£1.95p
☐	**The Master Mariner** Book 1: Running Proud	Nicholas Monsarrat	£1.50p
☐	**Best of Shrdlu**	Denys Parsons	95p
☐	**Platinum Logic**	Tony Parsons	£1.75p
☐	**Fools Die**	Mario Puzo	£1.50p
☐	**A Married Man**	Piers Paul Read	£1.50p
☐	**Sunflower**	Marilyn Sharp	95p
☐	**The Throwback**	Tom Sharpe	£1.25p
☐	**Wild Justice**	Wilbur Smith	£1.75p
☐	**Thy Neighbour's Wife**	Gay Talese	£1.75p
☐	**That Old Gang of Mine**	Leslie Thomas	£1.25p
☐	**Caldo Largo**	Earl Thompson	£1.50p
☐	**Harvest of the Sun**	E. V. Thompson	£1.50p
☐	**The Third Wave**	Alvin Toffler	£1.95p

All these books are available at your local bookshop or newsagent, or can be ordered direct from the publisher. Indicate the number of copies required and fill in the form below

4

Name _____
(block letters please)

Address_____

_____

Send to Pan Books (CS Department), Cavaye Place, London SW10 9PG
Please enclose remittance to the value of the cover price plus:
35p for the first book plus 15p per copy for each additional book ordered
to a maximum charge of £1.25 to cover postage and packing
Applicable only in the UK

While every effort is made to keep prices low, it is sometimes necessary to increase prices at short notice. Pan Books reserve the right to show on covers and charge new retail prices which may differ from those advertised in the text or elsewhere